FINDING MYSELF LOST IN LOUISIANA

FINDING MYSELF LOST IN LOUISIANA

Keagan LeJeune

University Press of Mississippi / Jackson

The University Press of Mississippi is the scholarly publishing agency of
the Mississippi Institutions of Higher Learning: Alcorn State University,
Delta State University, Jackson State University, Mississippi State University,
Mississippi University for Women, Mississippi Valley State University,
University of Mississippi, and University of Southern Mississippi.

www.upress.state.ms.us

The University Press of Mississippi is a member
of the Association of University Presses.

Photographs by the author unless otherwise noted

Copyright © 2023 by University Press of Mississippi
All rights reserved

∞

Library of Congress Cataloging-in-Publication Data

Names: LeJeune, Keagan, 1972– author.
Title: Finding myself lost in Louisiana / Keagan LeJeune.
Description: Jackson : University Press of Mississippi, 2023. | Includes
bibliographical references.
Identifiers: LCCN 2023024436 (print) | LCCN 2023024437 (ebook) | ISBN
9781496847331 (hardback) | ISBN 9781496850331 (trade paperback) | ISBN
9781496847348 (epub) | ISBN 9781496847355 (epub) | ISBN 9781496847362
(pdf) | ISBN 9781496847379 (pdf)
Subjects: LCSH: LeJeune, Keagan, 1972– | Folklore and history—Louisiana. |
Folklore—Louisiana. | Tales—Louisiana.
Classification: LCC GR110.L5 L454 2023 (print) | LCC GR110.L5 (ebook) |
DDC 398.209763—dc23/eng/20230524
LC record available at https://lccn.loc.gov/2023024436
LC ebook record available at https://lccn.loc.gov/2023024437

British Library Cataloging-in-Publication Data available

For my mother

CONTENTS

| ix | Acknowledgments |
| xi | Preface |

3	1. Homesick at Home
33	2. The Only Time Ben Lilly Was Ever Lost
61	3. Mister Unlucky, Mister Nobody
89	4. Into a Far Country . . . Close at Home
117	5. At the Shores of Eternity
145	6. Jack and Me and Coochie Brake
173	7. The Little Cajun Saint and the Closed-Down Resort
201	8. Land in the Slow Making

| 229 | Epilogue: No Matter Where You Go, There You Are |
| 231 | Notes |

ACKNOWLEDGMENTS

Deep thanks to all those people who shared their stories with me and hosted a wandering soul, especially Clifford Clark, Tony Maricle, Grayhawk Perkins, and Barbara Swire. Ricky Mahaffey, my heartfelt thanks for that fireside help long ago. I appreciate the work and help of all the state parks agents I met and the librarians I befriended. Thanks to Katie Keene and the press for believing in this project. My thanks to the support of the Louisiana Folklore Society. I want to acknowledge the mission of the Lamar University Center for History and Culture of Southeast Texas and the Upper Gulf Coast. I am indebted to them for their generosity and wish to thank them for the 2022 fellowship. Thank you to my friends at Manresa and the Montaigne Society. I am so grateful for my neighbors who helped me during the hurricanes. My deep gratitude to Marcia Gaudet, a most helpful guide. Thanks to all those Louisiana writers and researchers whose work inspired and directed this book. Obviously, I owe a special debt to Barry Ancelet, Carl Brasseaux, Ray Brassieur, Gay Gomez, and Malcolm Vidrine. I'm grateful to my former teachers at McNeese State University and University of Louisiana at Lafayette. To all those friends, colleagues, and students at McNeese over the years, you make the job a joy. Where would I be without Joe Cash and Leo Marcello? How would I have found my way without Ray Miles and John Wood? John, where are the words? Kevin Thomason and Jack Vanchiere joined me on parts of this journey. Without them, I would've never finished. To the good company of my family—aunts, uncles, cousins, grandparents, greats and great-greats and so on, my parents, and my siblings. I owe so much to Carmen and Jules. I would be utterly and forever lost without my wife Melanie.

PREFACE

We don't know our homes, our houses. It's not only the wildness of our backyards that I mean—the clandestine activities of the neighborhood tom or the quick-witted pranks the weeds pull while we're distracted one wet afternoon—but the normal things, the common stuff.

It's the dirt we overlook and the rich history of the soil our homes scooch their big haunches into. It's the loam and its past stitched with everything from mastodon bones and mollusk shells ground up in the loess to the plastic Davy Crockett figure forgotten by a child and buried over time.

We neglect the hidden spaces inside the walls and the rot advancing in an unnoticed corner of the eaves. We turn our thoughts away from the unseen nest of wires in the attic or the tangle of pipes occupying our home's underside. We're quick to pass over the everyday things happening in the background.

But if we ever had to sit across someone and confess what we fail to appreciate, we might feel ashamed: the heat and coolness, of course, rattling through the vents; the water raring to go when we slide up the kitchen faucet; the steady chirr of the fridge or the ceiling fan or the whatever-it-is-that's-making-that-hum our ears have learned to ignore.

We overlook the gift of a countertop we can sit something on and the bedroom door we use to close off the noise and the breathing room of a hallway we dip into. We forget how rarely we recognize the way space has been shaped to make us feel comfortable. We take for granted even the trust we have in the ceiling's tendency to stay put or our confidence in floorboards to hold us up. We assume the of-course-it-does sureness of plywood and the damn-right-they-will smugness of two-by-fours will always be around, until they're not anymore.

Why does it take grasping around in the dark for us to be grateful for the lights? Why do we need water to be up beyond the wheelwells for us to appreciate the street's dull concrete? We start to long for the callous routine of slipping our key in the lock and plopping down on the couch only after we're standing on the curb, lost in the rumble in front of us. We wait till then to promise that we'll never again come in the door without first planting a huge kiss on the fascia or the siding or the backsteps.

Why don't we hug the chrome doorknob or the welcome mat or everything we have, and do it each and every day we're lucky enough to have it?

I don't know, but it's funny how an evening's blackout or the gun-metal gray of a storm or the pluming smoke of a house fire can change that.

I'm proof.

In 2020 a complicated thing happened to me. That haze of ingratitude that I walked around in was engulfed by the greater fog of four federally declared disasters. Ironically, once that happened, I started to see.

I didn't notice it at first, but one morning I woke up and realized everything was already going, disappearing just like the marshlands and estuaries along the coast. The oak trees were dying from saltwater intrusion. The marsh reeds' roots were letting go. Whole football fields of them were floating away. The people were uprooting too, and I was one of them. The only difference between them and me was that my slow drift away from this place wasn't physical.

I've called Louisiana home my entire life, and sure, sometimes it has felt a little odd and alien and unusual to me, like a far country, but before the disasters of 2020, that strangeness had always been part of Louisiana's charm. But now I couldn't sleep. I couldn't think. All sense of direction in my life had vanished, and I found myself lost in my birthplace and stripped of my birthright.

I guess what I mean to say is one day I woke up, and my body ached with a homesickness that swept over me even though I was still at home.

At that exact moment, I was called to go on an adventure.

I'll confess now to the paradoxes of it. Very little happened on this quest. I didn't travel all that far. I was usually by myself.

I'll admit to my motives too. At the start, I held on to the idea that the trip's purpose might be to get myself unstuck from this mucky place I call home, but by the end, I was left wondering if the entire point of the journey was to get myself lost because that feeling was the only thing that set me right again.

I don't know. I could be wrong. All I know for certain is this: that journey is what comes in the pages ahead. You can judge it for yourself.

FINDING MYSELF LOST IN LOUISIANA

1

HOMESICK AT HOME

Once upon a time, in a place named Basile, which sounds far away but isn't, there lived a man named Potic Rider.[1]

I say, "Once upon a time," but this story is true, even though you might believe it fell straight from a storybook.

You might suppose the place isn't real. You might think the customs are too outrageous. You might say the characters, if not downright fake, seem at least the stuff of fairytales.

When you hear the words Potic says, you'll think they sound almost magical. The things he does, almost too fabled to have happened. But according to the people who were there that day, the events unfolded exactly the way I'm telling you. You'll have to trust me. Nothing is made up. Nothing at all.

It was a Tuesday in a dull Louisiana town during the drab middle of February. The grass was probably brown, the sky, a little gray. Birds sang workaday birdsong. The wind did what it lazily did. In other words, everything that day was in every way ordinary—except for this . . . a gaggle of costumed men marched the countryside.

A stranger to town was there, watching these curiously dressed men parade by. The stranger had a notepad and maybe a camera and probably a tape recorder, and out of the blue, Potic Rider walked right up to him to say, "I can't explain it. Mardi Gras doesn't come from the head; it comes from the heart. It's in you. Where it comes from . . . it's very deep."

The stranger didn't ask for that explanation, but Potic Rider gave it to him anyway. Potic wanted the man to understand what was happening. He wanted him to comprehend this *very deep* thing. "It's like Moses going to the mountaintop and seeing the burning bush," Potic told the stranger. "And the burning bush said, *I am that I am*. Well, I am that I am: Potic. I run Mardi Gras."

That's a true story, but it's not exactly the story I want to tell you. Not all of it anyway.

My story is part of that one. Or it's part of mine. I can't tell which, but either way, both stories mean that Mardi Gras revelry often involves bad weather . . . and running in the mud . . . and people feeling sick . . . and a few bystanders complaining that this year isn't as good as it used to be . . . and someone standing under a carport crying over the member of the Mardi Gras who passed away the year before . . . and by day's end people going home knowing that some things don't make the sort of sense the everyday world says they should. They don't resolve, they don't settle in as only *bad* or *good*, and most importantly, they can't be labeled as *back then* or *will be* or even *right now*. Some things just *are*. Some things, even when they don't seem to, mean *I Am*.

It was September in my story, or could have been. It's hard to remember. Whenever it was, it was only weeks after Hurricane Laura hit in 2020. During those days, I'd wake up before the sun and stay in bed alone. There was no power going. The whole neighborhood throttled with generators, their motors wheezing like a jumble of snoring cartoon dwarves.

My generator sat chained to a post on my back patio, and a thin orange extension cord snaked from it through a slightly opened upstairs window. At night, it kept a lamp, a window A/C unit, and a phone charger running.

But as soon as daybreak drove away the mosquitoes, I'd go outside, kick off the generator, then come back in to open the windows and make coffee on the gas stove. I'd light the burner with a candle and watch until the water boiled. I'd click off the burner and pour the steaming water into the drip pot, and while the water seeped the grounds, I'd fix a peanut butter sandwich, no jelly. Once I was set, holding the sandwich in my mouth and my mug in my hand, I'd walk back outside to sit for a while in the rose-colored dawn.

It was too early to bang around the sledge or make racket with the pry bar and not yet light enough to toss broken roof shingles and chunks of ripped-out sheetrock into the piles of debris on the streets, so I'd wait in the half dark for the neighbors to stir inside their homes, and while I did, I'd pick up my phone.

During those early mornings, I relied on my phone. It acted like a friend who tried to make me feel normal. It chatted about the weather. It brought up news about sports scores, world events, celebrity gunk. It kept me up on the local gossip. But then it began to change. It started getting personal. It started trying to relive old memories by showing me the pictures I had taken. It started dredging up the past to take stock of our history together.

There was an 1812 fort in Louisiana in the first picture, Rome's Colosseum from my one big trip in the next, then the rock formations located at a nearby state park. Each image sat there just long enough for my mind to halfway remember the place. A random brick wall overgrown with weeds. The ruins of a Pompeii manor. A cave too small to stand up in. The arches of an old Louisiana bridge barely reaching across a river.

Days went on that way. Weeks of my phone going through the places I had been. It seemed harmless at first.

It was the second or third week of October, I think, or might as well have been, maybe it was the week before my birthday, when my phone got serious. "Spotlight on Keagan," the alert said.

The first picture from the set it showed me was from five years ago. In it, I'm sitting at a table. My face is blurry. I'm barely looking at the camera.

Then, another picture popped up—my oldest daughter and I are in a neighborhood in Houston. It's the middle of summer. She's young enough to leap into my arms.

I'm somewhere else in the next frame. Nowhere I can remember. But I'm crouching on a stool positioned next to a cardboard cow, pretending to milk it.

My family's at a bonfire now—this time all four of us are posing for the camera.

The next one has just my hand.

The one after that shows a brother's backyard and a birthday party, his fiftieth. There are three of us brothers standing by each other. I'm the one in the costume.

I'm lost in a corn maze next, something small we did for my second daughter's birthday one year.

Then my wife and I are dressed up like Clark Kent and Lois Lane for a Mardi Gras ball.

I'm in a tux now. It's mostly my face, with the black tie and the shoulders of the black coat showing.

And then the slideshow went black. That was it. My life. My I Am.

The nights and days of October turned to November in a blur. I looked down. I looked up. It was December. I couldn't tell you where the time went. Most of the time, I couldn't tell you the time of day. It would be 3:30 in the morning, and I'd be wide awake, standing in a little back room in my house, looking out the window. I wouldn't recognize anything outside.

The streets had turned to mountains of glass and the trees grew upside down. All the blades of grass were nails. Houses had grown feet and wore hats. Every one of the buildings had taken up bags of luggage in their hands. One evening, they all just moved away.

I spent the last days of that strange year scratching my head at those changes until one night something happened. It was like the lousy jokes you find in a book you give a child. It was like a prank, but the ones in your dreams that you pull on yourself. It was a call on the phone, but no one was on the other end. It was the start of my story.

Once upon a time, I had a phone and I couldn't tell if it was a liar or a trickster or both because I couldn't tell what was real and what wasn't, especially in the pictures it showed me.

Let me explain.

It was almost New Years, and my phone came to me with a set of pictures it wanted me to see. "In the Woods," it said, and "Don't you remember," and it showed me a close-up of a honey locust, then a loblolly pine tree with green shoots, then a good bend of the Sabine River.

I tried, but I couldn't stop myself.

"Psst!" it whispered. "Shouldn't you rediscover this," and the shaggy edge of a woods at the geographic center of Louisiana flashed before me. "Or this," and the sun came through a cypress crown at a state park. Then it was a campground near a lake fed by a natural spring, then it was one of the oldest oak trees in Louisiana. "And this . . . in the Woods," and a patch of trash trees overgrown with trumpet vine captured me. Then it was a storm tree in Cameron Parish. Then the back of my house after the hurricane.

I swear I heard my phone laughing when it showed me that—my yard swallowed by the thicket of branches from the two water oaks that Hurricane Laura felled. The top of one tree punched a hole in my house and its trunk flattened my garage. Everything stored inside transformed into yard debris. All the tools my dad had given me disappeared into the dirt and leaves. The other tree, when it fell, was a magician. Its branches, almost like a spell, knotted my backyard into a snarled, twisted, tangled mess. And my phone was sniggering about it all—"Take a look, Keagan," it teased. "Your yard, your house. In the Woods."

After that, through the rest of January, I fought to ignore my phone's pestering. It was almost six months after the storms and nothing was normal, but my phone never stopped trying to make me pretend every strange thing was ordinary, that it was enough already and I should be feeling back to normal. "It's been ten years since this," it would say and show me something I was supposed to be happy about remembering; a birthday cake set on a picnic table in the corner of the yard, a candid shot of two teens dressed for a dance and miserable about posing for a picture at our front door.

It was the first days of February when my phone finally wore me down. "Do you remember it's Mardi Gras," it told me, and like a fool, I nodded my head. It had something special planned—a picture from 2013. I gave in. When I looked, my heart fell like a ball dropped down a well.

In 2013, my sister was working in Crowley as a dental hygienist. One of her patients, a man named Ed LeJeune, invited her to a Mardi Gras celebration in a place called LeJeune Cove.

LeJeune Cove, or L'Anse de LeJeune in French, is a tiny unincorporated community near the small Cajun town of Iota. Iota has only fifteen hundred people itself, so by most standards, LeJeune Cove is miniscule, not even a settlement, more like a neighborhood. The invitation was supposed to be a treat.

LeJeune Cove was homesteaded by my great grandfather and his brothers, which meant that in some far-off sort of way, my family was related to Ed LeJeune's. That's why he wanted my sister to experience Mardi Gras there. "Of course," he said when she asked about bringing me and my wife and our two daughters along.

I've been to Iota a million times. It's where my grandparents lived, but before that Mardi Gras visit, I had never been to LeJeune Cove, not that I could remember.

My mom grew up in Iota, so one afternoon I asked her about the name LeJeune Cove and what it meant. She lifted her hands, moved them apart like she was holding an imaginary bowl, and held them out. "It's a . . . it's like that," she said, moving her arms away from her belly. "I guess it's like a little tucked-away community where the people are together," her hands placing that make-believe bowl in the middle of a make-believe table.

"And *cove*? Why *cove*?" I asked.

"I don't know," she said. "I don't know how that comes because there isn't any water around. There isn't a major body of water." The crinkles of disappointment rippled across her forehead. "It's just like a neighborhood of people, like a set-off community."

The day my family drove out to LeJeune Cove, my mind was everywhere. I had to stop myself from speeding several times. When I parked, I barely missed the ditch and nearly rear-ended the car in front of me. The whole time I stood around, I calmed my nervousness by taking sips.

There was a hazy glow around the pair as I watched a costumed man take my oldest daughter by the hand to lead her to the dance floor. I remember raising my phone and the flash going off. I remember being almost happy. I remember looking at the image for a long time after.

In the photograph, she's thirteen, and full of nerves too. He's at least a foot taller than she is and more than twice her size. His arms jut out in front of his body. One hand cups her waist and the other clenches her right palm.

As the music chank-a-chanks, her shoulders loosen. Her feet start shuffling faster. The two of them edge closer together.

They're not touching, but he's near enough to make her turn and look at me. She's smiling so big her eyebrows are dancing too as her cheeks rise to build an expression I've never seen on her face before.

On his face, the man's mask hides almost everything. All I can see are his eyes. They're skewed towards me. His fake schnozzle looks like a pig's snout or a bull's nose. A string of beads loops from one nostril to the other. His teeth have a pronounced underbite, a bulldog's snarl. The eyebrows are two thick lashes of cut rope glued to make each a swooping arch. His beard's white yarn. Buttons and fringe and crinkles turn the sides of his face into a junk drawer I want to stick my hands into. His cheeks are as bright as a ripe, ripe tomato, a red that's as arresting as a splat of fake blood.

His hat is pointed, shaped like a princess hat—a *capuchon* people call it. A rim of moss wraps around its base and a tassel, colored the same brilliant vermilion as his cheeks, dangles from its tip. His clothes are camouflage, but with tie-dyed fringe around his ankles and emerald green fringe up and down the arms. His belt made from scraps of cloth is brindled. Only his hands aren't costumed, which he uses to grab my daughter the same way Mardi Gras grabs everything when it unfolds.

If I had my entire life to tell you what I mean, I don't know if I could. Mardi Gras can look so different from one place to another. In LeJeune Cove, they do it the old way. The man dancing with my daughter is a *Mardi Gras runner*. That's what people call him here, or just a *Mardi Gras*. His mask and costume are so complete maybe his neighbors won't even recognize him, or they will at least pretend they don't as long as that's the game. He'll spend the entire day that way—anonymous with the other runners, traveling from house to house, singing traditional songs about empty bottles of wine and dancing with the wives and daughters of the people waiting under patios or out in the yard or just at the end of the driveway. Some spectators will wave and maybe even give a little money as these costumed beggars parade by, and others will make a whole day of it. They'll throw a party at their house, setting out lawn chairs, cooking for everyone who plans to come over to wait with them, keeping the makeshift dance floor clear for when the Mardi Gras arrive. While they're waiting, they'll visit, drink, and stare down the road anxiously for the runners in the masks and all their strangeness to come knocking at their door so that all this silliness, all this playing around, can swallow everything, everyone.

Except it didn't. Not that day. Not me.

Mardi Gras goes back so far. I should know it by heart, should know it as *home*, the same way I should know LeJeune Cove, but that day, a part of me felt like I had always missed something. Like all of this had been lost to me.

I knew it was a trick. I realized my phone showing me that picture was the bait. It wanted me to remember the almost happiness I had taking the picture that day back in 2013.

Now it was February of 2021. It was the months following Hurricane Laura. It was a time of questioning, and my phone wanted me to question everything.

I bit the hook anyway. If my phone was going to do its prank-call routine, I was going to put it to the test and decipher what was real and what was a pack of lies. I knew that would be the only way to turn the question "Am I" to something like "I Am."

So that February after the hurricane, I decided to leave my house to find a place called by many names—the home-that-almost-was, and the home-that-wasn't, and the home-that-was-to-be. But to find that home beyond my own four walls, I knew I would have to travel to the place buried in the photograph, a place both impossible to go to but absolutely necessary for me to reach. But before I went, I knew what I would need—a gift from my dad, what counted as my inheritance—a Ziploc bag.

My mom gave the bag to me one day long after my father had died. "I know you're interested in these sorts of things," she said and told me what was inside—pages and pages of a genealogy book he had copied when he was on that kick.

I had skimmed the pages when my dad was alive. We were sitting at the kitchen table when he showed them to me. I didn't understand them back then, or didn't care to, and I'll confess that I didn't even open the bag when my mother handed it to me. I thought I knew exactly what was inside, so I stuck it somewhere in my house and forgot it there.

For two cold February days I searched the bookshelves spared from the leaky roof and looked through the bins full of papers and files and folders pulled from the places not spared from the rain. I rummaged through the drawers of my desk and hunted through what was left of the keepsakes in the keepsake closet. I looked through the junk I had to empty from the attic because of the tree branch, and even though I knew it wasn't there, I searched the three boxes I brought home from work six months earlier. I did that twice.

I was about to give up when I thought to look under a stack of books in a black basket by my desk. The size of the books stopped me from looking there at first. They were thick anthologies I use to teach sophomores everything from *Gawain* to "Prufrock" to "Church Going," and I didn't imagine anything could be underneath them.

Moving them was like rolling back a stone. At the bottom of the basket sat a Ziploc bag as long as a legal pad and roomy enough to hold three or four manila folders. Through the plastic, I could see the papers and envelopes and Xeroxes stuffed inside.

I took the bag, put it on the floor, then I knelt down to pull the Ziploc seal apart. After that, I turned the opened bag upside down, letting everything inside slide onto the hardwood floor. Then, sitting down and crossing my legs to spread the contents out around me until the pages and folders and copies encircled me, I settled in.

I picked up the two sealed manila envelopes first, but didn't open them. Too many loose pages to pick through already floated around me, so I set the envelopes off to the side. I grabbed one of the loose pages, read it, then set it down in a stack. I did this over and over again.

A violet sheet of paper was an invitation to a "La Famille LeJeune/Young" reunion. Three Xeroxes were of a *Lafayette Daily Advertiser* article about LeJeune history. Several typed pages offered different versions of the Leger family tree. I found at least seventy copied pages from John Austin Young's *The Lejeunes of Acadia and the Youngs of Southwest Louisiana*.[2] Most of the seventy pages were Young's chapter ten—"The Lineage of Francois Homer LeJeune and Celestine Vige." They were my great-grandparents.[3]

Going through all the pages took a while, and I was ready to quit, but then my fingers stumbled upon a transcription of an interview my cousin McBee Cooper did with my grandmother.

"I was christened Maria Coralie Leger at the St. Joseph's Catholic Church, Iota, La.," my grandmother started. "I was born August 19, 1894, at my father's country home near the present village of Egan, La."

At that time, people called that part of Egan Abbott's Cove, the document told me. My grandmother's father was born there on the homestead of his father. He later moved to homestead land not too far away. My grandmother was born at my grandfather's new place.

The transcription went on for eight pages. It told me the year my grandmother's father died. It gave her mother's name and that woman's birthplace, a place near Egan called Pointe Switch that some people called Canal Switch and others called Jonas Cove or Regan. It whispered the details about her mother's first marriage, which I never knew about, and listed the names of all my grandmother's brothers and sisters. It remembered her wedding day and the marriage to my grandfather Mark LeJeune. It pointed out where they lived right after the ceremony and where they finally moved to after a few years of married life. It described how Grandfather Mark LeJeune built their new house and what land he built it on. It gave the names of all my aunts and uncles, and then, in its last pages, included a half-empty family tree of their children.

After I read the interview, I redoubled my search, digging through the loose paper like a raccoon through the cat-food bin. I found a duplicate of my own birth certificate and several other *legal* documents—a probate for my grandfather Mark's estate; the succession for my uncle Myles who died in 1962; a plat map "showing the partition of property of the heirs of J. N. Leger," who I found out was my grandmother's brother Joseph Noe. There was also what appeared to be a 1965 reissue of an 1805 marriage certificate for "Joseph LeJeune (son of Blaise LeJeune and Marie Joseph Brau) and Euphrosine Carriere (daughter of Michel Carriere and Julienne Marcantel)." They were married in Opelousas.

Surrounded by those papers, sitting on the floor, my legs crossed, feeling lost and overwhelmed, a thought came to me like a gust of wind. I realized, whether it was Potic Rider or Moses or even the big "I Am," the first step in understanding something like that was the riddle of the name itself—the question of what it meant and why it was important and how it could define someone.

I couldn't answer that question for myself, not after Hurricane Laura hit Lake Charles in August, not after Hurricane Delta hit it again less than two months later, probably not even before, but looking into my Ziploc bag was like seeing through a looking glass because as I stared inside, I started to understand that all the documents built to a story. All the pieces of paper gathered to reveal a time that seemed to be out of time and a setting not of this world. The names became characters who seemed to be more than ordinary people, and the details became a series of breadcrumbs down a path. If I followed it, I would be following a tale of how once upon a time a LeJeune came to settle a place, which was more than just an ordinary place. It was a faraway place, even though it was only about a hundred miles from my house, and though it was new to me, it was an old place called *home*. It was a special place. It was a place that meant "I Am."

If I had any hope of finding an end to feeling lost, I needed to trace the path that began with Mardi Gras and my daughter's dancing and ended with me standing nearby, watching her, feeling homesick at home in that place.

So I did. I traveled back to that world named after LeJeunes.

There are a thousand ways to travel home, but even if I could describe all of them, what would be the point? All you need to know is back then, right after the hurricane, the interstate was a knot of snakes. It had tree crews from Florida pulling the long con and tarpers from Alabama promising to keep a bad situation from turning worse. It had fly-by-nights "just looking to help" and good souls who couldn't give an exact quote, who didn't need a contract, who were just "trusting folk who could take care of it no problem by simply billing you and your insurance company after" and then setting a lien on your house. It had F-150s with subcontractors who loved to holler in their phones. It had insurance adjusters on the first week of the job puttering by in their economy cars. It had mold-and-mildew men in logoed vans. It had general laborers in their dully trucks hogging the lane. It had big-boss contractors with their feet on the gas, trying to be only an hour late for their next appointment, not because they minded making anyone wait but because they knew listening to someone complain is this world's biggest waste of time. It had Houston roofing crews with single-cab Joad Toyotas—their truck beds stacked with rolls of roof paper and buckets of tar and ice chests and coolers and coils of air hose; with shovels crammed in so their noses stuck up in the air; with huge spools of roofing nails and spare squares of shingles left over from the job before; with cougar paws tied by their shoelaces to a rack welded to the cab; with strapped-down extension ladders on top of it all, one end snug against the tailgate and the other held tight to the cabin roof with bungie cords so the giant rectangles of foam under it would never blow out. But that wasn't all. It had you, who knew each and every one of them would bite your head off if you crept along at only ten miles over the speed limit or if you decided you shouldn't ride the bumper of a semi to let them pass or if you even thought about trying to exit.

So I avoided that ball of serpents. I took the backroads through tiny towns called Ragley and Stanley and Kinder, names that sound like what this place is. It's Highway 190, an old way to go, an empty one except for trash trees running along the fencerows and trash grass growing along the shoulder. A rundown way with buildings that used to be for something but not anymore. An overgrown way with elderberry thriving in rusted cultivators and unhitched disc plows and kudzu sprawling up telephone poles. An okay way to go. An ordinary way, which was just fine with me, which was just perfect actually, because at that time, especially when compared to the landscape unmade by a hurricane, ordinary in Louisiana felt magical.

But magical can be commonplace in Louisiana's Cajun Prairie, or once was.

Today the prairie is mostly rice fields and soybean crops and crawfish ponds and country settlements crammed with little houses sitting squatly on perfectly mown yards, but long ago, before railroads and combines and irrigation canals, before cotton and corn and cattle, the world of southwestern Louisiana was a sea of grasses, an ocean of wildflowers. Back in 1803, spanning nearly one million hectares from Lafayette to Lake Charles and from Ville Platte until it ran into the chenier marshes along the coast, the stunning prairies of southwestern Louisiana ruled the landscape with grasses high as a man on horseback and plant life boasting all the colors of the rainbow.

It was at that time that a man named Charles-César Robin embarked on what he called his *Voyage to Louisiana*. Robin didn't know who or what he might encounter here. When he arrived, he met the landscape the way someone meets a stranger.

As soon as he stepped foot on the Cajun Prairie, "the face of the earth" stared back at him in the form of a "new and astonishing scene." Its cheeks were "wide green plains." Its quirky smile, "an expanse of grass interrupted only by an occasional clump of oak or pine trees." Its singular voice, the winds that "breathe over the pathless waste of savanna."[4]

Charles-César Robin, himself, belonged in a kind of storybook. He was a man with a made-up name and no history, complete with pseudonym and anonymity, but he was one of the first travelers to write about the Louisiana prairie back when much of it was still actual prairie land. "Spacious prairies stretch out, as far as the eye can see, broken here and there by patches of woods," he wrote in his journal. "Crossing the wide prairie, strewn with flowers, whose stems raise them to the height of the horse on which the traveler is riding, one rides suddenly upon herds of cattle."

Sudden. Strange. Staggering. "Surprise follows surprise in this varied vegetation," he exclaimed about this new-fangled, fabled world. The cattle seemed to never be without milk. The eggs so big they almost talked. The grasses like a bottomless well full of riches.

But the Eden waited only for the brave because, Robin warned, "The Opelousas and Atakapas prairies are also substantially more beautiful" than the rest of Louisiana but "more wild and dangerous." Only "the vigorous Canadians have penetrated here," he explained.

To the outsider, the Cajun prairie's expanse seemed to stretch forever, but Acadians who first settled the region realized that "there were several interconnected prairie areas, divided like ponds by stands of distantly visible trees," as William Faulkner Rushton explains in his *Cajuns from Acadia to Louisiana*. The terrain of the Cajun Prairie "made the grass seem like the surface of the sea the Cajuns had left behind in Canada.... The line between the prairies and the trees seemed very much like the shore, that's how prairie villages like Robert's Cove and Church Point acquired their names."[5]

In other words, in this sea of grasses, a clump of trees in the middle of it looked like an island and might be called that. By extension, a place where a gallery of hardwoods poked out into the flat grasslands might be called a point, and in line with that, if the prairie in an area seemed to be surrounded by groves of hardwood, you called that place a cove. Why? A cove was a piece of flat land tucked into a pocket of woods. It looked like an inlet, a bay, a quiet harbor protected from the vastness of a harsh ocean, a good place to settle and make a home.

Cove, or *l'anse* in French, was an important geographic term for early Canadians. You can see it on the maps—the bodies of water and a few spots of land carrying *l'anse* as part of their names. But their naming patterns seem different than the Cajun way. *L'Anse aux Meadows* is a perfect example. While *L'Anse aux Meadows* in Canada refers to a location on land, it's also the name of the adjacent body of water. The coves on the Cajun Prairie aren't named like this. LeJeune Cove is a stretch of prairie. There is no nearby body of water called LeJeune Cove.

LeJeune Cove, Andrus Cove, Lyons Point, Roberts Cove, Gott's Cove—these were the names I grew up hearing, names of places settled by prairie Cajuns, and as I drove east on Highway 190, I started to wonder if this list of islands and points and coves that ran through my brain were more than simple markers on a map.[6] Could they be answers to a question? The features of this prairie landscape, the way this place was settled, these names—were they the start to finding my "I Am"?

But by the time I finally got to Eunice, which was only about thirteen miles north of LeJeune Cove, I found out that the same stuff that I use to keep myself guarded was shutting off Eunice from me. It wasn't any physical wall stopping people from getting into town, but a shyness, an insecurity, the hesitation to be what it is. It was the two-lane highway heading in and out of town that told you it hates how people must see it as never going anywhere. It was the city limits sign that told you it wonders if it's a disappointment to people. It was all the Louisiana-small-town junk—the electrical lines that look like a tongue tangled up by a thick accent and the short boxy clumps of grass poking through the concrete that betray how even the neat cement lot is likely an imposter.

If you looked, everything clued you in on this place's low opinion of itself. The ruined and rusted awning of an old pump station no one cares about anymore made it clear. Fred's and Circle K and all the other get-cheap-shit-quick stores trying to be everything to everyone reeked of desperation. Even the red light right outside of town told it to me plain—I need to get over myself. No one's banging down my door.

When the light turned green, I swung into a parking lot to head home. I needed to fix my house. To get on with things. To get practical. But then I heard a noise down by my floorboard. It was a rattle, a squeak, a chime—it was some sound that made me take my hand and dive it down near the floorboard to fish up my Ziploc bag that had fallen there.

Once I had the bag on my lap, I started digging inside. The Xeroxed *Lafayette Morning Advocate* article titled "Mysterious Deportation Locale Surrounds LeJeune Ancestor Jean-Baptiste" was the first thing I pulled out.[7] It spoke to me.

I don't mean that it seemed meaningful and touched my heart. It talked to me. It spoke. It said—and I can't remember the exact words, but it said something like, once, a long time ago, people known as the Acadians were driven from their homes. They were made to abandon their farms. They were made to leave their possessions behind. Some were loaded into ships and deported to places that didn't want them. Some tried to escape in their own way. Some were put in jail. Some died at sea. Some tried to avoid deportation and fought. Some were surprised by what was happening to them. They stood there frozen.

It wasn't that the frozen ones didn't know that France and England were at each other's throats, the article told me, but it was that the Acadians saw themselves as neutral. Acadia had been transferred back and forth from France to England several times before, and the Acadians never took sides, not really. Now that the English were taking over once again, the Acadians thought their history of neutrality would surely grant them a sort of autonomy.

To the English, it did not. Major Charles Lawrence who oversaw the transition quickly adopted a policy of exile for the Acadians. One by one the Acadian families were gathered up and deported from the land they had settled, the article said. Mine was one of them.

But did you know, the article asked, that "a mystery surrounds the eventual deportation" of your family, the family of Jean-Baptiste LeJeune? Early on, Jean-Baptiste, Marguerite, and their three children were living in Ile Royale.[8] The English aggression seemed to be focused on it at first, so Jean-Baptiste and Marguerite thought that if they moved their little family to Baie des Espagnols, they might be safe. They were wrong.

Once the French lost Louisbourg on Cape Breton Island, the British gained control of one area after another. Soon, British vessels moved against the Baie des Espagnols. The LeJeunes, like so many other Acadians there, were scooped up and expelled.

That's not the whole story, though, the article told me. Like many Baie des Espagnols Acadians, "Jean-Baptiste's mother and at least two of his sisters" were sent back to France, but Jean-Baptiste LeJeune and his immediate family were deported to Port Tobacco, Maryland.

Why?

That depends on the story you want to tell.

It could've been the luck of the draw. The first deportation boats went to France. The later ones brought the exiles to more remote places. The LeJeunes could've been late and unlucky.

It could've been just policy—the "carefully calculated British policy . . . to disperse the Acadians over a widespread area . . . to prevent their coalescing . . . to eliminate them as a group."[9] Lawrence's plan all along seemed to be splitting up families and scattering them throughout the new colonies.

Then again, it could've been personal. Jean-Baptiste and his brother-in-law Honoré Trahan might have been deported to Maryland, the article explained, because "their families attempted to escape deportation by hiding out" or by resisting British forces.

It could've been any one of those reasons, the article told me, but to me that's not the whole mystery anyway. There was a story inside the story. It went like this:

Once upon a time, after being deported to a faraway land, Jean-Baptiste and Marguerite lived with their children in Maryland. It was an unhappy-ever-after, but at least they were together. Then, it got worse. One day, people simply disappeared. The 1752 census listed Jean-Baptiste and Marguerite with their three children. Then POOF! The next census didn't.

The only details we know after that are a few about the children. A boy, "Blaise LEJEUNE, orphan," appeared on the 1763 Port Tobacco census. He would've been around twelve, maybe thirteen. His younger sister Marguerite lived there too, and so did his two younger siblings Joseph and Nanette.

Blaise wasn't living in the same house with any of them. He lived in the house of the "Honoré Braux family." Marguerite lived with the Pierre Launne family and Joseph and Nanette, maybe twins, lived with the family of Honoré Trahan.

Blaise's parents were gone. His oldest brother wasn't listed anywhere on the census either. At thirteen, Blaise became the de facto head of the family, the protector of his sister, the step-in father of the twins.

It was a hard job in a treacherous world. In Georgia and South Carolina, an Acadian exile like Blaise and his family would face indentured servitude. In Massachusetts, the Puritans wanted no part of the Acadian Catholics. In Virginia, the French-speaking exiles weren't even let off the boat. In Maryland, the deportees experienced a somewhat better welcome, but not by much. An orphan like Blaise confronted a dim future. Take for example the 1756 Maryland law that passed soon after the first four ships of deported Acadians docked in 1755. It said that indigent Acadians could be imprisoned, and orphaned children like Blaise could be, or maybe ought to be, bonded out to serve some local family.[10]

It's a kind of story you read to kids to scare them into being good, I blurted out. The stuff you say to them, so they never run away from you in a Target parking lot.

It gets worse, the article told me back.

The families of Honoré Breaux and Honoré Trahan—and the LeJeune orphans they cared for—had to decide between living "in a state of ... Misery, Poverty, and Rags"[11] or scraping together all that they owned and buying passage to somewhere that might take them in.

By 1766, even a young boy of sixteen like Blaise would have heard the news about the groups of Acadians who had reached Louisiana by booking passage "aboard Louisiana-bound English merchant vessels."[12] Maybe he overheard someone as they read one of the "numerous letters of invitation from Attakapas Acadians ... circulating widely among the Acadians remaining in exile in Maryland."[13] Maybe he felt the weight of trying to give his younger sisters and brother the chance of a happy life. Maybe then, he looked to the ocean, to a sea. But the article told me, we don't really know what Blaise felt. All we know is what happened.

That same year the Breaux and Trahan families booked passage on a ship called the *Britain*. The families' plan was that the orphan Blaise and his siblings would climb aboard with them when they gambled on finding a new home. And here you are, the article said, afraid to lose.

They were fighting words. I swallowed my fear of what people might think of me, and I pulled out of the parking lot. At the red light, I chewed back the worry of what was coming. When it turned green, I pressed the gas and resolved myself to finding my way to the I Am of LeJeune Cove.

In Louisiana driving south in the Cajun Prairie can feel like diving into another realm. It's because of the weather. It's because of the water. It's because of the world around you.

If it's a struggle to imagine, it may be because you've never encountered the giants of the Cajun Prairie—the rice dryers. They have a grain elevator that seems taller than a beanstalk. Silos too. They have a titan's bulk. They have a colossal mass. They last when so many of the fantasies about Cajuns' idyllic past have died.

Of course, I've seen the astonishing hulks before, but that day, it was like seeing them for the first time because they weren't just giants anymore. Having been shaped by the long history unraveling itself to me, the dryers transformed into huge ships at sea.

Three or four stories high and as long as a football field, a rice dryer is like an ocean liner run ashore. It's gargantuan, mammoth, and stagnant. It's a frigate drifting in an ocean of grass. The building's huge straight walls are like a ship's broadside. Its metal or concrete exterior is colored shoreline gray or surf-spray white. The huge dryer fans look like propellers that take it out to sea. The tops of the buildings hold little rooms and windows that sit high enough to be a crow's nest, higher even.

The windows sit far enough in the clouds to make you wonder about Blaise in Maryland. By 1767, "at least 689 of the 1,050 known survivors in Maryland and Pennsylvania . . . had boarded vessels in Chesapeake Bay ports for Louisiana."[14] Everyone was leaving. Would he be next?

You swear you see him alone, fidgeting, already having learned the restlessness that would pervade his bones for his entire life. Like me, like you, he had trouble sleeping, and you watch him creep out of doors in the early dawn to walk the streets. It gnawed at him; it must have—the lack of direction. The waiting. He could look around and see the neighbors packing their things, moving off and on to better things. So he walked. He paced.

By 1768, you can see how his stride and steps had changed, as if he suspected it was already too late to alter his fate. By November of that year, his anxiousness to taste the last of Maryland's cold on his tongue probably made him hate walking, but he couldn't help himself. By December, he must have been so eager to feel the last of the frost in his bones that he promised to shut himself indoors, but there was nothing else to relieve his restlessness but constant motion, so he walked.

One day, late in December, you swear you see him standing on the quay. A few days later, you're sure. On the 12th of December, you watch him and his unofficial guardians, along with a total of "thirty-four Acadians and forty Catholic Germans," stand on the deck of the English schooner called *Britain* captained by John Steele and commanded by Philip Ford.[15] It's the ship they've chartered for their journey, and everyone gathers excitedly on the deck, but no one is moving.

The ship isn't either.

Everyone's restless, and it doesn't take long to see why. The Acadians and Germans booked passage on the *Britain* without even seeing her firsthand, and before "the *Britain* left the quay," they discovered the lug "was not seaworthy."

Their stomachs sank while their blood boiled, but what could they do? They had already handed over their money. Now they were desperate. Their only option was to commit to the plan they had made weeks, months earlier. As much as it infuriated them, when Ford demanded the passengers make the necessary repairs, all they could do was to shrug their shoulders and roll up their sleeves.

"Refitting the ship . . . drawing the water . . . cutting the firewood necessary for the voyage"—the work Ford forced on the passengers in order to make ready for the voyage was hard, frustrating, difficult, but you can tell the emigres were not strangers to that sort of labor. They knew a maritime world and the effort it demanded. They had already settled a frontier of sorts in Canada. They would settle another one in Louisiana.

Blaise would settle what would amount to a third, but that would be far away from Maryland and a long way off from 1768. At hand was refitting the *Britain* and that took time—three weeks, three slow weeks that ate into the stores of provisions the emigres had purchased with their life savings. Three grueling weeks that, you can tell, ate at the heart of Blaise, not only because he was a young man, but because of his spirit.

After three restless weeks, the *Britain* finally slugged out of port on January 5, 1769. By then, you can see that along with all its cargo, the schooner carried a lingering "animosity between the passengers and the crew." The passengers mistrusted Ford, and Ford "bitterly resented" them. So much so that on February 21st when the *Britain* sighted the Louisiana coast, Ford refused to head north. He blamed "easterly winds and continuous fog" that drove the ship off course, but it was nothing but spite that made Ford follow that route.

You and everyone else could see it. The passengers "noticed that the *Britain* sailed in one direction while Steele was on duty and in the opposite direction when Ford . . . [and] the ship's pilot stood watch." One day, finally, proof of the treachery spilled from someone's mouth. "You think that you have arrived at New Orleans," the liquored-up pilot blurted out, "but you are wrong. I shall make you suffer before you get there."

The Acadians and Germans threatened to throw Ford and the pilot overboard. Fearing for his life, Ford relented the helm to Steele, but by then, the schooner was so far off course it was nowhere near New Orleans.

Without charts of the strange waters it found itself in, the ship skirted the coast. Several times it tried to come into a bay, but the shoreline was unforgiving and the weather was bad. Even from the distance of 250 years, you can see how misery set in. The already sparse provisions ran completely dry. Thirst took the helm. Hunger climbed aboard. Ford himself attested that in the end "passengers and crew were reduced to a diet of 'rats, cats, and even all the shoes and leather in the vessel.'"

Frantic at that point, way off in the faraway land of Texas, Steele made the schooner do something drastic. His will forced her into Matagorda Bay. Wild-eyed, he didn't care that the desperate act meant "grounding the vessel on the bar three times."

Run aground is the best way to describe what I did on my trip to LeJeune Cove too. I was speeding down the highway, looking for the turnoff, and suddenly I saw the green LeJeune Cove Road sign. Not wanting to miss the turn, I hit the brakes so bad the lurching of my car felt like a boat keel slamming into a bank.

Some would call LeJeune Cove a neighborhood, but Cajuns might use the words *le voisinage*, "a small, rural community most often located near a waterway such as a bayou."[16] It's a set-off community. LeJeune Cove's north edge is probably the bridge over Bayou Mallet as that waterway curves east. Its western edge is probably Bayou Mallet's southerly track as it runs to meet Bayou des Cannes. Its eastern rim is likely Grand Coulee Road running along des Cannes, and its southern end is maybe Big Leaf Road. This is all just guesswork, though. LeJeune Cove isn't the kind of place where the boundaries are marked. People there know it by feel.

I didn't. But if I had to make a stab at what the heart of LeJeune Cove was, I'd say it had to be that metal pole topped with the small green sign that read, "LeJeune Cove Road." At it, a skinny gravel road ran about twenty-five hundred feet all the way back to a wood jutting up against a bayou.

Nice houses lived on that road. Brick houses. Metal roofs. Tractors in the yards. Small stretches of rice fields spread behind them. One plot on that road was populated by a newish pumpjack. One house had "LeJeune" stenciled on the mailbox. Another had "LeJeune's" in big black letters nailed up near its door.

I shut my eyes for a moment and imagined myself living on that road. I made up a story about myself. I had a dog, a lab. My wife and kids convinced me to put a trampoline out back. The neighbors had kids who were always over to play. She was a nurse and he was a contractor. We were related in some way that neither of us could explain, but both knew. But it was even better than that. Another neighbor down the LeJeune Cove road did roofs. When the hurricane came, it was natural he did mine, and I helped him in whatever way I could. It was the old days and I was playing pretend. I was doing the old things—the *coup de main*, the phrase my dad used to say. It meant pitching in. It meant sharing the work. It meant something akin to a barn-raising.

But now I was the fool. So I opened my eyes, and left.

I only made it a mile or so on the highway before I turned around to cruise the gravel road again.

There was a man tinkering in his driveway, and this time I stopped.

I told him who I was, that I was a LeJeune, and he said, "I'm sorry for you," and we laughed.

After we talked a bit, mostly about who I really should talk to for answers to my questions, I left for good, traveling south on Highway 91 as it traced Bayou Pointe Aux Loups. That bayou and Bayou Mallet both crept slowly south to feed Bayou des Cannes.

Bayou des Cannes, Bayou Nezpique, Bayou Plaquemine Brulée, and Bayou Queue de Torte—these are the largest tributaries of the Mermentau River. They watered the Cajuns and the Cajun Prairie of old back when it was a recognizable prairie. Of course, that was more than a hundred years ago, nearly two lifetimes away, but still, it must have been magical.

"The most pleasing part of the state"—that was how surveyor Samuel H. Lockett described the prairies after four years of touring Louisiana. It was 1872. It was once upon a time.

Lockett's hope was to draw a topographical map of Louisiana's land, but the world played tricks on him. Before his very eyes, the terrain of the prairies transformed into something other than land. He couldn't avoid being bewitched. It was impossible to ride through the prairies "without having their striking resemblance to large bodies of water constantly recurring" to his mind. The prairie surface had small depressions known as *marais* (little marsh) and slight elevations known as pimple or mima mounds, but mostly the landscape stood as "vast, treeless expanses . . . covered with a luxuriant growth of grass. . . . Generally . . . level, but occasionally huge swells will cross them from side to side like the mighty billows of a deep sea . . . the green carpet . . . all around you . . . the distant horizon . . . terminated by the dark lines of a forest that project . . . like the headlands of a lake."[17]

It was a setting that teemed with life, and his body must have been drowning in the depth of its richness. The grass, it "waves in the wind and looks like ripples on the bosom of the ocean," he wrote, edged by "the dark blue borders of woods." The treelines and groves, they call out like "distant shores, the projecting spurs, like capes and promontories, the 'coves,' like bays and gulfs, and the occasional clumps of detached trees, like islands in the sea."

Cove, that word, he snatched it from something, from somewhere, maybe from the people speaking to him. Maybe he was quoting St. Landry Parish's David Courville who lived in "the Great Prairies . . . the ocean-like expanses." Maybe it was "Joe Chaumont who owned Chaumont's Ferry on Bayou Nez Piqué" or maybe "M. Pierre" and his wife, "a negro family" who lived in Pierre Noir "on the opposite side of the bayou . . . in a point of woods that projected into the Prairie like a cape into the sea."

Whoever it was, the quotation marks are proof of the nets he used—conversations with these early prairie settlers about their home. They seemed to look upon the cove, *le voisinage*, the "neighborhood," as a key factor in their sense of belonging.

Historically, in the Cajun Prairie neighbors all knew one another, probably were even related in some way. They shared various "communal activities throughout the year" that kept them connected. Mardi Gras, "the *boucherie*, the *échange du temps*, la *ramasserie*, *veillées* . . . treatments delivered at the hands of a local *traiteur*," even good visits and long cups of coffee at the kitchen table, became traditions people shared that kept members of *le voisinage* physically close and emotionally attached.[18] It was just one of their survival tricks.

But these people, my people, were full of dodges and deceptions. One of their most potent was seclusion, at least a certain kind of it. Already run off from a land they settled, they cloaked themselves in this one with a "sense of cultural isolation by establishing geographic isolation."[19] They lived as close as they could to their old Acadie way of life to protect themselves and preserve and maintain their sense of ethnicity.

Why? Because people judge other people. Because Acadian exiles knew what that felt like. Because they have for a long time. Because the feeling of being judged is hard to run from. Because it can feel like it's following you, even from one country to the next, even if you're speeding down a highway.

But the Cajun Prairie offered ladlefuls of protection from that. Its abundance was separation, and the Acadian settlers in Louisiana ate from that willingly "not only for cultural preservation but for familial cohesiveness and economic independence."[20] In this way, the little community that sat on a semicircle of prairie land buffeted on three sides by trees felt like an escape, like protection in a storm, like a cove. The little neighborhood of families felt enchanted.

It makes sense that many of these prairie coves were "named after the most predominant family in the settlement,"[21] like LeJeune Cove and "the first settlers there . . . Angelas LeJeune, Alcide LeJeune, Onezime Vige, Placide Leger, Michel LeJeune, Homer LeJeune."[22] Homer, that was my great grandfather—a man I never knew who settled a place I ought to know by heart, but don't.

But I had helpers. I had my bag and the pages inside that drew my hand down into itself until I was fishing out "Chapter 10" of the LeJeune genealogy. Almost like a summoning, those pages written by a man I didn't know brought me face to face with the great grandfather I had never met.

"The LEJEUNEs and most of the Acadian descendants are very conservative," the author John Austin Young told me as way of introduction to my family. "Their homes are modest, functional, comfortable, with little regard for show." Acadian descendants "husband their financial resources allowing the pursuit of financial opportunities as they arise," he explained. "Homer was no exception, although unable to read or write he acquired a considerable amount of land." Part of that was 160.16 acres "about 3 miles north of Iota that he homesteaded on 25 June 1890," the acres that would become LeJeune Cove.

My grandfather Marc (sometimes spelled Mark) was Homer's sixth child. I never met him either. He died in 1944 when my dad was only nine. Growing up, I always heard Marc got kicked out of L'Anse de LeJeune because of some reason my father didn't really know and couldn't or wouldn't tell me. I can't say if that story of Marc's expulsion is authentic. It might've just been easier for Marc to live where my grandmother was from.

My grandmother died in 1989. It was late July. I remember the mammoth fig trees that boomed in her backyard. They would have been very ripe that summer, but I don't really remember. I was in high school . . . and an idiot . . . and a fool with worlds of time.

They say that in the coves, houses were close together, "almost always within sight of each other," and that "the Cajun of the coves married the girl that he met at the *bal [de maison]* . . . or at a relative's house," and that the *coup de main* shared the work of each cove family assuring "everyone would make ends meet."[23]

When my grandparents were married in 1911, my grandfather was nineteen and my grandmother was sixteen. "My husband had the lumber sawed for the building of our first home," she told my cousin during that recorded interview. "My father furnished the logs. This house was located on my father's property," she reminisced.

"My father's house site was approximately 100 yards from the present house site of my son, Elmo LeJeune," she went on. "My father's 1st cousin, Jules Leger, supervised the construction of the house. My husband, Mark, my brother, Dominick, and Raoul Roy also assisted in the construction of the house."

My grandparents' first child, my aunt Wava, was born in that house eleven months later.

"My husband began to acquire land," my grandmother explained. "In 1913 . . . we moved our house from my father's property to my husband's recently acquired property."

By August, she and my grandfather were completely moved in. On August 30th, my aunt Mertrice was born in that new house. Several other children followed . . . Elmo, Verda, Hugh . . . fourteen in all. My aunt Charlesa was born in 1933 many weeks premature. She was so small my grandfather could slip his wedding ring up to her elbow—that's the story anyway. My dad was the last one, the baby boy. He was born in that same house. It was 1935.

For my grandmother's funeral in 1989, her children put together her obituary, laminated it, and turned it into a bookmark. It was one of the first things I pulled from the Ziploc bag the day I scattered things on the floor. "Mrs. Mark LeJeune" was what the obituary called her. Marie Coralie Leger LeJeune was her full name. She "was ninety-four at the time of her passing." She had forty-three grandchildren, sixty-six great-grandchildren, and seventeen great-great-grandchildren.

The year she died may have been the very end of the period of my life when I was closest to my extended family—all my uncles and aunts and cousins, all my godparents and half-cousins, my blood brothers. But at that time in my life, I don't think I knew enough to ask what "LeJeune" meant. Besides, I still had time. My father was still alive. So were many of his brothers and sisters. Weddings and funerals, weekend visits, drives to my dad's hometown of Egan—all of them seemed to be as abundant as figs in a rainy July.

By the 2013 Mardi Gras, all that had changed. My father died in 2009. My aunt Wava passed many years before that. The trips to Egan and Iota to see my mother's and father's families hardly happened anymore. Somehow, I made excuses for missing weddings and funerals.

It happened earlier to the Cajun Prairie, but by the turn of the twentieth century, it had changed. New Orleans was an old crone by then, nearly two hundred years old and needing a reliable supply of food. Up to that point, boats had handled all the foodstuffs the Crescent City needed, but the schooners and flatboats and barges faced treacherous seas and marshes and dried-up creeks. Every year that trip seemed more and more cursed. By the 1880s a miracle happened—the railroad with its coal-black engine and its steady-as-sleep coursing over the flat prairie. The iron horse appeared to everyone as a most beautiful dream, an answer to the prayers people said before bed.

Once the tracks were laid and the railroad route was finished, speculators ate up the prairie—Eunice, Iowa, Welsh, Roanoke, Crowley, Rayne, Esterwood, even Jennings where I grew up, they replaced the French names that once were. Abbot's Cove turned to Egan. Pointe-aux-Loups became Iota. L'Anse de LeJeune, if anyone said its name at all, transformed into English, mutated into LeJeune Cove.

Prairie lives also changed. People started farming, making crops to make a profit, growing and farming as much as they could. The prairie landscape started to morph from grassland to farmland. That changed not only the countryside, but the culture. Before the prairie was gone, as one geographer explains, "share-cropping neighborhoods once radiated outward from [a place like] Mamou in all directions. Each of these was a named neighborhood—l'Anse Meg, La Pointe aux Pins, Tit Mamou, Duralde, Grand Louis, Anse Johnson, La Pinière, Soileau, l'Anse des Priens Noirs, and others. . . . These communities, the *anses* (or the coves), as they are still called, were once the foci of the intensive daily interaction of the French-speaking farmers of the Prairie."[24] But now, "a casual observer might be easily persuaded that the Prairie has always had a low population density, with farmsteads scattered across the polder-like landscape . . . with the town limits now surrounded by wide expanses of rice and soy beans."

I say all that to say this: Once upon a time, a man driving away from the LeJeune Cove Road, looking for home, had a Ziploc bag that had run out of whatever power it had. He could look along the Eunice-Iota Highway and see the small homes, but they weren't neighborhoods anymore. He had heard what some wise people once said—that all throughout the prairie were "the clusters of small farms that still dot the landscape along major streams."[25] That was what he saw—dots, points, orphaned places, relics of a world that used to be. Farmhouses that now seemed stranded, deserted, adrift in the rice fields surrounding them.

And the man in the story had a father who used to close his hand to make a fist and say he could count his friends with it. At first, he didn't understand and thought his father meant he had no friends, but he saw the way his father visited with everyone.

As the son thought more, he assumed his father meant that he felt isolated, but the old man never seemed to feel too alone, or if he did, he never told the son.

Then, the son guessed the father meant to tell him something about family, but the boy never knew what that something was, not really. Now, the father was dead, and the son had no idea and had no one to ask.

It was a long time ago, it seemed, and far away, but the father and the son used to drive nearly every Sunday to see a grandmother in Egan, near a place once named for big bad wolves. Nothing ever felt lonely then. Nothing seemed too impossible.

But then the son drove away from LeJeune Cove Road one winter. He had to leave. He had no house there, no home, but then he remembered the old car rides, and wondered if he had misremembered them all along. The son thought that maybe when the father saw the one farmhouse out by itself on the edge of a rice field, the old man thought something other than what he let on. When the two finally rode all the way back home and pulled the car into a driveway that connected to a road running into Main Street but to none of the father's relatives, to his father, did that scene feel like a good story coming to an end or a sad story with an ending that kept going?

And that I say only to say this: In 2013, when I went to that Mardi Gras, I would've brought my father if he were alive then, but he wasn't. It was my sister, me, my wife, and my two daughters. It was a day when a few of my family walked LeJeune Cove again. It was a day surprise followed surprise and somehow, I ran into an old friend, Ray Brassieur, who was there with bells and a beard and a guitar.

The Mardi Gras run in LeJeune Cove dates back to 1900, and up until World War II, twenty or thirty men of LeJeune Cove would run it. After World War II, the LeJeune Cove run merged with larger ones nearby and almost disappeared for good. But people saved it. My friend Ray Brassieur, an anthropologist, was one of them, but I didn't know. It was one of this world's secrets.

Ray's research meant that even after a lapse of some fifty years, the 2003 LeJeune Cove Mardi Gras run looked very much like it did in the 1930s.[26] The male runners came upon the farmstead on horseback and on a wagon. They donned traditional costumes and disguised themselves behind masks with beards, huge eyes, and outlandish noses. Pointy *capuchons* sat on their heads. Everything whirled with fringes and bright colors and bells. They sang the communal songs. Everyone danced.

They kept dancing, every year. In 2013, my daughter two-stepped with them, and when I watched my girl hold the hands of the costumed man, when my head swam with something that seemed like a storm cloud, one of the strongest feelings I've ever had in my life sat in my stomach like a stone: my life was missing something; in this life I had built, there was something I had missed out on.

That ache kept me going on my trip after the hurricanes, but it didn't turn me south on the Eunice-Iota Highway. It didn't face me towards the interstate, back towards home. It sailed me east on Grand Coulee Road that swept up and across the prairie until I hooked a left onto Rupert Lake Road. Then I was in Frey Cove. Then I was in Mowata. Then I was on Cole Gully Road, which crossed Gumpoint Road and White Oak Highway and Prairie Hayes Road. Then it swung me south until I found a small gravel road flanked by a long stretch of pasture populated by a group of lucky cows who had found solace in a patch of hardwood. At the end of that road, Blaise LeJeune Bayou survived.

The water there wasn't deep, but I watched the slow current it held. The creases and purls and wrinkles on the water's surface watched me back. The side of the road had strong patches of Johnson grass as high as a man's head and giant ragweed, too, and privet, and hornbeam copperleaf. Clumps of goosegrass managed to thrive in the gravel, and turnsole in the culvert, and the chamber bitter and yellow foxtail and witchgrass built the place between the road and the woods into something strangely familiar. Webs made lace in the canopy of all the trees where something dark sat among the spangled sunlight caught in there. Black bodies of banana spiders cut with bright yellow stripes made homes in the branches. I hadn't seen them since I was a kid.

And then I saw it. That once upon a time when a pack of orphans, their good band of chaperones, two villains, and a crew of lost men found themselves stranded, basically deserted on an island of sorts. It was a shoal near Matagorda Bay, and I say once upon a time because what happened to Blaise next seems fairytale-like, but is history.[27]

Five Spanish soldiers found the passengers of the *Britain* on the Texas coast not long after the ship ran aground. The soldiers marched a portion of the shipwrecked passengers "twenty leagues inland" to La Bahia Presidio. The rest waited on their beach to hear their fate.

The Spanish commandant at La Bahia listened intently to the woeful story, wrote it all down in a letter to the viceroy of New Spain, then waited.

Without permission from the viceroy, the commandant wouldn't allow Ford to set sail with his cargo. Ford refused to give that up, no matter what that meant for the passengers, so the lost-in-Texas Acadians suffered a "four-month detention" while the commandant and Ford played chicken.

Eventually, the *Britain* was freed to set sail again, but by then, the ship was in tatters—rotten wood spotted the hull and ruined sails sat on the mast. The Acadians would have to walk the 380 miles from Bahia to Natchitoches, the nearest Louisiana post.

Following two Spanish guides named Francisco Pacheco de la Portilla and Martinez Pacheco along the El Camino Real, the Acadians left La Bahia on September 13th and marched every day. More than a month later, they reached Natchitoches.

In Louisiana, the used-to-be-lost-in-Texas Acadians ran into another obstacle on their road home. This time, it was Louisiana Governor Alejandro O'Reilly who had just quelled a rebellion supported in part by armed Acadians. He wasn't thrilled about more Acadians coming in to settle near New Orleans. He could see letting the Germans migrate to Iberville, but these new Acadians would have to stay in Natchitoches.

Blaise sat stuck in Natchitoches, and the men leading his group were enraged. The whole point in migrating to Louisiana was to be near family, reunite with friends, find home sites near those people once scattered but now gathering along the Mississippi River, but now an officious wall stood between them and their dreams.

It was a change in governor that changed things. Newly appointed Governor Luis de Unzaga told the stuck-in-Natchitoches Acadians that if they could find their own way to their Iberville claims, they could settle them, which they did.

Blaise was nineteen or twenty when he landed at Iberville in the late summer of 1770. It must have been hot, humid, far different from that Maryland December of his sixteenth year. By 1772, Blaise had received a land grant on the west bank of the river Mississippi in the county of Iberville. He met his bride Marie-Joseph Breaux in 1773. From the outside looking in, everything appeared idyllic in Iberville.

From the inside, though, Blaise and his family had seen enough of trouble and were through with being judged. Like many Acadians, they were looking for escape, for insularity, for a certain type of solitude, but not even those settlements in Iberville offered enough of that.

By 1774, Blaise had sold his land grant there. He wasn't alone. Around that time "many of the Acadians abandoned their riverfront farms at Iberville for the isolation of the remote and forbidding Opelousas prairies."[28] And just like clockwork, Honoré Trahan's family, Blaise and Marie-Joseph, and all the other orphaned LeJeunes moved to Opelousas as a unit.

According to the census of the poste, Honoré Trahan and his wife Marie Corporon lived in dwelling 100. Blaise's brother Joseph lived in dwelling 101.

Marguerite and her husband John Crooks lived in dwelling 125. Blaise and Marie-Joseph lived in 130.

The quest for loneliness wasn't done. In 1777, Blaise and Marie acquired a tract of land on Bayou Carencro, south of present-day Sunset, and left Opelousas to move there.

It didn't last. For some reason, that place wouldn't do either, and Blaise sold that land to his brother. Burdenless now, Blaise went west, pioneering to the very edge of Cajun migration. Finally, he planted roots north of Plaquemine Brulée, which is a waterway that sits about ten miles southwest of Church Point.

In *Founding of New Acadia*, historian Carl Brasseux explains that at that time "few Acadians sought homes along Bayou Plaquemine Brulée, and fewer still ventured into the wilderness beyond the prominent plains landmark." Blaise was one of them. He was isolated, but only somewhat. "Wildly scattered along Bayous Blaize LeJeune and Des Cannes," Brasseux writes, "this pioneer settlement comprised only four families totaling twenty-nine individuals."[29] In other words, Blaise was just the right amount of alone.

All of that should have mattered. All of it should've settled my restlessness. But standing at the bridge of Blaise LeJeune Bayou, I opened up my Ziploc bag, put my mouth to it, and asked, "Blaise, what was different about this place from all the others?"

But there was no answer. How could there be? There was nothing but a road, a patch of mixed hardwood growing along it, and a small bridge. There was only this place, where the gravel road disappeared and the grass swallowed the tire tracks. And silence.

That was when I looked up and at the far end of the road saw an opening where the trees fell away to open fields. I walked the hundred yards to them, and when I was at the edge of the road and able to look up into the sky without the walls of trees blocking my vision, I saw the birds of the prairie circling, reeling. A field was being cut somewhere nearby, and the cowbirds were in flight gathering for a feast.

A long time ago, once, the coastal tallgrass prairie that Blaise homesteaded "covered 2.5 million acres in southwest Louisiana." Today, it's been reduced to "less than 100 acres in small, isolated remnant strips along railroad rights of way."[30] But not too far from Blaise LeJeune Bayou, not too far by the timing of a car ride, not far away at all from LeJeune Cove Road, people are fighting.

And like the fight the English had with the French for the Bay of Fundy, this fight is about land. And like Acadians who conducted guerrilla warfare as they resisted expulsion from Nova Scotia, this fight is happening out of most people's line of sight. And like Blaise's march to Natchitoches, it's a fight for home. And it's happening right there in the middle of Eunice, and in Duralde too. It's happening right there on the Eunice-Iota Highway that runs by LeJeune Cove. It's a fight for the Cajun Prairie.

Malcolm Vidrine, Charles Allen, and a handful of others are the battle's champions. In the late 1980s, dedicated preservationists like them and organizations like the Cajun Prairie Habitat Preservation Society promised to return some of the majestic Cajun Prairie landscape to its natural state. The oldest project started in the heart of Eunice with a 4-hectare lot that had been left fallow for years. The city of Eunice leased it from the Union Pacific Railroad, mowed it, cleaned it, got it to a bare state, then the work began.

The volunteer groups sent out students to collect seeds from remnant strips of prairie found along the railroads. There were papsy grasses and love grasses and three-awn grasses. There were little and slender bluestem, big bluestem, and broomsedge. Wire grass, switch grass, and panic grass. Goldenrods and false foxgloves. Spurges and sundew. There were many more.

By December of 1988, volunteers were ready to sow seeds, add sod, and plant a few cuttings. Prescribed burns came yearly after that. Very little weeding was done. Bare spots were sown again. The tallow trees were cleared.

Today, in Eunice, down a road called Athabaska Street, which is an old word for "grass or reeds here and there," sits a field the Cajun Prairie Habitat Preservation Society keeps unmown and natural and unfenced so that someone, if they wanted to, could walk through and touch sneezewort and grassleaf rush, and dandelion, and southern dewberry, and bull thistle, and musk thistle, and all manner of sedge—globe flatsedge, blue wood, slough, troublesome.

Malcom F. Vidrine can tell you about the once-upon-a-times, how the Kingdom of the Prairie was made and when it was destroyed. Malcom F. Vidrine is bona fide, that's the word he uses in his book. Vidrine walked acres and acres of the prairie over the course of his lifetime to gain the knowledge and experience he has. He uses it to tell you all about it in *The Cajun Prairie: A Natural History*. He can tell you about the things you may not notice—like the Chinese tallow tree which is a "vicious weed" or "how the feral cattle, horses, and pigs" destroyed so much native vegetation. He can tell you about the large-scale impacts "of farming and petroleum production [that] were much more dramatic and damaging." He can go through the chapters of the prairie's story one by one—how over time it was grazed by cattle; then "dissected by irrigation canals and developed into rice fields and cotton fields." How it was "cut into lots for homes." Then drilled and made into oil fields. Then its bayous dredged, its rivers straightened, even its end-rows were removed. Finally, all its yards were mowed for looks and city ordinances. In the 1960s, "the last of the prairie plants essentially disappeared," and "by the end of the 1970s, the Cajun Prairie was considered lost."[31]

But there were a few corners where the wrinkled hands of time didn't reach, and that afternoon, I ended up at one of them. It was the intersection of the Eunice-Iota Highway and Fournerat Road where a car can pull off onto the shoulder and a driver can step out to see a patch of saved prairie. It was called Cajun Prairie Gardens, and I don't know how I landed there after I left Blaise Bayou, but when I saw the field and yard converted to the ancient prairie, it was like looking back in time.

A ditch separated the wildflower patch from the highway, and standing on the asphalt, I could see the awns of grasses and faces of flowers and the bees moving back and forth between them. There was Eastern gamagrass and white wild indigo. There was swamp sunflower and prairie blazing star and Lindheimer's beeblossom and rattlesnake master and gray goldenrod. There was biennial gaura that my mom calls evening primrose and wood grass she calls Indiangrass and partridge pea that she says as kids they used to call touch-me-nots. There were purple passion flowers that make maypops and people here used to eat their seeds, and there was coral bean that everyone around here knows as Mamou Root and uses for medicine, or once did.

But Cajun Prairie Gardens was private property, or so it seemed, and I was afraid to walk inside, so I stayed at the edge of the roadside ditch and stared.

For a long time, I did that, then I walked up and down Fournerat Road hoping the people inside the little house made of bricks might come out and invite me inside the garden. Or maybe someone driving by might see me and point the way inside. But it never happened. One man on a motorcycle waved to me but kept going. One work truck seemed to slow down enough to check me out, but didn't ask if I needed anything. So I walked up and down the blacktop several times, my feet in the ditch, newly mown, my toes on the edge of the flowering landscape.

Looking out at the Cajun Prairie project was like seeing through the eyes of early settlers. It was like walking in the steps of Blaise and Homer, taking in the slow undulation of the ground, gazing at lines of trees in the distance, seeing the sky for what it is—a bringer of rain, an endless mover of storms, a blue that makes you feel like things have gone on forever. It's the color of a deep well, the deep well of history that calls us back.

But that's a poisonous water—a water that's impossible to drink, a water like seawater that will make you thirstier for what you don't have.

Or at least, that's what came to me that afternoon. And that was what I carried home as I trekked up to Eunice, then back west on 190, then down into Lake Charles.

"The homesickness you have at home," that's how Glenn A. Albrecht might describe a feeling that some people have, some places. He coined the word *solastalgia* to describe it—the state you're in when you can no longer find solace at home due to the "sickness" of your home place. For Albrecht, that sickness often comes from a landscape that's been damaged or an environment that's been ruined or destroyed and is no longer recognizable. I don't know if that's what you would call Lake Charles and the Louisiana coast, but my stomach did sink a little when I pulled into my driveway.

There was so much to do to get things back to normal, and my Ziploc bag was empty, and quiet. Its tongue was gone, or someone had sewn its lips shut or a curse had dried up all its words. It couldn't even tell me if any of the house jobs in front of me were worth doing. It couldn't say if rebuilding my garage or my roof was or wasn't just building a castle of sand.

So I walked back to the black basket to rebury my inheritance. Maybe my daughter would know how to use it, or her daughter might, or someone else would be able to make the Ziploc bag talk again.

But as I tucked the bag away, I realized I had forgotten something. All the pages and pieces of genealogies had found their way back into the Ziploc after I looked at them, but the two sealed manila folders hadn't.

I sat down on the floor and pulled the folders close to me. First, I turned them over in my hands, then I saw my father's signature running across their flaps. I unpinned the brass brad pin of the first envelope, opened it, and slid the papers out. They were more photocopies my father had saved. "Prieres" was written at the top of the first page. "L'Oraison Dominicale" and "La Salutation Angelique" and "Gloiree au Pere" and several other prayers all printed very carefully by someone's hand, with accents and a few notes about pronunciation included.

When I tilted the other envelope upwards, several copies of the traditional Mardi Gras songs from different small Cajun communities and a newspaper article from the *Jennings Daily News* slid out. The article was dated January 20, 2005, and showed all the words of the "Traditional Mardi Gras Song" for the Grand Marais Mardi Gras run. Hurricane Rita hit Lake Charles and Jennings that year. Three years later my dad would find out about his cancer.

I don't mean to add the detail about his sickness except to tell the once-upon-a-time story I need to tell. You see, I know how the ocean was made salty, and it wasn't from a salt mill and a wish for it to keep grinding. Our tears come from greed and self-pity. What I mean is, I've heard the birds are dying—the common songbirds, the blue jays, the robins, the starlings, the grackles, all along the East coast, hundreds with eye and brain problems.[32] I don't know all of their names. Maybe it was the jewel-throated John Wood warbler or the full-breasted Leo Marcello cormorant or the Ray Miles-to-go swallow, but the birds are stumbling around, dazed, not eating, disappearing. And the lightning bugs are gone. People here have said that to me. And the bees collapsed a couple of years ago. And it's hard to find banana spiders. And I don't know how many people would recognize a Mamou Root plant.

And walking along the roadside ditch at Cajun Prairie Gardens was like watching my daughter at Mardi Gras or like being in LeJeune Cove but not running the Mardi Gras. It was like I was standing on the edge of a dance floor. I could hear the music. I could see the people dancing. I watched the steps, saw the bodies sway around the floor, but I didn't dance. I couldn't. And it wasn't that I wasn't asked. It wasn't that the dancers wanted the dance and the dance floor to themselves. It was that I didn't know the steps.

It was like standing on the edge of a great field both lush and golden. If I walked into it, I would be able to feel the tingle of the tips of the grasses against my arms and neck. All I needed to do was lose the greed and self-pity and step inside. If I did, I would be engulfed in the sweet smell of field grass. If I wasn't afraid, I would be swallowed by a wild pasture.

The warmth of it wasn't far. I only needed to take a few steps to become lost to the shoulder-high wildflowers, the grasses as tall as a traveler on horseback. Only a few steps and I'd be back inside a history not really forgotten, back in a place not foreign to me.

But I couldn't go. I couldn't step inside.

But worse than anything was that I wasn't a traveler who couldn't enter. I wasn't a visitor looking outside in. I was at home but dispossessed of it. I was homesick while being at home.

So while this whole journey to LeJeune Cove and Blaise LeJeune Bayou at first seemed to be an answer to a call, I realized that was wrong. It was merely the first steps I needed to take to go where I needed to go. If I was going to find myself, there were edges and islands and centers and all sorts of other places in Louisiana I had to reach and get lost in them.

Because once upon a time in a place named Louisiana, which sounds very far away but isn't, there lived a man named Keagan LeJeune who searched for a way to say, "I Am" and a place to say it in. His story follows.

2

THE ONLY TIME BEN LILLY WAS EVER LOST

> As soon as I write my book I want to go wild again.
> —Ben Lilly, 1931

Five months to the day after Hurricane Laura hit Lake Charles, I found the books in my office doing something strange. It was one of the first days faculty were allowed back on campus, and while some of my books sat politely on the bookshelves where I left them before I evacuated, the rest had changed. My folklore books had scattered around the room. My books of myths were on the floor, their spines broken, lying supine. *Fairy Tales from around the World* was doing cartwheels. My books of tall tales had doubled in size. *The Jack Tales* had the wrong book jacket on as a way of disguise. *The Hobbit* was buried under a stack of C. S. Lewis books. *Till We Have Faces* was on the top, face down. My books on Texas and Louisiana legends were sitting in a circle telling lies. *Gumbo Yaya* was hanging off my desk. *Swapping Stories* was standing on its head as if the world was spun upside down.

But this was a new world. It was late January, southwestern Louisiana, 2021. It was the land of rebuilding from double hurricanes. It was the realm of hollow buildings and emptied-out neighborhoods and ghost-town campuses. It was the kingdom of lost homes. It was the empire of what used to be.

It was, simply, my first adventure back into my office. Most of the other buildings on campus still sat shutdown—chains on their doors, the lights off, the yellow tape labeling it a total loss. But my building suffered only *minor* damage—a ruined roof, which was fixed now. The A/C was back on. The mold remediated. Contractors finally had cleared the building for reentry so faculty could check in on their spaces. It was the first swing in the fight to get back to normal. That's what the administration called it. That's what everyone said. It was time to claw our way towards typical, but what they didn't know, what no one did, was this was just a lull.

By late January, you see, this place was just two federally declared disasters down. By May, there would be two more. Of course, no one knew that yet. This hard-to-live-in home of mine had us good and fooled.

The upcoming semester strutted across campus like the cock of the walk. It twisted our shirt collars, pulled us close, and demanded things—like most of our money, and any time we had to spare, and all our attention, and every ounce of energy we had left.

I had met my share of toughs before, but this semester had come to outrun, outsmart, outfight, and outlast anyone around who didn't oblige, didn't toe the line, didn't get back to business as usual. To hell with what I wanted. I had two choices now—please or start getting pummeled.

I figured playing the fool was safer than being the rival with the black eye and busted lip, so I busied myself with juggling the start of a new semester with a world upended by two disasters. I threw my own house with cracked rafters up into the air while I caught an office jumbled by contractors, then my hands chased them both around a moving circle.

The tricky part was I didn't yet grasp how crazy this world had become.

That truth of that came with a knock on my office door.

It was a man as lean and taut as a railroad tie. His eyes were steel shot, a bluish gray with corners that glinted like the edge of a sharpened bear knife. His long beard looked like a patch of moss. His ramshackle hat sat tilted on the top of his head. He wore a woodsman's brown jacket and sturdy traveling pants hitched up by suspenders and a rope for a belt. From that belt ran another sturdy rope that connected to a passel of baying hounds, and all about his body hung the instruments for hunting.

But beyond all else, he carried the odor of himself and the outdoors. It was so strong it both shook me by the hand and slapped me across the cheek as he roostered himself through my doorway. After a few steps, he propped himself against my desk and folded his arms. He took a good minute looking around the room covered with the chaos of a hurricane, tsking and grinning as if he had expected as much.

I knew right away who he was. It was Benjamin Vernon Lilly, the legendary huntsman, born in 1856 and dead for eighty-five years.

I wouldn't mislead you. I couldn't. Even though the man everyone called Ben Lilly or just Ol' Lilly had died in 1936, he stood right there in my office, alive as ever, just like he is in the stories people tell.

There are all sorts of those. Tales of his incredible strength and stamina. Speculations about the record number of bears and mountain lions he killed. Praise for his keen naturalistic observations. Wonder over his ardent embrace of primitiveness. Head-scratching at his other unusual principles.

Lilly was one of those few people who became a legend even when he was alive. His hunting prowess made the national papers. For decades, people talked about his feats as if the man was still not adding to them. Southern bear chasers and western ranchers anticipated his arrival on a hunt with stories about his earlier exploits. Teddy Roosevelt, who once used him as a hunting guide, marveled over his "frame of steel and whipcord," as Teddy himself put it, and saw him as a walking tall tale.

Dead, Lilly's legend grew. Dead for nearly a century on the day he walked into my office, most of his legend couldn't fit through my door.

Sure, I know this sort of thing doesn't happen where most people live, but it does in Louisiana. Here, the unbelievable is as regular as anything. It's as normal as hundreds of acres of land floating on water or parades where everyone knows to turn the world upside down to make things right. In Louisiana, legendary Ben Lilly is just one of our neighbors. In Lake Charles, the can't-be often happens.

You grow used to it—misbelief, disbelief, wonder . . . wondering. Will the storm hit? Could it be as strong as they're saying? Should I stay? Should I go? Why do I have so much to pack up from my house? Do I have time to go to my office and box up what I don't want to lose? Can I believe this traffic headed out of town?

If you're lucky, once the storm's passed, you come home and there's still something to come home to. You go up to work. You count your blessings that the worst of it is books and papers simply rearranged. You struggle to take it all in. You try to accept this is the new normal now. Then you look up to see Ben Lilly perching himself in the doorway, or on your desk, or in your chair. But you're in Louisiana, so the surprise isn't that he's there. What beats all is that he's bewildered at what you're worrying over, what you're fighting to save.

"Property is a handicap to man": From across the room, I swear to you, I heard Ben Lilly say that, like he always did announce to people, explaining why he chose to live in the woods, without a bed or tent most nights, in such a primitive way.[1]

As a young man, Lilly would disappear for weeks or months at a time for a hunt. Without a word, he'd stay gone until he was nearly forgotten, then come back, only to settle for a bit before roaming off again without another word. Eventually, Ben Lilly gave it up for good—houses I mean, not roaming or hunting. One day, he just strolled out his door, walking away from his family and his land, and he just kept going, losing himself in the scrub and canebrakes.

But he never was lost, not in the way we might think of it. In fact, Ben Lilly, that legendary hunter and woodsman, swore he had never spent a single second of his entire life turned around.

"But were you never lost at all?" someone once asked him.

"No," he said, "but one time for about half a day I was considerably bothered."

So take that as proof that I wouldn't pass on a fib to you. I couldn't. Sure, I was stunned that day in my office when Lilly told me he wanted to take me somewhere special, somewhere off the road, somewhere out-of-doors, but when he told me he wanted to get lost, that was something I couldn't make up even if I tried.

You see, I know Louisiana. I expected something like Ben Lilly to come knocking on my door, but I didn't expect the man who despised the burden of traveling companions to invite me along, and I certainly didn't expect the person who never was turned around in the woods to tell me that for this trip he planned on doing just that, go blundering up Fool River.

I knew the place. Back in the 1840s, up in northeastern Louisiana, among the loops of the Tensas River, "when a tenderfoot lost his way in one of those streams he was said to have gone up Fool River."[2] For a time, any traveler, trader, or trawler who was lost was lost to that same wild place. I had a hard time figuring why Ben Lilly might want to go there.

My first reaction was any sane person's. I tried to talk everybody out of it, but all the while, Ben Lilly just stood there toeing the books on my floor and with a sneer on his face, fiddling with the few things left on my desk and nodding his head for me to hurry up and come along. Finally, I had enough. I told myself if Ben Lilly wanted to take me down Fool River, why the hell not. Besides, I knew the man's natural talent for letting go of things. After the hurricanes, I needed some of that.

The first thing Lilly showed me was that everything I thought I knew was a lie. He brought me to Fishville and Pollock, in the western part of the state, nowhere near Tensas River. This was Fool River 8, and it flowed into Fool River Bend. He showed me the old false river there and how when the water's right, it flows down into Catahoula Lake near the Kisatchie National Forest just to prove to me that I wasn't near as smart as I thought I was.

Next, he took me all the way east to Snake Bayou and Boggy Bayou and Buckshot Bayou, right there by Fool Lake. That was Fool River 2, which was meant to rub it in.

Then we went to the middle of the state to see Fool River Road in Jena, and then north up to Boston Fool River in Grant Parish. He shoved me south after that, sniggering and snorting and snickering all the way down to the coast near Galliano where there was John the Fool Bayou. It was all just salt in the wound.

I won't pretend about it now. Lilly had me over a barrel, but I was too annoyed at that point to let on. So, I parried. I told him I hadn't the time for such foolishness. There was hurricane damage to get back to. There was a home and office to worry about. Things had changed and he was getting old, and it looked like he was finally lost for real this time.

But I should've known better.

In 1928, Texas writer J. Frank Dobie heard Ben Lilly speak at the American National Livestock Association. Dobie was amazed by the stories Lilly told, and by the man's knowledge of the wild, and perhaps most of all, by Lilly's peculiarity and high opinion of himself.

Dobie wanted to turn Lilly into a research topic at that very moment, but life got in the way. It wouldn't be until around 1940 that Dobie could start on his own hunt, not for bears, but for the stories people told about Lilly.

Throughout the 1940s, Dobie traveled the trail of Lilly's life, tracking down those people who knew the hunter, recording their stories. It led to a pot of gold.

Few who heard about Lilly forgot his legend. Fewer still who met the man forgot a single detail about him—his strength, his stamina, his skill, his strangeness too. In 1950, Dobie, already a critical and commercial success as a writer, published *The Ben Lilly Legend*. Ben's legend skyrocketed.

The book recounted Lilly's early runaway life, his remarkable hunting career, and even his later days, including that 1928 talk Lilly gave to the Livestock men— "the first public speech he ever made, except for a talk to a Sunday school."

It was Dobie who said that Lilly knew the woods "so well and had such a sense of direction that he could on a drizzly day kill a deer in the middle of this forest-swamp, go off for hours over the trailless expanse, and then come directly back to the deer he had hung up."[3]

It was a skill Lilly himself admired. That old sinewy huntsman would boast about it and show it off. Almost as a parlor trick, he would enter a pathless swamp, stick a knife in a tree, exit, come in by another way, and promenade directly to that blade. It didn't matter the weather. The time of day made no difference. It could be the middle of the night. Driving snow. In any canebrake, he could do it.

"His sense of direction was not based on a knowledge of the compass, on observation of landmarks, the stars, currents of the air, or any other observable form of matter," Dobie claimed. "It was inside him." And according to Dobie, Ben's skill was something a step beyond the ancient seafarers' use of celestial maps kept in a navigator's mind. "It was instinct," Dobie wrote of Lilly's gift, "like that of a bear or a pigeon—something more elemental than reason—something that civilized man has almost lost."[4]

Truly, Lilly was elemental in his desire to be primitive. He was dedicated to that life. To him, all his years spent living outdoors were like sharpening a blade over a stone. "If we are not faithful to our talents," he once said, "we lose them."[5] What he was faithful to was tracking, and the woods, and the hunt. The man, in truth, was a walking anachronism—a never-tiring, dog-training, bear-killing, sleeping out-of-doors, dead-reckoning, knife-making, alligator-loving walking anachronism. And living primitively, out-of-time, kept those things glistening and sharp inside his heart.

All those Fool Rivers Ben brought me down were just a game. He had simply traipsed us around and around the state until the two of us finally found ourselves wandering down the streets of Mer Rouge, Louisiana, like he wanted us to.

Mer Rouge is a tiny village whose absolute center is occupied by the Country Cream Drive-In. Ben and I stopped walking its main street when we reached the town's post office. It wasn't the place I had expected, but I wasn't wholly surprised. Before us, no more than two or three feet away, stood a small monument. Erected in 1997, it was a statue of Lilly and a pair of his hounds pulling at their leashes.[6]

Frozen in stone but still alive, his bearhounds were sniffing out a fat black she-bear moseyed up on a log to his left. A set of boulders were to his right, and there, a slinking mountain cat straddled a staircase of stones. The bear had not escaped the dogs' attention. They stood ready, necks careened around the hunter's legs. And he was ready too.

Lilly was always about the hunt. He was famous for it. "Like Esau, Jacob's brother of Bible times," the monument's plaque read, "Ben Lilly was the ultimate hunter.... Not one to focus on acquiring 'things' and money, Ben acquired knowledge, knowledge about the outdoors and the four-legged challenges he found there."

Lilly wasn't born in Louisiana, but the statue sits here because he ended up in Morehouse Parish. That's due to his uncle, Vernon Lilly, who was a prosperous bachelor here and convinced Lilly to settle in Mer Rouge.

For Ben, nothing spoke truer than primitiveness, and even as a child, the legendary hunter searched for that. To escape the constraints of school and the enterprises his family pressured him to embrace, ten-year-old Lilly left his home in Alabama and walked all the way to his uncle Vernon's place. To many people's astonishment, he traveled the entire way basically unaided. He hunted along the way for food and slept in the woods at night. When he arrived, his uncle was so flabbergasted, the boy was allowed to stay for a time.

Eventually, Lilly was forced to return home, but that didn't stick.

The second time Ben left he was a young man. This time, no one knew where he had run off to, and for years, Ben was "lost to the family." As an old man, when Lilly talked about these missing years, he "referred to [them] as 'wild.'"[7]

Then one day, during a trip to Memphis, his uncle passed by a blacksmith shop and saw Ben Lilly's name on the sign outside. Uncle Vernon strode inside and told Ben that if he moved to Morehouse Parish, settled down, and took to raising crops and a family, Vernon would leave Ben his land.

The acreage Ben ultimately inherited was property the 1908 tax roll described as "three acres on the east side of Bastrop and Mer Rouge."[8] It's not too far from the monument where the bronze Ben Lilly looks as if he were alive.

The promise of a propertied life was enough for Lilly to fool himself, but not for long. In 1901, with a wad of money gripped in his palm, he walked through the front door of his house and handed the cash over to his wife Mary Etta Sisson. Next, he pulled out the papers and signed every bit of property over to her. Then, as natural as anything, he walked back out of doors, vanished into the forest, and took up the furious art of hunting fulltime, his new life being the "lonely, nomadic life of a 'mountain man' . . . a single camp deep in the woods his only home."[9]

It made a sort of sense. Lilly was never much of a farmer. Chickens, cows, crops, corn plots, coops, pigs, plows, plots of ground—all of them bound him to a place. He would have none of it. "Things ride mankind," he would argue. They would not ride him.[10]

Lilly enjoyed spouting his ideas about things and rarely shied away from opining. He was apt to proselytize. He often pontificated about owning things, about property, about obligations. He declared that he resented all "bindings."

But Lilly was a man of action mostly, and nothing speaks louder than how the man lived. He never would abide a life built begrudgingly, even if that meant leaving everything behind, and so after leaving his house and home, he never did return to his wife.

Ben found work eventually, found himself a living. Around 1904, biologist Ned Hollister had been hunting in Louisiana for specimens to send back to the Smithsonian's National Museum. Hollister met Lilly hunting in the woods, they say, and was overcome by the huntsman's skill and his knowledge of bear and panther and all the other wildlife of the Louisiana canebrakes. Lilly seemed to have an intimate understanding of these creatures, and as a hunter, Lilly was unmatched. It was a no-brainer for Hollister to hire him. All he needed to teach Lilly was the one thing about the wild the man didn't know—how to kill a thing and save its skull and skin to send back for science.

If I know anything now about Hollister and Lilly both, it's that they wanted to set down something on the page before it disappeared. Arguing the merits of leaving a wife and kids is a hard stance to take, but I've found it equally hard to blame Lilly for chasing what he loved, what he believed he was born for, and, despite it all, setting that down for posterity's sake.

But that's a farce—trying to save anything. I know that now. But people sometimes want to do that, want to try.

And I suppose I started mumbling something like that to Lilly as we stood in front of that monument. I specifically remember grumbling, "This isn't the Fool River I know. What's the point of you showing me this?"

For an answer, he just smirked, shook his head, then told me that I had misunderstood. We weren't going to Fool River, but down it.

A person driving west from Mer Rouge can't help but ease into the gas a little, with or without Ben Lilly as a guide, or at least I couldn't. It's a fat paved highway running along cotton and soybean fields that ripple like a blanket set in the grass. That day, my car swept around the lazy curves that bent themselves under a forever-blue sky, and I didn't care if a squall was riding hard in the distance. If I caught it, I knew it would dump just enough rain to cool me off and slick the asphalt black, black as Bayou Bartholomew snaking through the woods nearby.

Driving in such a languid way, only a fool wouldn't follow the cars plowing west on Highway 165. I'm not a fool, or so I said to myself, and without a second thought, nosed my way west into Bastrop, where everything turned to syrup, by which I mean everything slowed.

Bastrop is one of those Louisiana towns split by the railroad. I don't mean metaphorically split by the money the railroad offered, and I don't mean split by the this-side-of-town versus the-across-the-tracks-side-of-town mentality that oozes across the South. I mean the roads slice right through downtown Bastrop like a knife splitting open a watermelon. Madison Avenue heads west; Jefferson Avenue heads east—both pulling the center of Bastrop apart like a zipper undoing a pair of seersucker trousers.

It's a scandal—Bastrop is. The Tractor Supply Company and the Super Foods and the Bastrop Car Wash, all showed themselves starkly naked before Ben Lilly and me. "Trash," he could've said if he would've said a word. "Ruinous properties." But he uttered not a sound, and instead just nudged me to keep going.

Soon, we were squeezing through the oldest part of town to behold the stout workmanship of the Morehouse Parish courthouse and the ageless brick storefronts. And just as quick, we were waving goodbye to them, edging out of town, riding hard on Highway 425, running north, tramping ourselves to Chemin-A-Haut State Park, or so I soon discovered.

The name Chemin-A-Haut means high ridge or high road. It's an old French term early traders brought along with them. It references an early route cutting through the woods that the Native Americans here used to avoid the high waters of Bayou Bartholomew.

Chemin-A-Haut State Park is officially one of the oldest state parks in Louisiana, established in 1934 as a wave of interest swept through the state, the nation. That year, State Park Commission Chairman Robert S. Maestri wrote that "probably one of the most striking characteristics in the development of American recreation during the present century has been the manner in which Americans have become 'out-of-doors minded.'"[11] Much of it, people believed, was owed to the "vigorous and effective influence" of President Theodore Roosevelt who conveyed "that America's heritage of the out-of-doors is something that must be fought for if it is to be preserved."[12]

But that's in the abstract. In a very real way, Roosevelt had his own special connection to the land that in 1935 would become Chemin-A-Haut State Park, also known as Louisiana State Park No. 4. It turned out that Park No. 4 was surprisingly close to the home and hunting grounds of Ben Lilly, the man who would serve as his bear-hunting guide.[13]

Chemin-A-Haut Park began as five hundred acres of "heavily wooded, rolling land . . . fine stands of second growth pine, oak, sweet gum, hickory, black gum, red gum, cypress, beech, and maple." Before it even opened, people lauded the place "as a fishing and hunting paradise."[14]

Nearly all the original structures of Chemin-A-Haut were erected from 1935 to 1938 by the Civilian Conservation Corps Company 478 stationed at Camp Morehouse. They built the "club house, a park superintendent's residence, ten overnight cabins, shelters, foot and vehicle bridges, a bath house and a boat house."[15] When that work was done, the 160 enrollees of CCC men planted trees to reforest the bare patches made from lumbering and removed logs and snags from Bayou Bartholomew to increase its functionality as a fishing locale.[16] Finally, they turned to fire hazard prevention. They dug a well, built a fire tower, cleared fire lanes straight as an arrow through the woods, then ran telephone lines.

Back in the fifties and sixties, people used the hunting lodge for reunions, barbeques, picnics, get-togethers. There were hunts too. Once, I saw a good picture of seven men kneeling in front of that park's early hunting lodge. The photo was dated 1958. The lodge's screen porch is set behind them, and the men, all wearing hunting caps and crooking their shotguns under their arms or resting them atop their shoulders, crouch over a map spread out in the dirt and pose as if they're pointing out their favorite hunting spots.

I consider it an homage to the past. There was an "annual hunting event," a local man named Don Priest remembered. Don's grandfather Sanford Harrison served as the park's superintendent from 1949 to 1969, and Don recalled how "raccoons were released in the woods around the park and then chased down by the hunters' dogs."

I didn't need to goad Ben Lilly to know his thoughts on the matter. The man was partial to owning dogs, in his way. He liked a pot-licker strain, but no matter the breed, he praised a good hunting dog, defended it. He was never without one on a hunt and often tied his hunting hounds to his waist by way of a long lead rope. Once they caught a scent of a bear or big cat, they pulled the huntsman in the right direction. Galloping along with the passel, keeping pace with them, jostling through even the thickest thickets of woods, that man could run forever, they say.

They say too that Lilly loved to hear dogs baying in the woods. He thought dogs "had a right, like himself, to follow instinct for hunting." But maybe it was really an obligation. Any "dog without that instinct was to him a betrayer of the species." He would put that dog to death.[17]

I imagine he would tolerate a raccoon similarly. Likewise, a raccoon hunt. "Anyone can kill a deer," Lilly used to say. "It takes a man to kill a varmint." By that, he meant bear, mountain lion.

But there's no statue of Ben Lilly at Chemin-A-Haut. In fact, the agent working the park's entrance desk pretended like she didn't even see Ben when I drove up, nor did she speak or nod or glance in his direction when I asked her what Chemin-A-Haut's great treasure was.

"The Castle," she told me.

Again, no surprise. Everyone comes to that monumental cypress standing regal in Chemin-A-Haut Creek, the tree that once made the cover of the official visitor's guide for Louisiana.

When I drove beyond the park entrance, Ben let me know it was that highfalutin tree we had come for too, and when I whipped my head around to check for a wink or grin or a deadpan expression that might give him away, he was straight-faced about it.

I drove down to the middle of the park in a fit, anxious to get it all over with as soon as possible. The frustratingly narrow road ended in a loop of asphalt that encircled a level patch of green locals call the "ball field" because long ago fieldtrips or family reunions saw a kickball game or a round of cabbage ball sprout up there. I pulled into the grass. There had been plenty of rain lately and I knew chances were good my tires would leave ruts, but it seemed fitting. The whole trip was starting to sink with the feeling that I was wasting my time.

A sunken brick amphitheater and three sturdy buildings sat across the road from where I parked. "Back in the '50s the amphitheater was a living, breathing, maintained thing," Don Priest once explained. "There were several church groups who used it for campfires and singalongs," he said. "I used to go down there and sit with them."[18] Back in 1957, the first pool in Morehouse Parish was built here too. They also constructed a shower and laundry facilities. Now the amphitheater's mostly ruined bricks and weeds, and those old buildings have been replaced with three newer ones—a nature center, a hunting lodge, and a building for the new pool.

I rushed through my investigation of the buildings. They seemed unremarkable. They were square and boxy and sound. Their bricks held several good thick coats of cream paint, and their brown roofs had a mash of rust-colored pine needles around their chimneys. There was a blanket of brown oak twigs and cottonwood leaves covering the sidewalks and ramped walkways that led to their doors.

The nature center was the one I walked up to first. A good amount of daddy longlegs had worked hard to build nests in all the corners and crevices of the door frame. I eased my hand around them to try the doorknob. It didn't turn. I walked over to a large window opening into one of the building's two rooms, cupped my hands around my eyes, and leaned against the darkened glass.

The floor was caked with dirt. The walls were white. A wooden teacher's desk leaned against one wall, and a three-foot long desiccated hornet's nest sat on top. Other than that, the room looked empty.

The window peering into the other room showed a similar scene—dirt, walls, a desk . . . but this time, the room was littered with boxes and had a fireplace with a mantle. I couldn't tell what was in any of the boxes, but the mantle was cluttered with birds' nests and scat and two stuffed fowls. I looked for a long time, but from that distance, I couldn't see much detail about the birds. What I mean is, I didn't take the time to try to identify them.

The door to the hunting lodge was locked too, but the inside seemed more recently inhabited. Other than the shiny oak floors and the elaborate woodwork baseboards and crown molding, though, there wasn't much inside to see.

I didn't even bother over the pool building. It appeared to function mainly as a checkout stand for baskets or locker keys. Besides, the pool had a new black iron gate surrounding it and by then, Ben was urging me down the hiking trails of Chemin-A-Haut. He wanted me in the woods. That was no surprise. "Every man and woman ought to get out and be alone with the elements a while every day, even if only for five minutes," Ben Lilly often said. "I can't think at all except when I am out."[19]

The park had a few trails, but I had no idea of where he wanted me to roam, so I walked them all.

Or maybe it was that I was trying to avoid what he wanted me to see.

He won in the end.

My patience was coming to a close when I found the hurricane fence with a rickety gate at the back end of the playground. I pushed it open and traveled down the overgrown Boy Scout Trail to Bayou Bartholomew. I knew the tree was somewhere back in the waterways, but I wasn't about to turn frog and jump in the water, so I toed along the bank until I ran into a boat launch that slid into Big Slough Lake.

Bayou Bartholomew seemed about as empty as the park did that day. I didn't see many boats on the water . . . no kayaks, no canoes. A few fishermen came and went, all empty-handed just like me, and for a while, I just stood near the boat launch, befuddled about what to do, but then, one boat scooched up the ramp and while the fisherman loaded it onto his trailer, I studied the water dripping from the hull. It fell like melting candle wax or sand through an hourglass. That's when I understood exactly what to do.

I rented a canoe, slipped into Bayou Bartholomew, then paddled up Lower Chemin-A-Haut Creek with a plan. I was lucky. The rain and Beekman's Gage were with me, so I ran into no shoals. I skirted around the cypress knees in the water and scooted by the moss and vine spilling from the trees. I ducked my head to slip under low branches. I ignored the possible primitive take-outs. I went on and on, sliding by the tupelo and water oak and smaller cypress into the confluence of Chemin-A-Haut, which was a forest of giant Louisiana bald cypress. It was far, as far as I wanted to go, but beyond what I could imagine alone.

"Beyond the end of cultivation towers the great forest," Roosevelt wrote when he saw the cypress forests of northeastern Louisiana. "Wherever the water stands in pools, and by the edges of the lakes and bayous, the giant cypress loom aloft," he said about the landscape that had overwhelmed him when he visited the state. "In stature, in towering majesty, they are unsurpassed by any trees of our eastern forests; lordlier kings of the green-leaved." Ben Lilly had led me there.

Many huge trees surrounded us, but Lilly pointed to an old, old cypress with a gargantuan trunk large enough to fit our entire canoe—sideways. Inside, a hollow cavern formed from the tree's bowing cypress roots. It was both typical and otherworldly. Huge cypress trees often make these caverns as they grow, and the healthiest, largest, oldest cypress become essentially hollow at their base. But this one was special. It was an ethereal wooden cave.

I paddled closer and closer until I could reach out my hand and touch that wall of tree in front of me. "The Castle"—that's the nickname people have given this ancient cypress of Chemin-A-Haut. It deserves that name. The trunk measures about twenty feet in diameter, which means it's likely "older than the state of Louisiana. In fact, it may be older than civilization here as we know it."[20]

With my hand on the bark, I saw the tree clearly. The arches of the trunk looked like the sinewy tendons of an old courser's legs. The lichen along the bark like a hunting hat's brim. The short green moss might as well have been the film on an uncleaned tooth. The fibers of the flaking cypress bark, the bristles of a weather-worn beard.

I gave my oar one more good stroke, and as my canoe drifted inside, I could smell the wetness of a night out in the forest and feel the coolness of a dark woodsy place. At just that moment, with my senses swimming and my head spinning, Ben Lilly lifted his hand and pointed to a growth ring inside the tree, a ring that dated maybe from a hundred years earlier.

"Is this it?" I asked. "Had we gone down Fool River?"

But Ben had misspoken before. He wasn't taking me down Fool River, but up it.

In a flash, I realized we were now finally lost enough for him to show me what he wanted to, which wasn't happening now but in the past.

I know you won't believe it, but it's the God's honest. That was how Ben Lilly transported me to the past, back to the year of his big bear hunt with Theodore Roosevelt.

It all started with a train. In 1907, a locomotive rumbled into a place named Stamboul, Louisiana, in East Carroll Parish, a town that *was* near Transylvania, Louisiana. I say *was* because Stamboul's nothing now but a memory. It's called Roosevelt today, in honor of the time Teddy came to hunt bear there.

The famous Louisiana hunt was organized by New Orleans businessman, bigwig, and future Louisiana Governor John M. Parker. John A. McIlhenny, fellow rough rider and statesman and Tabasco heir, was there too. Parker's organized hunt would last more than ten days over a rough country that sprawled across land owned by the man. He enjoyed more than seven thousand acres of Louisiana soil.

It was five years since Roosevelt's famous "Teddy Bear" hunt in Mississippi, and this hunt, like that one, couldn't be kept quiet. The national papers teased it to readers. "President Roosevelt is considering an invitation to go on a hunting trip into the Louisiana canebrakes," one wrote that September.[21] "ROOSEVELT MAY HUNT BEAR."; it said, "Is 'Sorely Tempted.'" By the end of that month, Roosevelt decided. "Louisiana Canebrake Lairs of Bears, Boars and Panthers to be Invaded," the latest article cheered.[22]

When Roosevelt disembarked on that Saturday in Stamboul, he didn't mess about. He and a few other men mounted horses and rode hard for the campsite on the Tensas Bayou, trudging through an incredible landscape Roosevelt himself described. "This is in the heart of the great alluvial bottom-land created during the countless ages through which the mighty Mississippi has poured out of the heart of the continent," he wrote in a *Scribner's Magazine* article that appeared a year after the hunt.[23] "The canebrakes stretch along the slight rises of ground, often extending for miles, forming one of the most striking and interesting features of the country," he explained. "They choke out other growths, the feathery, graceful canes standing in ranks, tall, slender, serried, each but a few inches from his brother, and springing to a height of fifteen or twenty feet . . . they are well-nigh impenetrable to a man on horseback; even on foot they make difficult walking unless free use is made of the heavy bush-knife."

A canebrake is a curious place. It's a dense thicket made up of grass, or a type of it. It's a species of grass called river cane, a native bamboo. A canebrake likes best a low-lying area, not swampy, not dry, but the moist floor of a floodplain. In a place like that, cane grows quickly. Once seeded, in a month or two, the cane culms (i.e., shoots) reach their full height and their greatest thickness.

A canebrake can survive but might do meagerly in the shade of a forest's grand overstory; however, if fire or a hurricane undoes the trees and a brake suddenly receives ample sunlight, the giant cane booms. When a canebrake riots, cane stalks can reach up to twenty-four feet high, three times taller than any person. Undisturbed, a forest of canebrake may stretch as far as a river's entire floodplain. Standing there inside a thriving canebrake, hunters could easily suppose they were standing inside an endless thicket of actual trees.

But the rich floodplain floor of a canebrake has been both the reason for its birth and its demise. Farmers have long coveted the alluvial soil beneath a canebrake, and historically we've done anything and everything to turn the black fertile soil of a canebrake into a money-earning field. Over the years, Southerners have cut, burned, plowed, poisoned, hacked, attacked, grazed, dug up, grubbed, backhoed, cleared, dredged, and axed. Anything to get the cane out.

Today the canebrake ecosystem is critically endangered, reduced to fragmentary patches of wild thickets. Widespread agriculture and logging saw to that,[24] but that wasn't always the case. Once, there was nearly twelve million acres of canebrakes across the South. Once, there were many thick sections of this cane wilderness running on the acreage of the Mississippi delta. Once, inside them there were Bachman's warblers and Florida panthers and good fat bear.

And back then, knowing if a canebrake had bear and where that bear might be laired required someone who knew and could read bear sign. That meant Parker's hunt needed a guide. Roosevelt knew it. Everyone did. "No man could have threaded those swamps without a guide," one chronicler of Roosevelt's Louisiana hunt would say after seeing the landscape.[25] It was obvious that to kill bear in the dense cane required local knowledge. In Louisiana, that meant Ben Lilly. No man had more of that here.

But Ben Lilly was gone. He had fled Louisiana a year earlier. He was already fifty, already long famous as a one-of-a-kind bear and panther killer, but he was still chasing the paradise of better hunting grounds.

At that time, bear and panthers were nothing more than destroyers of livestock, no more than ferocious vermin. Killing them, to Lilly, was something akin to a vocation. He approached it with fervor, with a fanaticism, and committed his whole being to hunting. Usually, he was out on a game trail every day of the week as if ordained by God to kill varmints.

But Lilly was a holdover of a wilderness age, as if he belonged to a people and place that existed thirty, fifty, a hundred years earlier. He was a man of the woods. So much so that he believed a person ought not to sleep indoors. That notion developed in him early, and as he aged, it calcified. By the time of his legendary hunts, he was a certified roamer, completely turning his back on roofs and walls and comfortable beds. He spread that word to the world any chance he could.

"When I am around babies," Ben Lilly told Dobie, "I always tote them out on my arm in the evening and let them look at the stars and feel the wind." This was Ben Lilly's way. "They sleep better for that. They would sleep better still if they had their pallets on the ground. I always sleep better on the ground."[26]

What can a person say in rejoinder to something like that? What could I say, when the two sides of my mind were still at odds about it: one side regretting even having a house after the hurricane, relishing a night by a campfire, a long evening under a blanket on a porch swing, an endless black sky spread above me while I lie on a beach or on a rooftop or in the bed of a pickup parked in a rice field. The other side of me remembering the soreness and body aches brought on by sleeping on hard ground.

For Lilly, though, there were no two sides about it. If our body was a river, sleeping out-of-doors was the current threading deep within us. If our body was a farm, sleeping in the open air was a deep well that we must tap into to keep us green and growing.

How did he know that that necessity dwelled inside us for what amounted to eternity? Why did he think sleeping out was a naturalness we ought to embrace?

If an old bear has a clock within it that drives it out of the dampness of a cave and into the open night where it might stretch and sprawl its body beneath the riotous stars, Lilly figured we should too.

This was his proof for many of his beliefs. How the animals slept, what they ate, the manner in which they bathed and cleaned themselves—these lessons Lilly took to heart and emulated.

It was no wonder he was such a remarkable tracker of game. He knew their signs and behavior as well as any biologist who devoted a lifetime to the study of a creature because that's exactly what Lilly had done, obsessively.

And like any impulsive lover, he would drop anything to be near what captured his heart. Would move anywhere to be near it.

Snatches of Louisiana canebrakes still had a handful of bears, but it had nowhere near the number still inhabiting the wild spaces of Texas. Lilly would be the first to tell you that. So he migrated to the Texas Big Thicket in order to become an expert of that terrain and hunt the last remaining bear there.

They say it was a telegram that "summoned Lilly back to the land he knew better than any man alive" to help Roosevelt hunt.[27] In particular, they say it was a message sent by "one naturalist with the Bureau, Ned Hollister" who "put forth the name Ben Lilly" to Roosevelt. Who knows if that's what really happened. The truth of it is this—like a stranger, it would be by invitation that legendary hunter Ben Lilly would return to Louisiana, to his home.

When Roosevelt and his hunting buddies hoofed into the hunting camp on Bear Lake, they found the place already cleared of trees and the tents already pitched.

They settled in quickly and busied themselves preparing for an early start the next day. The president despised wasting hunting time.

Roosevelt stewed over the hot weather and the "steaming rains" and the "insect plagues...a scourge...of huge biting flies, bigger than bees." He was glad when after the first four days the weather turned and the bugs cleared. He was even gladder when Ol' Lilly strolled into camp.

"The morning after we reached camp we were joined by Ben Lilley [sic]," President Roosevelt wrote about that brisk October morning.[28] All day before, and most of the night, Lilly had "tramped" through the woods to rendezvous with the hunting party. "It had rained hard throughout the night," Roosevelt recalled, "and he had no shelter, no rubber coat, nothing but the clothes he was wearing, and the ground was too wet for him to lie on; so he perched in a crooked tree in the beating rain, much as if he had been a wild turkey."

"He had come on foot through the thick woods, followed by his two dogs, and had neither eaten nor drunk for twenty-four hours; for he did not like to drink the swamp water," Roosevelt observed. "But he was not in the least tired when he struck camp; and, though he slept an hour after breakfast, it was chiefly because he had nothing else to do, inasmuch as it was Sunday, on which day he never hunted nor labored."

No wonder everyone at camp found Lilly odd, even the hunters who knew him well scratched their heads at him, but probably President Roosevelt, who had no real knowledge of Lilly, was most confounded by the old huntsman, so dumbfounded in fact that he couldn't help telling someone. "There is a white hunter, Ben Lilly, who has just joined us, who is really a remarkable character," Roosevelt wrote to his sixteen-year-old daughter. "He literally lives in the woods."[29]

Roosevelt believed Lilly warranted a mix of incredulity and curiosity. "I never met any other man so indifferent to fatigue and hardship," Roosevelt noted. Maybe it was admiration. Maybe it was nostalgia. Maybe it was just misplaced hatred of getting old. Whatever it was, Roosevelt couldn't stop it from making him gush. "He could run through the woods like a buck, was far more enduring, and quite as indifferent to weather," Roosevelt told people about Lilly, "though he was over fifty years old."

Such stuff just rolled off Lilly's back. "My reputation is bigger than I am," he famously told Dobie when the Texas writer met him for the first time and told Lilly he had heard stories about the hunter. "It is like my shadow when I stand in front of the sun in late evening."[30]

But on that Louisiana hunt, there were two men like that around, two men with legends trailing about them like shadows. That was something I didn't expect, but it taught something valuable.

About seven or eight hours after the appearance of Lilly—rain-soaked and dragging the rank odors of wet woods and his two hounds behind him—another guide tromped into camp.

Leading a pack of twenty-two lurching, baying, feisty bearhounds and arriving alongside two white planters named Clive and Harley Metcalfe, that second guide was a black man whose legend in the afternoon's dying light spread across the camp, sending a shadow as long as Ben Lilly's. That second guide was Holt Collier.[31]

Collier was born a slave in 1846 and was a bear-killer by age ten. As a boy, his job was to feed the plantation of the Hinds family by hunting.[32] He "never learned to read or write . . . never learned how to sign his own name,"[33] but legend says Collier was the inspiration for Faulkner's "The Bear."

As a boy, Faulkner must have heard those old Mississippi hunting stories, must have heard about Holt Collier and bears, and so they say when the creator of Yoknapatawpha County wrote, "He was ten. But it had already begun, long before that day. . . . He had already inherited then, without ever having seen it, the tremendous bear with one trap-ruined foot . . . He had listened to it for years: the long legend," that southern writer, who was a legend himself, meant legendary Holt Collier.

He was one of the president's guides from that famous 1902 "Teddy bear" hunt. Ever since, Roosevelt was enamored with the man.

Every bit as wood-stuck and woods-loving as Lilly, Collier's lifelong obsession was bears as well. He hunted fall or winter, spring or summer. He possessed an equally deep knowledge of them—what they ate, where to set a deadfall trap for them, how they'd plainly refuse to bed down on a wet forest floor. He made a living on that understanding, selling hunted meat to slave owners and farmhands, to railroad workers and timber companies.

Holt Collier used to say, "Money don't buy nothing in the cane-break, no how, and a man's dog don't care whether he's rich or poor," which Roosevelt loved, maybe as much as hearing Collier's accent say "painter" for panther.[34] But what astounded Roosevelt most, they say, was Collier's time as a Civil War scout . . . for the Confederacy. Roosevelt often remarked about Holt's "having been the body-servant and cook of 'old General Hinds' . . . when the latter fought under Jackson at New Orleans." Collier "followed his master to battle as his body-servant . . . acted under him as sharpshooter against the Union soldiers." Roosevelt was amazed by all that. In truth, it was probably Collier's service in the Civil War along with his half-a-century's worth of knowledge about tracking and killing bear that made Roosevelt describe the man as a figure possessing "all the dignity of an African chief," as a person in his own way "as remarkable a character as Ben Lilly."

That comment itself pointed to how tensions were thick in camp. While their lives should have placed Lilly and Collier in a sort of fellowship, during the 1907 Louisiana hunt it didn't work out that way. They say one main reason for the animosity was the contention about who should be leading the hunt. Many of the papers covering the affair labeled Lilly as "Chief Huntsman," but other people argued that appellation was never a true assessment of the hunt's organization. They say Roosevelt put more stock in the Metcalfe brothers and Collier from the start. If so, "the reason [was] simple," some said. "Roosevelt was gregarious, while Lilly preferred to track bears alone."[35]

When speaking on Lilly, Dobie said somewhat plainly that Lilly was "thoroughly Southern." The man was a fundamentalist and kind, but believed that people like Collier "'should be kept in their place.' The orthodox location of that place is always down."[36] If that's the truth, Lilly's irritation makes even more sense. Lilly hated playing second fiddle to any hunter. Playing it to Collier would've felt harsher.

The animosity was also a matter of hunting strategy, or at least that's what some have argued. Some hunters there believed Roosevelt ought to hunt by stand. Others wanted to light fires to flush the beasts so they'd run to a spot where President Roosevelt waited. A few others argued the best way was to chase the bear with hounds. And a handful pushed for using the hounds to track the bear to its den.

And then there were some larger arguments, which hung around the camp like smoke from a fire. Some attendees didn't believe in these canebrakes anymore. They didn't believe there were bear in here at all. As soon as the Metcalfes arrived, Harley pulled Roosevelt aside, according to one account of the hunt, and told him, "You have plenty of good bear hunters, and lots of dogs, but you've got seventy-five miles of country and no bear in it."

"How do you know that?" Roosevelt asked.

"I sent Holt Collier over here to investigate it . . . Holt knows what he is talking about."[37]

It was weeks before the hunt when the Metcalfes sent Collier down from Mississippi to meet a man named Alex Enolds at Rescue Plantation. Collier was sixty years old, but he still helped with the labor of "cutting trails and clearing a camp site out of the canebrake in anticipation" and then he and Alex scouted for bears.[38] The landscape, though foreign in its way, must've seemed like home to Collier, except he saw no sign of bear in it.

The Louisiana black bear is a special kind of bear, though. It has a longer, narrower, and flatter skull than other black bears and larger molar teeth. Its snout seems longer too. It also has adapted to special habitat. Even before its numbers dropped, the Louisiana black bear never ranged outside of Louisiana, western Mississippi, and east Texas.[39] And in those regions, the canebrakes are an even more specialized habitat for this bear. Its habits being known only to a specialist.

Inside a Louisiana canebrake, bear disappear. Sometimes, the only proof that a bear exists at all will be the scraps it leaves behind: A black bear is an opportunistic carnivore. It will eat almost anything it can find. But a good bear tracker knows not only opportunity, but probability. Bears will always eat beetles, insects. In deep winter, an active bear will eat grass and vegetation, will scavenge for acorns and pecans in any area to be had. Soft mast—blackberries, dewberries, leaf buds—during spring, during early summer. In late summer, a black bear is apt to take to a farmer's fields—crops, corn. In late fall, hard mast: the fruits of oaks and hickories, Louisiana palmettos.

For the Roosevelt hunt, in an October's early fall, Lilly (and Collier too I assume) knew what a Louisiana black bear in a Louisianan canebrake was most prone to do—chances were that any bear left in that canebrake would be in the cane, eating the wild corn, gorging and about to den, sticking to places in heavy cover, the thickest thickets—a fallen tree, a hollow cavity of a cypress. They'd be close to water, but spread far apart from each other, way out and away from trails and commotion. They'd be hard to find. Hard to kill.

"When the President goes hunting there are two great essentials for his hosts to consider," a reporter once pronounced about Roosevelt's bear hunting excursions. "First, the chief Executive must be safe. Second, the guest of honor must kill a bear."[40] It didn't matter if this place in Louisiana was fundamentally different. Teddy wasn't going to change.

And so the hunt organizers devised their strategies.

For the first few days "Collier and the Metcalfe brothers planned to put Roosevelt on a stand and then jump and drive a bear toward him." It worked, to a degree. A beater did manage to scare a bear and make it run, but the creature didn't go near the stand, and then after that one good chance, days of nothing followed.

Roosevelt himself lamented that the hunters "waited long hours on likely stands . . . rode around the canebrakes through the swampy jungle . . . threaded . . . trails cut by the heavy wood-knives of my companions; but . . . found nothing." Those kinds of comments let everyone know something was going to have to change.

Lilly had his notions. He blamed all the failed days of hunting on too much commotion, too many hunters, too much noise, "too many dogs, scores of them."[41] He thoroughly believed there was bear near. He had seen the signs. What the hunters needed to do was to get primitive.[42]

It took a while for people to listen.

It was about a week after Roosevelt arrived when Lilly took over the hunt in an obvious way. People say it was Lilly who encouraged the camp to move from Tensas Bayou to Bear Lake, which was an old riverbed that was swampier and more difficult to maneuver and more remote than the other places around. It also happened to be only about a thousand feet from the loopy Tensas River where people knew Fool River to be.

A day or two after the move, a dense night "brought heavy rain," so hard "only Lilly wandered from camp."[43] In that solitariness, the huntsman seemed to find what he needed. The day following the rain, Lilly's hounds ran a bear to the spot where Roosevelt still-hunt, meaning he waited in a stand, but the matted vines making thatch work of the Bear Lake woods prevented Roosevelt from gaining a clear shot. It was a costly missed opportunity.

The way one reporter told it, Roosevelt knew he had only a few days of hunting left and then "called Collier to the fire."[44]

"Holt," the president said, "I haven't got but one or two more days. What *am* I going to do?—I haven't killed a bear."

"Colonel, if you let me manage the hunt," Collier said, "you'll sure kill one tomorrow."

"Whatever you say goes, Holt."

"He ain't no baby," Collier reportedly told Clive the next day about Roosevelt. "He can go anywhere you can go," instructing Clive to "bum" the president around in the woods and be ready for when Collier's dogs caught the scent.

The day after Collier took over, a Friday, the weather cleared. Raring to hunt for real, Roosevelt slogged through the canebrakes, spending hours and hours battling the bugs and vines and rough terrain with the other hunters, walking among the snapping turtles "heavy as man."[45]

It was late in the day when a guide's dogs managed to drive an old she-bear in the direction of where Roosevelt waited near bear sign they had found the day before. President Roosevelt and Clive mounted "tough woods-horses [that] kept their feet like cats" as they "leaped logs, plunged through bushes, dodged in and out among the tree trunks . . . now at a trot, now at a run, now stopping to listen for the pack."

In no time, the two men closed in on the bear and dismounted in a bound. Roosevelt, hearing the "babel of the pack" of dogs and hoping the bear headed towards him, "crouched down . . . rifle at the ready."

Luck was with him. The bear loped into his line of sight and Roosevelt stood and fired.

The bear, about twenty yards away, caught the bullet in her chest. She "went down stark dead," Roosevelt wrote, "slain in the canebrake in true hunter fashion."

The bear Roosevelt shot was slung over "Holt Collier's pony," as one reporter put it, "and the whole party rode back in high spirits." But not everyone was riding high.

When Roosevelt neared the camp, Holt Collier had the idea to stop his horse, dismount, and goad the president to hitch himself up on the saddle and "ride in with his game." One of the other hunters, Doctor Lambert, froze the moment in time, snapping a picture. In it, Roosevelt's mounted with "Holt standing beside him among the dogs."

"Holt never complains," that reporter wrote, "but he does say mournfully, 'The Colonel promised to send me one of them pictures. He give me a fine rifle, but I wanted a picture of me and him together.'"[46]

Lilly was no doubt mournful too. Lilly's dogs had jumped several bears over the fourteen days of Parker's hunt, but every single bear had evaded Roosevelt. To make matters worse, when Lilly spotted fresh bear tracks the day before, no one would follow him, so he drifted off into a canebrake alone, which meant he was nowhere near the spot President Roosevelt killed his bear, and by the time he returned to Bear Lake and the little shack the party was using as a hunting camp, the celebration was in full swing. Of it, he took no part.[47]

"I had rather be off in the woods and wild," Lilly would say to people. He thought "he had learned things there that other people do not know."[48]

That was the last thing I heard him say before he climbed us out of that giant cypress on Bayou Bartholomew and took us back to my own time.

The paddle back to the pier was like the air hissing out of a punctured tire. The walk up the road was worse. The rain-bright grass in the "ball field" seemed less vivid somehow. The nature center and hunting lodge more ramshackle. The guilt about the ruts my tires left sank a little deeper.

I couldn't help it. Lilly and I had traipsed around the state, gone to and down and up Fool River, traveled in and out of time, come back again, but the point to it all seemed to elude me the same way so many bears did Teddy. Sure, I knew Ol' Lilly thought he had learned a deep thing by being out-of-doors, a natural thing by sleeping under the stars, an important thing he wanted me to know, but my hands still felt empty. So I cranked my Rogue and kissed the park goodbye.

I'd like to say the drive home was a pleasant one. I'd like to tell you that about halfway down I-49, Lilly pulled the lever on his seatback, sat up as primly as a preacher, and started spouting off sense to me. But the truth is, we mostly just waded through silence.

What counts as fun was one of the first thoughts I had driving home. "Recreation means many different things, depending on the person who is thinking about it," Robert Marshall, the director of forestry in the Indian Service at Washington DC, told readers of the *Louisiana Conservationist* back in 1935.[49] "To some people" recreation means "climbing rarely scaled mountain tops to glory in the wilderness panorama and to become saturated in the feeling of the primitive." To others, it ranges from the banal to the maniacal: "driving at seventy-five miles an hour along well banked highways . . . to setting fire to the forest to hear the gigantic roar of pine trees bursting into flame." But despite that last extreme, most seem to agree recreation in the forest should be focused on recreation in which the forest is essential. Recreation in the forest should be recreation "that stirs the emotions of forest users."

The second thought? Emotion in a forest is a fickle thing, is a puny thing, even for something as grand as The Castle. Because that tree is just a matter of time. And maybe sooner rather than later, because in 2005 the Morehouse Lake Commission formed, and they sought to dam a portion of Chemin-A-Haut to form a recreational lake.

Naturalist Jeff Barnhill saw the plans. "I was dealing with chemo and radiation," he said, but there was so much at stake—his favorite spots, the Chemin-A-Haut cypress—that he couldn't do nothing. Sick, in and out of treatment, he fought. "I found old canoe pictures on the creek, scanned them and made it known that there were old growth Bald Cypress here. The big hollow tree is dated at 1,000+ years old. . . . Imagine what would have been lost here," he said. He won. No dam ever happened. Not yet, anyway.[50]

But mostly, amidst that silence, I just sat there thinking of Lilly.

Just about a year after that legendary hunt in the Louisiana canebrakes, President Roosevelt planned a dinner. Some people know it as the "Teddy Bear" dinner, but Roosevelt called it "the bear-hunters" dinner. To him, they were as "good hunters, as daring riders, as first-class citizens as could be found anywhere." He wanted to show "such fine fellows" to people and claimed, "[N]o finer set of guests ever sat at meat in the White House."[51] Ben Lilly, John M. Parker, John A. McIlhenny, the Metcalfes who brought Holt Collier to the Louisiana hunt—they were all invited. Many, many people who had hunted with Roosevelt were asked to come, twenty or thirty of them. They were all served Louisiana black bear.

I never learned if Holt Collier received an invitation to the "Teddy Bear" dinner. I did find out that Roosevelt encouraged him to come to Washington, DC, but Collier turned down that request. "Lots of negroes around here thought I was a mighty big fool for not going," they say Collier told people. "But I didn't have any friends in Washington," he said, "and I couldn't hunt up there. So I thought the best thing for me to do would be to stay right here among my own people."[52]

Ben Lilly also turned down his bear-hunters dinner invite. He was too shy for such an event, he said. Besides, he had already committed himself to traveling farther and farther west to be amongst the wilderness . . . to be hunting.

Topeka reporters who watched Lilly during the big Kountze bear hunt of 1906 said at that point in his life he had killed 118 bears. Ten, fifteen years later, that number could have doubled, tripled, quadrupled. After all, during his life the man delivered forty-two black bear specimens to the National Museum of Natural History alone. He had hunted and killed a great many more. By Lilly's own count, his number of killed bear was astronomical.[53] He wouldn't bat an eye if you said that by 1919 he had killed five hundred bears.

He would've turned sixty-five that year, and according to official records, he was the leading hunter of the "approximately three hundred professional hunters and trappers" employed by Uncle Sam "to exterminate predatory animals in the range country."[54]

To the stockmen of his day, Lilly was a godsend—that was a matter of simple economics. "On the accepted basis that a wolf kills $1000 worth of stock a year, a bear and mountain lion $500 each," Lilly had saved the western stockman a small fortune.[55] But that wasn't all. "At the turn of the twentieth century, Louisiana's vast natural resources—in the form of virgin forests and teeming wildlife—were besieged by commercial interests and others who lacked environmental consideration."[56] Hunters like Lilly were the only ones fighting for leaving some places uncut or unfarmed or unmined. In other words, Ben's "obsessive compulsion to kill bears and cougars" and his reputation as the best hunter of his day ironically crowned him as perhaps the greatest defender of the wilderness too, the great conservationist.

In 1920, at sixty-one Lilly visited his sister in Shreveport. It was his last visit to Louisiana and the local paper ran a news story about it. It praised Lilly for being titled World's Champion Hunter by *Illustrated World*. Lilly didn't stay long with his sister. He just couldn't. The man was "restless in the city, and is constantly looking forward to his return to the wilds," the paper explained.

By the 1930s, Ben Lilly was living in a home near Silver City, New Mexico. He was nearly eighty. Legend says Lilly always regretted not ever adding a polar bear to his list of killed bears, but he never bagged one, and by that time, it was too late. His eyesight played tricks on him. His hobby became making colored drawings of bears and lions . . . some with horns, some crayoned purple and red and blue.

"A bear brain is about the size of a pint bottle"; Roosevelt wrote in one of his hunting essays, "and any one can hit a pint bottle off-hand at thirty or forty feet. . . . If a man is close enough it is easy enough for him to shoot straight if he does not lose his head." For him, that was a mere fact of shooting.

It's the distance that matters in the end, Roosevelt added about shooting. "A novice at this kind of sport will find it best and safest to keep in mind the old Norse Viking's advice in reference to a long sword," Roosevelt counseled. "If you go in close enough your sword will be long enough."[57]

That advice, though, works not just on bears. It works on a landscape too. It can also work on someone's life, if you do it right, and get up close for long enough.

I see now that when Ben Lilly took me to get lost, when he climbed us up in that tree, when he drug me back in time, part of what he wanted me to learn was that the Roosevelt bear hunt near the Tensas River might have been one of the most remarkable events to have ever happened within the limits of the state because it was the confluence of all the qualities that make life in Louisiana ridiculous.

Theodore Roosevelt was a great many things, and I can't say that I loved them all, but it's hard to debate his central role in that hunt. What I mean is, his presence was like a great black hole. It was like a giant vacuum sucking up the stars and voiding light and time itself. Because when he came into that Louisiana canebrake, he brought with him a giant lens to show the strangeness that had given birth to the Louisiana wilderness. It was a magical lens that could show and even magnify how that wildness was coming to an end.

Because when he did come, Roosevelt brought unto him two legendary hunters, formed themselves by the exaggerations of the landscape that gave them life. Collier was the ancient bear, and the ancient bear was Collier. Surely each relied on the other to pronounce, unequivocally, their existence. The people who obsess over the bear keep the bear an obsession. Once those people are gone and silent, it's a good chance the bear may go silent too.

And Ben Lilly was the Louisiana canebrake, and the canebrake was him. Surely his eccentricities were the offspring of that land's preposterousness. Surely he was the natural progeny of a people audacious enough to settle along the Mississippi itself, people born of a wildly reckless plan to farm a floodplain. And the canebrakes are scions of the Mississippi too, where grass grows as tall as the trees and the soil's so rich anything tossed in it turns to a giant overnight. What I mean is, a canebrake is a world as impenetrable as the tiniest sliver of time we try to keep alive. A wild place that continues to surprise.

And just like that I was right where I started—my little office space basically the same as the way I left it before the hurricane, but no longer pristinely mine. The books sprawled across the floor in my office were men lying asleep by a campfire. They had spent a long day chasing a she-bear through an impassable thatch of cane and an even longer night by the fire celebrating. Sleep, it had unfurled their bodies before they had a chance to find their beds, and long into the evening, their sore muscles, the aches in their bones, night's cool weather, even the wetness of a morning had twisted their shapes until all around my office was the mess found before a campsite is broken.

Ben Lilly had found his place in my doorway, where he caught his breath before he said that he wouldn't lie to me, that he couldn't, but there was a true story he wanted me to know, that he had to share.

In it, there was a man, he told me. There was a boat. There was a captain. And this really did happen just this way, he promised, but one day the captain got turned around on the Tensas River where it "widens out to about a half a mile or so." Locals "call this wide place Tensas Lake," and the Mississippi-River captain had tried to "turn into that arm of the lake" because he was confident it headed somewhere.

"It don't run no wheres," some nearby plantation workers cautioned him, but like all outsiders convinced they know better than locals, the captain steamed ahead "until he had to turn back."

That turned him around worse than he was before, and then, thoroughly lost now, the captain eventually stopped at a plantation "to inquire the way."

"Stranger, where do you live?" the captain asked.

"Right here," said the plantation's worker.

"Oh, I know," said the captain, "but where is *it*?"

". . . mouth of Fool River."

"Yes, I'm damned if it ain't Fool River," the captain conceded, "and I'm one of them, too!"

My head dropped. It wasn't funny. I looked at my floor, my bookshelves, my books. I took a circle around my office, stepping over the piles, putting my hand on a bookcase, picking up *Swapping Stories* from my desk, debating whether to return it to its place of honor or throw it in the trash. I set it down. Finally, I looked up and, turning to the doorway, saw that Ben Lilly was gone.

I don't know why I walked out of my office to track him down. I knew it was a lost cause, but I trudged the first-floor hallways anyway. I climbed the stairs. I made a pass around the second floor.

Everywhere around me were the telltale signs of people leaving.

You see, where I work, at the small university so near the swamps and marshes of the Gulf, when someone decides to resign or retire, it's so predictable you can track it like a hurricane or an animal trail. If you're observant, there's sure sign.

It's an activity that goes on quietly in a corner of the building, in the small space of hallway outside the person's office. It's obvious if you know where to look, and it's a guarantee that the leaving isn't all talk.

It's the stack of books sitting on the linoleum like an old waypoint on a trail in the woods. There'll be textbooks and workbooks and paperbacks. Some will be new, but most will be used and show the wear of a professor teaching from them for years—the dog-eared pages, the broken spine, the markings with a pen. There'll be books for classes no one will teach anymore or copies of the classics everyone already has. There'll be hardbacks, the books the university presses put out for experts in a discipline. There'll be seminal texts. There'll be breakthroughs. There'll be the most important books for a person in that field. And that will be the biggest reason no one wants them, especially here.

It's easy to spot if you know how to read the signs. You'll pass by a suite of offices, maybe on the second floor, and you'll see the stacks of books so high it takes a good stride to step over them. You'll see them grow chest height. Shoulder height. You'll see the stacks become as high as a man. They'll grow like weeds, like giant grasses. They'll grow as tall as trees. They'll become a forest, and somewhere deep inside, something like a pile of stones, something like a monument, will be made. And that's when someone comes along to tape up a makeshift sign. Its letters are scrawled in marker and say, "FREE BOOKS," as if it isn't a fact that's already known.

They say Ben Lilly, with his giant bear knife in his hand, once screamed, "You are condemned, you black devil," before piercing a bear tied to a pole. "I kill you in the name of the law!"

And for some reason, standing in the second-floor hallway, those words are what came to me. All I could think of was Ben Lilly's bear knife, its blade, and his exhortation.

What I mean is, thinking of those words made me wonder if this was what Ben Lilly wanted me to see all along. I had been dispossessed of home. I had been let go of by LeJeune Cove, and I wondered if it didn't all tie back to Ben Lilly and Fool River and what he wanted me to witness.

"I like to think of the past," Ben Lilly would say. "I can think of myself as a barefooted boy standing before the fireplace with my hands spread out, and of my mother close by me, and I am happy. I cannot be happy trying to grasp the future, unless it's something like a lion that I am trailing."[58]

I was starting to understand that it was the same way with me—that while a close-up look might work on someone's life, some distance worked best for my own. Without it, I couldn't see myself for the damned fool that I am.

You see, there was a time when I used to wonder how a man might walk out of everything. How he could turn his back on his money, his house, his land, his career. Say so long to hot meals and a warm bed for the night. Use a rock for a pillow. Never need a roof and walls. Say, "Goodbye wife. Goodbye kids." And then the next sound would be the latch of the door scraping to a close.

But with twenty-five years of a work stuffed in my pocket, most of my life isn't much beyond a stack of books in a hallway, an accumulation of junk that works on me the same way a canebrake works on a landscape.

In one of the little games history likes to play, Holt Collier died the same year Ben Lilly did. It was 1936. Lilly was eighty. It was pneumonia.

He died on a poor farm owned by a man Lilly once hunted for. During his last days, he mostly stayed inside. On the day of his death, that "morning he . . . believed he would stay in bed." Later that day his "mind seemed to lighten," and then he was gone.[59]

His funeral was presided over by a "Methodist minister who had never seen him and had never heard of him." Eleven years later, J. Frank Dobie and a local Mer Rouge man named Tom Harp made it so that a bronze plaque honoring Lilly went up on a boulder in the Gila National Forest. It marked the site where Lilly's final hunts took place. The Mer Rouge monument took much longer.

The Mer Rouge plaque says that Lilly hunted "here on Bayou Bonne Idee and Beouf River . . . hunted south through Tensas swamp . . . then on West through East Texas, Northern Mexico and ultimately to Southwest New Mexico where he settled down." In New Mexico, where Lilly killed bears and lions for the last decades of his life, "the ranchers paid him, the government paid him, unlike back home in Louisiana, so he stayed." Why? Because there's a logic to leaving a place where you don't feel wanted. It makes a certain sort of sense to not stay where you don't belong, even if it's your home.

Before Lilly died, his dream was to set down what he knew about bears and lions and hunting in a book. He wanted to share it with people, wanted to put to posterity his wisdom about the wild. He finished about three chapters of it. He never found the time or energy or patience to sit still and write the rest. I imagine laboring with words on a page never quite matched the feeling of being in the thickets, hunting, no matter how much he tried to will it to be so.

In the end, during those last lonely and sedentary days of Ben Lilly's life, what would he have said if I had asked him if he would've traded some of that time in the primitive woods for more days at a desk, writing, so that his book could've been finished?

But I guess I know the answer to that.

Ben Lilly's whole life seemed to be a choking, suffocating crawl away from what he called the "rancid air of indoor living." But I could see it as a wild hunt too, a chase after something, a race to be so lost a person couldn't help but find themselves.

Because it's not that no one cares—that's not the reason the books will sit untouched in the hallway or the papers left behind in an office will never find a home. It's just that no one cares as much about the things I love as I do. Ben Lilly's long-bladed knife sinks into the heart of a bear—it's proof no one hates what I hate, at least not in the exact way I do, not quite in the way I can. What I'm telling you is, no one is as lost to my thoughts, perversions, predilections, obsessions as I am.

So why shouldn't I, like Ben Lilly, go off to Texas or New Mexico or anywhere else where at least I feel homesick for a good reason.

To be lost at home pierces the heart. So why not dispossess myself of what seems to be through with me?

But to do that, there was something I had to do first. I needed to plunge myself into the very heart of Louisiana and holler, "I kill you in the name of the law!"

3

MISTER UNLUCKY, MISTER NOBODY

> "Well, of course, Pop," answered the fool. "I understand exactly what you mean."
> —Jean Sot, right before he shoots the cows[1]

People say, "Luck," and I don't know what they mean. They say, "Worse." I just scratch my head. People speak as if they see something far off, beyond the here and now, but I'm too simple, I guess. I just focus on what's right in front of me.

It was that way after the double-hurricane days. People would see the six-foot-around water-oak trunk cricked on the edge of my house and tell me, "It could be worse." They'd see the pine that flattened my fence but missed the front of the house and say, "Whew." They'd see the cottonwood out back that lost its crown but didn't uproot. They'd see branches and leaves strewn everywhere like glitter at a New Orleans Mardi Gras. They'd see the rubble of my garage, none of it even bulldozed yet. I had friends who would drive in from out of town. I had family who would stop by for a visit. They'd see the entire mess, look at me, and say, "Really, it could be worse, you know. You should be smiling. You can't see how lucky you are."

When they'd leave, I'd walk around my place to find what I was missing. I'd go into my house to look up the words.

Because if there's a bee on the end of my nose, I see the bee. I see the stinger. I don't taste the honey being made in some way-off field. I don't picture the flowers that came before. I'm a simple man, but I know that can make me shortsighted.

It's always been that way with me. I can be too literal. With words, maybe more than most things, I can be too exact. I can be too focused on the trees. I can miss the forest. Especially after the hurricanes came, what was right in my hands became all I cared about. The debris my feet stepped over was the only thing that filled my hours. It ate up all my time.

Days passed like that. Weeks. Months. Finally, I started to look up. I started to be able to see more than two feet in front of my nose. Then the third disaster hit. It was February. It was almost an anniversary, almost half a year after Hurricane Laura, to the day.

It was a Monday night. The temperature dropped to fourteen degrees. I woke up early the next morning to an eerily still house and the thought that it was happening again.

I stood in the kitchen, looking out the window at my storm-battered neighborhood now in the middle of a record cold. Lake-effect snow slowly covered my front yard, my tarped roof. A stark white blindfold stopped me from seeing the old disasters and made me stare at this new one.

That morning electricity fled from the wires like birds before bad weather. Neighbors' pipes busted. So did the pipes in all the houses left vacant after Laura and Delta. My house's pipes never popped, but it didn't matter. Water pressure dropped all over town. If I flipped a light switch, nothing happened. If I turned a faucet, it was useless. Stores closed. The roads turned undrivable. We all made do, which meant I was at the gas stove, standing over a pot of pool water I had put on to boil when I realized just how little I understood.

If an angry person's cheeks burn and their blood runs hot, pots are that way too. It's common sense to me, so I stirred and stirred, agitating the water until ripples and swirls writhed around my spoon's handle. In fact, I stirred so hard a whirlpool formed around the bowl of my spoon.

My two girls like to sit in the kitchen sometimes and study me as I cook. They giggle when their mother asks me what I'm making and I say, "A mess." They giggle harder if I blow a puff of flour in the air or hang a ladle from my nose. So while I was stirring, I turned to find the jar of flour next to the stove. When I did, I took my hand from the spoon, but instead of stopping, to our amazement, the spoon whirled around on its own.

We watched in silence for several seconds until something sucked it to the middle of the swirling water. "Why? Why, Dad?" my girls shouted.

But I had nothing right in front of me to answer them with, so even though my mouth was open, no words came out.

My only thought was to try again, so I stirred harder this time. When I let go, I witnessed the same result.

"What? Why?" my yappers went. "What keeps the spoon going when it ought to quit?" the older one asked. "What pulls the spoon to the center?" the younger one chirped.

What could I do for an answer but stick my nose into the middle of it? Not only in the swirls, but in the idea of center itself. So I did. I looked in the pot, and when that didn't solve anything, I walked to the middle of my house. When that didn't work, I searched the center of my neighborhood. Then I biked to the center of town. Then I drove to the heart of my parish. Each time, though, I came home, hat in hand, with nothing to offer my little wonderers.

Call me a simpleton, but I didn't quit. Call me a fool, the one from every culture, the one in all the stories who keeps schlepping even when he shouldn't schlepp no more. It's okay by me because if the world's a joke, I'm the butt. I'm the laughingstock that takes things at face value—people's word, what they say, what they mean.

Because my dad used to tell me, "Be somebody," which I took to mean, "Don't be a nobody," and so I try not to be. I try to be a man who doesn't leave a question unanswered, a puzzle unfinished. Ask me a riddle and I'll keep limping along for an answer until I'm walking with a cane.

Because I am a try-hard even when the odds are all wrong.

Because I am a donkey and a dope and a ninny and a fool.

Because I don't see much else to do but go in search of what pulls a spoon, a person, a family, or anything to a place and holds it there.

Of course, at first, I didn't know where else to go. I couldn't think of a center I hadn't checked. But then I had an idea.

Some may say, "Luck," and some "A blessing," but I say it was coincidence when a day or two later I heard the TV in the living room making noise. It was the show with questions for answers and answers for questions, and one of that day's categories was "Geographic Centers." For $600, contestants needed to know the question to "In Avoyelles Parish southeast of Marksville." And with that clue, I had my answer, or question I mean: "Where can you find the geographic center of Louisiana?"

The next answer was, "Now," and the question was, "When should I go?"

So, in the middle of a disaster, as soon as the roads de-iced enough for me to drive and power came to the traffic lights, I went off to find out why some invisible thing, like that feeling inside me that home was the center of my world, could make a body keep spinning, keep going, even when the obvious thing to do was to stop. What I mean is, I went off to find the center of Marksville, which would lead me to the center of Louisiana, which would answer all my questions about the reasons why I felt the tug to stay here at home.

I didn't know it at the start, but by journey's end, I would learn that to find my way to the center, I would need to forget the map and lose my bearings and toss away most of what I thought I knew, even the meanings of certain words like *luck* and *worse* and *somebody* and *nobody* and even *center*. But that was all hindsight. In the beginning, all I knew was that if a place had a name, it had boundaries, and if it had those, it had edges, and if it had edges, it had to have a center.

I know that makes no sense at all, but sometimes the truth is the simplest lie to keep straight, and so off I went.

The closest thing I had to a trail to follow was a piece of WPA writing called "A Day of Home Life in Avoyelles Parish" written by an Anthony in the 1930s. I don't know more about the writer than that, but the sketch was supposed to capture a typical day at a Marksville home in the 1890s. It starts like this: "It is, let us say, early one morning on one of the Avoyelles farms, about five miles from Marksville." My brain told me I could start that way too.

So to start... it was, let us say, early one February morning on one of the Lake Charles neighborhoods, about five miles from I-10.

"The sky is dark, and except for the soft splash of the ever flowing well, there is no sound from the rambling house, that is near one end of the field."

And my sky was dark too as I sat in bed, and except for my wife's snoring, there was no sound but the dripping of snowmelt from the eaves.

"In the vague light the house looms large. It is a rambling, ample structure... there is an air of designed haphazardness which informs us that in forty years since it was built, the original structure has been added to many times."

The haphazardness of my house loomed large as well—some might say nothing loomed larger since everything was a rambling mess. Water stains hung on the ceilings that weren't pulled down. The garage was smashed under a fallen water oak. A smattering of debris still sat all over my backyard. A wrack of clutter collected against the pole of the corner's stop sign. Gangs of wayward shingles still loitered along the sides of the streets.

"Somewhere in the house there is a rustle. A man coughs. Padded feet move across the floor and a light springs to life. The father of the family has arisen and is dressing."

Somewhere in my house I was the one rustling. It was early—4:30, 5:00. Sleep was hard to come by for me. Dreams turned to lists of what needed to get done. In nightmares, I rehearsed the calls to insurance agents, how to win over the contractors. When I rolled out of bed, I said all the words again. As I dressed, my mind mulled over what to say when they answered back. No good comeback sprang to life as I padded around my room.

"The man has completed dressing now. He takes the lamp in his hand and goes down... and into the kitchen."

After Hurricane Laura, for twenty-three days, I fumbled around my house with a flashlight, but even after my hallway washed in electric light, I still fumbled with even the simplest things, the everyday tasks, like smiling while I stood in the kitchen or seeing the point in making anything, even coffee.

"The father has lit a roaring fire in the range, and is now parching coffee, over the stove's blaze. Holding a large frying pan filled with beans, stirring them he shakes the pan, to prevent beans from burning."

I didn't make a fire, but I scooped coffee grounds and clicked a button and watched the light on the machine next to the word *BREW* flare blue.

"Just as the coffee has parched to the right shade of dark brown, his wife appears in the kitchen."

My wife didn't appear in the kitchen. In fact, the busyness after the hurricanes had made us both disappear, in a fashion. She stayed in bed, like usual, and I walked out the door.

On that February morning, the sky was the frail black of a chalkboard. No letter, no word, no sentence—only the smeary white left by clouds dragging their lumpy bodies across it. No leftover stars. No morning moon. Only me—the dunce trying to head in a straight line to Louisiana's center.

Impossible.

I had to ditch the arrow of the interstate early on. Then I abandoned Highway 165's hard angling to cut through a small town called Midway. That just dug the hole deeper.

Small towns turned smaller, and the route morphed into a maze of crooked roads and their meaningless red lights. One place required me to take a pretty good dogleg. Another mandated I cut back and forth on several backroads. At one turnoff, I had to hook a left onto a junction highway swarming with roaring cars only to pull off again less than a mile away. At another turn, I zigzagged from one two-lane highway just to get to another one, only to bring me back to the first.

But that was typical with me. Not just in driving, but in life. I chase my own tail. I run in a million directions. Trying to please everyone, I satisfy no one, including myself. I'll cut off my nose to spite my face. What I'm trying to say is, for almost an hour, I herked and jerked and lurched at the red lights of the little towns, never building up enough speed to make any real headway; then, like usual, when I lost my patience, I took a shortcut through Cheneyville, which didn't do anything but make the trip more work for myself.

It's like the stories people tell me at work. It's like the questions they ask me. I'm the first call someone makes when they've decided to resign, and I'm the last person they talk to before they start the job in my department. Either way, it's always the same—their stories, their questions, their answers.

For the new hires, the salary is set—it's what the university is willing to pay people to teach English. NO arguments. NO exceptions. For an instructor, it's $38,000. The job ad will come out and say it. It practically screams it. "NON-NEGOTIABLE!" it hollers.

But it's always the same. People always ask. They have questions. They always wonder. "But this," they say. "But that." But what can I do?

And then the fool in me steps forward, the imbecile trying to please people, the dunderhead who doesn't get nuances, the one who can't utter, "It could be worse," or "You're lucky to have a job when so many PhDs don't." It's the simpleton who doesn't understand those words like everyone else does, who doesn't get it would be easier to lie. No, the idiot in me just wraps the phone cord around my fingers, takes a few deep breaths, and wordlessly waits for their answer.

But that's always the way with me—fumbling for the right phrases to mean what I'm trying to say.

And that's exactly what driving to the center of Louisiana felt like.

The whole route was one big loopy line full of mess-ups and turn-arounds. It was squiggly Highway 71. It was snaky Bayou Road along wormy Bayou Boeuf that bobbed me up and down. It was undulating Highway 1 that's nothing but a wave rolling up and down as it traces the Red River, which itself is full of curves, just like phone cords you twiddle in your fingers. It was the echo there that wasn't a real echo, but the town of Echo, which earned its name for the sounds that used to reverberate off the river many years ago when paddle wheelers chugged cotton down the channel and their sounds carried over the water, carried along the dock at Echo, carried into that small town backed up against the liquid throughfare. Those waves of sounds carried down the streets, carried into people's homes. Every day was full of those echoes, coming into town in rollers.[2] But those are gone now. In Echo, all you hear are the sounds of your own thoughts. And the whole route was just like that—like a phone call when no one knows what to say.

My face was turning green from the rollercoaster ride of Highway 1 and my lunch was about to play hooky when I finally reached the outskirts of Marksville, but instead of calling it quits, I chose to ride another ride—the merry-go-round of that town's streets.

Before I left Lake Charles, I had assumed the exact center of Marksville would be easy to find, and then logically, if I found that, I could find the exact center of Louisiana. But I was wrong.

You see, people say, "Remember to keep the main thing the main thing," but I couldn't in a town like Marksville where I found two main streets, one going east and west on Highway 115 and one going south on Highway 1. So instead of being sure, I couldn't help but second-guess myself. In Louisiana, at its center, where Main Street didn't mean anything anymore, I couldn't do anything but kick myself for being a dummy and, while idling at a red light on Tunica Drive West, bang my head on the steering wheel for confusing things again.

And by *again*, I mean always. And by *confused*, I mean being less help than no help at all. And by *confused things again*, I mean being my foolish self.

Because there are some things they never let you forget.

By *they*, I mean people. I mean everyone. Even myself. Myself, most of all, I mean. And by *things*, I mean every little thing. Every small mistake. Even the accidents. People won't even let you forget the times you meant well, the times something happened exactly opposite of what you intended.

It's like this story people tell at work. It's about a man who has to pick up someone from the airport. Let's call this man John and the visitor Boss, and in this story, John has to pick up Boss and show him around.

It's a bright blue afternoon, and I'd like to say John is elated, but he's too nervous for that feeling. The errand is a big deal, especially to John's job. The visitor is a big deal too, just ask around. He's the top choice considering taking the job where John teaches, and the university just really needs him, just ask anybody. And John knows himself all too well. He's bound to stick his foot in his mouth.

So the two are in the car, about a block away from campus, idling near a crappy strip mall and a campus building. John is desperately trying to think of something to say, some chitchat to fill the dead air, but he's also worried about the questions Boss may ask—the questions about salary. He doesn't want to answer those, doesn't even want to hear them, because John's always too honest during these times, too literal, too straightforward. That's the real problem. John always says just what he's thinking, especially when his emotions get the best of him (which is always, or I should say *again*), and so right there at that Podunk corner of town, John is struggling and stupidly says, "This is the center of town," meaning this is the geographic center.

Boss looks around. Frowns. "How can this be the center of the city?" Boss thinks but doesn't say a word. "If this is the heart of town," Boss says to himself, "there's no way I can move here."

Later that day, Boss meets some other people who show him the restaurants in town. In one, there's a jazz band playing. Everyone sits at a table and drinks beer. Boss gets to talk, and listen, and then talk some more. Boss understands downtown is the *real* center of town, that he can live in the town after all, that he can answer the university's prayers, and he realizes what sort of fool John is and how close John came to ruining everything.

Of course, he never lets John forget it. Even four years later, on a phone call, or walking in the hallway, or during some late Friday afternoon faculty meeting, Boss will bring it up out of nowhere. "John almost," he'll say, and then tell the good one about the time he nearly turned down the job on account of how foolish John misunderstands the word *center*.

That goes back a long way with John, but I understand how it can happen, how tricky words can be.

It's like when I was a kid in the backseat of my parents' car with my dad driving and my mom in the passenger seat. I used to get so confused.

My dad always kept a stack of foldout Louisiana maps packed in the car. He kept some in the glove compartment, but most were stored in the back of the driver's seat. A road would be closed, or an accident would be up ahead so we'd have to detour, and that was when my mom would call back for a map.

I'd reach into the seat's pocket, slide out a map, and hand it to her over the seatback. First, she'd unfold it so it fanned across nearly all of the dashboard, and then she'd fold it back until only the part she needed showed. In a glance, she could tie and untie any knot of highways and find a shortcut. In no time, she could tell how this or that byway connected to another one.

Once we made it through, my mom would hand the newly folded map back to me, and it was my job to refold the flaps and return it to its place.

But once I had the map in my hands, I couldn't help myself. Even though reading in the car made my head hurt and my stomach queasy, I loved to trace where the different highways ran. I tried to understand the roads and decipher the patterns. I enjoyed finding out where they ended. I relished sounding out the funny names of the Louisiana towns—Bastrop, Ball, Boutte, Bunkie. My favorite part was listening to my parents' stories.

There was one about how Bunkie got its name.[3] In it, a man named Captain Samuel Hass owned so much of the land in Avoyelles Parish during the 1880s that when the Texas and Pacific Railroad wanted right-of-way permission across his land, they had no other choice but to give in to all of his stipulations, no matter how silly they might seem, how peculiar. One of the oddest demands was that Hass would only agree if he could name the station they built on his land. Well, Hass had a little girl, who people say knew exactly how to get what she wanted from her daddy, like a pet monkey he bought her or her daddy naming the station after that pet. Only she never could quite work out that word *monkey* on account of a bad lisp she had. "Bunkie" is how *monkey* came out when she said it, which was what she called her pet monkey, which meant that was the word she made her daddy use to name the town.

Because names are made up. And so are routes and highways. And borders and capitals. Directions, too, in a way. Even the edges of maps are made up, which I realized long ago in that backseat.

And all that flooded back to me at the red light at Marksville—that backseat, my journeys, my ideas about words, the mistakes I've made with them, just like John's. Then it hit me. The center of something could be anywhere. It just depended on how a person saw it or what they understood that word to mean.

French anthropologist Claude Lévi-Strauss once wrote, "One's own world is the center of all worlds," and geographer Yi-Fu Tuan says that "people everywhere tend to regard their own homeland as the 'middle place,' or the center of the world."[4] I've met people, plenty of them, who see themselves as the center of the universe. If their world is a wheel, they are the hub; the people closest to them are the spokes; everyone else is the rim.

Humans for a long time have placed themselves in that same position. They've stood in the middle of a stage demanding the spotlight or climbed the soapbox at the center of a room or pointed to the stars to argue that only a fool would believe anything but that the Earth sat at the universe's center or that anything on the planet mattered as much as them.

And nations have also seen themselves as the point of it all, as the core of a circle. Greek historian Herodotus told us that long ago.[5]

And if a nation can be a hub, so can a city. But a city can also be a wheel. Old Rome was one, or planned that way. Plato's ideal city was one too—producers, warriors, and guardians in nice little rings. The growth rings of Paris also show a city as a wheel. It was made by planning and time and luck. Each fire over the years built a new circle of the city and its walls.

And fortune is a wheel, a spinning wheel we ride upon.

And life is a ride. It has spokes and a hub, which I figure is a home, and about that, I'm not alone. "An ideal sense of home," Tuan says, "lies at the center of one's life, and center (we have seen) connotes origin and beginning.... The stars are perceived to move around one's abode. Such a conception of place ought to give it supreme value; to abandon it would be hard to imagine."[6]

But abandoning home was the only idea that made sense to me after the hurricanes. There were forces spinning spoons and swirling water and undoing houses. I didn't understand most of them, so huge chunks of the world made no sense. Places unhinged themselves.

At LeJeune Cove, I felt the homesickness one feels at home, and up Fool River, Ben Lilly taught me that homes and possessions can ride a person. The answer staring me right in the face seemed to be undoing the life I had made.

So I sat in my car, going round and round about all that, idling at the red light where I couldn't keep the main thing the main thing, realizing that my whole plan to find the center was stalled, my foot on the brake, my forehead on the wheel, motionless when the light hit green.

The horns went off and my body jumped. Jolted, my reflexes didn't know what else to do but duck my car into a Chevron parking lot.

I positioned my car at the edge of the lot, out of the way of the pumps, near a defunct quarter-operated air compressor, my bumper kissing an empty field, and in a funk, I sat and stared at the store's glass door. My plan was to swallow my pride and go in to ask for directions, but a haughty Ford F150 was parked up near the entrance, so I stewed.

Outside my windshield, I could see how far the empty field ran before it hit an optometrist's office. Beyond that sat the rest of LA-1. There were strip malls and fast-food joints. There were the bright, but fake facades of Auto Zone and Capital One. Treasures Antique Shop sat there too, with its used bikes and rocking chairs and rustic oak barrels set out on the asphalt. I could see the signs for the Peace Pipe Smoke Shop and the Broken Wheel Brewery, but for the life of me, I couldn't find anything that pointed to the center of Louisiana, or even the center of Marksville.

Then someone's knuckles rapped on my window.

It was a man, a drifter, a vagabond, who had meandered into the parking lot from the field. I could see his shoes were still wet from melted ice, and so were the ends of his thick dark brown traveling pants. He had a traveling bag too, and a heavy coat that fell below his knees. He hadn't shaved in several days, and a great deal of his scraggily hair had been tucked beneath his cap.

On the one hand, his face looked forgettable, but on the other, it held an almost stately aspect, and even though on the surface he looked hard-up for cash, he stood in the parking lot like he owned it, and the field nearby to boot. But most surprising of all, when I looked closer, I noticed his callused hands folded like they once had money, and even though he didn't say a word, even though he didn't ask me to roll my window down, even though he just nodded to the field, or more precisely to one corner of it—a small patch that bordered the gas station and the highway and held one of the town's monuments—I did what he said.

Call me a sap, but to me a good monument is always worth a visit. Why? It's a good storyteller.

Some people may say that's impossible. They'll say that a monument isn't a person so it can't be a storyteller, but a statue has arms and legs and a body, so what else could it be? Or they'll maintain a bust isn't a real face. But I say a mouth and chin and nose and eyes form a smile or a frown and isn't that the whole story of a face? They'll claim a pillar can't speak like a man or woman can, but these are the same people who say colors speak, and so does the heart. Besides, most monuments have words, just like my wife and I do sometimes, and I imagine a monument means what it says, as much as anyone does, if you can read between the lines, even if they're not speaking to you.

The Marksville monument wasn't a statue or a bust, but one giant concrete wagon wheel, and it talked in circles. It had thick spokes going all the way around, except at its bottom right. There, two of the spokes were cracked and a good chunk of the rim had gone missing. That was the point of the story it told, I think, but it kept talking. The monument had a solid base, and on it, about three or four feet up from the ground was a plaque about the size of my head. The words there lost me.

The plaque's background was the color of a thunderstorm, with letters that same smeary color, but a shade darker. To add to that, the plaque's raised edges that were supposed to be a border were a steely gray that blended into the rest of the dull background, which made the words impossible to grasp from where I stood, so I picked my way through a flowerbed's skinny brown gardenia branches to catch it all. First a step, then two, then more tiptoeing, until I had my ear right up to the metal plaque where, finally, I could make out the broken wagon wheel sitting at the top of the plaque and right below it, the words, "1809,

MARC ELICHE TRAVELING THROUGH THE PRAIRIE THAT IS NOW AVOYELLES, HAD A BREAKDOWN ON HIS WAGON. HE STAYED. THE TRADING POST HE ESTABLISHED BECAME THE CITY OF MARKSVILLE."

That's word for word what the plaque said, but if I read between the lines, the story it told was "Luck, luck, luck, luck, luck." In fact, if I listened carefully, the plaque was singing.

It was a Jay Chevalier song everyone used to sing. It was a jumpy rockabilly steel-guitar rhythm and it started with two women singing. "Mighty, mighty man, ooh-ooh," they harmonized. "Mighty, mighty man, ooh-ooh." And then a twangy Chevalier joined in. "There was a Cajun named Marc Elishe. Harnessed up his horses and left Pointe Coupee. Loaded down his wagon with pots and pans, calico dresses, and fancy hat bands. . . . Marc Elishe was a mighty, mighty man. In the Red River valley, he built the promised land. He traded with some Indians on the top of a hill. Built a little town and called it Marksville."[7]

Chevalier's now in the Louisiana Music Hall of Fame, the Louisiana Political Hall of Fame, and the Rockabilly Hall of Fame, and in 2005, he even recorded Louisiana's official state recovery song after Hurricane Katrina, "Come Back to Louisiana." But before all that, back in 1959, Chevalier's first recording "The Ballad of Earl K Long" sold more than a hundred thousand copies. The other side of that record was "The Ballad of Marc Elishe."

There was a time when many people would have known that song. I don't know who remembers it now. I'm not sure who remembers what anymore. People don't seem to know the songs they used to. Families don't seem to gather around the piano in the front parlor and kids don't gather around campfires out in the woods and sing. I'm not sure if families even still take car trips.

I remember mine. I remember the drives I sat in the backseat and stared at the maps in my lap and gazed out the window to watch the roads and fields and city limit signs fly by. I remember on trips like that my father used to tell me, "Wherever you go, there you are." I used to think he meant that any place was as good as another—streets, houses, grass, dirt, people, all one and the same—but I'm starting to think he was trying to say something about how to keep yourself bolted to a place, affixed to the center of something. I remember when he used to tell me, "Be somebody." He told all his kids that all the time.

It's kind of like the story of the two somebodies who ended up in the middle of nowhere, in a "no place." In fact, the story goes that the place was so unimportant, so nondescript, everyone called it "Bayou No Name."

It was back in 1936. Mrs. Stephen Juneau had been wandering all around Avoyelles as a part of the Works Project Administration, that famous New Deal endeavor that put a few no-name artists to work, and one afternoon she stopped in to visit a Mrs. B. W. Hall in Bunkie who told the story of two lost somebodies, "two ministers named Huffpower who had come to Avoyelles Parish from one of the Eastern Seaboard states."[8] The ministers were trying to find a good place to start a church, and "they travelled by ox wagon and were crossing Bayou No Name in this wagon when they became stalled in the mud of the swamp."

They fought and they fought and they fought to get their wagon freed, but nothing they did made the wagon budge. Exhausted, knee-deep in the mud and all but absolutely hopeless, the two preachers finally took a breather to build up the courage to have another go at nudging the wagon forward, but when they looked up from their job, they noticed a stranger had been standing there the entire time, watching them brawl with the mud.

The two ministers didn't ask for help. Instead, all they wanted to know was the place's name.

The stranger didn't answer them. Instead, he "asked the name of the preachers."

"They replied, 'Huffpower.'"

"The questioner said, 'Well Huffpower you came a long way to get stalled in the mud so we will call this lake Huffpower.' And the place nearby became Bayou Huffpower."

That's the story of how Bayou No Name became somebody, which made more sense than some of the things my dad used to say to me, because I know there's a Lake Providence in northeast Louisiana, and I know there's a Lucky, Louisiana, in Bienville Parish, and as much as those two places are named for providence and chance, I know that Bayou Huffpower and Marksville are named for luck too. And it's not bad luck. It's good luck hidden in the bad. It's the kind of luck you don't know you have until something worse happens to you.[9] It's kind of like saying, "Wherever you go, there you are," but knowing that you'll never know you're there until something rubs your nose in it. Something important, like a monument, that you're gawking at. It's kind of like hearing that monument saying one thing, but having the dumb luck to know that the story it's really telling is that the only way for a nobody to be a somebody is for a somebody who's more important than the nobody to decide to give the nobody a name.

Which is a long story to tell you how I finally figured out where to go, but that was how it happened. I realized I needed to find the story behind the name Marksville. Once I had that focal point, I could find the edges of town. Once I had those, I could locate the center. A smarter man would've gone there quicker, but I was the best I had.

The Marksville courthouse, even at the end of February, still hung onto Christmas. The white bulbs someone shoved inside the evergreens growing on the lawn were not only still strung amidst the branches, but still lit. There were a few stray strands of tinsel left on the ground and one bow forgotten on a door handle. The neoclassical building had two flanks of impressive entry steps facing the road, and at the dead center of the first landing sat a slender fir topped with a bright star. Of course, all of it paled to the courthouse's square front doors, which were a bright blood red, but that shade had nothing to do with the season.

To the left of the doors was an imperious swinging bell. It was brass, nearly the size of a Volkswagen, and squat. It had huge oscillating mounts with very stiff haunches, and its internal clapper looked frozen in place, as if it hadn't been made to move in years. To me, it looked like a giant paperweight.

Farther from the building, along the sidewalk, were three separate historical markers—one for Solomon Northup, one for a Confederate fort called Fort De Russy, and one for the founding of Marksville. "Marcos Litche, a native of Venice, Italy and a traveling peddler," it told me, "migrated to the Avoyelles Post c. 1794. Because of a broken wagon wheel, the pleasant environment, and friendliness of the Indians and local residents, he decided to stay in the area. He established a trading post and eventually became known as Marc Eliche."

Maybe no man of Avoyelles had been dealt worse cards than Marc Eliché—that was what I learned at the courthouse. "In those days such a journey was a perilous adventure . . . when the railroad was unknown, cities and towns were built on rivers or at crossroads." Any trader like Marc Eliché would have preferred to find a spot on a river, "but, according to tradition, fate had somewhat to do in selecting the site" of Marksville's founding.[10] I know, Marc's fate doesn't sound so bad, that is until you learn the whole story.

For the town's 170th birthday, the book *Marc's Town* swapped stories with everyone in Marksville about the old days—about "Marc Eliché," "Indians," "Court Houses," "Main Street," the "Soil and Toil," even "*Joie de Vivre*." It gossiped that Marc Eliché, an Italian immigrant from Venice, was twenty-eight when he settled the town. "A merchant, selling to about 50 neighboring families in the Avoyelles area," peddled his wares by wagon, but when the wagon wheel broke, the temporary breakdown "turned out to be permanent." "Old Marc could have fixed his wagon and been on his way," the book says, "for there was a blacksmith at the nearby [Avoyelles] Post," but legend has it that what he had stumbled upon was just too good to pass up.

It was fate. Marc Eliché didn't intend for his wheel to crack. He didn't wish for his wagon to get stuck. It was luck. It was his good fortune. It was that "this was such a beautiful country with its green prairies and moss-hung shade trees along the bayous and lakes" that fated things turning out this way. You see, by the time Marc finished fighting with his wheel, "he could hardly leave."[11]

He found a wife, Julie Carmouche, a local girl from a good family, the "daughter of Joseph Carmouche and Madeline Ducote of Pointe Coupee Parish."[12] He had a house. He had a fortune. He "obtained Spanish land grants totaling more than 400 arpents." He had no sons, but he had a godson, Albert Gallatin Morrow, who was "bequeathed a certain tract of land which comprised the site of the Courthouse Square."[13] He had a business, a trading post, built right where his wagon stopped. He had a steady stream of customers, right off. It had its own name. "Marc's Place," they called it. "Marc's Store," they said. Then "Marc's Town" and then "Marc's Village." Eventually, to everyone the name became Marksville.

That's called *making your own luck*. That's called *thanking your lucky stars*, the ones "perceived to move around one's abode." Because people are resilient. Cities are resilient. Our ideas about places are resilient. Because, geographer Tuan explains, "should destruction occur we may reasonably conclude that the people would be thoroughly demoralized, since the ruin of their settlement implies the ruin of their cosmos. Yet this does not happen."

Resilient people just tweak the cosmos: "With the destruction of one 'center of the world,' another can be built next to it, or in another location altogether . . . it in turn becomes the 'center of the world.'"[14]

When the cow kicks over the lantern and some of the city burns, people say, *Providence*. When the dam breaks and the old part of town floods—*Good Fortune*. "A godsend," people will say when a tree smashes some of a house but not all of it. *Luck* is the word I'm supposed to use when rain drips from spots in my ceiling, but I still have a livable home.

And that would've been the whole story, except for the massive concrete patio connected to the courthouse steps. The patio was shaped like a diamond and made from large sand-colored concrete stones packed closely together. Most of the beige slabs were rather plain, but several stones held dark brown metal panels sunk into their centers. One, two, three, four, five . . . I counted seven stones with inserted panels.

Walking the patio several times, I read every insert more than once. Each panel commemorated some detail about the parish. One was a map of all of Avoyelles—its boundaries squiggled out in a thick gold border and the location of each town marked with its name and a fat gold star. Another panel described the establishment of "Poste de la Avoyelles." Another observed the settlement of the Tunica-Biloxi Reservation. Most of the other panels focused on the parish's individual towns . . . bits of the parish's story. The insert for Cottonport displayed a cotton boll and told me it was the "Home of the Christmas Festival of Bayou Rouge." Mansura's panel boasted a seal with a pig and the words "Cochon de Lait Capital of the World," which swirled over the animal's back and under its belly. The Marksville insert told me it was settled in 1809. It displayed a picture of a broken wagon wheel, and then the words of its motto: "Marksville—Where Everybody is Somebody."

Before that day in Marksville, I would have said that a vagabond owns no compass. I would've bet he just drifts with the wind. That he roams as he pleases beneath the stars. But a wandering man doesn't necessarily walk with pockets empty of plans. Even if we don't see them, even if he doesn't know they're there,

there may be schemes turning nobodies into somebodies and, of course, making the opposite true.

You see, the opposite, that was the gist of this trip, not seeing the good luck hidden in the bad, but seeing the bad luck hidden in the good. That was the point. Only I didn't understand it at first.

It's like the story about a man in Avoyelles, a man much like Marc Eliché.

Once, several years before Louisiana was a state, before it even was part of America, there was a young man who was a trader.[15] He lived in New Orleans, but he was not a native there and so had little prospect to earn a living. He had brought his life savings over from the old country, but in this new place, his money was like water in a sieve. No matter how much he tried to save, no matter how frugally he tried to live, each time the sun came up, the man found his pockets lighter than they were the day before. It seemed hopeless. He was desperate. Finally, one morning when the sun broke through the window, the young man "found himself penniless."

In the city, it was too hard to own a store, to be a trader, but around town rumors churned. Outside the city there was hope. Far from New Orleans, where there was less competition, a man could make a living. There, in the country, goods flowed back and forth, and stores, people nattered, "were springing up daily." Even the boat traders, the *caboteurs*, who "navigate the river in pirogues carrying sugar, coffee, tafia (rum), china and some cloth goods," found themselves with bellies full of food and purses full of coins.

The caboteurs, they came "daily to the inhabitants of the countryside ... some in carriages, with one or two horses, others on foot, carrying on their backs hardware, clothing, jewelry." "These are the peddlers," people would say. That's what they called them.

Life was not easy for the peddler, to be sure. If the horse needed care, the peddler needed to see to it. "Let the carriage become stuck in the mud, or broken, or let the harness be broken, and the unfortunate merchant must be porter, wheel wright, saddlemaker and harness-maker all rolled into one."

But this new place offered a chance, and that, at least, was good enough, the young man in the city thought, so he "took on credit in the city to buy goods" and set out from New Orleans.

The journey was hard. The man found himself alone in the country on poor roads and faced with dangerous travels; his pockets were empty too, but he did have one thing. He had hope.

Then hope muddied.

The man hadn't traveled more than four miles from New Orleans before the "road, which was slippery" had him "cursing his destiny."

Stuck, on his own, practically lost, the young man "was tempted to jump with his burden into the Mississippi."

But as fate would have it, the young peddler stumbled upon a nice house with a friendly face. The owner's name was Maccarti, and taking pity on the peddler, he bought a few goods from the young man. "You must stop with us," Maccarti said, then invited him in for dinner.

The young peddler was polite. He knew to decline, but Maccarti insisted, so that evening, despite his better judgement, the peddler dined with Maccarti at his table.

How did the dinner go? "The cheer was excellent. The wine was an old Bordeaux." And when the weather turned while they ate, Maccarti invited the young peddler to stay for the night.

The next morning, the invitation was extended once more. This time it was a seat at the breakfast table. And then, once that meal was done, and after Maccarti had purchased a few more items, the peddler moved on, much the same as he had started, but with a few items sold and, more importantly, with a new resolve to pursue this prosperous life.

The planter? His next day was very much the same as the day before. He didn't miss the wine. He didn't notice any more wear on the bed. His pantry seemed as full as it ever was.

The moral? It's supposed to be, "It is not always money that people down on their luck require. A kind word and good counsel may be enough to settle the destiny of such a man." It's supposed to be a story about everybody being a somebody, a lesson in how a somebody can help a nobody stick it out until he is a somebody.

But sticking it out can sound better in a plotline.

In life, so many endings go the other way.

It's like the stories everyone had after the hurricanes. For weeks afterwards, for months, my phone kept ringing. *BRRING*, and it would be another colleague resigning. *BRRING*, and a person was taking sick leave. I would need to find a replacement. *BRRING, BRRING*, and someone was deciding to retire. *BRRING, BRRING, BRRING*—it was a graduate student. They weren't coming back to teach next semester. They weren't coming back at all.

I started to hate answering. It rang. It whined. I started to plug my ears to it. When I ignored my office phone, it became my cell. It rang. I silenced it. It rumbled in my pocket. I pretended my leg was numb.

But I couldn't ignore it forever.

BRRING, and it was someone who had been teaching at McNeese for ten or so years. He was first a graduate student, then an instructor, and then a couple of years ago, he finally landed his dream job—full-time, tenure-track, teaching what he loved to graduate students.

His recent promotion meant his salary went from something like $37,000 to $42,000. I could use the word *lucky* for that, but his wife was a teacher too. They hadn't felt like they could afford to buy a house before the promotion, and after it, the money still had been a little tight.

Maybe in another year or so, after their debt had been paid down some, if the price of houses didn't keep going up faster and faster, or if they could find a fixer-upper in a good part of town, they would be able to buy a place. They could feel it. Their luck was about to turn: that's the kind of things they would say before the hurricanes.

Then, Hurricane Laura hit. Then, Delta. The place they had been renting needed "to go down to the studs," which was the phrase everyone used after the storms. *Down to the studs*, but I could never understand that phrase exactly because sometimes it meant things could be worse and sometimes it meant things could be better. Except for the person I worked with. I knew what he meant because after he spoke those words to me, he apologized for having to leave. He told me how he and his wife had to evacuate to her sister's place somewhere in Illinois. They were going to stay there until they could find another place in Lake Charles, but then the high school where she worked called. The school didn't have much damage, and they told her she needed to report back to work in the next two weeks. If not, consider her contract void. His phone call to me was to let me know their decision was made. Only there was no choice, not really. There was no place to move back to. So she was quitting. He would teach online until the year was up. "Sorry," he said. "I couldn't make this work."

In 1869, when Samuel Lockett rambled around Louisiana to survey the topography of the state, he slogged his way through Avoyelles Parish too, and like Marc Eliché, he was in a wagon. "No effort at description could possibly convey an adequate idea of it," Lockett wrote about the roads there. "Words would utterly fail to do justice to the subject . . . forcing a passage through the muck and mire of the swamps."

But wasn't it worth the grief—wandering, getting lost, risking a wagonload embrangled by mud to see the "panorama of considerable beauty" present in the bottom lands along the great rivers? To Lockett, it was. And to "visit the deep, silent bayous, overhung with moss-covered cypress, willows, and liveoaks," a wanderer "must ramble along the clear quiet lakes whose surfaces reflect with perfect fidelity everything above . . . and he must penetrate the tangled swamps . . . and if he had anything of an artist's eye, he will see new and peculiar beauties everywhere."

Only, an artisan's labor can be so tedious. The Red's waters "are excessively turbid . . . its current is swift; its banks are constantly washing away at one point and building up at another; cut-offs are frequent; islands, old rivers and abandoned channels are numerous; bayous are sent off from the parent stream; overflows and crevasses often occur." In other words, like luck, the water here is always changing. What I mean is, working here can feel lonely. For some of us, living in Louisiana can feel like being on your own.

It can be like this with me. In Avoyelles, in Marksville, "Where Everybody is Somebody," I emailed the mayor to set up a meeting to hear stories about Marc Eliché. I called the local tourism office. I tried to reach someone in city hall to tell me about that wagon wheel and teach me about the history of the town.

I *was* trying to stick it out, to make it work. I wanted to understand the attachment I had to Louisiana, the pull the landscape had on me. Even if it took me in circles. Even if I needed to find a geographic center to *center* myself, to figure out how a *nobody* could be a *somebody*, like my dad wanted me to be. I was willing to do it. I planned on slugging it out.

But I never was lucky enough to get a callback or an email from Marksville. I couldn't even find a pamphlet. I don't blame anybody. Everyone's busy. Life gets in the way. I consoled myself that it just wasn't meant to be.

Then I discovered in Marksville even books are somebody. They can talk as much as any other thing. They all know one another and make for good company. Maybe a single cup of hot coffee will be the only thing served and maybe I'll be the only invited guest, but a spread of Marksville books around a table is all it takes for a good party. Enough conversation will go around that even a fool can just sit there and pick up a thing or two.

At the party, I listened to *History of Avoyelles Parish, Louisiana* the most.[16] "Some say that [Marc's] store stood several blocks from the courthouse square, about where the Ford Motor company is at present," it told me in its papery voice. "Others say it was on the north side of the square, where the Bailey Theater is now." Whatever it was, one thing seems certain that it was near the courthouse. Judging by the number of his signatures on documents, he must have been at the courthouse very often.

I scooted myself closer and tilted my head in its direction. "Just when he arrived is not known," the book rasped, but his name, it's on document after document. They're mixed notarial acts dating back to the Avoyelles Post. Every exchange at the post needed two witnesses, *temoins d'assistance*. "Those who performed this duty most often" were Marc Eliché and Francoise Tournier, two early merchants. Many of the older Acts are written in Spanish and French. The later ones are in English. They are all housed in the courthouse of Avoyelles Parish, and Marc Eliché's signature appears on several of them. Anyone looking at them could see how he was a *real nobody* here.

"A nobody?" I said, scratching my head. "What sort of nobody signs court documents?"

The same sort of nobody who owned a store, was the book's rejoinder. There were "several stores at the post." Marksville "from the earliest time was famous all over central Louisiana for three things: stores, hotels, and education. Marc Eliché, founder of the town, was its first merchant."

The same sort who donates the land for the courthouse, another book supplied.

The same sort who uses his home for one of the earliest meetings of the jurors and justices of the peace to meet, *History of Avoyelles Parish, Louisiana* added. "Just what took place at this meeting records do not tell," but it was at Marc Eliché's home.

"But I don't understand," I said. "He sounds like a somebody to me."

No, not at all, one book corrected. Because many times he stood as a witness to a marriage.

I tried to grasp what they were telling me, but I was the kid in class who raises his hand to ask what everyone already knows. The one who struggles with one plus one or when he reads, the clock goes by slow. "It doesn't add up," I stammered.

It does if you unlearn everything you thought you knew, *History of Avoyelles Parish, Louisiana* went on. In August of 1797 when Jean Baptiste Lemoine married Marie Else Ducote, Marc Eliché was there. When a price was set for the husband's horses and mares and the bride's cows and oxen and even the "outfitted bed worth $60," he was there. When everyone agreed that "everything to be done had been done according to Spanish law" and "the contracting parties make their marks," he was there and signed his name. He signed it again when the "inventory of Mr. William Gauthier, directed by his widow," was sold. "One bed, completely outfitted," was let go for $39.

"But isn't a witness a *somebody* in a town like this? Isn't that how history works?"

No, he was a nobody because he was also legally a somebody in court, a book sitting across the table said with a smile.

Confused, I turned to *History of Avoyelles Parish, Louisiana*.

There were times when things did not go well, when things were not "done according to Spanish law," the book said. There were times when Marc Eliché was sued. There were times when he sued back. Sometimes he proved he paid a debt. Sometimes someone else proved he hadn't. On an October day in 1799, someone charged him with making rails "off of the place of de la Morandier." That "place had been seized for debt."

"But to sue or be sued, a person needs a name," I pleaded, and then, hoping to rattle sense back into it, I knocked my head a few times with my hand. Then I said, "To sue or be sued, a person is an entity. In the eyes of the court, an owner of property is a real somebody. Am I wrong?"

This is sold, that is sold, and Marc Eliché signs his name—true, a book responded. He's a seller or a buyer or a witness. He's a man of standing, an entrenched part of town, a true . . . *nobody*.

I was almost in tears.

Consider this, *History of Avoyelles Parish, Louisiana* cut in. Once, Francis Tournier wrote the governor about Marc Eliché. And once, on January 20, 1798, when a list of men "declare that Mr. Baptiste Mayeux and Mr. Joseph Joffrion, sindics at the post, have always acted with justice in all cases involving them, and that their honesty and integrity are unquestionable," Marc Eliché signed his name to pronounce the same.

"The governor," I said shocked. "Wouldn't that make it obvious that Marc Eliché had made a name for himself?"

Then all the books began to murmur. Sure, sure, one finally said louder than all the other voices. Making a name for oneself is an important thing for a person to do.

Sure, sure, they all agreed . . . sometimes.

Because, one of the books piped up, sometimes a name can be changed.

Because, another added slyly, sometimes there can be worse things than a name meaning nothing.

Because, one finally said, sometimes a name can be dangerous. Sometimes it might be better to have no name at all. There was a time in Louisiana when the law cared about a person's name, kept watch over it. There was a time when the Code Noir forbade observance to any religious creed other than Catholicism and called for the expulsion of all Jews from Louisiana.[17] True, not many people cared, not until 1795 when Governor Carondelet wanted to make a new post on the Red River. After that, a person's name could be a dead giveaway.

You see, the book said, Carondelet sent Carlos Luis Boucher de Grand Pré up and down the Red to find the perfect spot for his new military outpost. After several surveying trips, Grand Pré wrote back. Avoyelles was "the key to the river and in the center of all its posts and settlements," Grand Pré told Carondelet. "The beautiful island settlement of Avoyelles. . . . located on the first high land which occurs along the Red River after leaving its mouth at the Mississippi" would be an ideal location. There was only one problem—the illicit trade there.[18] But for Pré, that had one simple solution—eliminate the clandestine movement on the river. Eliminate the unlicensed traders. Eliminate the transients. Eliminate the itinerants, the vagrants, the vagabonds.

A paper-thin voice began to chime in. It was a book sitting at the far end of the table, and quietly it said that the word *vagabond* was an interesting one. It could mean different things. It could mean someone like Marc Eliché, with his wagon and his back-and-forth crossings of the Red River, his going in and out of the Poste de Avoyelles. That word could mean him, or those like him, peddlers who put down few roots at first because they came from an Old World that did not allow them to own land, men who did not buy farms because Old World laws gave them little experience with farming, men who learned the business of traveling, of trading, by necessity. And then, after they had saved enough money, these young peddlers would pick out a spot, open a store, turn into a merchant.[19]

"But what's that have to do with Marc Eliché, the Cajun from Pointe Coupee?" I asked once it finished.

Almost in a whisper, the quietest of all the books said that many say Marc Eliché also was a Venetian Jew who came to America, a Sephardic Jewish trader whose name was recorded as Marco de Elitxe by the Spanish and changed to Marc Eliché only after his trading post was established.[20]

"They changed his name?" I said.

"His signature appears on a document in 1822," *History of Avoyelles Parish, Louisiana* said, but after that, his story is unclear, like the writing on a smeared chalkboard.[21]

I stood up from the table. The party punch had soured, and so had my mood. My eyes were blurry and my tongue felt like lead. Arguing held no sweetness anymore. My back ached and my head hurt so bad it was hard to think, but I was starting to understand.

It was like the story of that young trader who left New Orleans to find a host, a bed, and a bottle of good Bordeaux wine. Was that bottle just a detail to arouse the senses? Was it a clue? Was it a nod to Bordeaux's important role as a trade center for New France? By the 1750s, Bordeaux was a major French port. Was it a reference to that commercial city's feelings about trade and its status as a *havre de tolérance*, "a harbor of tolerance" where a French Crown allowed Protestants and Jews to trade? Was it a coincidence that in Bordeaux, Jews could obtain French naturalization and the special title *bourgeois de Bordeaux* that bestowed commercial privileges? By the second half of the eighteenth century one merchant out of every four or five in Bordeaux was a Jew.[22] Was it all just chance?

I walked to the library's door, opened it, and in the space of quiet between my body leaving the building and the door thudding shut, one book called out, "Beyond this nothing else is known of Marc Elishe, and he flits into the past like a shadow."[23]

After the library, I spent an hour or two drifting around town. I was sinking down a drain, turning randomly, drifting up and down roads, aimlessly going where the wind took me. I dodged traffic near the courthouse without even thinking. I darted back and forth across a few major roads just for the hell of it. I used Martin Luther King Drive to navigate a roundabout path through a residential neighborhood of identical single-family brick homes for no other reason than to remind myself of the dull life I had built for myself.

It was down those streets where I started to wonder if even the stars grow bored of places like this. That when they look down on this neighborhood or mine, do they laugh? Or even yawn? Even when people like me look up and say something essential, don't they just turn their heads to cast their light on some more important place? Or maybe it's that the stars themselves are confused. In a place where one home looks the same as any other, how could they ever tell "which abode to move around"?

I know, I was being too melodramatic. Call me an idiot, a pitiful fool, but I didn't know how else to feel or what else to do. So I kept driving, deeper and deeper into the nondescript *noplaces* of the Marksville neighborhood I found myself in.

I drove one block, then two, then three. From my windshield, I investigated the yards, peered down their driveways, studied what homeowners keep under their carports. I even tried to see into the houses' windows.

It wasn't long before I saw two children roaming through one of the house's front yards. As I got closer, I realized it was two brothers tromping across the icy grass to hunt robin. The older one cantered with a pellet gun leveled underneath his aiming eye. The younger one, barely up to his skinny brother's waist, struggled to keep up, switching his attention back and forth from his brother's aiming eye to the female thrashing in a pile of oak leaves and ice-snapped branches.

I kept track of the boys with my rearview after I drove by, and by the time I shifted my eyes forward, the road dead-ended into a park. Most of the park's property was separated from the road by a split rail fence running along the edges. A wrought-iron swing gate barred the entrance, but I knew where I landed.

The Marksville State Historic Site, also known as the Marksville Prehistoric Site, is a sprawling forty-two-acre park made up of grassy fields, sparse runs of trees, earthen embankments, and seven prehistoric burial mounds. Local legend used to claim the earthworks here were fortifications made by Hernando De Soto and his men during one of their earlier expeditions, but archeological excavations showed those old stories were wrong. The mounds were signs of an earlier people here.

In the 1920s, when several Ivy League archeologists explored this set of mounds built on a bluff running along an abandoned channel of the Red River, the scholars celebrated it as a unique, archeologically important example of the Woodlands period, a site to rival the decorative Hopewell culture sites of the Midwest. The elaborate earthworks, the pottery with intricate geometric designs, the other finds that proved a grand trading network existed here, and the tombs—the discrete burials so unique during this time—all of these stood as a distinctive, identifiable Louisiana culture known as the Marksville culture, stretching from around 1 to 400 CE.

From the gate, I could see one of the larger mounds about a hundred yards away up to my left. It was one large circular platform. A few oak and pine poked up along its rim. A flat patch of knee-high grass grew on its top.

I took a few pictures, but they were uneventful. The magic of a mound is what's buried underneath it. Pottery, pipes, stone points. Crafted objects of shell, bone, stone, even copper. Bracelets, necklaces, earspools. Figurines. People of honor—earlier excavations here proved this is who was buried in these mounds. Archeologists even found one or two dogs laid to rest alongside the people, but no one really knows their purpose.

Today, the park's purpose is in limbo. After years and years of watching fewer and fewer visitors come, after watching the budget fall lower and lower, the State of Louisiana decided "it would likely never be able to operate it as a park and historic site tourist attraction" again, so on August 20, 2020, Louisiana finalized the official paperwork "returning the park to city ownership."

The city couldn't take care of the park, though, so the site still sits closed. It could be turned over to the Tunica-Biloxi tribe, which is federally recognized and owns the Paragon Casino Resort in town, and no one would be surprised if that happened, even State Parks Director Brandon Burris, but it hasn't happened yet.[24]

It's like the old saying, "Whoever is crying for the past is praying in vain." Or the story about a father who doesn't know how lucky he is, the man with twelve kids who thinks the noise inside his house can't get any worse. He visits a rabbi who tells him to take his chickens and move them into the house. When things don't get any better, the rabbi gets him to move the geese inside, then two goats, then his cow. After that, the father learns what loudness really is. He learns that it can always be worse.

Because as bad as it is for one somebody to disappear into a nobody, worse is an entire people. Worse is the Avoyels people, who seem to have gone by various forgotten names—Avogel, Avoyelle, Avoy, even Tassenogoula, even Petit Taensas—and who themselves seem to have vanished. Disappeared. Gone. Extinct, maybe. But no one knows for sure.[25] And no one, it seems, even knows for sure what their name meant. Did it mean Flint people? Did it mean "people of the rocks"? Did it mean little vipers?[26]

It's all guesswork, isn't it? Certainty about the past. Certainty about anything.

It's like the story of Carol Mills-Nichol who was raised in Long Island and traveled to Avoyelles in 2002. She knew her family had connections to Louisiana, but not much about them. With research, with trips to France and Germany, with interviews of several locals living in Rapides and Avoyelles parishes, including Jim Levy the retired editor of the *Bunkie Record* who "remains as the Jewish presence in Avoyelles" and Rabbi Arnold Task at Gremiluth Chassodim in Alexandria, with all this work she discovered a history and a giant family tree. "To go from no relatives to a tree with over 30,000 of them is quite a revelation," she once said. It happened because she moved past the limits of what she had been told, what she knew, and began to explore. After that, the past, once so confined to false boundaries and fake divisions, opened up to her.

Mills-Nichol says that her work on her family "grew into the history of all the many Jews who lived and worked in Avoyelles Parish." While her one story centered on her family, it soon became a story of "assimilation and loss of the religious identity of so many in that area" because according to her research, many of the very early families of Pointe Coupee and Avoyelles were Jewish, but that history had been overlooked or erased.

She turned it into one large story: her book *The Forgotten Jews of Avoyelles Parish*. In a way, it's a complement to the older *Fourscore and Eleven: A History of the Jews of Rapides Parish 1828–1919*. Both try to recenter the history of the area, complete it, write people like Marc Eliché back into it.

His name is nowhere in her book, though. "Whether or not he was a Jew is just speculation," she said. "I did not mention him as I have no way of proving one way or another his true ethnicity or heritage." About Marc Eliché founding Marksville, giving the town its name, his decision to settle there, especially the broken wagon-wheel part, she considers that "legend."[27]

It's just another story.

East of Marksville, beyond the edge of town, down Highway 1, there is an old road named Cocoville Road. Off of it, Old River Road runs a hundred feet or so before it reaches Little Cemetery Road, which rambles through the grounds of St. Paul the Apostle Catholic Cemetery. Dedicated in 1796, that cemetery is one of the oldest in Avoyelles. There are rows and rows of plots, and a small mausoleum of brick and glass. Behind it is an open field, and in the dead center of that field sits a tall thin monument.

The base itself is made of a sturdy white brick. A plaque there reads, "Sacred to the memory of Marc Eliche, 1766–1819, founder of Marksville and his wife Julie Carmouche Eliche, 1766–1837." At the plaque's top are two dates, 1809 and 2009, and an engraved image of a wagon wheel, the lowest spokes broken. At the plaque's very bottom are the words, "Requiescat in Pace."

The monument is telling a story too, a story like any other.

The fact surrounding "Marc Eliché's death are as mysterious as his arrival." His actual burial site is unknown, flitting through the past like the man. Some say Marc Eliché "was buried in the old cemetery on the post located near Mansura, but a fire which destroyed all wood markers might have destroyed his, unless it is one of the many nameless iron cross markers."[28] Some say it's actually in the older cemetery near Mansura, and some say it even could be in St. Paul's, maybe even near the monument.

But the monument isn't a gravestone. It's only a symbol, a sliver of memory. It's simply a base and a slender white column of marble rising six or seven feet. Perched on top is a pelican made of that same white stone. She tucks her beak into her chest so that her bill pierces her breast. Below her hungry young wait for her, for the pieces of her heart.

At home, my daughters waited for me that day, waited for an answer to why people, like spoons, get sucked into some place, get stuck and can't move.

But even though I had a few stories to tell, the pull of center still had me speechless.

From the gas station monument to the courthouse to the library to the mounds to the cemetery, my journey had led me in circles and I wanted to quit. It was a good time for it. But it's like how people say, "Do not be wise in words—be wise in deeds," so I tightened my belt and retied the laces of my shoes. I climbed back into my car. I put the key into the ignition, peered over my shoulder to back up, and all at once it came to me—the memory of the vagabond boy in the backseat.

My fingers dug themselves into the pocket on the seatback, and before I knew it, a book of maps—*The Roads of Louisiana*, an old Christmas present one year from my mom—sat on my lap. "All the Roads of Louisiana from the Interstate to the Backroads," the cover promised. The pages inside kept the vow.

I was lucky. Was any man luckier? The book's pages showed me the road I needed to get to the center, and that road was the one I was already on—Old River Road.

All I needed to do was dive down a little more into the story. So I did. I dove.

Old River Road ran through empty countryside, and I dove. It cut through a patch of unpeopled woods. It crossed Bayou La Cabane. I dove. It passed by the river camps built along the water. It made a broad swoop south. And I dove, holding my breath, hoping, until finally, I found the geographic center of Louisiana. It was the very end of a dead-end road.

Not metaphorically. Literally.

A small blacktop circle spread out to form a little pad. Beyond the asphalt, the ground drifted into dirt and then the detritus of seedpods, oak leaves, broken palmetto fronds, and running cords of poison ivy, greenbriar, pokeweed and pepper-vine and then smartweeds and maiden ferns that were waist high and then the vines thickened to become a curtain growing between elms, ash, hackberries, and all the other hardwood trees that formed these woods near Premier Bayou. On one of the trees, nailed to its trunk, I saw a small square white sign: "*Wildlife*—STATE MANAGEMENT AREA."

I climbed out of the car and shuffled my feet in the dead leaves cluttering the middle of the roadway. If this wasn't the middle of nowhere, it was close enough.

The scrubby patch of woods sat in a low-lying, poorly drained area composing part of the Red River backwater system. Other parts were lakes or coulees or bays or small rivers or bayous or canals or sloughs or ditches. All of these waterbodies and low places were "relict channels of the Red River," but this one swampy patch was, as luck would have it, Louisiana's center.

About two thousand years ago, the Red River decided it, I guess. In a river's fickle way, it did. The center could have been underwater, but the river broke into a right-angle bend, cut northeast. The diversion "isolated a piece of highland that became Avoyelles Prairie and created bluffs."[29] People used those bluffs to make crossing the river easier. Marksville, sitting on the edge of the Avoyelles Prairie, stood as a bluff Natives chose for a town and ceremonial grounds. "The Avoyel Indian knew a good place to live when he saw it," is the sort of thing the local histories say.[30]

Good fortune, the flip of a coin, the way things turned out—call it what you want, but looking around that February, I realized it could have been different. The center of somewhere else could be, would be somewhere different—a mountain, a monument, a museum . . . somewhere impressive, somewhere not part of a backwater system, somewhere not soggy or sinking. Mine was this. Mine was what it was.

Avoyelles is called a "crossroads parish." It makes sense. Avoyelles is a crossway. It's a crosshatch. Its history is a history of a place where people came to trade and swap goods, where their lives met. It's still a place where three rivers meet, where waters meet, where every road seems to curve along a bayou or stream or waterway.

It's a place where Highway 114 swoops and loops in Moreauville. It's a place where, in Cottonport, Front Street follows the wiggles of Bayou Des Glaises. In the town of Evergreen, Hill Street and Main Street and even Burns Roads seem to tie together in one fine knot to make a bow out of Rouge Bayou and Bayou Huffpower.

It's a curvy place. Roads curve, rivers curve, the track of a hurricane is one long curve to shore, life throws people curveballs here.

Maybe that's why I couldn't quite tell when I finally left that parish. I missed the parish limits sign, and unlike maps, the actual roads I took never seemed as clear to me. Just more proof of why my life has taken the path it has.

Sure, there was a time when the word *luck* made more sense to me. Twenty years ago, if someone asked me how I was, how I was getting along, I probably would've said I was lucky to land a job so close to home. I vividly remember the day twenty years ago when McNeese called me. My old boss was on the phone. He knew I was close to finishing my PhD, so he asked if I'd consider moving back to Lake Charles. The job wouldn't pay much at first, he cautioned, but there was a good chance I could get on fulltime. One or two years later, that happened. I was making $31,000 grading one hundred essays a week.

It didn't matter. I was one of the few lucky ones to be teaching in Louisiana and also wanting to write about it, but twenty years later, back from Marksville and

Louisiana's center, pulling into my driveway, seeing the debris still left in the road and the home repairs left to do, the meaning of a word like *luck* left my eyes bleary.

I used to feel lucky to get a call from a former student sharing that she landed a job. It wouldn't matter if it was at a community college, or in the next-door state of Texas, or even in another Louisiana school. You could bet she would be making five, ten, maybe fifteen thousand dollars more than I was. It wouldn't matter if the person just started. Chances were good her salary might even be double mine. It didn't matter. I was happy for her. We were both lucky. She had her life. I had mine.

But these days that vision of the world stood blurry. The roads I had gone down years ago with such conviction didn't seem to be the right ones now. If I had to draw my own map of the world today, I couldn't promise you I would know what the core of it would be.

And worst of all, I was going to have to walk into my door and tell my daughters what I had learned, what I had discovered about the center of my home, about the center of Louisiana.

One year my family and our neighbors took our annual Thanksgiving trip. That year we chose to visit Poverty Point. We rented a cabin at the nearby state park and used up one whole vacation day walking around the UNESCO site's impressive configuration of mounds. We used the brochure and followed the path, read all the kiosks. We climbed the stairs leading up to the largest mound and looked out. Our kids took selfies of themselves at the top. We ate a picnic lunch. We spent a good long time inside the interpretive center.

Poverty Point was named in 1873 after the plantation on which it was located. It's interesting to think about the sentiment of that name—a plantation associated with poverty, a place we think of as a grand estate linked to shortage. It turns out many plantation owners took that ironic tone. *Solitary, Hard Bargain, Hard Times, Hard Scrabble, Solitude,* and *Poverty Point*—that's a sampling of some Louisiana plantation names, and those were just in Tensas Parish.[31] Why? Many of these were owned by pioneers who sold their possessions back east and gambled on making a fortune in Louisiana. They wanted to give that anxiety a name.

I remember after walking around Poverty Point, we piled into our two cars, the kids blending the families like a bowl of mixed nuts. As we drove away, they kept checking out the back windows to see how long they could still see the mounds. When we reached the cabin, it was already late, late afternoon.

That night we had planned on a campfire in the park's picnic area, a short walk from our cabin's doorway, so we rested a bit, waiting for the dark to set in, and then we grabbed our supplies. Someone packed up the marshmallows and graham crackers. Someone found the matches and our little sticks of lighter pine. Someone stuffed the ice chest full. A few of the kids grabbed their solar-powered lanterns. And then, once we had everything, all of us walked down the road to the fire rings.

Were there nine of us in all? Yes, nine. Our wives and kids walked up ahead, wagging the lanterns they carried and singing the songs we all knew the words to. My friend and I lagged behind. There were no streetlights there, so the lanterns glowed like beacons, and the moon was a big fat shiny disc, all its light pinpointing us, spotlighting our families' simple walk down that road. For a moment, I felt like I was standing at the center of the world.

It isn't easy to think of a story to tell. It isn't easy not to feel like a fool when you look for something and can't find it. When you're asked a question and don't have an answer. When the way you see things doesn't make sense. When you don't understand the basic words people say.

So when I walked inside and heard my daughters asking about what I learned about the center, I said to them, "Do you remember this story?" and I told them that one time, there was a man watching his daughters walk down an empty road with nothing but lanterns in their hands. They were going to make a fire ring and sit beside it to tell a few stories. The lucky man felt like he was the center of the universe.

It's a story, like any other.

Flag Island at Hodges Garden

Carmen and Mardi Gras at the LeJeune Cove Mardi Gras

Restored Cajun Prairie at Cajun Prairie Gardens

The dead-end road at the center of Louisiana

Ben Lilly Monument in Mer Rouge

Ben Lilly Conservation Area in Chemin-A-Haut State Park

Bayou Bartholomew boat slip

The Broken Wagon wheel at Marksville

The courthouse in Marksville

Patio insert for Marksville

Occupy #1 church sign

Roadside marker for Occupy #1

Gravehouses at Talbert-Pierson Cemetery

A newer gravehouse at Talbert-Pierson Cemetery

Sunrise near Grand Chenier

An oak at Pecan Island High School

The Chenier Plain

Bird observation tower at White Lake Conservation Area Bird and Nature Trail

Giant thistle at White Lake Conservation Area Bird and Nature Trail

Curtain of pine needles near Coochie Brake

Interesting rock formations near Coochie Brake

Rock outcropping in Kisatchie National Forest

Gum Springs Campground

Jack crossing a tree at Gum Springs Campground

Pavilion built by CCC at Gum Springs Campground

Charlene Richard's grave

Plexiglas box on Charlene Richard's grave

St. Clair Baptist Church sign

Lost road to Hot Wells

Marker and Benches for Pere Rouquette

An oak on Bayou Lacombe

4

INTO A FAR COUNTRY . . . CLOSE AT HOME

So there I was, parked on the shoulder of an empty road, staring at a maze of black gum and slash pine. This time the job was way out in the sticks in a town so small everybody knew each other's dirty secrets. Actually, it was my wife's hometown, but that evening, I wasn't out for family business. It was personal. That night I wanted justice. I wanted revenge.

It was after the double hurricanes, and I had spent the day at my mother-in-law's trailer checking on the place. I was fixing a leak, ripping up carpet, chain-sawing three gargantuan crepe myrtles at her property line and dragging them to the highway. It was March. Go ahead and call it the ides since it was already hotter in the year than it should've been, and I was so rank and dirty that the acrid taste of sawdust on my tongue was like a match striking my heart aflame.

All day long, my brain kept working back to the object of all the vile and violent things I burned to do. The so-and-so wasn't too far from her trailer's lot. So I finished, packed the car, and drove straight to that darkening side of the road, then spent half an hour thinking how the target of my revenge was no more than a long, steady walk through a curtain of hardwood.

Someone could call it trespassing if they wanted to put a fine point on it, but I was in no mood to worry about details, about particulars. My hands were wringing the steering wheel. My teeth were champing at the bit to settle things. My Rogue was shifted into park but idling, and the rumbling felt like a bedmate shaking me awake to go take care of a noise in the dark.

But I didn't move.

I couldn't say exactly why. Maybe I was savoring the purplish evening sky coming on, relishing it the way someone brags on having a black eye. Or maybe

I was wondering how I got myself into this mess. Maybe I was trying to let cooler heads prevail. Or maybe I was just working up the nerve.

In truth, there were reasons to second-guess my plan. First off, the woods. They were a waxy shade of green good enough for going unseen in, but maybe they were too dark. What I mean is, if I got out the car, there was a chance I would never find my way back to it, which meant another reason was the fear of getting myself turned around in the woods. The worry at the forefront, though, was the darkness and the chances it gave of me blindly stumbling into someone with an intent as lowdown as mine.

So this is a confession, I guess. It's an account of what happened to me and I'm going to get it off my chest, but it's also a warning because I'm going to be truthful about it all. Mostly, I'd say take it as a lesson of what not to do—which is mainly don't get lost somewhere in Redbone country and ask for help or you might find yourself in a cemetery. Because that's what happened to me. I was poking around someplace maybe I shouldn't have and the next thing I knew, I found myself staring at a grave. Hell, I was inside it. My two feet were kicking dirt. My body was cramped into a square of wood. If I looked up, I could see the wooden planks above me. If I stuck my arms out, my palms could feel the splinters. If I squinted, my eyes could catch only the smallest cracks of light sneaking through my prison. Worst of all, it seemed to be on account of a misunderstanding.

But I'm getting ahead of myself. Let me go back to the start, go back to the time before I was in a grave, back to even before I was sitting in my car at the edge of the woods. Then maybe you'll listen.

I don't know what to unload first. There are clues, there are red herrings, there are mysteries, and they all seem to be part of this convoluted story, but in my heart, I know this is a simple case of payback. No, it's not exactly about a man taking the law into his own hands, but it's about anger and hate, and someone holding a grudge and taking action, and deep down, it's a story of retribution, and maybe like all stories of vengeance, it's a story of a reckoning too.

But I guess the whole thing began when a lady named Barbara strolled back into my life.

It was the first day I unlocked my door after Hurricane Laura and stepped inside. One of the streams of water dripping through the ceiling turned out to be directly above the bookshelf where I had crammed the papers and books and pamphlets I've dug up over the years. I could call it "research," but that word seems too fancy for what I've got. It's a newspaper clipping of a reunion or a flyer for an event at a rundown church or an old map of a place in Louisiana now shutdown. What it is, isn't much to most people, I'll put it like that, but I sorted through it all to figure out what to salvage. I took things off the shelves at random, tossing the too-wet papers in the trash and dropping what I could save into plastic bins one of my brothers gave me.

The trash bags filled up fast; the plastic bin did too, and so I slid over another one, then the pain sank in. Under that leaky roof, as I studied the mess I needed to weed through, so much of that stuff seemed to say, "Mister, you ought to know better."

But that's a hurt I'm used to. The harsher sting came when I put my hands on a black binder. It was bulky, musty, maybe a little damp, definitely destined for the trash, but as I was chucking it, a CD slipped out of the binder and landed on the floor.

I couldn't help myself. Written across the CD's surface, spelled out in black marker, were the words "Bear Head Creek Incident," so I picked up the CD and fished the binder from the trash.

The binder had a manila folder labeled "Redbone Research" written in neat cursive loops. I didn't recognize the handwriting, but inside the folder were several pieces of research: blogs and websites printed in pale jet-printer ink, pages of a manuscript, printouts of a local newspaper dated 1884, a Xerox of a paperback book about a famous 1882 Christmas-Eve fight between "Whites and Redbones," and a copy of a 1953 *Newsweek* feature titled "Redbones and Dynamite" with a cutout of a local newspaper's 1953 story titled "Magazine Story Irks Two Parishes" taped to it. It was a sore reminder.

I sat for about half an hour, flipping through the contents, reading, ruminating.

What could I tell you about any of it to help you understand? What could I say even about the name *Redbone*?[1]

It's complicated, is maybe all I might say. It's got a past. It drags around a history. It's a word in a lot of the papers I've collected over the years, and though some people use it still, it's a word I don't say, not unless I'm trying to explain a past. The word's a knife, I guess is the best way I could describe it. Or it's a tool. Or a weapon. Or it's an heirloom. It's a word whose weight depends on who's wielding it.

A 1953 *Newsweek* article says it's "a purely local term applied rather loosely to the native sons of Allen and Rapides parishes." The article appeared after a local paper workers' strike turned violent. Machines were being destroyed. People were being shot at. Locals were turning on each other, and by way of explanation, the article told readers *Redbone* was adapted from "redskins" and meant people had "mixed blood" and were part Native American and other things down "in their bones." The writer acquiesced that locals may say something different, that local legend suggested "redbones" were "Spaniards and Mexicans from pirate bands and Gulf Coast shipwrecks, American fugitives from justice.... adventurers" who mingled into Central Louisiana. But it didn't matter much to the writer anyway. Or at least it mattered less than what was happening at the time and why.

"Redbones are still an eccentric people," the Newsweek article claimed, "suspicious, secretive, and contemptuous of the law and its agents. When they stray, it is almost impossible to get any evidence on them; when they disagree, they settle their own scores, using the knife and the shotgun in their private quarrels and feuds.... Whenever a shotgun blasts or dynamite explodes (which is too frequent for comfort) in strike-ridden Elizabeth, La., somebody always blames the 'redbones.'"

Local people were annoyed—pissed, you might say. "Magazine Story Irks Two Parishes" proved it. Everyone in the local newspaper's response "branded" those comments "as 'utterly ridiculous,'" and everybody, and I do mean everybody, wanted to know where this "out-of-town writer" got off, "whoever he was."

I guess it was three familiar issues the local paper took umbrage with, three old wounds that resurfaced. For starters, locals wanted to know who this outsider was who used the term *Redbones* and where he came up with that definition he used and what gave him the right. The second thing was this "mixed blood" stuff. And finally, people wanted to know if the writer knew most of the locals supported the strikers, and if he did know that, why had he "omitted ... that the strikers are deeply religious. Little churches can be found less than two miles apart in the rural areas of these parishes."

There was no need for the writer to answer any of this, though. Locals didn't care what he had to say anyway, not anymore. The omission of the churches and the good side of people proved his intentions. Good riddance to him, locals thought.

Which is what I'm trying to tell you. Old grudges are hard to let go of. Especially here. Especially with me. I've never been called a *Redbone*. I'm not one. But with that word, it's still a gut thing. It takes me to a place I maybe ought not go, to places I maybe ought not visit. It's a flight-or-fight kind of place. It's not real. It's a landscape dredged up inside me, built from regret, erected from fear. It's a landscape of my mind, which makes it a place hard for me to explain, but it's a part of the story you need to know, so I'm going to try to fill you in on how I went from holding that binder in my hands to waiting near that stretch of black backwoods and how trouble ate into me.

One thing you need to know is that I faced a stretch of sleepless nights. It was months after Hurricane Laura passed, maybe two or three weeks after the roof was on and the leaking ceilings stopped, but I couldn't let it go.

To be truthful, it was a good long stretch. It was the rain. It was the weather. It was hearing a thunderstorm roll in and wondering if the new roof the people put on my house would leak or not. It was seeing that I was right, people do cut corners. It was the trickles coming through the ceiling making me grit my teeth. It was cursing myself at first for being duped, then it was scheming on what I ought to do. It was resentment that kept me up. It was kicking myself that had me walking the floors.

It was hard at first, but the sleeplessness grew close to a routine. I would find myself fiddling around the house's dark, trying to turn all the late hours into an old habit. It wasn't easy when it started, but I grew methodical about it.

The yellow light above the kitchen sink showed me the well-worn way to the cabinet and the cup and the faucet. I wasn't thirsty. It was just something that felt familiar, normal. Piddling around at two in the morning was like a good alibi. Nothing was out of the ordinary. Nothing was strange. It wasn't anything if it wasn't a pattern. It wasn't me who was obsessing about my house. I was the guy busy wondering why the pillow felt so uneasy, so out of sorts. I had an everyday excuse for kicking off the covers, lumping out of bed, and walking the dirty floors. It was just how nights were now. How things were done here at home.

The TV could vouch for me. I learned there was nothing wrong with the hubbub of a rerun's conversation to step in for the thoughts I was dragging around from the day before. There was *Mannix* and *Cannon* and *Barnaby Jones* late at night to help me put away the list of to-dos for tomorrow, or even help me scheme on what to avoid.

And it all went according to plan, until it didn't.

It was the commercials. They threw a wrench in the gears and made the mind start to wander, start to roam out into a far country of thick woods and wild grasses, into dark places. To be precise, it was the memories that came rushing back while the commercials ran. Those old thoughts were old hands at setting an ambush.

"I have been acquainted with people of this country ever since the year 1835," a Louisiana preacher once wrote. The job set before him was to record the origin of a small cemetery in the far western portion of Louisiana. It was 1927 and he feared the past might be lost, "grown over like a field of weeds and turned unrecognizable."

"In my early days there were no churches, no schoolhouses, no preachers, not anyone who would offer prayer in public," he explained, but "people had to die, and I well remember when the people were called to bury John Martin's infant child. This place was selected to lay the precious body . . . here lies the body of the old and the young resting."

"Here the body of William Martin, with his wife, also many children and grandchildren lie buried here," he wrote. "And the old wayworn traveler Saul Williams, who had been to market to get supplies for his family and was taken sick . . . His children from Texas came . . . and laid his body here to rest."

"J. W. Franklin's two bright little boys whom I have often nursed to sleep, their bodies have been lain here too, with several of his grandchildren. W. G. Franklin has one lain here. J. P. Mitchell has lain five of his children here. Elmore Kay has two children here. Abel Dixon one. Thomas J. Franklin two."

"I feel it's my duty to give a short history," he clarified, then said, "And here lies our father . . . and by him our mother has been lain . . . three of our own babies, one boy and two girls have been buried here."

It was a look in the mirror for him. It was his honest account. "To our disgrace and shame," he confessed, "we let this grave-yard grow up though it had been once pailed in and wire stretched around it. Still it has gone down."

You see, it was the paradox of *home*. Of *home* in Louisiana especially, where *gone down* is routine and shame is regularly scheduled.

I mean, the detectives on TV, the ones with the sidekicks who need all the explanations or secretaries who end up kidnapped, were the lucky ones. I didn't have a partner. It was me going around and around with myself to work things out. One part of me smarting off that having trouble sleeping wasn't like murdering someone so there was no need to get bent out of shape about it, but then the other part stuck its nose in and claimed the sleeplessness was the surest clue of all the things I had failed to do. It was my graveyard grown up though it had been once pailed in.

What I mean is, I saw those detectives and they solved things. I wanted to do that.

When the power came back up in Lake Charles after the storms, I had to scrounge for a computer with a CD Rom drive. My laptop didn't have one, neither did my home desktop or the tower in my office, not that I could get to it—the hurricanes saw to that. Eventually, I found a PC up at school in one of the two computer labs left standing, rooms all the campus faculty were meant to use. On the last row, four coal-black machines, all about the same age, lined up against the wall. One Saturday I had some extra time, so I picked the workstation closest to the window.

When I pressed the CD Rom eject button, the slot clicked open like a beer tab. I put the CD in the drive and mashed the disc holder shut. The system whirred for a moment; then, a folder popped open on the monitor.

My little cursor hovered over several files tucked inside the folder. Some were jpegs labeled "redbone news article" with a date. Some were unlabeled Word docs. I could also see a handful of .txt files, and for some reason, my mouse floated to those first.

The documents turned out to be a batch of old emails, and for a second, I hesitated to read them. Then I asked myself, "What would Mannix do?"

"Barbara," the first one said, "I was talking with Carolyn last night and promised to write you about something I found last year. . . . I found undated newspaper articles on another Redbone fight which occurred between Lake Charles and the

Bearhead community — over toward Newton, Texas.... Do you know anything about it? Exactly where it occurred?" It was signed, "Don Marler."

Barbara, whoever she was, wrote back. "That is interesting info that you found," she said. "I should be going into Lake Charles on Friday (we are going camping close to LC) and I will do a search in the index for Bearhead."

A few more emails sallied back and forth before one, sounding a little defeated, admitted, "I had to make myself quit researching because I had a few other things to do." It was the Barbara again, adding another sentence or two of apologies, then a few spaces that I swore sounded just like a long sigh, before she closed with, "Tomorrow I will put you copies of two other articles and a map in the mail." I realized she was referencing the jpegs in the folder.

I dug around until I found the scans and started reading them. I couldn't tell which newspaper ran every article or the exact dates of some of them or even the sequence they belonged in, but the first of the series seemed to be the one titled "A Desperate Battle at Lock, Moore, & Co.'s Log Camp, 'Redbones' Try to Drive a White Man from the Camp." It happened in 1891.

The newspaper's account of the affair was mysterious and murky, and I felt like I needed a code ring to read between the lines. "Our town was thrown into an excitement last Monday morning," the story began. The facts, "as nearly as we can get at the facts" the reporter said, seemed to be that "a party of about twelve people of a very low class, well known through this portion of the state as 'Redbones,' headed by Austin Ashworth went to the home of one Mr. G. W. Morris, a gentleman employed by Lock, Moore & Co. about 11 o'clock Thursday night and informed him that he would have to leave the place before daylight or take the consequences."

Morris didn't leave. Or as the newspaper put it, he "did not care to give up his position." What he did care to do, it appeared, was "to take in a stroll," which is what he did. He and "his friends being desirous of taking a walk, started in the woods," but "knowing the threats of these treacherous, mix-blooded people, they took their guns with them."

Morris and his pals ended their late-night meandering at a neighboring store. There were Redbones there, "a party of Redbones who wanted to know if they came to fight." The way the newspaper told it, Morris and his friends said they weren't looking for a fight, but that wasn't the answer the Redbones were waiting for. "One of the Redbone party reached for his gun and said he could kill any —— in the crowd," the newspaper claimed, but "Mr. Ward, of the white party, being too quick, shot him dead and then a general and fierce battle ensued."

People can be a mystery. A place can be too. But trouble never is.

Before people knew the facts, fear spread a haze. It made people stir and worry their hands. Rumors swirled. People nattered. Speculation was that "these pesky Redbones were massacring every woman and child in the camp." Folks heard Dr. Meyers and "other well-known people around Lake Charles and Calcasieu had been killed," which whipped up everyone. Then, a "report that the Redbones were murdering old and young brought out reinforcement from along the line of the Calcasieu, Vernon, & Shreveport railroad."

Worry sparked a frenzy, and the reporter seemed to be fanning the flames. "The white people in those parts are indignant at this outrageous and murderous affair," he wrote, "and it only requires about another such move on the part of these low, miserable mixed bloods to cause the white people to rise and literally wipe them from the face of the earth, as it were, every mother's son of them."

The only problem was all the rumors about the dead women and children turned out to be just that—hearsay. Gossip. Lies. It turned out the supposed truth "proved to be without foundation, as there were only six killed in all . . . 2 on the white side" and four "on the Redbone side."

Just the facts didn't seem to be enough, not to the paper, not to the "Lock, Moore, & Co." and the "500 men employed," not to three white men in jail who claimed they "offered no resistance whatever" and whose "host of friends in Calcasieu parish felt sure that they can prove clearly that they were on the defensive and not offensive side."

The reporter concluded that "what we can learn is such a war is brewing all the time as these Redbones push themselves into equality with the white men of that section, which should not be and will not be tolerated," and with that, the article had said its piece. Well, it did add one more predictable truth about trouble—"More trouble is expected at any time."

So I waited. Not for the trouble of the past, but for the mess that I knew was coming. I could tell my brain was sniffing around something. I just didn't know what it was yet. I should've left it alone, but when my brain nabs something, it's like a dog with a bone.

After a hurricane, there are nights you sleep alone. You stay behind in the empty house to keep an eye on things, to be there if anyone walks through the broken gate at night, to listen for someone trying to climb through the boarded-up windows. Or, you tough it out just for an early start at cleaning.

It's a chore you don't ask your wife or kids to do, so you watch them pull out of the driveway to go stay with family out of town and tell yourself there's no point for more than one person to stick around to be miserable, except maybe you won't end up talking to yourself too much, which you do after a hurricane. You talk yourself to sleep. You talk to get yourself out of bed. You talk to make it sound like the TV's on. You talk because your brain hurts from the mess in the house you're trying to set straight. You talk to gnaw at the trouble.

If you're lucky, the talking loosens the knot, wiggles something free, some memory. One moment you're struggling, biting your lip and squirming around, and the next, some problem imprisoned in your head is finally untied.

That's how the identity of the woman in the emails came flooding back to me.

When I was just starting my job, when I was teaching maybe my first or second class on Louisiana traditions, one of the students was a woman with the brightest eyes I've ever seen. I think her face was the cheeriest when she wore blue—a short-sleeved button-up chambray top and blue jeans. Her name was Barbara Swire.

I remember her hair was black with thin wisps of silver woven through. Every day when she waltzed through the doorway it was perfectly in place, I'm sure set weekly at her hairdresser. She carried her books in a canvas bag that swung down by her knees. It had two long straps, but she never slung it on her shoulder. She clutched it primly with her hands and placed it neatly by the side of her desk when she sat down. Her back was a pin when she did.

She was simply coming back to school to read, she would tell me when I got to know her better. She hoped to learn all the things she didn't appreciate when she was younger. Whenever I asked how her classes were going, she'd tell me how much she liked to hear what all her professors said about the books they had read, the details about history they knew. She admired someone who took good care of what they loved, whatever that was, she used to explain to me. She enjoyed listening to people who had spent a long time with something.

She was a Herbert, I think, originally. Maybe her relatives were Bass. I should've paid closer attention to the details. She took a few of my folklore courses and was often too kind about them, giving me more credit than I deserved.

It can happen when you're part of a class like that. Day in, day out, students talk about their traditions, share their histories. Everyone's stories swirl around the room. It can feel meaningful, rich. I don't do much when that happens. My routine is to just stand there.

I knew she enjoyed the class, but I was still surprised one day when she interrupted me in my office to ask if I might take a job. Well, it was an opportunity, she would've said. Anyway, she wanted to know if I might be interested in giving the keynote address at that year's Redbone Heritage Foundation Conference.

I was happy to accept, flattered really, and probably a little smug too back then. It must have been 2003 or 2004. I was too young and dumb then to realize just how unqualified I was.

I remember the weekend of the conference, driving there, pulling into the Alexandria Holiday Inn, wandering around the swanky hallways, smashing my soles into the tight-woven Berber carpet, counting door after numbered door, inventing stories about the travelers behind them, rehashing those old legends of wanderers through western Louisiana. . . . squatters, desperadoes, black-market smugglers, frontier peddlers, circuit-riding preachers.

If I remember right, it took me about twenty minutes of trekking the hallways to finally find the room arranged with chairs and a podium. I peeked inside, and that was the first moment fear of what I was about to do started to creep up on me. I gathered myself, squeezed through the door, then scanned the faces in the chairs. It was too late then to tell Barbara I couldn't do this thing she asked of me.

At the podium, as the projector fired up, the room's lights dimmed, and the audience came into focus, dread sunk its teeth in me. That word *Redbone* would have to come out of my mouth. My ears would have to hear me trying to explain something about that name. I would have to listen to myself go on and on about it in front of people who had always heard that word, who had felt it being used, who had lived it firsthand.

Don Marler sat among them, his arms folded and head cocked as he listened to me. He had written more about Redbones than any other person I know, maybe more than any other person alive. Most of that he had collected into *Louisiana Redbones*. The man could stand at the podium and talk for the entire conference.

But it was more than Marler. Everyone in the audience had combed through family trees and rummaged through courthouse records. They had scrounged up countless birth and death certificates. They had found all the old books, transcribed the notes written in people's Bibles. They had scrutinized the small country cemeteries and recognized the names on the stones, knew them personally. They had even typed up the stories their own families had told year after year, even the hard stories full of hard truths. And my idea was to stand in front of them and say a few words that every second felt more and more like a preachy sermon?

I improvised a little, cut some words, and did the best I could to stumble through the talk I had planned, which was meant to be a testimony about the way people can collect traditions and why they should. Maybe I talked about buried treasure stories too. Maybe I made the point that the real gold to find was the stories people shared, the customs they preserved. A very original and astute oration, I know, but I was trying to tread water until I could push away from the podium and dogpaddle to my own chair. There, I could catch my breath and just listen for the rest of the afternoon.

It was a good rest of the day. Someone talked about their family line. Someone talked about common Redbone last names. There were two talks, I think, about cemeteries. Towards the end of the day, someone stood and delivered a presentation on Joseph Willis. I saw stars.

By all accounts, Willis was one of the very first Baptist preachers west of the Mississippi River. He "first appears in Southwest Mississippi in 1798," historian W. E. Paxton explains. "In 1804 he came into the Attakpas [sic] county . . . the following year he settled in Bayou Chicot, where he gathered the first Baptist Church west of the Mississippi in this State."[2] People called Joseph Willis "The Apostle of Opelousas" since his work called him to Louisiana when it was still mostly wild territory, areas still known as the Opelousas and Atakapa districts of Louisiana. That nickname and the names of the churches he started have haunted me ever since. There was Beulah Church and Half Moon Church and then there was the name that punched me in the gut—Occupy.

Despite everything Joseph Willis did, there is one story I always circle back to when I think of him. It happened, so the story goes, one night at a boarding house after a long day spent preaching in a remote western Louisiana location. These boarding houses offered travelers a tolerable meal and a relatively safe bed off the road, but it often meant a large, shared room with several cots. On this particular evening, Willis shared his sleeping quarters with a grisly group of strangers, callous enough that they barely even noticed one of their own so terribly sick he was fretting for his life.

Willis comforted the man the only way he knew how. He set himself by the man's mattress, then opened his Bible and read, praying with him and witnessing to him until the sick man fell asleep.

When Father Willis woke the next morning, he found all the travelers gone except the sick man, who told Willis that while the preacher slept, the men could be heard planning an ambush for him down the road. The sick man begged the preacher to take a different, secret road the sick man knew. Willis heeded the advice, and his life was spared—the sick man became a believer for life.

I can't remember if the conference presenter told that story or if it was one I learned later. Either way, it's occupied a part of my mind ever since, almost as much as the lesson in humility I learned that afternoon at the Holiday Inn.

Legend says the name *Occupy Church* came from the very last sermon Reverend Joseph Willis gave there. That was around 1854, and Father Willis was known to everyone by then. He was an old man, more than ninety, but preaching was like breath to his lungs. When he could no longer stand, "he sat in a chair and preached." When "he became too feeble" to walk to the services on his own, "the people carried him." When traveling to the service became too much for him, the congregation "came to him." In a chair, from his bed, almost blind, he preached to the end.[3]

And at the very end, when he delivered his very last sermon, he said, "Occupy. Occupy till I come." His words threaded into the fabric of that little town, a place called Slabtown after the hunks of waste a sawmill produces when it cuts timber into boards.[4] I don't know why the town was named that, but I wouldn't be surprised if it was meant to be a putdown. Redbones seem to get that a lot. So did Joseph Willis. Maybe that's why for his final teaching he chose Luke's "Parable of the Ten Coins."

The Bible story tells of a man of high rank planning a journey into a far country. "Occupy till I come," he says to his servants before placing a gold coin in each servant's hand, then leaving them to travel into an alien land to receive his kingship.

Joseph Willis was a man of high rank too . . . or sort of . . . for a time. Around 1760, he was born to a white Carolina planter, a man of wealth and influence, but his mother was a Cherokee slave. It was that lineage that dispossessed him of his father's estate. Randy Willis, a descendant of Joseph Willis who describes this story in detail, explains that "since Joseph's mother was a slave, he was born to a slave-status" but it's "clear from Agerton's will that his father considered him as his only son and loved him as one. This fact did not sit well with some members of the family."[5]

It was Joseph's own uncle Daniel Willis who refused to let a "mulatto" inherit his brother's land and property. He even wrote the state legislature and Governor Richard Caswell. "I have a small favr. to beg," the letter starts. "My Deceas'd Brother Agerton Willis gave the graitest Part of his Estate to his Molata boy Joeseph and as he is born a slave & not set free Agreeable to Law my brothers heirs are not satisfied that he shall have it."

The whole affair turned into a historic civil rights case. Joseph Willis won, I guess. He earned his freedom. But he lost most of his inheritance.[6]

In the story of the "Ten Coins," when the nobleman returns after having received his kingdom, he calls his servants to him. Whatever those servants had done in his absence is called into account. One's gold coin turned to ten. Another's became five. One hid his. The good stewards become rulers of their own cities. The poor steward, with the same gold coin still laid up in the same worn napkin, admits to fear, says he knew his master was an austere man, so he buried the money. The master takes the gold coin and gives it away.

After the trial, Willis decided to spend whatever money he had left to travel as far west as he could, or as he might say "to come among these people" who lived at the edge of things without the benefit of church buildings and "labor for their spiritual good." Legend says Willis preached "the first sermon ever delivered by an evangelical minister in Louisiana west of the Mississippi River." It was in "Vermilion, about forty miles southwest of Baton Rouge. At night he preached at Plaquemine Brule . . . at the perils of his life."[7] Louisiana was still a wild country then . . . and a very Catholic one, a place dominated by the Code Noir. Under that code, the only sanctioned faith was Catholicism since the French crown believed any other undermined the region's stability. Officials forbade any Protestant preaching. Anyone caught could be punished.

And there were spies.

In Louisiana, if Willis was caught preaching, he was beaten, run out of town. He could even be exiled to a foreign land—Mexico. He had a friend this happened to.

But Willis was full of zeal. He had already lost his first kingdom. He was prepared to go into one farther still or lose his life. Whatever the danger, Willis desired to do good work. He wanted to baptize. He wanted to preach. People say Willis often walked from place to place to spread the gospel.[8] Miles and miles he would travel on foot, by mule, moving ever onward to share the Good News, even if only to a handful of people settled in a far-off wood, near a river. He would traverse the coppices. He would cross the waters. It didn't matter. Legend says sometimes he rode logs to travel downstream and sometimes he swam his mule across a current dangerous as a serpent. Legend has it he even swam his mule across the Mississippi, muscled and black and roiling.

You see, Willis was a licensed preacher, but he wanted to do more. He wanted to establish churches. But that meant being officially ordained by the Mississippi Association of Baptist Churches. That meant traveling to Mississippi.[9]

The first time he made the long journey, he made it for naught. His request was rejected. Some say it was his skin color, his low birth. But even though he had failed, this man in exile would not falter. A few years later he slogged back to Mississippi with a petition signed by his own church members who testified to his devotion and upright character and good standing in the church. The second time his prayers were answered.

"I came into Louisiana with nothing but a horse, bridle, and saddle," he would reminisce as an older man living near Pitkin. "Children," he would say, "you can slip away from me, but not from God."[10]

It was funny how the years slipped away from me. Was it ten years ago? Maybe fifteen. Could it have been twenty years since Barbara left that binder and CD with me?

It must have been two or three years after the Redbone convention when she came into my office with her bag. She didn't say much, or I don't remember what she said. She probably knocked lightly, smiled, then asked if she might bother me for a moment.

I probably was preoccupied. I'm bad for that. I didn't know it would be the last time I would ever see her.

Thinking about it now, I wonder if it wasn't right after the last big hurricane here, 2005's Hurricane Rita. Back then, maybe she was like me, and clearing out things. I wonder if her house saw damage in that storm and she thought the materials might be safer with me. Maybe she even hoped I would do some good with them. I guess that's what kept me awake those months after Laura, wondering if she'd be disappointed in how little I had done. I guess my mind was also trying to work out what she had found.

It was late one night when I started to piece together a few things. I had spent the last few days digging through the files on the CD and had hit a dead-end. I hadn't slept much, and that night I was moping on the couch, trying to let *Barnaby Jones* lull me to sleep. All at once, like an episode's final scene, all the clues fell together, and I saw it clearly.

It all connected to Willis and Occupy, but most importantly to the stories people tell about Redbones—the stories of fighting, feuds, and property disputes people still pass around. Take for example the earliest source everyone always throws in your face when you mention Redbones. It's a treatise in two parts written by a man named Webster Talma Crawford.[11] The title's a mouthful: *Redbones in the Neutral Strip or No Man's Land, Between the Calcasieu and Sabine Rivers, in Louisiana and Texas Respectively, and The Westport fight between Whites and Redbones, For Possession of this Strip, On Christmas Eve, 1882*. Like the title, the whole second part of the book concerns a legendary shootout in Westport, a small Louisiana settlement about two miles from Pitkin, a.k.a. Slabtown. "A most peculiar and clannish type people," Crawford calls Redbones, "ever a baleful enemy of the intruder; malicious, resentful and revengeful; constantly to be feared . . . who considered their country a private domain over which they held sovereign authority."

But one thing you learn when you're chasing the truth at the end of a story is that there are two sides to everything, even the reputation Redbones have. One thing you learn is to do the legwork. One thing you learn is that it may take a few days to put your hands on the master's thesis about Redbones that sits in the college's library archives.

But I read it, eventually, and in it I found new evidence. "The two public tragedies for which the Redbone community is widely known are the Rawhide Fight and the Westport Fight," the thesis said. "The Westport fight of 1881 is offered as proof of the group's allegedly belligerent and exclusive nature," but that fight "for which the community is remembered is a case . . . [with] no documentation and [only] few allegorical interviews."[12]

"How a people view themselves is affected not only by their own perceptions of the past," the thesis went on, "but also by the perceptions of outsiders. It has long been the style of the Redbone community to define itself in reference to the usually negative things others say about them," but at the same time "the present-day descendants would prefer not to have [that reputation for a violent heritage] continually directed towards their community."

In other words, it's what you learn in *Cannon* or *Mannix* or in *Barnaby*—you can't always trust the witnesses. You can't even always trust the killer's confessions.

So I lurched up from my couch, thinking of Barbara and what she left me. First, I chastised myself about how wishy-washy I was being about what I'd fight for and what I was willing to do. Then, while I was brushing my teeth, I asked my reflection if there was any grit and sand left inside me or if it had all fallen out. Then I sneered and bit my lip and clenched my fists. I went off to bed like that.

The next day I went farther, deeper, not that the files on the CD were buried any lower, but I dug with abandon. Way down in the folders, I went. Down and down and down until I found three files without an extension—the ones I worried about getting a virus from and was too scared to open the first time I saw them.

Now I didn't care. I tried four or five different programs, but each time my clicking spit back gibberish all over my screen. "Damn," I thought, and then I tried the simplest program I could think of—Word. I felt like a fool when the files cracked open.

One file was a survey. I guess Barbara was asked to look it over, so there were multiple drafts, and even a preface. "Nearly every group in America today has developed a written history," one of the first sentences said. "One exception is the group known as Redbones."

It didn't take many sentences for me to realize this survey was really an ambush. "My name is Don C. Marler," the author of the survey explained. "I plan to write a book on the history of Redbones and to publish it through Dogwood Press."[13] It was an attack on history. It was an assault on my own past.

You see, Barbara had come back to me after all these years. She wasn't knocking on my door, sitting across my desk, asking me to chase down information about a topic, but she was sending me on a hunt just the same.

She had discovered a set of articles about a fight between "Whites and Redbones," a different fight from the Westport fight, a fight known as the Bear Head Incident, and while finding a newspaper's account of a fight was the kind of expected trouble people have associated with Redbones, the puzzling details of the article seemed to show a different side to the same old story. Redbones didn't look like the antagonists. They looked like people who were fighting for their homes, for their lives. It seemed like the "miserable mixed bloods" had simply known "more trouble is expected at any time" and prepared themselves. Maybe they knew that any other "push . . . into equality with the white men . . . which should not be and will not be tolerated" would "cause the white people to rise and literally wipe them from the face of the earth, as it were, every mother's son of them" and so they pushed back. It appeared the Redbones were a people who were just trying to "occupy."

It wasn't that big of a puzzle, or even that complicated, but now it was mine.

If there's a gut instinct for poking around unlooked-for places, if there's a certain type of spirit that's required to have the courage to ask uncomfortable questions, it seems like some people are just born with it. I wasn't, but Don Marler seemed to possess it. In fact, he seemed to have it in spades, which you might expect from a retired Navy Frogman—an ace at plunging into murky depths unafraid.

I say that because the survey I found on the CD stuck its nose in some private and hidden places. Right off the bat, Marler wrote, *"Please complete this survey only if you consider yourself a member of the Redbone community,"* underlining and italicizing the words for emphasis. "We are well aware that the term Redbone has in the past had a negative meaning," he reassured, but "REMEMBER YOU DO NOT HAVE TO IDENTIFY YOURSELF IN THIS SURVEY." It was all so touchy, but he was dogged and full of zeal and hope. "That is changing as we all learn more and take pride in our heritage," he vowed.

But change can be slow. And history can be a thorny thing to rummage through. And Redbone history can be the thorniest. For one, "little documentation exists"—that's how Steven D. Smith described it when he wrote a history of the area for the Department of Defense's Legacy Resource Management Program. Redbone history "has yet to be wrestled from regional folktales," Smith cautioned, "so tightly intertwined with folklore it is impossible to sort fact from fiction."[14]

Webster Crawford complains of that too. "It has been a very difficult task to penetrate the thick haze of obscurity surrounding the Redbones," he lamented, "to lift even a little the heavy cloak of mystery in which he is so completely developed" was onerous because, to him, part of that heavy traveling cloak with hood and cape was "the wilderness region between the Quelqueshoe (Calcasieu River) and the Sabine . . . the whole area . . . of rapidly shifting scenes, of vague, ambiguous agreements; of colossal uncertainties." People call this area No Man's Land, and for Crawford, "The Redbone is so much a part of the environment that created him that he can not be understood apart from it."

True, the history of western Louisiana is a thorny thing too, full of scoundrels and cowards and fools, prickling with good outlaws and bad liars, barbed with trespassers and folks ready to do whatever to make them pay. Yet alongside those sits the other side of the story—the founders and pioneers and those of hearty stock. The reliable stewards and lawful sheriffs. The pathfinders and the first churchgoers and the other early people settling a land.

But among all of them, there is one character I can never escape. The one figure that keeps dogging me.

Who is it?

The detective.

What sort?

The not-so-hot one. He's doubtful, and daunted, and ever unsure of himself. He's not bumbling enough to be funny. He's not all that lucky. He's not tough at all. For that matter, he's not all that good at detecting. But he means well, if that's enough. And he tries. He spends a lot of time driving. He's bad for burning up gas. He always feels he's right at the edge of something, but he's usually not. He's typically preoccupied. He can miss the obvious. No one would call him fearless. Most of all, he's slow.

You see, a few days after I rediscovered Barbara's treasure and unlocked Marler's survey, I was still dragging my feet. I never wanted to dig around or write about Redbones. The topic just seemed too fraught with the danger of offending people. Too boobytrapped by race. Besides, my brain told me someone else could do it as well as I could. Better.

Into a Far Country... Close at Home 105

But I still couldn't sleep. It was hour after restless hour of hearing names of people and places hissing at me from the corners of my mind. It was Barbara's bright eyes. It was Marler's questions. Every night while I was in bed fighting the sheets, they would roll around in my brain. Then late one night, I slammed into it.

I had been seeing the survey all wrong. It wasn't a window into history or a view into the past, even my past. Instead, it was a good look in the mirror. It was a chance to stare at the figure looking back at me—the overly polite detective.

It's no surprise that it took me at least two weeks to pick up the next piece of the puzzle. Or that, to try to make it fit, I needed to head out to Occupy. I didn't know exactly why, but everything had got me thinking, and as much as I wanted to delay it forever, I knew Willis and Occupy and the fight Barbara researched all connected somehow. A part of me felt like I owed it to her.

If life was really like the black-and-white crime shows on TV, the scenes of that trip would've done more to give away the ending. I would've been prowling down a rain-soaked alleyway with ominous shadows darting against the walls rather than pulling down a sunlit asphalt road with a white pea-gravel parking lot at its end. The mockingbirds and their background music from the trees would've told everyone to get ready for the big reveal instead of sounding just like birdsong. And the remote church building and the sign out front would've been the moment when the curtain is pulled back or the mask comes off; instead, it was a case of mistaken identity because when the camera panned, if real life had camera pans, it showed that this wasn't Occupy Church No. 1. No, despite my top-notch sleuthing, this was Occupy Church No. 2.

You could call it a mystery—that there are two Occupy churches, but it really isn't. The explanation is that Occupy No. 2 Church formed around 1936 "as the membership grew" in Occupy No. 1, but that's just one story. Another one is that some disagreement split the churches a long time ago, and they haven't reconciled since.

I don't know which story is the truth. People keep it close to the vest.

I bet Marler knows, and if he doesn't, he probably isn't afraid to ask. He doesn't seem afraid of much. His survey is proof of that. In it, he asked people to note their church affiliation. "Baptist, Catholic, Pentecostal, Other, None"—he expected people to circle one. He asked people to tell him how much of their church's congregation was Redbone.

Occupy No. 2 sits on ten-mile Creek Road, and some people even call the cemetery Tenmile Cemetery because running nearby is a waterway called Tenmile Creek. It's named that because it marked roughly a distance of ten miles from the historic town of Hineston, Louisiana, which was the last stop before people traveled into No Man's Land. There's another fork of the river four miles closer to Hineston, which is named Six Mile. People here have been calling Redbones

Six-milers and Ten-milers for a long time. It's just one of the ways to talk around things, but it's all part of the story, the case.

"Would persons who are thought of as 'All White' be welcome in your church?" Marler asked in his survey. "Would persons who are thought of as 'All Black' be welcome?" he pushed. "Would persons who are thought of as Indian?" There were spaces to check, "Yes," "No," or "Uncertain." He counted on an answer.

I've always relied on a subtler approach. I like to call it that. More accurate might be saying I've employed a lot of standing at a distance and watching, a whole bunch of raising my hand and waiting to be called on. At Occupy Church No. 2, my strategy was mostly reading the church sign out front.

The first couple of lines didn't tell me much—"Sunday School 10:00 a.m." and "Worship Hour 11:00 a.m."—but I kept asking, politely as I could.

The next few lines were more of the same: "Training Hour 5:00 p.m." and "Worship Hour 6:00 p.m." and "Wednesday Prayer Meeting 6:30 p.m." I could see that it was going to take some doing, but I was used to that.

I stood around in the gravel, making myself a nuisance on the sidewalk. Taking pictures. Rereading the sign. Eventually, that stoolie of a church sign coughed up something interesting. It was way at the bottom of the placard—two lines in red block lettering that confessed to being a reminder of a calling. "COMMITMENT TO WIN AND DISCIPLE IN OUR LORD JESUS CHRIST" sat on the top line. "OCCUPY TILL I COME," right below.

Behind the church, there was a fenced-in cemetery. It had a sign that read, "Occupy No. 2. CEM_TERY, Est 1936." The gate was unlocked. I assumed it always was. I went inside.

The graves were clean, mostly new. I saw concrete bases and granite headstones and many with two sturdy vases standing aside the memorials. Some of the graves had small crosses on them. Some had stones. Some had figurines and statues—angels, bibles, dogs, cats, deer. It was just like Marler said it would be, in his way.

"In my opinion Redbones have some beliefs/practices that are different from those of the larger society," Marler wrote in his survey. "These beliefs/practices are in the following areas. Religion, Life, Death, Burial, Child rearing, Medical Treatment, Marriage, Other." He wanted the people answering to be the *my*, to circle which one they thought was different, and then he told them, "Please Specify."

I took my time inspecting the graves, reading all the tombstones. West, Perkins, Thompson, Johnson, Strother, Cloud, Maricle, and Willis—those were some of the names gathered on the single graves and in the family sections. There were also several double headstones, and they helped me understand why Don Marler decided to include a section on marriage in his questionnaire. "In the past Redbones married mostly Redbones," he wrote. "Marriage outside the group was disapproved," he explained, but then he asked, "Is this practice and the disapproval of outside marriage ____ as strong as ever, ____ about the same, ____ not as strong as in the past." He meant for the person answering to make a checkmark or X by what they thought. Marler was nothing if not upfront.

I could probably learn a lot from Marler. You can learn a ton from guys on late night shows. I'm always amazed at how direct a TV detective can be. Mannix does it with a sly, suave grin. Barnaby seems to bumble around, but it's a straight line to the bottom of things. Cannon can be politely rude. With a smile on his face, he'll mouth off to a crooked sheriff or keep asking the widow all the questions until the story pops out.

Marler peppered people with his survey questions.

"Question 24. If you are married did you marry a person with a heritage similar to yours? _____ yes _____ no."

"Question 25: If you are not married would you consider marrying a person with a heritage different from yours? _____ yes _____ no _____ undecided."

"Question 26: Would you object to your children marrying outside your group? _____ yes _____ no _____ undecided."

At the end of his preaching career, not long before he passed, Joseph Willis was met by one of his sons, his boy named Lemuel. By wagon he came to his father and asked him to leave the home of his fourth wife. "The story was repeated to the writer's boyhood ears," Greene Strother wrote in his work on Joseph Willis. On the day Lemuel asked his father to come and live with him, "Father Willis lay in the wagon when being carried to the home of his son, and sang as the wagon rolled along over the rough road."[15]

Greene Strother was the maternal great-grandson of Joseph Willis and seemed keen to use his family stories to write the history of the preacher. The work became his unpublished master's thesis. He called it his "Argument,"[16] and I guess he knew he was wading into something difficult because in the very first sentence he wrote, "Well does my brother, J. H. Strother, say, 'I fear that you have not given yourself enough time to write a thesis on a man about whom so little is written.... It will take quite a lot of time to gather the material, arrange it and get the historical significance so as to give it real value.'"

But Strother was determined, undaunted, full of zeal. To be blunt, he seemed zealous, anxious, like he had something to prove. "I would not presume to present facts so poorly arranged and call it a thesis," Strother wrote, "were it not that press of many duties does not allow me the needful time."

You see, it was 1934, and Strother was in a state. He was in a hurry. He was worried about what had been collected about Willis and what might happen to it. He feared the people still alive who knew the preacher, what firsthand knowledge they had, might die, and then what would be lost? And he was unnerved by the recently published *Negro Year Book, 1921–1922*. About it, he seemed especially concerned about the "Church Among Negroes" section listing Joseph Willis among "Noted

Negro Preachers," so much so that at the end of his thesis, Strother included a letter from the editor of the *Negro Year Book* explaining that based on Strother's urging and research he had expunged Joseph Willis's name from that book.

"In recent years the descendants of Willis have denied that he was part Negro and have contended that his father was English and that his mother was part Indian," Glen Lee Greene's *House Upon a Rock* clarified. It was written in 1973. In that work, Greene labored to prove "Joseph Willis' father was an Englishman and his mother part Indian and all the other blood in his veins was Anglo-Saxon." He built his case from the testimony of several of Willis's offspring, many of whom became prominent preachers and members of the Baptist faith. "A granddaughter and a grandson of Willis who, as youngsters, attended to him in his last days" told Glen Greene they remembered "hearing their grandfather say that his mother was part Indian" and Willis's youngest son, "who was seventeen when his father died," said the same.[17]

But life can be complicated. And history can be puzzling. And solving either sometimes takes a long time. Marler's survey suggested as much. He ran into the same sort of questions Greene Strother did. "If you have information regarding your ancestors who migrated to Louisiana/Texas please answer the following questions to the best of your knowledge," Marler's survey asked. "If a person (stranger) moved to your community who had a name similar to those in your community and resembled the people in your community, would you A. ___ Welcome him, B. ___ Reject him, C. ___ Distrust him, or D. ___ Tend to trust him." "Would persons who are clearly not Redbones be welcome to settle in your community?" "In your community is there prejudice against persons who have dark skin color?"

A red-tailed hawk is a conspicuous thing. It'll hunt on the wing. It'll perch on a utility pole in plain sight of God and everyone, then it'll catch flight and circle and circle and circle, maybe just so you know it looms overhead. It doesn't care if you see it. Its prey never does, or if it does, it's too late.

That's not a red herring.

When I drove up to Occupy Church No. 1, that was who I saw first, a hawk. I couldn't tell if it was watching me, but I do know I was watching it, and I guess, overly much because it wasn't until I quit looking at it and dropped my head that I saw the white truck sitting in the center of Occupy No. 1 Cemetery and that there were people there pretending not to notice me.

Joseph Willis died not long after he delivered his sermon on "The Parable of Ten Coins," but he was already something of a legend by then. He had been fruitful, multiplied. He had built various churches: Half Moon Baptist Church on the Bogue Chitto, Calvary Church at Bayou Chicot, Beulah at Cheneyville, Vermilion at Lafayette, Plaquemine at Branch—churches scattered around like little tombs in a graveyard, each with a name, and a history, and a long line of families buried deep inside. He built Occupy too. But it was special. Because it held so many of his children's graves. Because this is where he was buried.

I wouldn't call it snooping, but I was searching for Willis's marker when Tony Maricle confronted me amongst the gravestones.[18] I was at the far end of the cemetery, rambling in the north side of the grounds. Cats, dogs, bowls of fruit, cherubs, a boar leaving prints as it trotted across the top of a grave, and a collection of other figurines distracted me. The grave-top piles of stones, too, I studied those, and the names etched into the markers. By the time I looked up, he was no more than twenty or thirty yards from me, striding towards me, all business, holding a metal carpenter's level in one hand.

When I first quieted through the gate, I saw him sitting with a woman on the cemetery's south end. Like a good well-mannered detective would do, I was trying not to intrude, so when I started walking the graves, I skirted around the living people there. That was a fool's plan.

Tony sought me out. In fact, he crossed the entire cemetery to address me. When he was ten or so steps from me, he hollered. I nodded and waited for him to close within earshot to explain that I was looking for Joseph Willis's grave.

He raised the spirit level up near his head, and saluting with it, spun on his heels, then waved me close. "I know right where it is," he chimed, and made a beeline for it. That's the mystery of Tony Maricle, as no nonsense as a straight edge and as friendly as the day is long.

What words I said about Joseph Willis while we strode through the burials, I don't recall, but I do remember it was of no surprise to him that a stranger with a camera might come searching for Willis. It was a matter of course for him to lead me there. Almost immediately, he asked me for my name again, and then, after we had rushed nearly halfway back across the grounds, he turned to me and stuck out his hand. He was missing a pinky.

As we trampled a path through the grass, he told me that all his people were from around there and showed me where they lay. He pointed to their names cut into the headstones, and what sort of shape the graves were in.

Care work in a cemetery is a delicate thing, a careful thing. A person has to be gentle. A person has to be mild with what they do. A reckless man on a mowing machine is like the grim reaper to a graveyard. Its wheels and motor know no good time. It comes without warning, swinging its heavy body like a long scythe. It jerks, it spasms, it convulses as the driver works the pedals, shifts the gears, wrangles the levers, and then a tombstone is guillotined, a footplate run over, a wolf stone nudged just enough so it leans and begins to backslide. Over time, it cracks.

Tony Maricle knows that to be true. When I met him that afternoon, he was agitated because a slew of graves had mysteriously been toppled over. Some of the very oldest ones had fallen and cracked in half. Some of the newer ones had simply shifted. Was it the storm? Was it some kids? Was it the groundskeeper? That was what Tony Maricle maybe thought. "He's got too many irons in the fire," he told me. "Too many irons in the fire if he can't come back and tend to it as it needs to be."

A few years back, even Joseph Willis's tombstone had been tipped over. "The white marble monument" placed near the "older graves in the cemetery" was meant to be a permanent testament to "this elder's ... determination and profound faith" and persistent, "intense desire to preach," the papers said about Willis's new gravemarker.[19] The memorial stone contained a few plain phrases—"Pioneer Rev. Joseph Willis—Born 1764–died 1854, Psalms 119:103—First Baptist Preacher of the Word in Louisiana West of the Mississippi River."[20] It was erected in 1961, and though it was damaged a few times over the years, it was upright now. Tony showed me the seal around the bottom where it had been fixed after he and ten other men reset it.

When we left Joseph Willis's grave, Tony Maricle showed me the mystery he wanted to solve that day. The matter in question rested at the opposite end of the cemetery, near the gate. It was the brand-new grave of one of his relatives, and it was the reason he held that level in his hand. He wanted to see if the stone was built crooked or not, if it sloped a certain way. He wanted to bend down and take a reading of it. He wanted me to come along, and so we marched back across the graves.

He had cousins all around the grounds, he told me as we stomped through weeds. He was from Ten-Mile, near Westport.

"I've heard of it," I said.

He told me there was some rough stuff there once. He heard a lot of stories about it, the roughness, the place. I should've tried to make him talk more about that, but I didn't want to push things. Would you expect anything else from No Man Land's most mousy detective?

Tony Maricle kept talking as we trooped. He told me, kicking his foot up and pointing to his sole, that he "had some cousins dark as my shoes," but I didn't push that either. The too-polite detective let that fall like a seed into rocky soil.

Sure, I could blame the weather, but there was good sun. I could blame the time, but there was plenty of afternoon left. I could blame his level—we were eager to prove something, but that wasn't the reason.

What makes a good detective? It's right to be suspicious, I think. It's helpful to wonder about the lady who wakes you up on a park bench or the person flagging you down when you're headed down a gravel road or the man who walks across the broken ground of a cemetery to see what you're up to do. I think it's prudent to be curious. I think it's normal to be skeptical.

And for all those reasons I'd like to see the surveys that came back to Marler. I'd like to believe a flood of them were returned. I'd like to think people were so bothered they answered all the questions. But I'm skeptical.

In his survey, Marler asked, "Have you or any member of your family had any illnesses or diseases which are unusual or have been identified as more common in the Redbone group—such as Sarcoidosis?" He wondered if they or someone they knew were born with a bump on the back of their head, or with a dark spot on their back or shoulders, or a ridge behind the front teeth a person could feel with their tongue or fingernail. "Were you or any member of your family born with 6 fingers or 6 toes?" he asked. "Do you have an extra fold on your eyelids causing a slight Asian look?"

I'd like to know why he asked all those questions. I'd like to hear, in the end, if he thought asking them solved anything. I'd like to say I would read the answers people mailed back no matter how many there were. I'd like to say I'd make the time. I'd like to say I would follow up on what people circled or checked or the comments they made, the things they said. I'd like to believe a good detective learns from past mistakes.

"But the Redbones' origins, as described by Marler and McManus, stretch plausibility," one person wrote about Marler's *Redbones of Louisiana*. A couple of people seemed to pick pieces of that book apart. "That Native Americans (Apache!), Mediterraneans (Portugueses!), Spanish, and Blacks could intermingle in the Neutral Ground and form a homogenous culture within a few generations seems incredulous."[21]

But everything is a mystery with Redbones, it seems. "Please note that the book may explore where families came from, when they came, etc.," Marler wrote in the survey, "but it will not be a family history in the usual sense." Because nothing about Redbone history ever is usual. Nothing was ever said without some argument, some questions left unsettled. Maybe that has been what I've shied away from.

Nerves will do that to me. I'm better when the stakes are low. When nothing's on the line, that's when I shine. I do well when there's not a crowd around. When someone's telling me something important, like pointing me to another cemetery to check out, I'm better when it's a one-on-one conversation. It's ideal if we're standing in the St. Augustine. I'm better at things when there's more unanswerable things involved. I'm best at leaving well enough alone, I guess. At leaving things unresolved.

But when I left Occupy No. 1, I was worried. It was going to be more sleepless nights on the couch. More reruns of *Mannix* and *Cannon*. More cases my betters found a way to solve while I dug and dug around but came no closer to settling anything. I had schemed to pay back Barbara in some way, but the more I dug, the farther away I seemed to go.

I was anxious about the restlessness, but I feared the mornings more, looking at myself in the mirror. I dreaded the expectations. Geographer Yi-Fu Tuan once said, "Anticipation is a source of anxiety,"[22] which I take to mean, long-range plans are the tools we use to dig our own graves. Maybe that's why I had faltered this whole time.

But then I saw a sign for another cemetery and the Redbone conference came back to me in a flash. My soles were smearing into the carpet, my sweaty hands were holding onto the podium, my heart was racing as I took my seat and listened to one of the presenters talk about Talbert-Pierson Cemetery, the mystery of the tiny houses there, and their secret connection to the Redbones.

Talbert Cemetery Road was a country road, the narrow kind, the kind that was one-car wide, the kind that when I saw a set of headlights up ahead, I shimmied to the shoulder and sucked in my gut so we could both squeeze by. Its surface wasn't gravel, but a bone-pale asphalt that was flaking away. Its shoulder of clay was as red as an open wound. A long grave-deep ditch ran the length of the road, and the telephone poles along one side seemed like alien crosses and the scrub pine on the other convinced me the world was closing in. I was a hair's breadth from turning around when I saw the small one-room white Pine Grove Church building and behind it, the tiny cemetery.

The Talbert-Pierson Cemetery was placed on the National Register of Historic Places in 2003. It's known for the strange dwellings built over the graves of several Talbert and Pierson family members, and while it isn't the only cemetery where these structures can be found, it's especially famous for the comparably large number of these small, curious buildings a visitor can find there—fifteen. That might be the most a person can find in a single cemetery in the entire country.

But that's debatable. In fact, most of the details about the place are. If you ask about the origins of these structures, about the history behind this tradition, you'll hear debate. Different scholars have pointed to various sources—European, African, American Indian, French, Catholic, Protestant, the British Iles, Redbones.[23] If you ask what you might call these house-like structures, that's its own sort of mystery. Gravehouses, graveshelters, a grave shed, a shelter house, board mausoleums, spirit houses, *les petites maisons* in Louisiana French cemeteries, lattice huts, a grave box—all these monikers have been used. And in some places where the tradition itself has fallen so far into mystery that no one knows what to call the thing, the building may not even have a name.

But even there, I imagine, the deep-seated reasoning behind constructing such a little house over the grave is clear—someone was loved, the person burying them worried over the dead body, and so the living person made plans to make it safe in a house of its own.

In Talbert-Pierson Cemetery, the tiny structures are positioned in what amounts to three rows, each running near the rear of the cemetery. The first row contains seven wooden shelters, the second has six; the last row contains only two. A few other gravehouses have been added over the years, but these first fifteen are the most historic. Surrounded by walls made of fence pickets, each with a diamond shape at its top, the oldest gravehouse, built for James Talbert, Sr., the patriarch, dates from 1889. You can see his name inscribed across his whitish stone.

Over the years, people have made some slight alterations to keep the structures standing here, but the gravehouses maintain an incredible degree of original work. The walls are mostly French Gothic fence pickets attached to wooden sills that run along the ground. The roof is often a metal roof, a sheet of tin. The gable end is sealed with clapboard siding. From it hangs ornamental edgework or even the pickets themselves, turned upside-down and dangling like ornate Victorian eaves. Covering the grave itself—a layer of shells, pebbles, and crushed stone.

Why were they built here? That's another mystery.

An old legend tells the fate of a homesteading family. They could have lived close to this place some call home or could have stayed in a far country, but the story is the same. Once, long ago, a man lived the hard-scrabble life of a pioneer. What were those days like? The sun was bristly as a horsehair brush. The moon as cratered as hardtack.

But he persevered. His whole family did. He married a woman as independent as he was; she had to be. The couple had a fierce and prideful bunch of sons and daughters who loved their parents, not despite but because of the hardness of it all. And then, finally, when the tough old man faced death, his people gathered round.

Gravely ill, coughing on his deathbed, he spoke as best he could. "My children," he said, "my time is short."

No one said a word in argument. Honesty was a staple in that house.

"When I go," the father said, "bury me in that corner of the pasture with the big oak trees."

Maybe there was a pause. Could have been someone nodded yes.

Then the father said, "And don't let the rain fall on my face."

What Dad said, his children felt they ought to do, but this was more than obligation. They built a pine box to hold his body, dug a hole in his favorite corner of the farm, then to keep the rain from falling on his face, they cut and nailed and fitted boards together to build a small house to cover his grave.

To me, that's what the Talbert-Pierson Cemetery is, a place for the dead who are afraid of the rain. It's not strange, I don't think. If a cemetery is a place where the living can communicate with the dead, as some claim, Talbert-Pierson is a story of a land people have set their hopes in. Pickets, sill, and roof come together to form a "shed" or a "little house" meant to mirror the actual home these people built, and inside these enclosed spaces, mourners often place flowers, small potted shrubs, honeysuckle vines, evergreens, crosses, or any meaningful mementos of the living world. All this, in a way, is just more of what people do with a place of their own, a spot where they've planted roots, because as soon as hope is planted, I think fear is sown too, even if by accident. I think that's the landscape people build when they erect a cemetery—a landscape erected from the fear of losing what you love, fear of watching it fall through your hands like sand.

The afternoon I roamed Talbert-Pierson a felled pine that had crushed the benches outside the small white Pine Grove church building still sat there. There was another huge trunk lying prone against the cemetery's fence line. Along the small path set between the rows of spirit houses, torn-away pieces of roofing carpeted the steppingstones. When I came closer, I noticed some of the gravehouses' pickets had been ripped away. A gable was falling in. Plastic flowers had been blown around. When I ducked my head inside a house, I saw snatches of poorman pepperweed growing on the grave.

I couldn't help myself. I crept inside one of the little houses, sat down, and looked around. I didn't want to do it, but I couldn't stop asking myself if places like this will survive the storms. Will we remember them when we rebuild? Who will go the extra mile in keeping them *alive*? It's an anticipation that is built of anxiety, or it's the other way around.

But now you know it all. You've heard about the months and weeks and days leading up to the time I was inside a grave. Now you've seen how I nearly buried myself alive among the pepperweed to see the sun drift through the cracks. I didn't stay for long. It was getting late in the afternoon, and I was tired.

It wasn't too many days after that I found myself at my mother-in-law's trailer. For months I had been fooling with my own hurricane-damaged roof and my destroyed garage and all my crap stored in it that was scattered in my yard, which made me ignore her place longer than I should've.

After a hurricane you rationalize. You bargain. You make excuses. You understand that facts don't sleep well and neither do you. That wasn't going to change. I could keep turning that over in my mind to try to solve it, but why? Something was going to keep me up at night. It could be a fit with the blankets at two in the morning. It could be some noise—a trashcan tumbling outside or the dog muzzling the curtains on the French patio doors. It could be the sound of a faucet running or a drip, I swear, I heard coming from the ceiling. It could be anything other than the truth.

So you try to keep yourself busy. You lower your expectations. You visit a cemetery to understand how long, peaceful nights of sleep won't ever come again. You recognize the cracked cedar trees and the tilted iron fences overgrown with weeds are just more of the same. You accept the toppled marble statues for what they are. But then something pushes you to the edge.

I don't know exactly what it was. I spent the whole day at my mother-in-law's and then I felt a shove. Was it that the chainsaw kept biting down on me? Was it the sickening smell of burning gas? The myrtles that belonged to someone else but were somehow mine to cut?

The truth is, it's all an edge.

The gravestone someone decided to use and the details they wanted it to say. The little reasons people laid the plots the way they did or where they set the cemetery. It's an empty church. It's a broken sign.

It's one random day when I'm looking at an archived newspaper. It's an article from 1897, a tiny blurb in the *Abbeville Meridional*. No title, no bold type, the words forming just another paragraph, resting there at the edge of the page, but impossible to escape. "There was an immense affray in the neighborhood of Pot Cove this week," the paper read. "It is said that over one hundred pistol shots were fired—resulting in the wounding of two. Deputy Sheriff Hargroder went over to investigate bringing back nine persons with him. The fighting was among a class of mixed-breed, who if living in Calcasieu, would be called 'Red Bones.'"

It's the end of a page—that's an edge too. You print it out; you pick it up; you read it back. You think about what you've said and what you haven't. What you've made and what you let fear get the better of.

You see, I realized something standing in my mother-in-law's yard. It wasn't Barbara that sent me on a path. It was the storm. It was the hurricanes. It was my animosity against them.

Because after a storm, you don't think straight. After a storm, you just hate and want reprisal. You open the hatchback, shove in the chainsaw, throw your gloves in the passenger seat, crank the Rogue and drive—gritting your teeth the whole time.

You see, after the storm, you flail your arms around and hope to catch something on the chin, which is why I ended up on that empty road outside Merryville, looking out the window at an iron-gate of a woods sitting between me and the object of my retaliation—a place named after the thing I despised, a place called Hurricane Creek.

The way I had worked it out was that it was a place named for the forces that had done all sorts of dirty deeds to the people and the places I cared about. Hell, it may have even been the cause of all the bad people have ever done. I couldn't say for certain. All I knew was that it had ruined my house and pissed all over my plans, and the least I could do, I figured, was to piss all over it.

It was a sick joke, I know, but it was the only thing that I could feel way down in my gut.

But the joke was on me, only I didn't know it yet. I knew that about a thousand feet west of me was Hurricane Creek, but what I didn't realize—what my rage had blinded me to—was that about two thousand feet east sat Bear Head Creek, where Barbara's job waited.

Call it a missed opportunity. Call it one of life's little mysteries. Call it anything you will, except for what it is.

I set my car into park and sat there with my pal Rogue shaking beneath me, trying to nudge me right over the edge.

Because I had come into this far country and expected my inheritance. But what my home had handed over to me instead was trouble.

What did that deserve? Revenge? Hate? The courage to follow through on a promise?

I killed the engine, looked out the windshield to crank up my mettle, and what do you think the overly polite detective did then?

There were fence stakes in the ground and posted signs, but that wasn't what shook my nerve. It was the hollowness of trees that put me off my laughing mood, the peoplelessness of the place. In the sky, I could see how far dark was getting on. Evening's reach stretched deep into the thicket. Then I listened. For a long time, I did that. I heard the great emptiness of my home. Only the racket of night bugs came back to me.

5

AT THE SHORES OF ETERNITY

On the Monday before spring break, I teach Hebert's "Easter Wings," Donne's "The Flea," and a few poems by Milton. On the Wednesday, I pick up the class's exams, stack them into a stately pile, then start the swearing. I vow to put off grading. I promise myself I won't check an answer. I put my hand over my heart and pledge that I'll kick myself if I even take a peek at the tests before I've taken at least a few days off. You see, it's postdisaster 2021, and it takes real commitment to take it easy.

So I stuff the papers into my school bag and slump back to my office. I fumble with the keys. I free the door. I plop down at my desk to let my brain spin its wheels. First, it lists the schoolwork I need to do, then it's the house repairs still unfinished from the double hurricanes, then the calls to the contractors who haven't showed after guaranteeing they would, then the insurance company's request for estimates, then the mortgage company's letter asking for evidence of the progress that's been made, then the city permit that hasn't been granted yet. It doesn't take me long to double down. "That's it," I say. "I'm not working at school until after the break."

It feels great, postponing the inevitable. I take a deep breath, then exhale. Procrastinating feels like a fluffy cloud.

After that, I start planning my "lazy days," working hard to forget the busy calendar showing on my phone. On Thursday I have something I can't get out of. And Good Friday is booked too. Easter Sunday's no good either. The following week is so slammed. But Saturday? The Saturday before Easter Sunday? That's a day for wastefulness. That's a day with nothing written down. I could sneak away for a while, forget everything, float on a cloud on my own sweet time.

I'm typing "day off" into my calendar when my office phone rings.

I suppose it's a reasonable question, at least the people calling make it sound that way: Why live in the path of danger? Why rebuild when disaster is bound to come again? Why would anyone ever decide to stay in a place so lousy with hurricanes? They can make it sound so logical. It seems so simple when they ask it that way.

I don't know what to do with these phone calls. A part of me questions the common sense of living here too. I've debated throwing in the towel and moving away, especially lately, especially today. But I've also pondered not moving on at all, but just giving up and giving in. Because I've watched rooms and rooms of people's homes being brought to the curb. I've seen the flattened houses. I've tracked how someone's whole life can end up stacked by the road. Because, despite all of that, I've wondered where else I could go.

I don't say any of that into the receiver. I don't say much of anything. Mostly I just sit there, examining why I'm a glutton for punishment and keep picking up the phone.

Because does it even matter what I say?

If it's wise, it's not a sound bite. If it's useful, no one really listens. If it buys us all a little more time to come up with a better solution, it takes too long.

The truth is, the real answer seems impossible. Why do we set our keepsakes on our shelves? Why do we hang things on our walls? Why does anyone do anything at all when we know since we borrow everything, a place isn't ours, even if it feels like home?

But I don't say that. "Good question," I mutter instead. Or, "Hmmm. I'm sorry. I don't know."

But what I really mean is that I know the things people say, what they've always said, about life on the Louisiana coastline.

"This sheet of country is cut up into hundreds of islands by a network of bayous," Dan'l Dennett told readers of New Orleans's *Daily Picayune*.[1] It was 1883. "Numerous lone fishermen lie on these islands in the sea-marsh," he said of the people making a life on the coast. "They have pretty lonesome homes when the storm howls in the night and the waters rave . . . But these people seem to have the instincts of beavers in protecting themselves against disasters from floods and storms."

The veteran agricultural editor had visited the coast and found it all so strange, so odd, so perplexing to a person so sure about improving one's station. "Oranges are raised," he said, "and lemons, grapes, figs and other fruits and cauliflowers. . . . They can raise bananas here, and other tropical fruit." Yet so much more could be done with it, that man who loved progress surmised. "Rotten leaves, green crops plowed in and ashes"—all of it given back to the soil would improve it so much. "But the inhabitants take but little interest in these things," he lamented, befuddled by their disinterest in it all. "The chief object here is to live an easy and quiet life," he scribbled in defeat, "—to float listlessly through time to the shores of eternity."

But lately that's exactly where my thoughts are wandering. Like sometimes, when I'm walking my neighborhood and stepping around the mounds of ruined sheetrock on the sidewalks, I wonder about floating in the tub for hours. My eyes glaze over with thoughts of detaching my brain and zombieing off to work. When every day is a new building being bulldozed and every drive to campus is an empty lot where a house used to be, I dream about forgetting where I've actually ended up.

And I don't mean the place itself. I mean the daily things I've done and where they've led me. I mean the path I've taken. The road that began twenty-something years ago. The road that meanders through a career spent at a Louisiana college on the coast. The road running near the marshland south of Lake Charles where I've raised a family. A road under a sky that can appear to go forever. A road graced by patches of marsh wildflowers that can number in the thousands, vast expanses of innumerable water hyacinth and American lotus, but at the same time, a road cursed by storms darkening in the distance—a lowering ceiling, a black anvil on the horizon, cumulonimbi slouching this way. A surreal road in a surreal world marked by an unearthly mix of sublime live oaks and storm-damaged skeletal trees. A road that ends with a house.

So lately I'm questioning what to do with this kind of coastal world, and what to do with what people have said about it, about their arguing that it looks like a good place to leave and a dumb place for a home. But mostly I'm debating if I'm tough enough for the Louisiana coast. I guess the word I'm mulling over is *resilient*. I'm asking myself what use is it, and if I'm that.

That's why the Saturday before Easter Sunday is a day full of doubt. It's a day for not knowing how to answer the telephone calls and taking a drive down that road to the coast instead. It's a day for balancing the massive oaks against all the lotus plants. It's a day for taking those oaks and weighing them against the wisdom of eating those flowers. What I mean is, Saturday is a day for deciding to dig in and build like an oak or "to float listlessly through time to the shores of eternity."

And there's only one place for that—Pecan Island.

"Pecan Island is not an island," Geographer Alex Schou writes. "It has never been an island, and it is not very likely that it ever should become an island." No, Pecan Island is a chenier.

Chenier is a local word. It references a series of elevated ridges running through the marsh here. These hard, shell ridges became stranded over time. As millennia passed, the soft soil around them eroded due to the Mississippi's deltaic processes, but these elevations remained as fingers of solid soil surrounded by a squishy, marshy world.

Deriving from the French word *chene* meaning *oak*, the name *chenier* celebrates the primary feature of these rises—the oak trees that grow there. It's a bit of local wisdom. While these elevations might be called ridges anywhere else, local Cajun experience has aptly named these "conspicuous ... sharply localized, well drained, and fertile ridges" cheniers because they "support naturally a luxuriant vegetational cover [of] large evergreen oaks."[2] This in turn celebrates these marsh ridges' primary psychological feature—their ability to provide solid ground to sustain life. In other words, the fact that oaks have rooted on a chenier proved to settlers they could put down roots there too.

As many as five series of ridges run parallel to Louisiana's western coast, each chenier separated from another by broad marshland, all five spreading across the marsh like the digits of an open hand.[3] This world is known as Louisiana's Chenier Plain.

As a landscape, the Chenier Plain stretches from Marsh Island near Vermilion Bay in Iberia Parish to the banks of the Sabine River.[4] As a mentalscape, it exists as a level vastness that extends uncut forever and forever, often beyond the horizon. It can be a study in steadiness, and the deception one finds there. It's an immensity that just may send a viewer into a state of dread, but then, in the distance, a chenier will rise. When it does, the line of faraway oaks stands as a beacon of hope.

If the Chenier Plain is a dread hand, the cheniers are fingers, and Pecan Island is a fingernail, clawing to a way of life.

At one time, Pecan Island was one of the most cut-off locations in Louisiana's coast. No road ran to Pecan Island until 1951. Before that, getting there usually meant hitching a ride on the mail boat that traveled there two or three times a week. Even today, from where it sits at Vermilion Parish's westernmost edge, completely surrounded by marsh and practically at the dead center of the plain, Pecan Island exudes a feeling of solitude, of escape.

The ridge Pecan Island sits on runs about eighteen miles long and ranges from a quarter of a mile to two miles wide. The ridge's front faces a span of boggy brackish-water marsh that extends for six or eight miles until it reaches the tides of the Gulf of Mexico. Its back runs against the open water of White Lake. Then a swatch of marsh spreads twenty-five or thirty miles north until it rises again at another ridge.

It can be a peaceful, slow-moving place. It can be a lulling place. Just listen to its sounds—*chenier*. It might as well be a siren's song.

Because if paradise exists anywhere in this state, it exists in Pecan Island— bizarrely beautiful. Lovely and alone. The epitome of Louisiana's infamously inaccessible, peculiar, otherworldly, stuck-in-time sense of place. And, for all of these qualities, mesmerizing.

For decades, people living in that small settlement on that thin strip of elevated land found cars useless, TV and radio antennas pointless, electricity needless too. For a good long time, many things in Pecan Island seemed to matter less.

Imprisoned in a way by idyllic beauty, Pecan Island can be a place that'll plainly ask, "What's wrong with an idle life?"

Not a thing, I tell myself, and turn off my work computer. It's decided. I'm decided. My spring break getaway will be a Saturday drive to Pecan Island. There's nothing left for me to do but pack up and stroll out the office door.

I refuse to let myself organize the papers on my desk so the next time I come in to work I'll know what I'm looking at. I don't stick a note on my keyboard about the job I need to do first thing. I don't even put all the papers I'll need in my bag. It feels so light when I sling it over my shoulder. I'm almost whistling as I promenade to the door. I'm letting it swing shut when the department's administrative assistant sends me a text.

Shouldn't we have a party for our English professor who's resigning and moving away after the hurricane? Because of the hurricane? After all, he won't be here many more days. We could have a going-away breakfast—muffins, coffee, crullers, juice, a card, some socializing, something simple, just a chance to say goodbye. We could have it there in the conference room. We could start at 8 on the day we come back from spring break. We could get it ready over the break. Shouldn't we?

I put my bag down, trying to think of the text to send back, but my fingers can't move. Nothing comes to me but a flood of memories.

My building's conference room has an imperial ten-seat mahogany table, and too many chairs. On a typical day, maybe fourteen or fifteen of those bulky black ergo-types list around the room. For a "goodbye party," we'll drag in four or five more chairs from a nearby room, and if the retirement party is for several people (because we usually lump everyone who's retiring in Liberal Arts together), we'll also lug in a bistro table for the punch and the 20-cup coffee machine that's usually just too much of a pain to fire up. When the room's that crowded, whenever you walk inside, the first thing you have to do is whirl a couple of chairs out of your way, and then usually you need to swing your hips sideways to squeeze between the tables, and sometimes it's even necessary to suck in your gut, as much as you can. (That last part, I hope no one sees, but I do what I have to do.)

It was 2019 at our last goodbye party. The big mahogany table floated in the middle of the room with its surface stacked with towers of finger sandwiches and bowls of chips. Someone had crammed the coffee pot and electric tea kettle and sodas and ice and a structure of red plastic cups onto the bistro table. I grabbed a red Solo to look normal, then squeezed my way to an out-of-the-way place.

That year, I wasn't close to the people who were retiring, but I felt a little obligated to go anyway. (Why not? It's to say congratulations. It's to wish them good travels. It's to fill up the room with bodies and small talk. It's to make it feel exactly how I might want it to be when it's my year to retire—a room that feels eventful. It's so I don't worry so much that when my time comes, the day will matter somehow.)

But I didn't show it. I sat in the corner, clumsily holding an empty cup, and smiled. I looked around the room, calculating how many minutes politeness required that I sit there, trying to count where the time goes, and rolled with it, pretending to be unconcerned.

Then a kind of miracle happened—my friend Gay Gomez who retired four or five years earlier walked through the door. It was like watching a bird fly back for the winter.

During her time here, Gay was McNeese's resident specialist on the Louisiana coast, especially Cameron Parish. A cultural geographer with a deep love of the natural world, she wrote two lovely books about southwestern Louisiana's marshland, and I often found myself asking her questions. She seemed to know everything about that landscape, but mostly, I just loved to hear her talk. Listening to her lecture about Louisiana was like hearing birdsong, but understanding all the chortles and chirps as conversation. There were days I would stalk her classes to loiter unseen in the hallway within earshot of her words.

The last time I saw Gay, she was volunteering at the Creole Nature Trail Adventure Point in Sulphur. I had driven my kids over as a staging point for our last-day-of-summer trip. Maybe that was in 2016. I planned on walking the trail as a family, but Gay thought the biting flies swarming that section of the trail might make our outing miserable. She suggested the Pintail Wildlife Drive instead, a three-mile driving loop that included a small boardwalk running through a marsh carpeted in water hyacinths. In that place, at the close of summer, Gay told me, the bugs shouldn't be too bad.

"Thanks," I said. "How's retirement?"

She told me she liked it, but she was moving away from Louisiana. She was going west, maybe as far as the Pacific Northwest because it was just too hard for her. All of it. Seeing the changes to the coast, to Cameron, the liquid natural gas projects, the storms.

It was a shock to me. Gay grew up in the vast lowlands of Louisiana. "It is my home by birth," she would say, "and for nearly half a century had been my home by choice."[5] She could get wistful about the weekends spent outdoors at the camps her family owned, first the one at Lake Hermitage in Plaquemines Parish, then the one at Grand Isle, them finally her family's camp at Lafitte. "Grand Isle was my favorite," she'd recall, "and I will always remember swimming, beachcombing, crabbing, shrimping, fishing, boating, boiling seafood, playing cards, and telling stories with beloved family members and friends."

The last of the barrier islands to have permanent residents and the only one that's still accessible by road, Grand Isle was a loquacious teacher for Gay, and she a dutiful student. Through Grand Isle, Gay's grandparents taught her to see the coast as a place of recreation and education. Her father used it to show her how to cast a line and cast for stories from the "longtime coastal residents and learn from their many years of experience." As she grew older, those familiar longings for the coast never left her. "I live for the weekends and the chance to breathe air that has a tinge of salt," she'd tell people. "In other words, I live for my time on the coast."

She left her home in Louisiana to earn a PhD in geography from the University of Texas, but returned to write her dissertation on the Chenier Plain of southwestern Louisiana. That was the early 1990s. The dissertation eventually became *A Wetland Biography: Seasons on Louisiana's Chenier Plain*, a book devoted not only to the "daily surprises" even a lifelong resident experiences along the coast, but also to celebrating the people's "traditional ecological knowledge."

When she wrote her next book, a beautiful naturalist guidebook *The Louisiana Coast: Guide to an American Wetland*, Gay's old family ways reasserted themselves. "I want the readers to see the coast through my eyes, to fathom its beauty and variety and complexity, and to understand the threat this land, people, and culture face from coastal land loss," she wrote. "I want readers to care about Louisiana's coast as much as I do."

In her books, Gay takes great pains to listen to locals. "There's nothing more beautiful than the marsh; it's so flat you can see forever." But "is this flatness bland and unattractive?" she ponders. After a meaningful pause, almost with a grin, as if she's motioning to a crowd, she responds, "The answer depends on the observer."

So when I saw her again in the conference room, I smiled. I beamed. I held my cup in my teeth and used my free hands to sling an open chair in her direction, the way someone scooches over on a park bench to make way for the birds. I was lucky when she perched near me.

The two of us sat for a while in the conference room, talking about a few things, mainly what we had read recently and liked. A few days later, three slim books found their way into my office mailbox. One was a book about Cameron Parish written by the Cameron Parish Development Board. One was a history about the rise and fall of feather fashions and all the birds slaughtered for ladies' hats. The last was Tabasco heir and conservationist E. A. McIlhenny's fine book *The Alligator's Life History*. "Thought you might like these, based on our conversation at the Soc. Scis. retirement party several weeks ago," she inscribed. "If not, feel free to pass them along."

The trip to Pecan Island in 1905 took reporter Arthur Pipes nearly thirty-six hours,[6] but for me, it's a hop, skip, and a jump. The drive runs maybe an hour and a half from Lake Charles. There's rarely a car to pass or not to pass. If there is, I just slow down. I don't worry about making good time. If there's daylight, I'm too occupied gazing out the glass. If it's early, before the sun comes up, I'll turn off the radio and roll down the windows. Sometimes I'll drive even slower than I should to cut down on wind noise. There's the swamp music happening outside. When I lose myself listening to it, the drive ends too soon.

For me, from old Lake Charles, the drive begins with a deep dive south, almost straight down, for about forty miles. Coasting down that road can feel a little like being in a sort of ocean. On that April morning of my spring break, the early clouds catch just enough of the orange sun to tint the sky the color of a redfish—a beautiful warm copper color. It's windy, and the cows have buoyed themselves near the fences. The marsh palms and trees left standing are wrapped in grasses swept up by the storm's tidal surge. So are the fence posts and the barbed wire taut between them. The blobs of tidewracked grasses caught there look like sludge-brown reefs of coral. The tarps flapping on the roofs of the houses wave like someone calling SOS. About halfway there, I drive by a trailer full of scaled-away roofing shingles. It's crippled with two flat tires, stuck on the side of the road like an abandoned shipwreck.

I can't help it. Everything that April Saturday reminds me of being adrift. The broken bookshelves, the dresser-drawers, the coffee tables, the waterlogged mattresses, the ruined couches, the swollen bits of pressed-wood furniture—all of it drug from home after home and set roadside forces me to see how much I've avoided. Whole living rooms brought out to the end of the drive shows the extent to which local families have put their lives on hold after the storm. The bedroom sets stacked alongside the ripped-out sheetrock make the world here seem desolate.

Because after a storm, your own house can feel a little like a deserted island, and if you walk outside, you try to stay leeward. You try to stay on the safe side of the house, the side that wasn't too damaged from the storm. The other side is a lonely place. There's the slab where the garage used to be and the salvaged water heater and the few tools unearthed from the debris. It's a scary place. Every ruined thing looks like a stick stuck in the ground with an impaled head on top.

That's why you feel like you've become a castaway, someone trying to survive until they can find a way back home.

To do that on this exiled island is to decide on the basics, the essentials. You eat even without an appetite. You drink to feel normal. You decide what to fix first, which is like deciding how to erect a shelter when you're stranded on a beach. You do the roof at a price that's hard to believe and then you collapse into the sand, accepting how lost you are.

If you somehow survive the shock of getting a roof over your head, you lie in bed at night the same way you position yourself by a signal fire. You try to sleep.

You try not to look up. You try not to stare at the broken ceilings, because, just like a night sky, they go on forever and make you feel just as small.

If you stay abed long enough, you hear a voice asking you questions about when the repairs are going to come, if you've called the contractors that day, if you've stayed on top of things. If you stay in bed after that, you roll over because you realize the talk's nothing but a mirage. Nothing's being settled at that hour. Like a message in a bottle, your phone calls aren't reaching anyone, but you don't want to tell your bedmate that. You don't want to admit to your wife, or to anyone, that like a rescue boat out of earshot, no resolution's coming.

"No prospect can be more awfully solitary," US government surveyor William Darby lamented about the Chenier Plain. In 1816, after trudging through Louisiana, he stood staring over the eastern end of the cheniers and sighed, "From the boundless expanse of the gulf, and equally unlimited waste of the prairie . . . the scream of the sea fowl [and] the wind sighing mournfully [are] the only sounds that interrupt the otherwise eternal silence of this remote region."

Or Catholic priest Theodore Brandley's 1931 observation that what awaited him while he tended his Chenier Plain flock was "only flat, endless expanse of marsh and low ridges, washed by the muddy waters of the ocean running away to meet the sky in a cold, pale glare."[7]

But to an insider's eyes, the cheniers offer up something close to awe, and the grace that comes with it. As one writer puts it, "To the so-called marsh dweller, the chenier was a refuge from the recurring tempest and storm, a means of economic livelihood, and a favorite home site."[8]

For an early traveler adrift in the marsh—asea in an ocean of wiregrass or disoriented by the huge sweeps of giant cutgrass waving endlessly in the distance—a chenier must have seemed like a little island of safety, a chance at survival.

Against the flat marsh that unfurls until the horizon, the three-meter elevation of a chenier juts upward. It might as well be a shrine, a summit, a ziggurat. On the horizon, a chenier rises as a dark line, becoming clearer and clearer the closer a pilgrim comes near it. Soon the dark lines fill out to form the crowns of oaks, "broad, dark green . . . supported by a tracery of brown branches." Hackberries, black willows, honeylocust, and all the lower trees come into focus next. Then, once feet are finally standing atop a chenier's solid ground, a wanderer finds groundsel or blackberries, his hands touching palmettos or prickly pear, his eyes landing on wild grape, marsh elder, and honeysuckle. Even without the understory, a traveler under the unbroken sky of the Chenier Plain finds the simple shade an oak provides to be a refuge.

Imagine someone trudging miles through boot-stealing gumbo mud and gushy marsh bottom. Every move is a slosh. Every footfall gurgles. All around the brackish water supports nothing sturdier than bulrush, bulltongue, black rush, common weed, wiregrass, cordgrass, three-cornered grass. Every step is a sink. Each one deeper. But, suddenly, on the edge of giving up, the traveler's boot presses into sand and shell bed. After that, every step rises higher and higher until the trunks of trees appear. Soon, the walker is atop a relic beach ridge, feeling the hard soil under heel. Feeling the rough bark of an oak trunk after that kind of journey would be like touching the ghost of a long-lost someone only to find that it isn't ephemeral. It's real. In other words, coming upon a chenier has always been like coming upon a miracle made of land.

Obviously, the natural world of the cheniers is difficult to capture in words.

Gay Gomez does a better job. She's the one who taught me about the rarity of this place, explaining that the region stands as "one of only three extensive chenier plain systems" on the planet, equating the wonder of seeing "a chenier from afar" to "seeing a mountain range from across a broad plain."[9]

To Gay, even the word *chenier* is laden with meaning, its consonants full of pageantry, its vowels nearly ceremonial. "To most ears, the word is strange, exotic, difficult to comprehend," she explains, but to the coastal inhabitants "the term is as familiar as home, family, and community."

It took a self-reliant marsh dweller to make a home of any of these isolated elevations in the marsh, and settling them appears to have been a matter of resourceful island-hopping. Early residents first homesteaded places in the marsh closest to the Gulf or navigable rivers; then, by foot or by horse or mule, they braved the slog to explore deeper and deeper into the marshland, eventually taking up residence on the most isolated and remote locales.

Pecan Island's oral history claims that a man named Mr. Veazey was one of the place's earliest homesteaders. It was around 1840. He was living on Chenier au Tigre, which ran along the coast, when he traveled inland to find a new home. For miles and miles, he marched through the marsh to make it to Pecan Island. He had nothing more than "an ax, a horse, and a gun and built a lean-to and stayed there three weeks."[10] Mr. Veazey finally left Pecan Island to return to Chenier au Tigre, but he didn't stay gone long. A few days later, he ventured back to Pecan Island, this time bringing along his wife and children.

For these first pioneers, a chenier must have felt like a harborage, a firm place to anchor oneself, an island of hope for one's home. There's no surer proof of that then how these people named the world around them. Maybe it was a feeling of thanksgiving that molded the words in their mouth. Maybe it was the swell of accomplishment. Maybe it was fear, and these names helped them feel secure, as if uttering the name might reinforce that this solid foothold did in fact exist amidst this marsh. I don't know. But whatever the reason, what they called a town, what they named the place where they made their home, seemed to be a daily reminder of the surprising gift this landscape handed them—Grand Chenier, Little Chenier, Chenier Perdue (Lost Island), Oak

Grove, Hackberry Island (now only known as Hackberry), the uninhabited Mulberry Island, the eroding Chenier au Tigre, the washed-away Belle Isle, and of course, Pecan Island.[11]

After an hour of flat, solemn southerly driving, I make it to the nearest town that sits atop a chenier. It's Creole. Its population of about seven hundred people live only four or so miles from the Gulf's open waters. Of course, since the storm, no one lives there now.

A staunch little settlement, Creole waits at the westernmost point of the one major road that runs east to west through this portion of the Chenier Plain. Built around 1951, the road itself is built upon a ridge. It's Highway 82, sometimes called Hug-the-Coast-Highway because it skirts so near the Gulf of Mexico.

Positioned as it is, Creole can seem isolated, lonely, uninhabited, especially after the storms. As one geographer put it after his visit in the 1960s, "For long times, the chenier islands were isolated localities," and even when you visit now, "you still have a feeling of coming to the limits" of the inhabited world.[12]

Those are old feelings. An 1883 reporter described Creole and its neighboring communities as "a strange country and a strange people" because to him, it was a land with so much richness nothing seemed real. A place so lush it grew beyond comprehension.[13] That's one reason these cheniers have been touted as a tantalizing Garden of Eden, Gulf-misty lands with good things just hanging out of reach.

Creole can feel enigmatic. It can seem strange. Of that, there can be no doubt . . . because here in Creole there is no doubt. There are no what-ifs. When a strong storm hits Creole, it means devastation. Houses shift from their slabs. Storm surge strips the rooms of all their insides. Campers and cars and trailers disappear, swept away to a canal to be buried under muck or water or both. It's a fact of life staring you in the face. Being so far south, people know that when the weather goes south, their homes are the first to go.

Directly east of Creole is the community of Grand Chenier. As its name suggests, Grand Chenier sits on one of this marsh's biggest ridges, measuring nearly nineteen miles long. After the double hurricanes, that community's mostly deserted too, except for the trees. The mammoth Grand Chenier live oaks tower over the flat landscape. Draped in moss and standing for hundreds of years, they look like little histories, the drawings you see in books when people talk about family lines—the clumps of relatives who haven't died out, the ones that have.

Some of the oaks made it through Laura. Some weren't as lucky. Theirs are uptilted root balls. Theirs are the trunks that have split in half. Theirs are cracked branches that have fallen tree-side, home now to watersoak and rot and beetles. It's enough to tell a story of how much is forgotten in those family histories, how much of the past is always lost.

"But don't worry," the oaks tell me. Mild-eyed, they whisper in my ear to never trouble myself with that. "Take a load off," their moss-draped branches say instead. "Sit down. Settle in. Stay."

Because these are the sentries of the Gulf—the good stewards, the good guardians of homesteads here, a good place to build a home beneath their shade. They've weathered the storms—most of the storms, most of the trees have. "You could too," their leaves speak easy to me. "Under us, it's always afternoon."

Because with oaks as examples, the Gulf's waves don't come to me in crashes but in the words "Cajun strong," which means the strength to rebuild my house and not move on. That's what the moss utters. That's what the crowns proclaim. The acorns all around, they whisper, "*Telos. Telos,*" which means plopping right down by the trunk and living up to your potential, growing into a sturdy oak. "Sit. Rest. Stay." That's what the Grand Chenier oaks say.

"Lies," I shake my head and tell myself. "The oaks are liars." If to be under the bearded oaks of Louisiana is to be sunk in layered light, and looking up means drowning in a storm of noon and the sun's furious gold, to be under a Grand Chenier oak is to be on a ship at the bottom of that ocean where the world operates almost as it should.

To be under these Louisiana oaks feels somehow familiar, like the grown-up's return to his childhood home or the child sitting at her grandmother's vanity looking both in and through a mirror. To be there, beneath the limbs, looking up, is to see the state's most elaborate cabinetry, its own ornate furnishing. The roots are like molded doorstops, the moss like blankets stored until someone needs one. The branches are like pantries and junk drawers and root cellars and attic closets, and the resurrection fern growing along them is like a clock that keeps its own perfect time, and that time can make even the most familiar home seem out of place. Because to be under the oaks is to be an evacuee in a brother's or sister's house where you find all the things you might have owned but sitting misplaced on the shelves. To be under these oaks is to sleep beneath some other family's quilt. And lying there, voiceless, being not unaware of the nameless motions of the air.

Because no home has roots like an oak. Nothing does. No manmade house can outlast . . . then I forget what I want to say.

Because the oaks are speaking again. Because I'm listening to the branches and what they bear. Because the resurrection fern is thriving there. Because the words the oaks say make the raging of the Gulf seem so far, far away. Because it's no worries beneath their shade. Because I can mimic the roots they've set here. Of course, they tell me, mine can be as strong.

There's never enough time to soak in the beauty of the cheniers, to just lollygag and poke around, not when I'm driving, not on Hug-the-Coast-Highway, because as soon as I'm saying hello to Grand Chenier, I'm saying goodbye. Plunging even deeper east on Highway 82. Farther east into the marsh. East . . . across the Mermentau River where all the oaks disappear. East . . . past the wildlife refuge. East . . . for thirty sluggish miles as the side of the highway becomes one large drowsy marshy field until the calm water of White Lake takes over. East . . . until an imaginary line yawns two parishes apart. East . . . until I find myself at the highway's easternmost point—Pecan Island.

There, the highway becomes Front Ridge Road. I can see a few homes along it still. There were more some years ago. And historically, there were several ranches or vacheries, since the marsh is surprisingly good grazing land, but now the road's mostly lined with fishing camps built high up on ten-foot piers.

I can read the names of some of them. There's The Roost, Camp Brasso, Woo-Woo's, and Camp David. There's Porky's Place and Great Escape II. There's Tavin Oaks, Twelve Oaks, Four Oaks, and Twin Oaks. There's Duck Head, Pecan Island Yacht Club, and Fowl Play. There are all sorts of names that let you know that they know that you know what they're doing: They're taking a break and taking some time away. They're shutting things down. They're running on idle. Because if you're in Pecan Island and need anything, there's You Forgot It, We Got It Pecan Island Food Store. There's Southern Leisure, At Da Camp, and Time Out. Because the camp's a way of life here. People rely on it to take it easy.

So why not visit Pecan Island on spring break? Why not, right as I hit town, look for Pecan Island High School and its turnoff built alongside the road to scoot my little car into. It's a horseshoe, and so it's easy to pull off the highway and then back on. It's perfect, really, and perfectly ironic for a teacher ditching classwork to catch his breath.

All around Pecan Island are small pockets of elevated land—Kochs Ridge, Roberts Ridge, Forked Island, Lost Island, Long Island—and little roads connect most places now, even though a putter boat is still plenty handy. I usually choose the school, though, as an anchoring point. After driving an hour on that only road into town, to stop my car and put my feet on solid ground feels good.

Besides, the school's a useful place to study how people's houses finally pop up here after miles and miles of soggy marsh. It's an apt place to meditate on the flat pastures of wildflowers and level clutches of sedge grass undulating in the wind. It's a suitable place to look around, to register each time what has and hasn't changed—the camps built higher and higher up on the piers, the debris from the last hurricane uncleared from a canal, the slabs where homes used to be but now swept free of them—and sometimes, to say a few words, maybe under my breath, maybe only to myself. It's appropriate, I guess, to whisper, almost pledge-like, "I swear to leave this place alone."

But that has never been the case.

Because someone will always stand up and stamp around. They'll roll up their sleeves and dab the sweat from their brow. They'll flail their arms around and make pronouncements. And when that fails, they'll crook their elbow into yours to drag you into a corner of a room. They'll whisper, or they may even pass it around on secret little notes. Either way, it'll happen. Because no matter how it comes out in the end, it's all the same game: Someone will always hawk. Someone will always shill. Someone will always mutter into your ear, "I SELL THE EARTH."

In 1905 it was "The Real Estate Man." He hashed out bargains on the earth and told anyone who would listen, "If you want any part thereof Address:—D. D. Cline."

He purchased ad space on the banner running atop the *Abbeville Meridional* to be certain no one missed it, and he wasn't the only one. Those days it seemed like everyone was "selling the earth," selling "paradise."

Actually, a lot of the Eden they wanted to make a buck on was the marsh around Pecan Island. A lot of it, in fact, was land owned by Jabez Bunting Watkins, Seaman A. Knapp, and Henry G. Chalkley. Watkins was from Pennsylvania, Knapp called the Midwest home, and Chalkley had ties to London, but despite their disparate pasts, all three rushed together to form the North American Land and Timber Company.

They had to move quickly. In 1849 the first "Swamp Land Grants" began transferring federally-owned Louisiana swamplands to the state on the condition those lands be reclaimed,[14] and North American Land and Timber had big plans—reclaim the edges of wetlands by dredging canals and pumping water and moving soil, then lure prospective farmers into purchasing the new dry land . . . maybe not even in that order.

They set the capital stock at $100,000 and divided it into a thousand shares of $100 each. Once a good chunk of that capital was raised, the company would start buying the twelve-thousand acres of land it needed to "as soon as possible thereafter" put to work "a small 18 feet by 70 feet orange-peel dredge boat . . . [to dig] a canal 20 feet wide by 4 to 6 feet deep along the middle of a strip of land from White Lake to Pecan Island."[15]

When the *Cameron Pilot* shared the news about someone digging a canal between those two places, folks around turned giddy. The canal promised "to do away with the horrors of a winter passage in the marshes, and the mosquitoes and deer flies in the summer season." The *Cameron Pilot* flirted with the idea that the channel might open the island to "strangers,"[16] and the *Vermilion Star* opened the gate wider. It titillated prospective buyers by claiming that US Deputy Surveyor O. Elms would soon submit his report that placed "Pecan Island lands . . . on the market, subject to homestead."[17]

That explains why in 1905 a crowd was forming in Pecan Island—that's what the papers said anyhow. Word of the throng appeared in an article running beneath The Real Estate Man's ad. Not just a few, the paper said, but "all the people on Pecan Island turned out at the meeting . . . to organize for the purpose of digging the canal from White Lake to Grand Lake . . . so as to provide open water communication with Gueydan." After that, people started to talk. "The Richest Land in the World to be Reclaimed," another article gabbed. Pecan Island, White Lake, Gueydan—these Edens were slated to become "The Holland of America."[18]

All the while Knapp and Watkins frantically developed a new technique of canal digging, a technique to open the gate wider and wider still. A steam-powered dredge placed on top of a barge would be floated up and down the existing waterways. That machine could cut and plow an elaborate grid of new canals with all sorts of chutes and channels that could connect even the most remote places in the marsh to one another. Once that happened, everything was full steam ahead. Every piece of the world could become newly cut canals . . . and huge pumping stations . . . and fresh water sucked out . . . and sudden pockets of dry land, or at least it was billed that way. Schlank! The gate flung wholly open.

Because broad is the road that leads to destruction. Wide is the gate you can't get closed. Back then they called it land reclamation . . . dredge the canals, pump out freshwater, watch the saltwater come right on in. Now we know it as something else. Because that's the way it goes.

Today, a person staring at an aerial photograph or even scrolling Google Earth can still see evidence of that grand scheme—the straight lines of canals crisscrossing the marsh around Pecan Island.[19] For that matter, even at ground level, while driving the Hug-the-Coast Highway, I can see signs of the hatchwork of canals. True, I can't see White Lake canal from the road, but I know it's there all the same. I can tell because all the trees have disappeared—saltwater has backflowed into the canal and killed the vegetation, or the straight canals have stopped the water from eddying at a bend. It's the eddying that aerates the water. Without air, everything dies. So the proof is there, if I'm paying attention, if I know how to look for it.

But I don't. I forget all that. I forget whatever's in the way of my spring break. I listen to the oaks. I sail down a memory. I float on a dream.

I remember in 2000 when I gathered with a crowd of people to hear Gay deliver a lecture about her book *A Wetland Biography*. That night, my mentor professor John Wood introduced her. I remember how he talked about the photographs she had taken. I remember how he cradled the book in his hands the way he would a lily or hyacinth or a cluster of marsh marigolds.

When John retired off to Vermont, he invited several of us over to his home to turn us loose on his walls and walls of bookshelves. "Take what you want," he told us. "Carol and I can't move them all."

On the shelves I found a copy of Gay's book. I already had a couple, but I had developed the habit of buying one anytime I saw it on sale, each time promising myself to pass along the copy to someone. I had already given one to my dad and another to one of my brothers. I think I also gave one to my father-in-law ... maybe a cousin too. There would always be people who I thought needed to read it, so I picked up his.

It was hard. Standing in John's living room, where I had sat so many times as he gave me advice or encouraged me to keep writing or even just sipped mulled wine and listened to an aria played so loudly I couldn't hear what he was saying about it, I didn't want to take the book. Part of it was that scooping up any of the books from his shelves felt a little like throwing dirt on a grave. But the real issue was that I didn't like to think of John without it. I wanted him to have Gay's words and pictures with him in Vermont. I wanted him to have all the books he loved. It's silly, I know, but it was how I felt.

In the end, I could only bear to take three books that afternoon—two essay collections about photography and Gay's. "I'm glad that one is going home with you," John said, looking at Gay's book, patting me on the back as I left.

Once I was at home and my fingers were flipping through the book's pages, I ran into two sets of notes. One was immediately recognizable. Composed of a printed shorthand made of dashes acting as vowels and cryptic swirling lines masquerading as consonants, John's handwriting was notorious among his students, and while completely indecipherable to me, so much so that I usually needed a classmate to translate them, the note's author was clear, even if the message wasn't.

Gay's note to him, on the other hand, was both perfectly legible and a perfect representation of her. "John, if you could deliver a brief introduction on the photos in the book," she wrote. "I am so pleased and feel quite honored that you find them of merit. Will you accept a copy of the book along with my thanks for your efforts?"

Gay was always gracious like that, humble. It was just like her to give a thank-you gift, to be considerate of John's time and save him the trouble of buying a book.

"My title is 'Beholding Beauty: The Challenge of Wetlands," her note explained to him, and then "I wanted to describe the presentation." She followed that with a few sentences of summary, hoping to help him compose his remarks, but I doubt John needed much prompting. He was never at a loss for words.

Still, I'm struck by what she wrote to him about her goals for that night. For her presentation, Gay wanted most what she always wanted most. Whether her hours fell away to her eyes pressed against binoculars or her hands cupping a good hand of cards or to her mind setting down its impressions in a field notebook, Gay always wished the same wish for the wetlands—to "illustrate the beauty of this place so 'close to home'" and "suggest some ways a visitor ... may discover their subtle beauty."

For Gay, that meant experiencing the cheniers ... in photographs, in visits, in the words she recorded from its longtime residents. In other words, she wanted to "capture and communicate the essential character" of the cheniers. For her, that was only possible by capturing and presenting the thoughts and actions of its people. "Understanding is the product of both time and intimacy with place," she believed, "yet it is not beyond the reach of the person willing to learn."

I was willing to learn from the marsh. I was willing to learn from Pecan Island. I was willing to let go and let the lessons pour in, just like water when a dike breaks, just like a flood after the first tear.

But in an easy way. In an idle way. Because isn't that the right way? I was hugging the coast, drifting by the fishing boats and the don't-worry-if-you-forget corner stores and the hideaway camps up on stilts. I was chanting their names. I was soaking up all the leisure life Pecan Island promised. This was my time away, my spring break. I was kicking my feet up and just going along to get along, and I was ready to learn, but in a big stretch, big yawn, big fat pencil kind of way.

It came in the form of a story. To be precise, it came in what we might think of as history, specifically the history of how Pecan Island earned its name, a history that seemed to be rubbed over several times by a bright pink eraser.

In the 1930s, Humble Oil began its first foray into offshore drilling. It wasn't even offshore yet. It was the marshy world of the Louisiana coast—a funny world to try to build a rig in. Pilings sank and pavers couldn't build roads and surveyors couldn't even ride around in their trucks to take a survey. It was a pipedream. It was a gamble. It felt like a risk that would likely never pay off, but then in 1933, the word *allowable* started flowing from all the oilmen's mouths. Secretary of the Interior Harold Ickes decided that northern Louisiana's *allowable* oil production would be 24,300 barrels a day, but "southern Louisiana's proration allotment" would be set "at 44,528 barrels daily." That one word, *allowable*, or *proration*, "touched off a great oil boom" in places like Pecan Island and the Chenier Plain.[20]

One newspaper of the day described the bustling oil scene awakening those sleepy marsh communities. "Trucks rumble through the streets, restaurants are crowded, hotels are filled and business houses are busy," it wrote. "Out in the network of navigable streams, barges and boats of all descriptions are traveling to and from the marshland fields and seaplanes dot the skies."[21] Pecan Island, specifically, was waking up, rubbing the sleep from its eyes to watch the people stream in like too-early sunlight through an uncurtained window.

In 1935, reporter Dean Tevis *braved* a long trip by boat "across the treacherous reaches of southern Louisiana's Big Marsh" to see for himself what was happening to Pecan Island. He was going to sell the earth. He was going to sell "Pecan Island—Once a Weird Burial Ground of Man-Eating Indians Is Strangely Isolated Community of Louisiana Marsh," or so his title went. He was going to share the local legend of how Pecan Island was settled by "adventuring Jake Cole . . . from the raw country of the lower Neches in Texas" with the readers of Beaumont's *Sunday Enterprise*, now suddenly interested in the oil-rich marsh.[22]

Tevis claimed Cole, a rugged East Texas cattleman, was sailing "along the beaches of the outer coastline" when he saw the chenier's grove of hardwoods in the distance. He anchored at nearby Grand Chenier, which was accessible to the Gulf by the Mermentau River, and once docked, swore to turn the distant too-good-to-be-true paradise into his new home.[23]

Cole didn't have any guides. He had "two companions . . . stranded on the tip of Grand Chenier." There, "they had climbed high into gnarled oak branches. Off in the distance, they had seen, dimly outlined in the haze of a spring day, clumps of oaks to the south."

Cole believed the stories the chenier oaks tell. He believed in the promise of trees on the horizon, so "with his life in his hands . . . crossing the deepest part of the marsh," he and his companions traveled "over the boggy ground" until "they found themselves on what later became known as Long Island."

Standing at the edge of Long Island, Cole's companions "through yellow coastal haze . . . caught mirage-like glimpses of other seemingly greater oaks" but did not have the will to keep going. Cole, however, even though his "friends refused to go farther . . . struck out alone" and eventually reached Pecan Island to find a coppice of trees and vines and brush so thick the man was in awe.

Tevis painted Cole's Pecan Island as "curiously beautiful." It was "entirely surrounded by impenetrable marsh, cut off from every avenue of intercourse with the mainland . . . a last frontier." But it also "teemed with wild life. No coast line nor inland marsh of the continent had so many ducks." The "flora was rich and in endless profusion. Palmettos grew in thick mats on the marsh edges. And scattered from tip to tip of the island," Tevis wrote, "were wild pecan trees by the hundreds, and all bearing when Cole saw them . . . the first white man . . . to step foot on the island."

Cole "walked slowly among the trees," Tevis explained, "like shelters of gnomes . . . scores of hoary old oaks, twisted and corpses of those which couldn't stand the buffeting of the winds and water." Among them, the Texan found "a landscape at once frozen in time."

Cole's "lonely travels had taken him into many of the queer, unexplored nooks of the Louisiana and Texas coasts," but even he "became oddly fearful" of the chenier's "peculiar stillness." He found the place almost eerie, almost unnerving. "No other spot had resembled this strange island," this "fairyland . . . changed little by time." But despite the stillness, despite the island's emptiness, or perhaps even because of it, no other place "had drawn him with the appeal of Pecan Island."

The wild pecan trees appeared "almost as though they had been set as tiny saplings by some larger intelligence," and there were mounds of "dry, bleached bones." Those were the signs Cole could've seen, but the man instead "determined that Chenier Pecan was wholly un-inhabited" and simply chalked up Pecan Island's "peculiar stillness" as "one of the mysteries of the marshes."

For Tevis, Cole became the only one brave enough or gritty enough or just clear-eyed enough to possess the vision to venture into Pecan Island. Its stillness didn't unnerve him. The loneliness didn't faze him. Cole, according to Tevis, saw beyond Pecan Island's remoteness and emptiness. He looked through its oddness to embrace its potential.

The cattleman would have stayed there forever if he could, but back he had to go to Texas, to his wife. Before he left though, Cole readied himself for his trip home. He "filled the pockets of his ragged buckskin jacket with fat, wild pecans" and returned to his family "to prove he had reached his goal."[24] With these pecans as inspiration, "from all the rich choice of names, he called" his new home Pecan Island—as if the place weren't already named. As if the place weren't already known.

If there's one truth of the Louisiana coast, if there's one lesson to learn, it's that the oaks aren't the only ones who lie.

Because there's another version of Cole's "discovery" of Pecan Island. A different version. An older one. It's from the 1920s and told by Sarah Vaughan, a descendant of Chenier Pecan's first families.[25]

Vaughan also said that Cole traveled first to Grand Chenier, but what he found when he got there wasn't the same. In Grand Chenier "old Mr. Jake Cole . . . met two residents, Valcour Miller and Damon Miller." In other words, the place was already settled and that's what made Cole want to move on.

According to Vaughan's version, the two Millers agreed to act as Cole's guides to the mysterious spot the Texan spied from the sea. The three men started early, searching "the marsh for high land . . . fighting the tall grass and animals most of which were alligators . . . vicious looking . . . twelve or fourteen feet long . . . as many as twenty-five in one hole." They struggled all day through the marsh, "cane and sawgrass . . . high as a man on horseback," hacking a trail where there was none, "under constant attack by swarms of mosquitoes," not to mention those congregating alligators.[26]

Finally, they reached a small island known as Long Island "at almost sun down." They spent "a weary night" there. At daybreak, Cole woke and, after a quick survey, realized Long Island's narrowness wouldn't meet his herd's grazing needs, so he stood at the edge of Long Island. In the flattening distance, Cole spied Pecan Island.

The two Miller men were insect-bitten, beaten up by the reeds, and pure worn out. It really didn't matter much to them what Cole saw out there. Even "against Mr. Cole's begging them to continue their search the following day," the Millers refused to travel anywhere but back home to Grand Chenier.

Without them, Cole chose not to press on and returned to East Texas.

He came back later to Grand Chenier with "two slaves" known to be "good cowboys." The Millers laid out the route for them to follow, and with that, Cole and his cowboys reached Long Island. This time, without the Millers along, they didn't turn back. Cole forced everyone to slog all the way to Pecan Island.

When they reached it, the chenier was "so thick with vines and brush that the men were obliged to tie their horses and travel the ridge on their hands and knees cutting their way" to move through it in fits and starts. After slugging on their bellies for a while, the men eventually found a clearing.

Cole "had never seen so many different kinds and beautiful fruit. There were also many animals such as raccoon, opossum, bear, deer, and wildcats.... There also were many different trees of all varieties consisting of pin oak, live oak, pecan, willow, wild peach, hackberry, magnolia, large flower, tupelo, elm, toothache, cypress, and wild china."

He scooped up a few pecans in his hands and named the island after those little hard nuggets. By the next spring, "his cattle [now moved to Pecan Island with his family] were wild and fat as butterballs."

But the lie both stories tell isn't that Jacob Cole was made up. History shows us he was a wealthy rancher, well-heeled enough to have a series of legal cases develop after his death to decide the inheritors of his fortune.[27] At the end of his life Jacob Cole "led the life of a hermit, feeble, almost entirely blind, and attended and nursed by an ex-slave," and when he died in 1884, his sons James Cole and Jacob Cole, Jr., faced a litigious struggle for Jacob Cole's "wealth ... land and cattle ... at his death estimated to be worth at least $15,000."[28]

The lie is efficiency.[29] It's telos. It's potential. The lie is it takes an outsider to see what Pecan Island is worth.

The lie is also a lesson, and that lesson is that defining Pecan Island in terms of the "usefulness" of the land has always been what outsiders want to do. The lesson is Texas is always winning. The lesson is if my "chief object here is to live an easy and quiet life—to float listlessly through time to the shores of eternity," I've got my priorities all wrong ... just ask everyone who's not from here.

The lesson is it's the early 1900s and Arthur Pipes comes to visit Pecan Island. Jake Cole is nothing more than a "rancher, living in the southern portion ... of this parish ... who by accident stumbled upon the island after being lost several days when out looking for a bunch of cattle that had strayed off."

The lesson is it's 1905 and the canals are being dug. The lesson is "the importance of this drainage opportunity to investors can hardly be overestimated." In what was promised to be the Holland of America, "lands which five years ago had no value at all, and which now have a value of from $3 to $8 per acre, will be made worth at least $100 per acre on an average."[30]

The lesson is it's the early 1920s and Sarah Vaughan remembers Cole's local companions who guided him.

It's the late 1920s, the early '30s, and the lesson is Tevis turns Cole into a Texas trailblazing pioneer.

The lesson is it's the height of the cheniers' 1930s fur boom when "Cameron Beavers" are the "Next Big Farm Industry."[31] People are beginning "to wake up to the hidden wealth of the desolate marshlands" here. "Man's wanton wastefulness and encroachment . . . had greatly depleted the resources of the northern fur lands." Now "eyes of fur dealers everywhere [have] turned towards Louisiana and the coastal wastelands."[32] Outsiders are rushing in from all over to take advantage of what locals had not.

It's the 1940s and the lesson is fur is turning to oil. By 1942, the desire to promote the untapped potential of Pecan Island only escalates. Humble Oil drills No. 1 Louisianan Land and Fur Company rig. Slant drilling comes next. Then someone improvises a way to drill by way of a floating platform. The lesson is now marsh drilling is possible. Offshore production is feasible and profitable. Oil companies scour the marshland for oil-bearing formations deep under the soggy soil. To access oil pockets deep in the marsh, oil companies rely on that tried-and-true method of digging canals. These petroleum canals are even larger than drainage canals. Bucket dredges and spud barges move huge amounts of sediment and vegetation to carve them.[33]

The lesson is Pecan Island is never the same.

It's the 1950s and the lesson is when Dean Tevis visited Pecan Island fifteen years earlier he heard "some vague talk of a highway across the miasmic wilderness."[34] By 1951, those whispers had become a "16-odd mile" shell road "from Cow Island to Pecan Island."[35] The lesson is the construction of that road seemed to be nothing short of a miracle.

One Louisiana paper after another ran a story about that wonder of a shell highway.[36] Louisiana stood on the precipice of change—that was the good word that swept across the state. Roads, electricity, TV—it was all "opening" up South Louisiana to far-off places.

The lesson is Cajuns had turned atomic—that's how historian Shane Bernard describes it.[37] Bernard explains that along with the road to Pecan Island, electricity arrived in "May 1954 . . . spurring Pecan Island's four hundred residents to embrace consumerism with a vengeance." Pecan Island had been transformed "from the primitiveness of yesterday to the luxury of today as quickly as it took to flip a switch."[38]

The lesson is Cajuns learned about "A-bombs" and "oil" and "electricity." They learned how quickly those things encroached into even the farthest corners of the state. They learned through television. It "offered Cajuns a seemingly magical world populated with fascinating people from distant places like New York and Hollywood." They learned through an "era of consumerism" and an era of "patriotism and Americanism." They learned through an era "when joining the mainstream meant more to people in South Louisiana than being countercultural or even holding fast to their localized traditions."[39]

By the time the shell was being dredged and offloaded for that cambered highway, Pecan Island stood as the symbol of Louisiana's readiness to take a leap into the modern world. Or at least that's how the newspapers were pitching it. It was a new lesson on how to sell the earth.

Margaret Dixon was a 1950s reporter for the *Morning Advocate*. Like me, she liked to visit Pecan Island and during her time as a reporter, made several trips to the chenier. Something about the little island on the doorstep of change intrigued her, or so I'm guessing. Maybe it's that she wanted to witness something momentous.

"Grand Isle . . . and Pecan Island," she wrote, "represent two of the last frontiers in the state" about to "get a taste of civilization." She knew that "life at both places [was] still somewhat primitive." Pecan Island, especially. It was "still almost as isolated as it was 135 years ago when a Texan named Jake Cole cut his way through the marshes to the high ridge," she thought, but "a hard surfaced road has brought considerable conveniences to Grand Isle," and at Pecan Island, a "highway bed had been built through the marshes."[40] Change was coming. "Good things" were coming, she believed. Big things.

During her 1952 visit to Pecan Island, she sang the praises of the little town's "appurtenance of civilization—a library." Officially, the library was open each afternoon from 1:00 to 3:00, but since the librarian "Mrs. Tom Conner, the former Olga Veazey," also worked next door at the Conner General Store, the library unofficially opened "at the drop of a hat or at the request for a book." If that happened, Mrs. Olga Conner just walked over.[41]

Olga Conner was one person who looked forward to the creation of the new road, but she knew not everyone felt that way. "Some of our people were not so sure," she told Dixon. "But I believe it will be a good thing." She thought it had to be.

"It was different before," Mrs. Conner told Dixon. In the past, Pecan Island would go stretches with no doctor. "I had 10 babies and lost six of them. I lost twins who were born on the mail boat as I was going to Abbeville . . . Now when someone is about to have a baby, her doctor sends her to Abbeville to wait. . . . I guess the road will change everything," she said, "but I figure if we do right we haven't anything to worry about."

Roughly a year after her first visit, Dixon returned to Pecan Island. The shelled road had been completed and Dixon touted how "the islanders are getting a new taste of civilization."[42] She sauntered around town. She poked her head in the library again. She asked people what they had learned. "What we want next," the people of Pecan Island told her, "is electricity, and then blacktop. Then Pecan Island will get somewhere."

But the lesson is there *was* something to worry about. The road was a good thing, but it also wasn't. The lesson is that sometimes where you get to isn't where you thought you were going because the lesson is Mrs. Olga Conner's own brother George Veazey started to realize something. It took him a long time, but something sunk in by the time he was an older man.

In the 1990s, when Gerald Sellers interviewed him, George Veazey interrupted his own stories about the isolation of Pecan Island in the 1950s—his memories of no electricity, no local doctors, of the island's dentist also serving as the town's blacksmith, of the mail boat visiting a few times a week being the only access to the outside world. "We survived on our own," he said, but then, as if something had snagged his tongue and thrown it in a cage, he stopped himself in the middle of that sentence. He cleared his throat, took a breath, then he said, "We're missing something now." And then another pause. Then he said again, "I think we're missing something."

"When I went to work for the oil companies, I couldn't conceive of it," he told Sellers. "When I went to work for the oil companies, I couldn't conceive of them ruining our marshland the way they're ruining them today."

The place he loved, the place his ancestor settled with an axe and a horse and a lean-to, the place his cousins and siblings lived and worked and hustled back and forth to unlock the library doors, the place his father Ulysse Veazey made sure had a school and church—that place was missing something that was there before.

Pecan Island had been changed by the road and the canals and the progress it all brought. "The oil companies . . . they're ruining them today," he said. "It was something I couldn't believe to have been taken place." And now there was something about his home that seemed so strange.

It was in 1992 when Gay, still a student at Texas, found whooping cranes to be the perfect subject to sketch people's shifting attitudes about the cheniers. Whoopers is what some researchers call them. *Grue*, Gay tells us, is the French word "chenier residents in their seventies and eighties remember" using for crane.

As she drew a deeper and more detailed picture of the birds' history in the region's huge stands of maidencane, the value of longtime residents' experiential knowledge about the landscape also took shape for her. For Gay, maybe no better lesson about the locals' traditional ecological knowledge existed beyond the understanding they possessed of the whooping crane, and the story of that bird's survival.

Gay's whooping crane research eventually led her back to 1939. Most specifically, it led her to a day in May—a spring day perfectly suited for biologist John J. Lynch to scout the land by helicopter. He had taken to the air, hoping to cover more ground, hoping to confirm what local fur trappers and club hunters told him, that in the nearby cheniers he could hope to see the last of Louisiana's whooping cranes.

After hours of flying, he found the birds, not too far from the chenier called Pecan Island. In an inaccessible freshwater marsh north of White Lake, Lynch witnessed a group of thirteen whooping cranes—eleven adults, two juveniles. He was astounded. The bird's steep decline in the 1880s started rumors swirling that perhaps the days of whoopers in Louisiana had come to an end. On that bright May day, those rumors were suddenly squashed.

Sadly, the following year a hurricane displaced the flock. Only six cranes returned after the storm. By 1947, only one was left, a whooper called "Mac" who was named in honor of the helicopter pilot who in 1950 chased the bird, captured it, and relocated it to Aransas National Wildlife Refuge.

Six months later, Mac died.

But that wasn't the end of Louisiana whoopers. There was a larger plan to save *la grue blanche* in Louisiana, and that plan developed into a larger story, one that included Gay watching LDWF agents don "crane costumes (made by a local seamstress who volunteered her talents in support of the project)" to hand-delivering crates of birds to a spot near White Lake. It was 2011, and Gay proudly watched the agents carry the boxes in their arms the way someone totes a baby to bed.

The people on site that day, including Gay, operated in dead silence. Everything mattered. Each step, each noise, anything could make the difference between successfully reintroducing whooping cranes into the acclimation pens built on a sliver of levee near White Lake's canal and having the entire mission fail. Some of the success was owed to Gay.

The story of her contribution begins with the 2001 rediscovery of John Lynch's interview notes.

Lynch's 1939 typed field observations about whooping cranes' habitat, feeding behavior, and nesting sites stood as the last firsthand record of whoopers in Louisiana. That fact made them immensely important for the biologists wanting to follow in his footsteps. Even ornithologists like Robert Porter Allen, who garnered national attention in the 1950s as the man who saved the whooping crane (and who actually rode along in the helicopter with Mac and Lynch), relied heavily on the "Lynch records," as these typewritten notes came to be known.

Allen had long commended Lynch's work preserving traditional ecological knowledge. "The keen recollections of men and women of that generation," Allen wrote, "through Lynch's patient and intelligent research, have given us an incomparable picture of the status and habits of the whooping crane in this and other parts of Louisiana in the early days."

However, while Lynch's fieldwork was undeniably important, a large portion of his interviews and notes had never been seen. People had access to Lynch's synopsis, but not the transcriptions themselves, not words of the locals. That changed when Lynch's two daughters, Mary Lynch Courville and Nora Z. Lynch, discovered Lynch's unpublished notes of seven of his interviews with locals. As if scales fell away from their eyes, people reading those notes suddenly perceived the true depth of local people's knowledge.

The success of Lynch's famed 1939 aerial survey that "documented the existence of a non-migratory population of whooping cranes" owed a great deal to the everyday attentiveness locals possessed about their land and the wildlife there. Lynch learned, for instance, through an interview with John Gaspard and his grandmother that "the whoopers nested in abundance" some time ago and that "nests were built in the '*Paille-fine*' (the local word for maidencane) and also in '*Fouets*' (the local word for bulrush)." Gaspard told him that the area the grandmother meant was near White Lake.

Lynch also interviewed O'Neil Nunez who confirmed the information about nests at White Lake. "O'Neil Nunez was born in 1882," Lynch recorded, "and started trapping and hunting gators at the age of eight." Nunez was still running traps when Lynch talked to him. Nunez was "a very good observer, with a keen memory," Lynch noted, and the trapper relied not only on his knowledge but information from "three generations of the Nunez family [that] have lived in this region." Lynch saw him and his knowledge as incredibly reliable. "Whoopers always nested in a . . . marshy swale in the prairie," the fifty-something trapper explained to the ornithologist.

Lynch's fieldnotes show just how much he learned from locals about the whooping crane nests, but a keen eye also notices Lynch gleaned something else—words. Local names for flora and fauna and places flood Lynch's notes. Locals called the marsh onion a *glaieul*, "from the French for 'gladiole.'" Andropogon was called *Paille rouge*. Smooth cordgrass, that was "popping cane." And when Lynch gathered from his conversation with O'Neil Nunez that the Louisiana cranes predictably made their nests in a marshy swale in the prairie, Lynch also learned the local word for it. Nunez called that landscape feature a *platin*.

Nunez also explained the arrangement of the prairie outcrops to Lynch. "A series of 'islands' or prairie outcrops surrounded formerly by marsh, extends east to west thru this region," he told the ornithologist. Some of the names of these places were "Isle nid-d'aigle, Isle Cordonnier, Isle Cerisier, Coteau du Chene, Isle Perdue, Isle Mulet."

Names again, memories of a gift.

Around 1910, when North American Land and Timber Company partner Jabez Bunting Watkins "retired" at sixty-four, "he converted most of his Louisiana assets to cash, married his secretary of more than thirty years, and moved back to Lawrence, Kansas." He died eleven years later. His fortune—the wealth of one of the richest men in the west, grown from the Chenier Plain, and now managed by his widow—built "seven academic buildings, two museums ... a campus hospital," and a fat endowment supplying scholarships for needy students—all at Kansas University.[43]

In 1908, Seaman Knapp left Louisiana to move to DC to work for the US Department of Agriculture. Henry George Chalkley stayed in Louisiana, keeping the North American Land Company going, eventually also building Sweet Lake Land and Oil Company before he retired.

When John and Carol Wood retired, they didn't tell anyone until the summer. There was no party, barely any goodbyes, just one warm summer afternoon picking through their bookshelves the way a beachcomber gathers shells. What can I say, some people don't want a fuss.

I'm not sure if Gay fell in love with whoopers more deeply than she did with other parts of the Chenier Plain, but I confess that my mind can't separate her from those birds. When I first met her, I think her hair must have been the color of a crane's newborn chick, a blanched golden-brown. The color could have been the black of the primary feathers at the ends of their wings. It's hard to remember so far back.

When she retired, her hair was the gray found at the edges of those primary feathers. Her eyes, though, they were still beak-bright, as they always were. And to see a whooping square-dance in a field—stork leg up, stork leg down, stork leg up, promenade in a circle to mash the marsh grass down, then crank out the wings to break into the sky—was to see her smile break across her face.

Maybe that's why when I heard Gay was retiring, I wondered if it was a mistake. She seemed so young to me. There was so much left for her to write. She taught me about the Chenier Plain. She taught me to think so differently about so many things. To me, it seemed like she had so much more to teach.

After Pecan Island, the Hug-the-Coast Highway doesn't go east anymore. Highway 82 climbs north to Cow Island, then Kaplan. On my spring break trip, I take it, just like Gay taught me to do—to go, as she would write, "where spring and its accompanying green-up commence," where "even in decline" these lands and these waters "remain one of the world's natural wonders."

Gay taught me about spoil—that's the term for the dirt and sludge pulled up when dredging a canal or maintaining a road. If spoil is stacked on the side of a canal, that elevation means plants can grow there that wouldn't normally grow in a lower elevation. It can mean diversity. Spoil can also mean decimation. Spoil banks can impede water flow, which can mean preventing the annual movement of freshwater. A canal can mean saltwater intrusion too. Either can mean the destruction of a marsh.

She taught me to think about coastal management plans—the projects parishes along the Gulf are implementing to confront land loss, the things people are doing, and not doing, to help save the coast. Vermilion Parish's plan considers how "building a series of levees to prevent flooding is likely to encourage more intense land use."[44] Turning useless swampland into productive farmland can sound like a good idea, but it may not be. Building levees to prevent flooding may be the worst thing for a marsh. Build levees and more people will want to build there, will want to transform the land. Leaving land idle, leaving it alone, not building those levees and berms, might be the best thing for it. Gay taught me to see that too, the power of not doing.

And maybe that's the lesson—that there is no lesson. That's my opium for the afternoon.

Because the best way of describing the salt marsh surrounding these ridges is to say it is a sort of a sea . . . a sea impossibly made half of land and half of water, a sea formed from brackish and freshwater tide and head-high marsh reeds and mud so thick locals call it gumbo-mud. "If you step into it, you'll sink right into that mud," one local described it to me. "Sink right up to your chest."[45]

Doubt is what emerges then—doubt about what is and isn't land, what is or isn't water. Various lagoon lakes dot the landscape, but flotant-vegetation covers many of these watery pockets so they look almost like huge fields of wildflowers.

Doubt.

Several rivers cut through the marsh too, but the silt-rich water is muddy brown and sometimes looks like a huge patch of liquid soil flowing by.

Doubt.

My spring break Saturday drive ends west of Kaplan at a series of short birding trails located at the White Lake Wetland Conservation Area.

It's warm. Nearly hot. No one else is around.

Though the conservation area has a pen nearby, I don't see any whooping cranes that day, but I'm not surprised. Rather than for seeing a crane, the two-story birdwatching tower at the end of the park's small trail is meant more for spying a White-throated Sparrow or a Common Yellowthroat or a Loggerhead shrike, maybe even a White Ibis.

When I park, I see one of those cross the road. It ambles across the shell, not quite knowing what to do. It bobs its head. It hesitates. It eyes something in the high weeds along the roadway. Should it go there or fly off to wade through the distant marsh reeds?

It's a good lesson, the ibis's crossing and the Saturday afternoon I spend in the tower. Without too many birds to watch, I think about those exams in my bag and Milton's advice, which is like Gay's in its own way: In this dark world and wide, it's easy to misunderstand what's useless and what's not. To leave? To stay? To let it all be? To be resilient and rebuild in exactly the same way we always have? To decide everything is beyond my control? Do I listen to the oaks and set roots? Do I eat the Lotus flowers and float to eternity? Is there a third thing I could do?

Gay once taught me that "many travelers have pondered the nature of these islands in the marsh, asking questions about their origin, resources, inhabitants, and history."[46] Many have pondered how to save this place.

But it's spring break, and there will be plenty of time for that later. Besides, like a patch of fallow land, people also serve who only stand and wait. Isn't that true, what Milton said?

Where was I, anyway? I wish I had some good answers to people's questions. I'd like to tell you how Louisiana might make it through. I'd appreciate some time just to sit and think about what to do, but my office phone is ringing. I know who it is; I don't want to answer it. My friends are calling to tell me they're afraid the university will close the writing program here. "They can't ruin what John Wood built," they'll rage over the phone. I won't have the words. "I know," is all I'll be able to say. "The people in charge seem to think it doesn't make any money, or a difference anyway."

6

JACK AND ME AND COOCHIE BRAKE

The El Camino Real is a backbone. It's a spine. It's a cord that holds up central Louisiana. If you flayed a man and saw the avenues of blood we call veins and arteries, you'd be looking at something similar to the web of roads jutting off that main highway. If you pulled back skin to study the network of nerves woven closely to the bone, you'd have an idea of the often-told stories branching from that historic "Royal Road."

But don't let my melodrama confuse things. The King's Highway was very real. One branch ran from Mexico City (the Viceroyalty of New Spain) to Natchitoches. There, it opened to wilderness, disputed territories, and the French, and as it did, it acted as a gate or a door or hidden entryway, like a bush-covered mouth of a cave. Soldiers, bandits, roamers, raiders, out-of-touch autocrats, monks, caravans carrying ingots or colonial pieces of eight—all poured through the thoroughfare.

And this is where the drama slips in.

Gold. Silver. Other treasures untold. These wanderers left it there, or so people say, stashed in various hidey-holes scattered around Natchitoches.

You can find it. That is, if you have the eye, if you know the way.

The problem is I've never had a mind for treasure. I mean, I've heard the stories. I've seen the maps. I've flipped through the pages of *Tales of Louisiana Treasure*. I've read every word of *Louisiana-Mississippi Treasure Leads*. I've even pen-palled with a prisoner who deciphered an old diagram that supposedly led to Laffite's strongbox buried near historic Sallier Oak in Lake Charles. But when it comes to actual treasure hunting, I don't have the guts for it.

True treasure hunting, I think, requires two simple things—courage and conviction. But when my car's jostling down an unpaved road or I'm trudging through a patch of scrub pine, they peter out on me. As for my lack of courage, my problem's been the fear of wasting time. For conviction, it's either been no faith that a fortune's actually out there or not enough faith to take a risk.

It's a concern, I know. The real trouble is, though, it's not just in treasure hunting.

When I was first hired for my job twenty-five years ago, I felt so lucky to land work close to home that I never worried about the salary. Our first place was a duplex my wife and I rented. I remember the day the stove and washing machine, which were both in the kitchen, fell through the floor. We didn't care. I was teaching with all the teachers who taught me. It seemed like I struck gold.

My dad wasn't so sure. He was a public health inspector—a member of the Louisiana Department of Health—and when I finished my undergrad with an English degree, and nearly enough hours for a second major in biology and a minor in chemistry, he figured I had the sciences for a good state job, one like his. His plans didn't stop when I told him I planned on working on a graduate liberal arts degree. It couldn't hurt, he thought, to have a steady job warming on the backburner.

The week before I started as a graduate student in creative writing, he sat me down at the kitchen table so we could fill out the mail-in application form to be a licensed sanitarian. When the certificate came in the mail, he told me to keep it in a safe place. When I was working on my dissertation for my PhD, he asked where that safe place was.

Sometimes on university recruitment days, I'll meet the hand-wringing dads. I'll be standing at a folding table, passing out brochures for our degrees, answering whatever I can for the students. I have a spiel about the concentrations and the clubs and what joy even an English minor might bring. Most of the dads will hover over their kid's shoulder, waiting for my shtick to run its course, lunging the moment I take a breath to ask the question that makes me cringe: "What kind of job can you get with an English degree?" Dads worry like that. I guess they can't help themselves.

My last run-in with a worried dad didn't happen at a recruitment event, though. It was after we hired a new professor—a person to take over John Wood's old slot.

The competition for the job was stiff. The hiring committee's top candidate was a person from Detroit. After telling the committee their first choice accepted, which is never a sure thing, I remember the committee cheered.

It should've all been hunky-dory, but once the official rejections were mailed, a university booster was bent out of shape. He called my dean twice, wrote several emails, set up meetings with the university's president and provost. His son had applied, and he couldn't understand how after everything he had done for the school, his boy wasn't hired for the job. Besides, he was a local boy, after all.

I remember when I was hired. No one I worked with knew my dad, but it still seemed like nepotism to some people, the good old boy system at work, cronyism.

Why? Because I earned my undergrad degree at that school. It didn't matter that I went on to get a PhD somewhere else. It still seemed like an inside job. Actually, people felt like it was worse than that. The place I finished my PhD was in Louisiana too. I was wholly a product of Louisiana—detestable.

I used to overhear snatches of my colleagues complaining in their offices as I moved through the halls. "We need new blood," they'd say. "We need to escape all this inbreeding."

I remember the day I went into the copy room and found the cartoon about me that a history professor drew and posted around the building. In the poorly drawn scene, John Wood was a scheming puppeteer. Me and another new hire danced as marionettes on a set of strings. And sometimes I think of the time an entrenched female professor told me how surprised she was that I was an official member of the OBCC (Old Boy Coonass Club). I remember that I smiled, but I still can't explain to myself why.

I fought like hell to prove people wrong. I tried to dredge the accent from the mouth. I pledged to work hard at being worth the job. I scrambled to make up for the fact that the university hired someone who grew up thirty miles away. With every ounce of me, I struggled to defend someone studying and writing about Louisiana and how that might be as important as caring about Victorian England or Medieval France.

Some days I wonder if it wouldn't have been easier to have chosen something different, gone somewhere else. On those days, I dig through the job ads, polish up the résumé, type up the letters of application. On my worst days, I believe all those people I heard in the hallways. Most of the time, though, I take it all and try to make one of our new hires feel at home, like the woman who filled John Wood's budget line.

When she was looking for a house down here and asking me about parts of town, she mentioned several times that she wanted to be sure to find a place by the water. It was one of the things she liked about Lake Charles—the lakes and rivers and bayous running through it. "If I can leave from my door for a jog and be able to run by a pond or creek, that would be great," she said. Michiganders live for their time on their waterways, I learned.

I wanted to tell her Louisianans never feel estranged from the water. One day someone turns on a celestial spigot, and the streets don gray capes of the stuff. Back yards become lakes. Ditches, backing themselves into a corner, puff up and promise everyone they're coulees, or canals, or even bayous. But I figured that lesson about Louisiana is better learned on your own.

She took it to heart after she had to evacuate for Hurricane Laura.

It's late April, nearly a year after the double hurricanes and the historic freeze, when she calls me on the phone. All I hear coming through is the will to move back, the surety that Lake Charles is her new home. I don't know how long that can last.

The online class she's teaching that semester on eighteenth-century seafarers is titled "Sailors, Slaves and Saints: Writing the British Atlantic World." It's probably the most popular class we've had in years. In it, there's everything from sea shanties to captivity narratives to salty dogs and sunken chests, and I just can't help myself. Before we hang up, I ask her what she knows about pirates.

She tells me first about Blackbeard's Island off Georgia's coast and the rumors of gold buried in the sand there. Then she asks me if I plan to go hunting for it, to go to Georgia or the Carolinas to find gold.

I tell her I have enough searching to do here for my own lost things.

And I mean it.

And so I start. So I plan. So I scheme. So I begin my search for treasure close at home.

There's just one thing I have to do first. I call up my newfound friend Jack.

Jack's a graduate student. He's a poet. He's a walker of wild trails, a forager for funny mushrooms, someone as curious as I am about stories, and one of the only people I know willing to go camping with someone like me, someone who's okay with settling for cold food and cold nights of uncomfortable camping, at least for a few days, if it means we don't need to haul along too much junk.

"Want to help me hunt for Coochie Brake?"

"Sure," he says. "Definitely. . . . What's that?"

"There's a place in Winn Parish called Coochie Brake," J. Maxwell Kelley told writer C. Renée Harvison when she interviewed him in 1990.[1] A swampy wood running more than seven hundred acres, Coochie Brake sits only about fifteen miles outside of Winnfield, but it's so damned hard to get into, even many locals have never actually stepped foot in it. As the former mayor of nearby Winnfield, Kelley had heard his share of stories about the legendary place, even if he preferred to keep his distance.

Legends say otherworldly trees and odd-looking rocks and a profusion of fauna can be found there. Some claim the world's largest tupelo gum was discovered there in 1913.[2] Some say a high hill in the brake, a spot called Robber's Roost, stood for years as "a great vantage point" for bandits watching "travelers along the old wagon trail or the law."[3] Some even believe, or at least say some folks believe, that parts of Coochie Brake are "voodooed or had a hex put on it . . . whereas anyone who goes near it, something bad happens to them or a member of their family."[4]

"It's supposed to be a strange place," I say to Jack. "A weird place." And then I try to explain to him exactly what a brake is.

I stammer. *Brake* refers to the physical aspects of the landscape—a thicket, a swamp, an impediment. Early travel writer William Darby used *brake* in 1816 when he described swampy portions of Louisiana, but Samuel Lockett seemed to be the first in Louisiana to apply the term to mean "trees of considerable size."⁵ *Brake* appears on a Louisiana map around 1895, and the use of the term quickly spread through the Tensas and Red River basins. There, the term meant either a thicket, a canebrake, or a low wetland abundant with gum and cypress trees. In every case, the point was clear—when you run into a *brake*, you run into the same thing—a wall of a landscape, an impenetrable barrier, an untamed stops-you-dead-in-your-tracks.

I like the word *brake* for a place. It's a good little metaphor to me. It originates from a German word meaning rough and broken ground, and to my ears it perfectly describes what this sort of landscape does to you . . . or your horse . . . or your wagon . . . or even your little Nissan Rogue.

Telling Jack any more than that seems impossible, or pedantic, or simply just beside the point because when scavenging for silver, especially in Coochie Brake, there's real work to do, and it's a good idea to stay focused.

About treasure hunting, everyone will tell you to keep your eye on the prize, and they'll spit out the same advice about Coochie Brake, or sort of. In the brake, about the best thing you can do is keep your eyes peeled, and your wits about you.

Coochie Brake, you see, has been everything from a "haunt of moonshiners to the hideout of gangsters."⁶ It's been a home for spirits and a haven for outlaws. Loggers and quarry operators and roustabouts have tried to make big paydays working the area, the "big opening" people call it, and have found themselves stymied. Hunters have marched in there and come out with a string of crazy stories. Gold hunters have tried and gotten turned around. Even local boys have found themselves lost in there.

Hidden in plain sight, Coochie Brake holds an almost supernatural atmosphere for Louisianans. The State of Louisiana's Office of State Parks acknowledged that many locals have heard of the "wild and eerie nature of the site" that held "an aura of history and mystery . . . within its rocks, forests, and creeks."⁷ But few know it firsthand.

One local confessed that Coochie Brake was so dense and so impenetrable that "most Winn citizens have never seen this marvelous phenomenon of nature . . . 700 acres . . . an ostentatious display of winding creeks, trees, undergrowth, birds and boulders, caves and tunnels."⁸ Even to those "who had the courage to venture into its weird interior," another person said, the place has remained "something of a mystery."⁹

Back when he was a younger man, Darryle Kent Lacour had the wild idea to trek into it. "My discovery of Coochie Brake occurred while hunting in the area in 1970," he recalled.¹⁰ "I noticed a large section of trees. It looked like the perfect place for hunting game."

Lacour did a stint in the Army from '64 to '67, so he didn't mind marching through the thicket. In fact, he enjoyed being out in the woods, when his work at Winn Dixie allowed it. He liked to hunt and fish a little, but as a Civil War buff, he spent an equal amount of time with his metal detector rooting around for artifacts.

It was during his very first foray into the brake when he encountered something strange. His hiking had run him into the waters of Nantachie Creek creeping through the woods. Opting for adventure and discovery rather than calling it quits, Lacour decided to travel the bank until he found the spot in Coochie Brake that held the mouth of that creek. "It was like walking into another world," he said. "Or like finding a new island in the Pacific Ocean. Strange sounds came from the brake, and trees of all kinds grew in thick abundance for miles." He plunged deep into the dense woods before he decided to turn around. But it was too late. Lacour was bit.

From 1970 to 1973, Lacour's curiosity lured him into Coochie Brake several times. Each time he'd go off wayfinding through the brush; each trip seemed to unearth a new surprise. "Deep in the brake were large rocks," he said, "which appeared to be an old house or foundation." Huge clumps of wizened trees greeted him. On several outings, he encountered strange animals, larger than normal, with unusual markings. Flocks of parakeets too, he claimed to have seen. "Their calls were lonely and eerie," he said, but they paled against the other sounds. "Standing there at the edge of the brake," he said, "I could hear large splashes in the distance and sounds of bullfrogs or alligators bellowing, that rattled my eardrums."

His last trip came in 1973. He put a canoe in the Nantachie's goopy water and ladled for a bit with his paddle. It was meant to be an extended hunting trip, but it lasted only thirty minutes. "I came to a small mound in the brake covered with alligators, stump tail water moccasins and giant swirls in the water everywhere," he told people. "I took a compass reading," he confessed, "but the needle would never stop spinning."

After that, he wouldn't go back.

I pack the tent, sleeping bag, matches, lantern, and the other this-and-thats into a bin on Saturday. On Sunday, I play with a map and some old newspaper clippings. On Monday morning, early, before dawn, I load the bin into the car. Around ten, I hear from Jack that he's ready. By 10:05, I'm driving over to pick him up.

Two and half hours of two-lane highways needling us north is what we have ahead of us. During that time, after we get settled a little, we wonder about Coochie Brake some. Mostly my tongue's a lead weight when I try to describe it. That's a puzzlement to Jack, so he does some digging.

His phone-scrolling finds a story online about Coochie Brake. "My personal opinion is that the brake was formed by a fragment from the Giant Meteor that hit the Gulf of Mexico thousands of years ago," is how Lacour explains it.

It's a story people like to tell—that the impact of an otherworldly rock created the huge swampy depression in the brake and the pieces the meteor broke into are the odd-looking rocks and boulders visitors see still when they roam the grounds. The story also accounts for the swirling compass needles and bizarre creatures, that is to people who subscribe to it, since the meteor would likely have strange magnetic properties and maybe even radioactive decay emitting from it. It sounds scientific. Maybe that's why people like that story. It sure makes Jack's eyes light up.

But the meteor is only one theory about why the brake is the way it is. Other local historians claim that the entire brake formed when a fault line buckled. Some layers of rock shot up, and others sank. The latter forming the depression which over the years turned into a massive cypress swamp with a shallow lake at its center. The cypress trees inside the swamp became giants because they were fed by the lake's mineral-rich water. The fault line eruption also exposed deposits of granite and sandstone and filled a portion of Coochie Brake with boulders and rocks and outcroppings.[11]

And then there's the people who simply say Coochie Brake is cursed, and that explains it all.

It's enough of a debate to get Jack's eyes roving and my hand off the wheel. "So where is it?" he says. "Where are we going?" He starts poking his phone and I start rummaging in the backseat, my fingers wiggling to find the edges of the map stowed in the seat pocket.

When I pull it up front, I swerve just a tad trying to show him the roads I want to try and the infamous spot we absolutely must find—Lying Horse Rock.

Of all the places rumored to be in the brake, Lying Horse Rock might be the most legendary, and the spookiest. It supposedly holds the buried ill-gotten gains of outlaws. The pockmarked ground around it stands as hard evidence. Every shovel mark is someone's missed chance. Every hole is someone's whole night spent digging. Add them all up and they reach to the heart of the eager years people treasure hunted here. Put them in a sack, and you have all the old ghost stories that go along with them, all the hearsay, all the what-ifs of what happened that one time, all the things that match just what Maxwell Kelley said: "We've had some say that old so-and-so died because he got too close to Lying Horse Rock, but I don't put much faith in all that superstition."

Jack's ears perk up when I mention that, and now we're both anxious to find that mysterious boulder, me a little more on the nervous side. Proof of that is I have a bottle of holy water stowed in my car's center console. That's a secret I don't share with Jack.

What I tell him instead is how lost I'll likely get us. It's a running theme with me after the hurricanes, but on this trip, there's so little real information about the location of that rock to go on. I don't have more than a few fuzzy map coordinates, which I've translated into one large circle drawn on the map. It's nothing more than a stab in the dark, but I think it's our best bet.

It starts with Harrisonburg Road, which is an old colonial trail splintering from the El Camino Real. The current version of Harrisonburg runs a good portion of the course we've planned, or so our fingers sliding around the map tell us. If we hit it, we can cover all the potential spots we want to try, my circle included.

But some places don't seem right for circles. Some places don't fit in the boundaries we draw for them. They seem to wiggle free of the normal world. There, the ordinary and the supernatural overlap, just like shades of a Venn diagram, and the everyday mingles with the strange. When they do, a plain-Jane walk turns into something eerie. A noise doesn't stay just a noise. A rattle or a moan or even birdsong becomes a sound unusual, one that's full of the unexplained. We know not how. It just happens. And when it does, this weird space, this uncanny place, becomes full of opportunities. Maybe power. Maybe gold. Maybe memories of old ways now gone. Maybe ghosts.[12]

Coochie Brake seems like the right sort of place for that. Its topography, its terrain, its giant trees and curious rocks, its unusual tunnels, its ostentatious display of raw nature creating a rugged and evocative natural world—all these features mark Coochie Brake as a place where the commonplace shakes hands with the bizarre.

So like Alice traveling down the rabbit hole, Jack and I tumble along Louisiana's highways, and like her, there are people on our trip—mostly Jack—drinking and eating and smoking funny things. And there are people trying to taste adventure and bite off a little fun. And there are people, like me, who are looking for an opportunity to be transformed . . . to grow giant, or to shrink. To take a risk. To set doubt aside. To prove to myself that my mundane assumptions about what makes the world go round are wrong.

Within the kingdom of Coochie Brake, you'll meet people who amount to royalty, and once, many years ago, you could peeping-tom a king of sorts as he held court. That king's name was Harley Bozeman.

A confidant and childhood friend of loquacious Huey Long and his colorful brother Earl, Harley himself had a knack for storytelling. When T. Harry Williams wrote Long's biography, Harley was an indispensable source and recounted story after story about the Long brothers and his own relationship with Huey as high school friends and bookselling partners and traveling pals.

Harley was also a former member of the Louisiana House of Representatives and a well-known columnist for the *Winn Parish Enterprise*. His column "Winn Parish As I Have Known It" offered Winnfield residents a string of truths and lies about the area. I mean that in the most flattering way. You see, Harley was a speculator of the mind. He made people wonder what was and wasn't real about that swamp called Coochie Brake, about what could and just couldn't be true. He made people ponder. He made them care about their home place. He made them think of its possibilities.

Harley often opined how the brake's putrescene and outcroppings and oddities were a source of local pride. He frequently praised its astonishing features—the "tupelo in the area [grown] to a height of 200 feet, doubling that of other specimens," and the labyrinthine rock formations full of mysterious "passages and tunnels." He realized the richness of the parish's up-and-down past, its rich and thorny political history, its storied life near the El Camino Real. His Sunday column chronicled that entire span, and until his death in 1971, he never tired of reminding locals of the pull his home had on people. It was thirteen days after his eightieth birthday when Harley Bozeman passed away. His obituary said it all: "Harley Bozeman interviewed old-timers, dug into old manuscripts, letters, and other historical source material, and used his own remarkable memory of the past to present a fascinating account of Winn history."[13]

While he was alive, Harley strove to know as many Winn Parish residents as he could and to see every corner of its pine hills. He drove every inch of its red clay roads. He poked around its hard-to-find and hidden places. He loved discovery. There was just so little time.

In 1937, Harley and former parish representative Dudley D. Lang visited the mysterious Coochie Brake woods "to look over 160 acres which Bozeman and Lang were considering to purchase." The two men took a guide, "a man called John Morgan."[14]

While surveying the land, Morgan asked Bozeman and Lang if they wanted to tramp a bit deeper into the woods to see "the much talked about Lying Horse Rock" rumored to hold "valuable stolen loot" and where "for a bicentennial the shroud of mystery and superstition has hovered over." Having always heard the legends about "the fossiliferous rock . . . in the shape of a gray horse in lying position," Bozeman warily agreed.

And so, the trio picked their way through the woods and after a long slog through the thicket finally reached the notorious rock. While Harley and Dudley looked on, fighting to catch their breath, John Morgan did something rash. He clambered up the side of the boulder and found a seat on top of the rock. Was he simply showing out or was he showing up the two town officials? I don't know, but the man then pulled a pint of whiskey from his pocket and uncorked it.

"The spirits are guarding it," Morgan said, and when Dudley teased if Morgan meant the whiskey, Morgan replied, I'm "talking about the real spirits that 'haint' you."

Morgan meant the haints or ghosts or spirits standing guard over the rock and the treasure beneath it, but I imagine not a person there needed much explanation.

By then, nearly everyone knew the stories swirling around Coochie Brake and Lying Horse Rock. Like me and Jack, they were just willing to risk it.

The trio didn't stay at the rock long. After they had their fill of the brown, and I'd surmise the creepy surroundings to boot, the three men trudged back to the car, drove home, then parted ways, each eventually finding his own home and bed.

"The first thing I heard the next morning," Bozeman told people, "was John Morgan woke up dead." After that, Bozeman swore he'd never go back to Lying Horse Rock. And didn't.

Jack and I can't go back either, not to our beds and home, no matter how much of this trip might be a waste. It's Jack's first time inside the brake and my first time seeing Lying Horse Rock, and that counts as adventure, a chance at a little fun. After the hurricanes, I need that worse than anything.

So we hit Ball and then cross over to Creola and then drive north to Prospect. One of the scraps of information I have says that Lying Horse Rock sits just a mile from Iatt Bridge, but our fingers can't find that bridge on a map and neither can our phones, so we settle for the next best thing. We head for Iatt Lake.

No bridge to be found.

So we scour Iatt.

Nothing.

We crisscross a ton of tiny roads, the red dust blanketing my back window, so much so that when we come to a dead-end on a rutted logging road, I must stick my head out my window to back up. It goes on like that. On an old military road, we go nowhere. On grown-over spur cut-through, we nearly get stuck. On and on, all the tiny backroads running us in one big circle.

On Buddy Taylor Road or some other gravel boobytrap feigning to be a roadway, we pass a sheriff's cruiser parked in a driveway. The owner just happens to be walking his trash to the end of his drive, so we stop and ask for directions.

He's friendly, and as helpful as he can be, even though he hasn't heard of Lying Horse Rock. But he does know Coochie Brake and conjectures about the roads we need to use to journey there. Most of all, he tries to warn us—driving there in my kind of car is a fool's errand.

Harrisonburg Road is indeed a misery to travel. The ruts and gravel knock my little Rogue for a loop. My chassis is a bouncy house. The weeds roadside slap my fenders. Sometimes the windows too. Mile by mile the width of the road grows thinner and thinner. Two lanes, one lane, no shoulder, and then at some little town, maybe New Bethlehem, the road transmutes into a tiny pathway skinnier than a car and walled on each side by a thicket of black gum, pine, and climbing vine. I turn around. . . . Excuse me, I *brake* and turn around.

I tell Jack we ought to try to drive Coochie Brake Road itself. It's going to be the closest we can come to the swamp, I think. On it, maybe we'll see something. Maybe we can get out and take the air.

Jack agrees, and after the great waste of tiny roads we've traveled, Highway 34 looks like an oasis of asphalt when we arrive. Jack and I zoom, eating up blacktop, until we reach the little town of Wheeling. I don't want to tell tales out of school, but our partnership hit a rough patch there.

Jack had been dutifully navigating, holding his phone in his hand, following the little blue dot that meant us, but over the last five or ten miles, the steady rocking of my Nissan and the pillowing shadows of the trees thrown against the road and the sun, warm as a blanket, had turned Jack's eyelids heavy, which means at Wheeling we miss the turn and go right past Coochie Brake Road, which means I have to swing around, but that's just a treasure in disguise since it turns out to be an opportunity to read the "Nightriders" historical marker posted at the crossroads.

While Jack and I stretch our legs, we learn that from the 1840s to the 1860s, John West and Laws Kimbrell led a gang of outlaws operating by a set of secret signs and special passwords. Legends say they robbed and even murdered countless victims lost on the lonely roads branching from El Camino Real.

The marker tells us that "in the daytime, the Nightriders were known as upstanding citizens of their communities." At night, they did their deeds. Most members of the gang formed an outer ring of watchmen and patrollers, but a few select members formed an inner circle. The outer ring enforced law and order in a region reeling from pre–Civil War chaos and post–Civil War poverty. The inner circle was a clandestine band of criminals and murderers. They waylaid unsuspecting travelers and terrorized uncooperative residents and defied any efforts at Reconstruction.

They were no fringe group. They included the local constable and West himself, who served as a Methodist church deacon and was elected justice of the peace for one Winn Parish ward. The secret group also included a gang of Kimbrell brothers, whose father and mother ran a boarding house where legend says many a weary head went to bed at night only to dream its last dreams.[15]

Most of these stories and legends about the Nightriders can be found in the 1968 book by Richard Briley.[16] The people who had lived in the area for a long time heard the West and Kimbrell Clan legends their whole lives, so by the 1960s, nearly every person in town had their own tale to tell about a person either killed by the Clan or about a part of the landscape that had been hexed by way of those murders. So, to write his book, Briley interviewed several of these old-timers, and when he did, like Bozeman, Briley found a patchwork landscape stitched together by pieces of property cursed or haunted because blood had been spilt on that ground or a water well there had been tainted by a dead body being thrown into it. That led to even more stories—people's run-ins with ghosts, close encounters with spirits, someone wandering down an eerie road or too near a sinister well and feeling uneasy, a fellow trying to dig for treasure at Lying Horse Rock and encountering the haints tangled up in that place.[17]

Or maybe it was the other way around. Maybe it was that the landscape bewitched the upstanding citizens and turned them into outlaws.

In fact, that's just how it happened one night, or so the story goes. It was in the bedlam following the Civil War. It was by accident. It was "Elbert Weston, now calling himself John West," and Laws Kimbrell. The two of them formed a "volunteer organization . . . to act as a police force" to protect Winn Parish, which "had always been poor" but was now "defeated, overrun with carpetbaggers and even poorer." Their sensible plans, however, shift during one hunting trip "in the nearby swamp" when "the pair of young men decided to rest on a rock formation shaped like a side-lying horse."[18]

Time got away from them. The two sat ruminating about all they had gone through and what they might become. Then, afternoon changed to early evening. Then, early evening darkened to night. They chattered and chattered, and without realizing it, didn't stop until all the stars left the skies. Only once the sun broke through the dewy wall of trees the next morning did the two men grasp "that they had been on that rock all night," and that at some time during that stretch they had been altered—"a dark mood [had come] over them."

The pair of men "had entered the Brake full of spirit" but would leave "feeling victimized by the events outside their control—the poverty, the war, and the chaos—and were determined to take back the life that was owed to them. Coochie Brake had changed the men forever." The next night, West and Kimbrell would kill their first victim.

I tell Jack some of that. It's not on the sign, but makes for good traveling noise as we drive around and around until we find what we've been searching for this whole time.

Unpaved, dusty, red, and steep where it meets a culvert or a ditch, Coochie Brake Road is a ruination. It's one long string of loose gravel, knee-deep ruts, break-your-axle potholes, and other sorts of bad news. After only a mile, I swear it's cursed—voodooed by rain and runed by skidder tracks and, most of all, foredoomed since it too is in the path of hurricanes.

Jack and I can see the snapped trees in the nearby fields. If we squint, our eyes spy a tangle of leaning pine in the far woods. Their broken crowns loom like a gothic castle. But there are more pressing matters. The road right in front of us is plagued by broken branches and leaning trunks. There are places where avoidable pieces of storm damage lie in wait, but there are others, in just the same way a murderous band of men might conspire to erect a roadblock out of logs and brush and tree limbs, where the deadfall completely blocks our path.

Ready to turn back, I protest about pressing our luck, but Jack won't have it. He seems like a man possessed. Giggling, eyes strangely bloodshot, he laughs when I throw up my hands and blurt, "I give up." When the laughing doesn't work, he hits below the belt and questions my sense of adventure. It works. Every time I pause, his snigger goads me to drive around the bottomless mud puddles or aim my axle so it straddles ruts deep enough to bottom-out. A few times I hear the chassis guard scrape the ground and my foot inches toward the brake. Thump—Jack elbows me right in the gumption.

But then, even he can't deny this one roadblock. There's no way to go around, and I thank the stars my little Rouge is going to be spared, but just as I do, Jack, wild-eyed and lank, climbs out and tosses away a small pine tree blocking our progress. The second time, I say to hell with it, and we both get out to work the trees clear of the road. Because why not chase the money. Why not chase the what-ifs of what could be.

I keep my Rogue dancing around the potholes, and Jack keeps outsmarting the traps laid by the hurricane, the both of us sneaking past the cracked and tilted trunks and creeping under the cantilevered juvenile trees and trashing anything daring to stop us.

Finally, we make it to a turnoff near the road's center. Even though our eyes are bleary with pride, we can tell by the map the offshoot goes a bit then makes a loop as perfect as a lasso. We take it.

We park right where the loop begins its knot and ramble down the only path we find. It's a strangely dark place. The pine trunks grow so close together they form a heavy screen of brown, and as we look around, clumps of the fallen brown needles, like thick folds of fabric in the branches, stitch any gap between the trees closed, and any light that does brave itself through the curtain is sucked up by the forest floor's carpet of pine needles so deep they pool around our ankles and swallow the noise of our steps.

In that silence, a sudden crash is magnified, and Jack and I freeze. It sounds like it came from about ten yards off the path, so we peer into the draping needles. For a long time we do, trying to undo that covering pulled over our eyes, but both of us flounder at that sort of handiwork.

When the air seems right again for talking, I say to Jack that a racket like that is convincing. It's a good reminder, I chuckle, of how in years past the dense cypress swamp and thick pine of Coochie Brake made a good hideout for those wishing not to be seen.

We devote a good hunk of the afternoon hiking around, investigating, exploring, running into one posted sign, then turning around only to run into another sign blocking our way.[19] But that's another thing that makes me a bad treasure hunter. I don't trespass. No, I'm quick to abide by the rules. Extra quick. Too quick, sometimes. I guess that's what makes me a bad outlaw too.

There is one law that's hard to accept. No matter the country, it's the rule of the land. No matter the time, it holds sway. It's a law everyone knows and lives by but tries to ignore. It's the law of entropy. It's the law of change. Tame places go wild. Wild places go tame. Naught may endure but . . . what's the word?

"Man has made his impact on Coochie Brake," Kelley says. "Many of the old trees are now gone," taken by logging companies "from the Midwest and Northeast . . . setting up mills, cutting up timber."[20] Assistant District Forester Lonnie White explains that, in fact, the area was once called Edenborn Brake because railroad tycoon William Edenborn sold the timber here to the Avoyelles Cypress Company, but as stipulations of that sale, Edenborn refused "to allow the company to cut the four largest trees," which became known as the Edenborn Giants.[21]

In 1979, J. D. "Dude" Shelton was 68 when a local reporter asked him about those giants. Dude told the reporter that he knew the place well, very well. He had traveled in and out of Coochie Brake all his life and had been "turned around a time or two, but never lost," even in the densest pockets. For that reason, Dude had a sinking feeling about those trees. He knew one was struck by lightning and one was cut down anyway, but the other two he could never find. That was proof enough for him that all the giant cypress trees were gone.[22]

But monster trees are only half of what makes Coochie Brake what it is. The legendary rock formations at its "north end" where the deposits hold a "labyrinth full of underground passages and tunnels" turn the place into an odd meeting ground of rock and swamp, and into a place of mystery, or once did.[23]

Change. Entropy.

People will try to argue against it. "Even the giant machinery could not destroy the spectacle" of Coochie Brake, reporter Wanda Cornelius contested. "Some of the giant boulders still stand, towering above the excavations and they make strange sculptures, illuminated by the shafts of sunlight through the trees." One "massive stone hill" remains too, and "stones that look like ruined foundations" and one boulder that is a unique horse-shaped rock can still be found.[24]

More than any of the landscape's other implausible features, those rocks are what Jack and I seek. And there are hints. There's a feeling under our feet that feels like sudden elevations. A few grassy fields with exposed hardpan stretch out from the roadway. There are patches of pine that could be that way because they grow on pockets of stone in the ground. But it's a pipedream. Deep in my heart, I know it. The landscape never gets anywhere close to rock formations. Jack and I never come near the gold the stories promise.

Striding over storm-wracked trees and looking over our shoulders and reminding ourselves there's nothing really out there, we press on until eventually the path ends and even Jack concedes that we've run out of walking space. We do find a little golden sun around 5:30. That's about it. The day's waning light slants through the trees, and it's enough to convince us to set our minds to scheming on dinner.

The drive out of Coochie Brake is as bad as the drive in, but it's all a repeat, so I'll spare you. The point is once we finish it, we traipse down Highway 84 for Gum Springs Recreation Complex, which is part of the Kisatchie National Forest system and boasts sixteen campsites stretched over a series of hills shaded by pine and oak and tupelo gum. There are picnic tables and little fire pits at every tent site, a few of those overlooking a smallish lake that sits at the center of the park. The lake is cool and clear and fed by natural springs, and Jack and I pick a campsite close to it. There's no one else around.

As soon as we hammer our tent pegs in the dirt, we stand right back up to drive into Winnfield. Our brains and bellies work on buying a dinner we can burn over an open fire, which boils down to brats and bread and beer.

Back at Gum Springs the cooking commences, but Jack forgot to wear socks so his heel is sprouting a blister, which I discover means he can't help collect firewood, or fetch drinks out of the car, or even throw logs onto the fire, so he sits while I skewer links of meat and turn them black.

When their skins are spitting grease, we bury them in rolls of po'boy bread and drink the beers we bought. Our mouths are almost too busy to talk. Almost.

The story about how Coochie Brake earned its name is just too good. *Brake* is a little odd, but *coochie* is downright weird, so the telling has to get done, and fireside is the right place for a story like that.

I'm not sure exactly how the legend was started, but I know that nearly fifty years ago Harley Bozeman's brother Eck wrote it down that from 1767 until 1803 the area was home to a Spanish fort known as Fort Coutier, and the name Coochie came mainly from that.

Eck said that once the Spanish discovered the massive and mysterious rock formations in the brake, they intentionally established the fort inside it so that "quantities of gold and silver bullion" could be stockpiled "in the natural caves and in the many tunnels which had been dug into the rock escarpments abutting the old fort."

Sure, the fort sat in the middle of nowhere, but that was El Camino Real's doing . . . and intentional. The bullion was transported first from "Mexico by mule pack train" along that royal road, then stored at the Spanish fort until it could be "transferred to Poste De Concordia (Vidalia) on the Mississippi, where it was loaded on ocean-going sailing ships bound for Spain."[25] Some people claim Fort Coutier was "a dazzling and perhaps desperate gesture by the Spanish" since it was located "between civilization and the frontier" and others that it was the longshot "scheme of the Spanish governor of Louisiana," who desired "methods of bringing bullion from Mexico other than through the pirate-infested waters off the coast of Texas and Louisiana."[26]

Current oral tradition still holds "the Spanish used the massive stone hill as a fortification and to cache deposits of gold brought from Texas," reporter Bruce Schultz argued in 1979, saying he heard it from John Wiest, a state naturalist. Wiest said, "I really don't know if there is any factual data for that, but that kind of information has been handed down."

"But there's a darker side to the story," I tell Jack.

Even this far north, the hurricane's winds had uprooted huge oaks and pines, so all about Gum Springs are stacks of fallen branches and sawed-off chunks of tree trunks the park ranger has arranged into burn piles—seared and sooty and camouflaged in the blackness stretching out around us.

At first I need my flashlight, but it's not long before I can stumble away from the fire to collect wood without a light. The catch is after each scrounge, I come back with more and more ash on my shoes and grime on my hands. Sometimes a smear of smut finds my face. Sometimes it's a good-sized smear. Soon, I'm sitting by the fire, painted in shadows, unfolding the darkest tales I know, like the one reporter Robyn Jones told about a "mad Spanish monk" of Fort Coutier who "hoarded treasures of gold and silver."

Like the ranger, Jones had been at work making piles, but hers were mounds of "interesting tidbits" about central Louisiana, and in that stack, she included the garish tale of the monk, his personal servant, and "several Mexican workers [who] lived in the wilderness area . . . on Beech Creek near Coochie Brake."

The monk's job was to direct the storage and safekeeping of the Spanish gold and silver at Fort Coutier, but eventually greed got the better of him. Mad with money and power, the monk commanded that the fort's workers "kill the Mexican drivers and their burros and steal the loot." After that, the monk "loaded up all the gold and silver and buried it by one of the creeks near the Fort" so that "the 'mad' monk and his servant were the only ones who knew where the gold was buried." It was a string of deaths that kept it all a mystery.

First, all the workers and drivers died. Some say it was poison laced inside "a sumptuous dinner . . . of delicious dishes" the monk served to his men. Some even say that the monk himself "cooked the deadly feast."

And then the monk's loyal servant died. It was abrupt and unexpected and out of the blue—the wonder of it matched only by the monk's sudden turn.

Once he was gone, even if you could wrangle someone into telling you where that treasure was, no one was left around who knew.

That didn't stop people from looking for it. Plenty of people did, though no one found it. What they found instead is a hex, a "voodooed" landscape cursed because of those Spanish soldiers, their Spanish gold, and the treachery of that mad Spanish monk.

But there's still the mystery of the name, the puzzlement behind how Fort Coutier becomes Fort Coochie. That goes back to No Man's Land and the Louisiana Purchase. After the Louisiana Purchase, when Spain and the United States were bickering over what the US actually bought, both sides argued over the western boundary line south of Natchitoches. The quarrel almost came to war, but instead of fighting, both sides agreed that until the borders could be settled, each would remove all their troops.

The abrupt handover of authority from Spain to France prevented the Spanish soldiers from being "able to move out all the gold and silver bullion from the tunnels" in time, and so, not wanting the gold to go to the new owners, the soldiers "sealed" the entrances by *rolling* "rock boulders in and around them until the treasure-laden tunnels were hidden."[27] By secret deal, the fort went from France to the US, and when those English-speaking soldiers moved in, they found no gold, just as Spain intended.

Actually, it was worse than that. The Americans didn't quite come up empty-handed. They had no gold weighing down their coffers, but they did find themselves burdened by this odd-sounding name, Coutier, which they "interpreted it as 'coochie.'"[28]

It sounds like lies, but like the best ones, it's flaked with glimmers of the truth. There's the historian who argues there used to be a fort here. There are the people who study names who say the word *Coutier* could have existed here as a corruption of the Koroa or Courois Indians or as a translation of the Choctaw word *kŭska(k)* meaning *reed*. There are the 1887 newspaper reports of a Louisiana gold mine discovered nearby when "a cigar box full" of dirt and rock reached the assayers of the United States Mint in New Orleans whose tests showed traces of gold and silver. There are the stories of Natchitoches attorney Colonel William H. Jack who in 1890 operated a silver mine in the Brake that, locals say, produced five million dollars, and there are the legends from local families with relatives who have found a single silver ingot or a shot bag full of gold nuggets. And then there are the old maps. The ones with the word *courois* written across this area. Or the oldest one—John Bew's 1781 *Map of East and West Florida, Georgia, and Louisiana* that includes two dots not too far west of where "Naquitoches" is marked and the words "Silver Mines."[29]

It's all a long story to tell, and by the time I'm working on my second beer and struggling to keep my eyes open, Jack's heart is balancing between aching with how little we found and throttling with a wild surmise. I don't blame him. It's enough to get the brain racing and the body in gear.

But to me, it all seems so meaningless. Not just the word *Coochie*, but history itself, which I know is often not a record of the past, but people's interpretation of that record.[30] But it's more than that.

You see, there's another truth hidden in the Coochie Brake story. Monks and mines and buried gold—it's a legend you can find throughout the Louisiana territory. It's so widespread some people even know it by name. They call it the Legend of the Lost Louisiana Mine. In other words, the story's so outlandish, it appears in nearly everyone's backyard, flirts with so much mysteriousness that it's cheap. Money, buried treasure, hidden gold—it's all so commonplace. Grubby almost. It's blatant—the worth of a place for most people is in how much money it can make.

But how to say that to someone sitting across a campfire? Instead, I just sigh. "Jack, I'm just not cut out to be a treasure hunter. Sorry about that."

"It's okay," he laughs.

Coochie Brake, Coochie Brake, Coochie Brake.

If you say it too many times, which Jack and I do by the fire, the words lose all meaning. That's probably one reason its story keeps going and going. Maybe it'll go on forever. I don't know. I do know it outlasts a fire, though. And the strength of my eyelids. So, as much as I hate to do it, I tell Jack I'm going to make my move to bed.

But right before I crawl into the tent, I think about how rare it is to find anyone interested in wandering trails and identifying trees and thumbing flower petals. So few people are willing to waste a day or two on a wild goose chase. What I want to say is, "Jack, you're as good as gold." What comes out instead is, "Night, Jack. Today was fun."

The next thing I know I wake up to him settling down for the night. It's a second chance to tell him how thankful I am for his company, but this time my mouth pours out bits of the dream I'm having as I drift back to sleep. It's about a woman. She's following us around. Early in the day I see her threading the trees. Later, she's kneeling at a crossroads picking wildflowers. I see her at the grocery when we're looking for food in the brightly lit aisles. Do I see her when we stop for gas? I know she's making camp on the other side of the lake. She'll be there tomorrow too.

It means nothing. It's just a dream. But I end up telling it to Jack. He likes those sorts of things.

I wake up the next morning restless and needing to perambulate. It's early enough for the dew to wet my shoes, but as I'm leaving the campsite, I see the lights of the ranger's pickup swing into the park. They loop around the roads before stopping in front of the camp's water faucet. In one fluid motion, the ranger opens his door, bounds out of the cab, cranks on the spigot, then climbs back in and drives off.

Jack's awake when I make it back into camp, and the first thing he asks me about is the faucet's spewing. I only have time to say, "All I know is that it's been on about twenty minutes and that the ranger did it" before the ranger drives up.

By the time I reach the ranger's truck, he's putting the cap on his sample bottle. I'm not sure striking up a conversation is a science, but I manage to work up to a question about Lying Horse Rock.

The ranger hasn't heard of it, but knows all about Coochie Brake. "It's a lot of old wives' tales about outlaws in there," he tells me. He used to get down in there more but lately he's been too busy. There's loads of hurricane damage here and all the upkeep has fallen on him after the storms. He's the one who's been burning the piles of branches, the overgrown yaupon undergrowth, the Chinese tallow scrub. He's the one who knows how handsome this campsite was, how handsome it can be.

"Down at the bottom there is a historic spot," he says, pointing to a small section of the lake at the center of the park. There, in the direction of his outstretched finger, I can see the cement steps someone's built. They're climbing up and down the sides of the hills circling that end of the lake. I see the small pavilions, too, then I spot the wooden pilings in the water he's talking about. "I have to be careful about how I clean that up. By all the photographs, it used to be real pretty there."

Jack and I learn that back in the 1930s, the Civilian Conservation Corps worked this area. Locals had known how this small depression between the hills collected water fed by a spring, and it was a local tradition for people to gather here and swim. The water was so clear you could see way past your feet while you treaded water. Sakes alive, it was cold. It felt so good.

The CCC built wooden platforms out into some of the deeper areas. In the shallower sections, they used slabs of cut stone and thick wooden planks to line the lake bottom, which became a popular wading area. To access the wading pools, the CCC laid five or six long sets of cement stairs that climbed up and all around the hills encircling the nearside of the lake. For years, families would come and picnic at the pavilions the CCC boys constructed. Parents would build compact campfires in the small cement fire rings built into the ground so their children could sit around the fire, and when it was time, the stairs would lead the families down to the cool green waters.

The cement steps and rolled steel fire rings and the sturdy pavilions occupying the hillsides around the old swimming area remain, but are buried that morning under fallen trees and storm debris. Huge gum trunks crowd near the natural springs and entire crowns of pine close off sections of the shore. "It might take an act of Congress to get some of the machinery down in there and pull those big logs," the ranger says. "But I'll get it cleaned, if it all doesn't rot before that."

After the ranger leaves, Jack and I spend half an hour or so admiring the CCC boys' handiwork. We teeter our way down the closest hillside until we reach a pavilion and its set of stairs leading to the glassy lake. A huge white oak had fallen to make a bridge across the skinniest section of the swimming hole, and Jack and I take turns tightroping across it, posing for pictures as we balance. Even though aquatic fern blanketed the bottom, we could still see far down into the water, and staring into the gleaming, I couldn't help but think how hard it is to blame anyone for chasing something shiny.

After a bit, we climb a set of stairs on the opposite bank to reach a vantage point at the highest pavilion. We both can't believe how picturesque it all is, or might be, if we just shut our eyes and imagine how it once was.

It was back in the 1970s when Coochie Brake experienced what I would call big plans. To be precise, it all started on April 23 of that year. That day the *Winn Parish Enterprise* announced to local readers that they would soon have the opportunity to buy a piece of that legendary landscape—or at least would be able to buy a piece of a company with plans to buy it. "A total of 200,000 shares of common stock at $10 per share" went on sale only three days before, and the paper warned people that now was the time to get in while the getting was good. But locals didn't need the paper to tell them. They had already heard the rumors.

A few months earlier, Coochie Brake Attractions, Inc. had formed. It was led by building contractor Ronald Skains and corporate president/attorney Charles Bice, both of Winnfield, but in truth, the corporation would operate under the collaboration of several other "natives of Winn Parish."[31]

By the end of April, Coochie Brake Attractions had already lured plenty of heavy hitters, signing on a few entrenched local contractors and even the presidents of Merchants Insurance Company and Winn State Bank and Trust to back the proposal. Attorney Bice, or someone else with clout, had also already secured a commitment from the State Highway Department to "build an all-weather road to the site of the new tourist complex," and President Skains himself told the public the would-be "largest tourist complex in Louisiana" also had "encouragement from Governor McKeithen and Louisiana Tourist Bureau Director Morris Ford."

It felt like a fait accompli. The soil tests had come back. The engineering work had been done. Valley Electric had completed its initial surveys. Coochie Brake Attractions even published a brochure "in full color." With flair, it laid out its ambitious vision of transforming the "winding creeks, trees, undergrowth, birds, boulders, caves, and tunnels" of the brake into a one-of-a-kind grand tourist attraction. Contractor Ronald Skains described it as "'something out of this world,'" which fit Coochie Brake. The corporation even set an anticipated grand opening—June 1, 1971.

A five-year plan outlaid the phases of expansion beyond that point. "The first phase of the multimillion dollar project" involved purchasing 950 acres and building on that site, but those wheels were already turning. By September, the company owned 160 acres, a portion of it containing "the fascinating rock out-cropping and a portion of the brake," most of which planned to become "the central area of the proposed tourism mecca." The corporation intended to construct replicas of an old grist mill, the old "Gaars Mill cotton gin," the first drilling rig in the brake, a French settlement, a lagoon with a pirate hangout called Cat Island, and Coochie City, which was "an old logging town of 1900."

The schemers would also build a museum for Winn Parish history and take visitors through the Brake's "scenic surroundings" by way of a "floating railroad believed to be the only one of its kind in the world." That train, the Coochie Brake Limited, a replica of a Civil War locomotive, would set out from a hospitality house and travel "across the reflecting waters of the swamp" so people could "get a better look at the alligators," the deer, the giant bullfrogs, the immense pines, the flowering dogwoods, and the towering cypress and tupelo gums.

If things went according to plan, the complex would boast a pedestrian mall of cobblestone streets, a restaurant, live entertainment, shops, a mule racetrack, local craftspeople selling goods, reenactments of shootouts, and "a Night Rider pageant" recreating "the West Clan episode in an outdoor theater." Anything and everything the attraction needed to "give free-spending tourists places to buy souvenirs and things to see" would be there. And of course, the park would have a restored version of the "Spanish-built Fort Coutier" originally erected "to protect Spanish gold being carried overland to Florida" and now reconstructed "on its original site in the mammoth rocks."

Anyway, that's what the board members imagined. That's what they sold to locals.

Sure, these were big dreams, but the visionaries behind the project believed they had a few things in their favor. They trusted in the "energetic young men" of the parish who would be "willing to devote most of their time to it and to make running the complex their profession." They knew Coochie Brake was "well located near U.S. Hwys. 167 and 71," and they thought "other tourist attractions in the area," like Melrose Plantation in Natchitoches and Prothro Mansion in St. Maurice, would not only share tourists, but ultimately would draw more and more tourists to the area because "tourists like to visit where there is much to do."

I guessed it all seemed like finding a type of treasure buried in the woods. After all, in one estimate President Skains expected "half a million visitors the first year, with at least a million the second year." Another leader gave a more conservative estimate: "a quarter of a million people in the first year, each spending about $10 per day."

With figures like that, of course local papers supported it, but I'm not sure anyone believed in it as much as Eck Bozeman. About a year earlier, Eck addressed the Downtown Lions Club of Shreveport about the "800-acre tract of land . . . called a natural phenomenon and known as Coochie Brake."[32] He told the crowd about the trees and the boulders and the silver mining operations and legendary millionaire Colonel Jack and even about the "rubble of an old Spanish fortress which stood there from 1767 until 1803." It's no wonder the board of Coochie Brake Attractions brought Eck on as a consultant.

But that wasn't all Eck offered. Yes, the former Winnfield postmaster flashed around his knowledge of local history and held strong political connections—after all, Huey Long had hired Eck to drive around his father, Hugh Long—but Eck had another ace up his sleeve.

Some years earlier, Eck had a guest spot on one episode of *The Beverly Hillbillies*. He was working in Silver Dollar City, a tourist complex at Branson, when the show's producers had the Clampetts visit the town. In the episode, Jed and Jane Hathaway mosey up to the grist mill Eck is manning and have a conversation with him.

"That millstone must weigh a ton," Jane says.

"Yes, ma'am," Jed says, "and they's mighty hard to come by. Right, Eck?"

Eck responds with his only line, right on cue, "That's the truth."

Coochie Brake Attractions saw Eck's experience at Silver Dollar City as a real boon. That man had witnessed firsthand how these sorts of places work, and when the visionaries needed some vision, Eck answered right on cue. He corresponded a few times with *Beverly Hillbillies* producer Paul Henning about Coochie Brake's potential as a tourism site and was convinced that even though "lumbering operations have denuded it of most of the impressive virgin forest," and even though its "population of alligators and turtles is almost extinct," and even though most of "the boulders and much of the loose rock have been removed," in the face of it all, "enough of the original character remains," enough to attract annual visitors and make Coochie Brake "an exceptionally popular recreational area."

Eck trusted in that. "Give people something to come for, to see and do," he explained, "and they will come. It is as simple as that. Look at Disneyland, Six Flags, Astroworld! Once they were just ideas, and now they are household words."

Other people agreed, right on cue. How couldn't they? Besides, wouldn't it all work out just like President Skains believed it would? He said, "I know of no major tourism project that has ever failed." Do you?

Probably there are a great many reasons why tourism projects fail (and businesses too), but Coochie Brake Attractions faced the most common one—cash. The group couldn't even attain the initial level of investment it needed for phase one.[33] Sometimes ready money, like millstones, is mighty hard to come by.

I don't blame the people of Winnfield for believing in Coochie Brake. It's what Jack and I begged for the whole time we drove around the day before—a chance to experience the brake firsthand. Like us, Skains, Bice, Eck, and all the other board members of Coochie Brake Attractions had a faith in the brake's landscape, in the land itself. Essentially, they believed they had the dazzling combination of a rare terrain and an intriguing history on their side. But it wasn't enough.

After the tourism idea fell through, some crazy, fluky stuff happened to Coochie Brake. In August of 1973, locals learned "the virgin timber in the brake and the presence of the red wolf there . . . brought on the nomination" for the land to be included in the US Department of Interior's National Landmarks series. No one knew who nominated the site. Locals only knew that people owning land in the brake had been receiving letters from "a New Orleans plant ecologist" asked by the Interior "to help evaluate the site, and if certified, the designation would stand as testament of the locale's ecological, biological, and geological uniqueness."[34]

Then, a year later in 1974, a "quarry of sandstone rock . . . materialized where the amusement park didn't."[35] The old strange-looking boulders and legendary rock formations began supplying the Louisiana Corps of Engineers with the crushed sandstone it needed for revetment work on the Red River, a process that would arrest the river's east bank in Grant Parish from constantly caving in on itself and eroding into the water. The project leader, Guy Wright of Zarah Quarries Company out of Kansas City, believed Coochie Brake's rock was the only supply in "Louisiana that passes the Corps of Engineers standards for revetment work." The company planned "dynamiting the larger boulders," then trucking the rubble to the riverbank.

What followed was a particularly wet summer. The waterlogged ground meant the excavators couldn't get into the deepest parts of the brake and in the quarry, the bulldozer bogged down, which limited operations to the quarry's older sections and meant that all the workers could do that summer was gather that old broken stone into "a vibrating, screening machine known to the workers as 'the grisly.'" But as soon as the rain quit, Wight promised, the "blasting starts," then workers would "rip apart" about "50 boulders . . . at the same time."

I'll admit that a dry summer back in 1974 would have been a tragedy to me. I would've hated to see the rock formations turned into roadwork and the oldest boulders blasted to bits. Lucky for me, it never happened. When the rain stopped at the end of 1974's summer, Coochie Brake suddenly found itself as a part of a ground-breaking development put forth by the State Park System.

That year, the State Parks and Recreation Commission published an official "fifteen-year Capital outlay Master Plan" booklet.[36] Its nice cover was an image of a moss-covered cypress swamp, and inside, readers could find thirty glossy pages of color photographs and details by the ton. The booklet included a brief history of the State Parks system and a clear description of the organization's new goals and objectives, and the commission's "firm conviction that Louisiana *need not* rank 50th in state park land per capita and *need not* be tied for last place in capital expenditure."³⁷ The Master Plan also has a punchy ending:

> The challenge is clear.
> The method is at hand.
> The task awaits.
>
> It was an unmistakable call to action.
> It was a complicated idea.
> It still is one.

"Wilderness," cultural geographer Yi-Fu Tuan explains, "cannot be defined objectively: it is as much a state of the mind as a description of nature. By the time we can speak of preserving and protecting wilderness, it has already lost much of its meaning."³⁸ When the wilderness seems vast and untamed, as it did to pioneers, overcoming the wild means overcoming chaos and disorder. It means confronting what's dangerous and unknown. Challenging it becomes discovery, security, carving out a home. When the wilderness disappears and raw nature fades, when the wild grows less and less natural, mystery in the world slowly vanishes, possibility seems to lessen, and, especially for those with ancestral ties to the wilderness, its loss means a challenge to the fabric of the past.

But the past is impossible to hold. And change is inevitable. You can try to stop it. People try. In a way, the State Park Commission took a swing.

At the top of the organization's new list of goals was "to preserve and portray the significance of some of our most unique natural features and landscapes." These areas "of exceptional scenic value," "rare natural scenery," and "unique characteristics should be preserved," the Master Plan argued, and Coochie Brake became one of the first sites "because of its unique geologic formations coupled with a mysterious yet colorful history. The area, in central Louisiana, is rich in folklore, having served at one time as a favorite depository for Spanish gold and silver bullion." The plan suggested purchasing more than two thousand acres of Coochie Brake at a cost of $2,220,000 and scheduled the project as a first-year priority.

In 1975, the Louisiana Legislature officially passed Acts 657 and 298 and embarked on the fifteen-year Master Plan outlaid by State Parks. As promised, Coochie Brake became a central project. In March of 1976, the state spent more than $300,000 to purchase nearly twelve hundred acres in the brake.³⁹ Later that year during a good November, the state spent another $240,000 and bought another five hundred acres from Georgia Pacific Corporation.

Leslie Kent, the chief landscape architect for the Parks and Recreation Commission, guaranteed locals that Coochie Brake, "the first state preservation area," would offer plenty of things to do, but he also assured them their well-known spot would "be left, for the most part, in its natural state." It will, he promised, "afford the visitor various experiences in the natural state without damaging the resources."[40]

His words reflected a change in not only the brake's future but also in what people considered to be the value of place. In the past, people saw these sorts of places as commodities, but in the 1970s, this view started to shift, which might be most apparent in the National Environmental Policy Act of 1969. The attachment people felt towards a place and a concern for preserving certain areas for their intrinsic ecological and cultural value began to matter more than the profits a place could earn.[41]

Sure, what people witnessed in Coochie Brake might seem to be the same old story, as Tony Shelton reminded Winn Parish residents. Certainly, people might see "in the 1980s campers [coming] in with their silvery canoes and trailers," which might appear to be "the 1780s [and] the Spanish [coming] in with their gold and silver" or "the 1880s [when] Col. W. Jack came in with his silver 'mining' equipment," but Shelton assured them "the State Park system would be focused on protecting the tangible and intangible aspects of Coochie Brake more than trying to make money." Maybe that's why the state decided to put up all the posted signs that Jack and I ran into. Maybe that's why it fenced off as much of it as it could.

But that's okay. Jack and I have Gum Springs and its clear water. We have the swimming hole and the white oak to balance on and the rock stairs we climb up when we're finished looking around. We have a fisherman we meet at the top of the embankment, and we have the two of us thinking, "What the hell, we'll give it one last shot."

But the fisherman doesn't know where Lying Horse Rock is either. He's fished a few ponds in the brake, though. There was an old Dr. Collier he knew who owned a good bit of land down there, and the doctor let him fish those spots long ago. But he knows that's of no use to us. Old Dr. Collier is dead now, and all the land down in there that the fishermen used to go to is posted. "I think owned by the State," he says.

I don't tell him what we know firsthand. Instead, when he asks us where we're from and where we're headed, I just say, "We're going into Kisatchie today. We're just poking around. There's a spot . . . we might try to find these caves I've heard some old stories about."

The fisherman has seen caves out Kisatchie way, but he suggests we stop at Kisatchie Falls. "It's a pretty little place," he tells us. "People go swimming there."

There's not much to pack up at the camp. Jack and I fold up the tent, stir the ashes, and load up the car in about twenty minutes. On the drive out, we check the kiosk at the ranger station to look at a few of the maps and brochures stapled onto the corkboard behind the Plexiglas. Once we have our bearings, we swing onto Highway 84 and plunge into Natchitoches to hunt for gold one more time.

For years, treasure hunters ventured into the Kisatchie Hills to find a set of legendary caves supposedly hiding the treasure of a famous band of outlaws known as the Mystic Clan. People found the caves, and made a habit of exploring them, but around 1942, the US Forest Service dynamited the caves for the public good.

So, you can probably guess how much treasure Jack and I find. But that's not the point.

The point is, right when the two of us are riding the backbone that is the El Camino Real, Jack turns to me and asks if I remember mumbling something to him last night right before I fell asleep.

He's a good sport about it—all my babbling. He's a good sport about many things, but maybe most of all, he's good about what I promised him we would discover on this trip compared to what we actually do dig up. That's something worth setting down—that detail about Jack.

But this I want you to know too. Here, on El Camnio Real, here in Kisatchie, here among the pines, I unmask the woman in my dream. I had been thinking so much about writer and environmentalist Caroline Dorman, who basically convinced the US Forest Service to establish this natural forest, that she haunted my mind on our trip.

And because of her, Jack and I do unearth some beautiful things that day—wild azaleas as pink and bright as tropical birds, the cool water of Bayou Kisatchie, the pretty little rapids of Kisatchie Falls, the electric green Six-spotted Tiger Beetle that makes Jack think of Mardi Gras, the Longleaf Vista trail with rock formations that makes me imagine I might be an outlaw holed up in a hideout or a hobbit on Weathertop, flowering dogwoods so lovely they seem like another sort of siren waiting deep in this dark green wood, the five tiny stones of Airhart Cemetery tucked off a very rough road Jack goads me down, and beyond all that, I discover Jack.

Like a lucky penny, there's something he keeps hidden in his pocket. It's an easy smile, a quick laugh when the road gets rough, a ready appetite for a new trail to run down, a curious mind. "Gnarly," he says about the boulders and outcroppings we find at the top of a hill off Sheard Branch Road. He says it too about the yucca plants we stumble upon, about the yaupon and holly and locust trees we pick our way through on a trail, about the bright orange slime mold that looks like construction spray foam, about the sweetbay leaves and the taste of them, about the butter-yellow wild indigo blooms that seem to grow the wrong way down, about spring itself and how it's pulling its riot act in the forest here—an act so unruly the rangers are burning it back with torches so the whole trip smells of woodsmoke and charred pine.

Keeping a little weird in our lives, there's something to that. It's like the smell of a distant fire—it makes you wonder who's doing what. It's Jack who reminds me of that.

The story of people going into Coochie Brake, whether to quarry rock, log pine, or drill oil, or even to attract tourists or hunt for treasure, has always been a story about the place's unusual landscape. The stories of that "mad monk" behind the name Coochie Brake and the hexed history of Lying Horse Rock are strange enough and strong enough to be the glue. But for me, there's something else that pulls it all together. And it's Jack who helps me understand that like a fire, it's our knowing a place like Coochie Brake is out there that can give us direction.

Which brings me to the real point of what I'm trying to tell.

When I was struggling back in college as a science major and coming home from classes each day doubting what I was really supposed to do, I took a camping trip. My big plan was to go off, maybe into the Kisatchie, maybe somewhere else, and camp out alone. I needed some time to get my head straight, to sit by the fire and take in the woods and go to bed in the quiet dark answering only to the company of trees.

But my dad, he didn't like the thought of me off in public land all by my lonesome, so he asked his friend Mr. Mahaffey who worked at a health unit in a different part of the state if he had some land I could use.

Once the semester was finished, I met Mr. Mahaffey on a stretch of pine scrub south of Kisatchie that was his family's old homeplace. A rickey house still stood out there. Part of its roof had fallen in and some of the floorboards had rotted, but it was still shelter. If it rained hard, I'd find a room on the side of the dogtrot where the roof was intact enough to keep some of the sky from peeking in. I'd sit in there. When the rain stopped, I'd go out into the woods again and make a fire.

During the day, I'd tramp around the woods as much as I wanted to. At night, I'd try to sleep. In the early morning or in the late afternoon, I'd meet Mr. Mahaffey coming down the gravel road in his truck. I can't say for sure, but I bet my dad put him up to coming out each day to check on me. Dads are funny like that.

To my dad, the whole thing was peculiar. All he knew was that I was having trouble in school and was debating changing my major from science to English, but he didn't quite understand why I wanted to be alone in the woods.

He had even a harder time explaining it to Mr. Mahaffey. I remember overhearing him while he was on the phone with the man. To my dad, changing to English could only mean that I wanted to write a book one day. There was something about that desire that justified why I might be the sort to go out and get lost in the woods by myself. I don't know if that sort of clarification made a difference to Mr. Mahaffey. I imagine I still seemed like a real odd duck to him, but they both agreed. Maybe they did know. Maybe they understood.

My dad never mentioned the strangeness of it all when he drove me up there. Mr. Mahaffey didn't say much either, but the day I arrived, he showed me around a bit. He was the one who taught me about fatwood or lighter pine. He called them pine knots. They're the resinous hunks of a pine left once a tree has fallen and decayed. The sap settles into a deep pocket and crystallizes there. If you throw a pine knot into a fire, that sap-dense wood will burn forever. It'll start any fire too, even in the rain, even with wood as soggy and ruined as a shot-down dream.

Those little yellowed pine nuggets are prized by people. They're as prized as anything in No Man's Land. People will make a pine knot pile in their backyards, and they'll go searching into a deep wood for them because pine knots can be a little hard to find. It takes local knowledge to know where to go to have the surest chance at locating them. It can take an old knowledge to know how to recognize the kind of fallen pine trunk that holds the golden nuggets of sap buried there.

Mr. Mahaffey called them pine knots. Some people call it fatwood. Some people call it lighter pine because of the way it burns, the way it keeps a kindling going. It goes by many names, but no matter what you call it, in my book, it's the sort of treasure you find when you really know a place, when you know a landscape, when you cherish it not for what it gives you, but for what it is. Some people, because of where the sap sits in the wood, call it heart pine.

7

THE LITTLE CAJUN SAINT AND THE CLOSED-DOWN RESORT

On a Sunday, I'll find my way into my office early. During the right time of year, I can arrive in time to watch the false dawn scrape its gauzy hand across campus. From the parking lot, I'll walk through the sandy glow of the lampposts. On most days, the predawn wetness feels like thick bandages wrapped close to my skin. The whole site can seem mummified then. When that happens, an oily quiet slows everything.

Once, several years ago, my earliness set me up for a scare. I'm always a little jumpy walking across campus in the dark, but maybe that morning was worse. No one was around—no students, no cars, just an empty lot with a trash dumpster in one corner. It was not yet light out, and something about the emptiness felt uneasy. My eyes darted back and forth. My walking slowed. Each step closer to the dumpster felt like a mistake. Then, when I was only an arm's length away, I heard a noise. Was it metal scraping over metal? Was it a chain scratching the ground? Was it a growl? Scuttling claws?

Then a body's thud hit the ground. Thump. Then a horrible tearing came from the oak leaves. Hiss. My legs hopped up and my feet skipped and I broke out into two big strides before my eyes found the family of possums pouring from the dumpster's window and running away from me.

It leaves me feeling a little foolish. And not just that one time, but any early morning or late night when I find myself alone in my building. People whisper several portions of the campus are haunted, but the hallways I must walk through might have the most stories—the presence on the third floor, the white woman roaming the staircase, the noises in the east-wing bathroom. If nature calls and I know the rest of the building is empty, I'll be sure to close every door behind me, and my trip down the halls is an exercise in self-talk. A bang from somewhere in the building becomes three solid minutes of me reminding myself of what there's no such thing of. A walk to the exit means looking over my shoulder and quickening my steps and my mouth preaching about what I do and don't believe.

Because if I'm being completely honest, I'll admit that to me being a ghost seems easier for some things. For the wind to be a ghost must be so natural . . . in a cold snap, ooohing in the crowns of trees. With their hollow bones, birds seem close behind. Bats, too, I guess. A ghost dog seems to be an unnatural thing, but then I wonder about its hunger and the times down a back country road I've heard barking and seen the flash of something running heavily in the woods or skittering away from a pile of bones. Or in an alleyway, in a rundown part of town, the ribs and skeletal frames rattling the trash around, it's enough to make me think of a phantom black dog padding up out of nowhere. Couldn't that happen, even to someone like me who doesn't quite believe? After all, it goes back so far.

But of everything, humans have the edge at being ghosts, I think. They have the lives they've worked hard to build and have watched fall apart. They have the hopes they've held and can't let go. It's the stories that they have. Once I've heard the whats and whens and whos that have occupied a place, I'll start to catch something out of the corner of my eye. It happens every time, despite my doubts and reasonings.

Because as awful as they are, those stories are my stories too, and once I hear what happened to the person who turned into a ghost, I say to myself, "Okay, I get it now. The misery. The hope they can fix things someday. Because of that, they stay."

It's like that on a Sunday in 2021. It's early, just after dawn when I swing my office building's door open and the murmur of the twenty-ton A/C unit moving air around the vents whispers to me. It's the only noise I hear.

It's a reminder of the days as a kid when I came in the back door and heard a similar sort of thrumming. It came from down the hall or, if the mumblings were louder, from right there in the kitchen, a simple room away.

I knew the source of the hushed talking. Around the table, there would be my mother and the ladies from the church. One of the ladies' husbands might be there too, and sometimes so would a priest. Everyone would be holding hands, or maybe each person would be clutching a rosary. If there was a sick person there at the table, the circle might reach their hands out in his or her direction. They might move closer and hold their hands over the person's head or heart or part of the body that was suffering. Someone might even rest a hand on the sick person's shoulder or arm or maybe even his or her chest. It would be late on a weekday, after work and dinner were over, or in the middle of a Saturday or Sunday afternoon. At least, this is how the memories come back to me. And it might be a grown person they would be praying over, or it might be a child.

If my mother's prayer group gathered in the front room, the child might be lying on the sofa and the people might be kneeling on the floor. My mother would be the closest. I remember her that way. She would have her hands over the child's throat or hovering them along the arms and legs to get at the bones. Or her palms would be pressed against the child's temples. Or her hand would be cupping the back of the skull. In those positions, she would whisper the prayers that came to her.

My mother often prayed with people. She prayed mostly for their healing. People would ask her for these sorts of prayers. They'd call her on the phone or stop her after mass. They'd pass a word to the prayer group she was in. Sometimes she visited a person's house. Sometimes she prayed from her home. It happened several ways, but she prayed for the sick and the sick felt better—that's how I remember it.

I can't say they were healed. Honestly, I don't know if they were. But I do know people thanked her. There were so many times I stamped my foot in line at the grocery store or fidgeted impatiently after church when someone stopped her on the steps to say how grateful they were. I remember that.

There was a time when I might have seen folk healing as something opposite to modern-day medicine, but my mother never saw her prayers for healing that way, nor did the people who knocked on our back door. What they did just existed alongside what the doctors did. Something extra. Because doctors are busy, and some can act very busy, but the way I remember it, healing with prayer was a phone call in the middle of the day. It was stopping after work for an hour or so, not too long to be in the way, but long enough for the caregiver to step away for a while. It was an afternoon spent in someone's kitchen or several hours sitting in a chair by someone's bed.

The prayer group filled in the gaps for people. A lot of times, it involved a holistic approach to getting better and to taking care of someone. It was asking someone if they had been feeling better or how treatments were going. It was talking about the medicine someone was taking or driving them to the doctor. It was bringing gumbos or casseroles over on the days they went in or came out of the hospital. It was holding their hands and letting them know you were praying for them. It was sitting down, bowing your heads, and saying the prayers for the ailing person when their words just wouldn't come.

Like a kitchen or den is to a house, my mother's faith was a central part of her life. She woke at four every morning to pray before the rest of the house stirred. She went to mass every day she could, usually in the morning before she went to work. Believing was a simple part of her routine: an everyday thing, like resting for a bit in the sofa chair with a cup of coffee or grading papers for her fourth-graders or passing the broom across the floors.

She would always say that her deep faith came to her as a gift, even as a little girl, and the signs of that faith were never far from her. Always, there was a rosary in her pocket and a prayer book with dog-eared pages lying facedown near the coffee pot. The source of that faith was never far from her either. She saw it in the way the roads in town were built around the old churches. She saw it in the faces of her relatives that came to her in wedding pictures or first communion photographs. She saw it in the St. Joseph lilies or groundsel or whatever else she grew in her flower beds. She saw it in the centerpieces she made from them for her tables.

I couldn't shake those details about my mother's life when I walked into empty Kaufman Hall after COVID and the hurricanes and the other disasters, but during that time, the strongest memory that came to me were the stories she used to tell us. Many of them were about the miracles she had known—the ones she had prayed for that were answered in a way she understood and the ones that were answered in a way only His understanding could explain—that's how she would put it.

The stories of Medjugorje and Fatima and Charlene Richard were common in our house, but Charlene was ours. "The Little Cajun Saint," that's what everyone calls Charlene here.

Charlene was a young Cajun girl who died of leukemia in 1959. She's regarded by many in South Louisiana as a saint, but she's not officially recognized by the church. "There are a lot of unrecognized saints," my mother might say. "There's a lot of saints in the world you will never know about."

Charlene suffered a painful illness and death, but to people who know her story, who share it, Charlene's suffering was extraordinary. Sister Theresita Crowley supervised the pediatric floor of Lourdes Hospital in Lafayette when Charlene was a patient there. "Of all the beautiful, sick children I have tended to in my career as a nurse," Sister Theresita said, "Charlene stands out in a special way. . . . In all her suffering, she was always more concerned about the welfare of her family than about herself."[1]

About suffering, for those who see the child as a saint, Charlene was remarkable in her honest appraisal of it. She didn't want it. She was often frightened of particular tests or certain procedures. She dreaded the long needle of the bone marrow exam that would pierce her chest's muscles. But her attitude never soured. "She knew that death was imminent," Father Joseph Brennan said. "But she showed no bitterness."

Father Brennan visited Charlene several times while she was in the hospital. He prayed with her and took her communion. Along with his friend Father

Floyd Calais, who believed he was healed through Charlene's intercession, Father Brennan was most responsible for spreading stories of Charlene's saintliness. To him, Charlene's acceptance bespoke plainness. That made it powerful. "There was nothing extraordinary about the little girl," he once said, "besides her simplicity and her faith." Maybe Charlene's brother John Dale says it best: "My sister was the most extraordinary ordinary person I ever knew."

Charlene's grave sits in a cemetery positioned alongside St. Edward Catholic Church in the small Cajun settlement of Richard, Louisiana. Richard's official designation isn't a city or a town or even a village. It's an unincorporated community in Acadia Parish, a place known for rice, crawfish, and traditional Mardi Gras—ordinary in every Cajun way. Driving there can feel like you're headed to the middle of nowhere. At least ten miles from even the smallest of two-lane highways and flanked on all sides by huge swatches of farmland, it's so secluded it might as well be a secret place. To reach it, buried deep in the heart of Cajun Country, first you crusade east or west on the interstate. Then, you pilgrim north.

For those of us wandering, driving east or west in Louisiana can sometimes be a religious experience. The long ritual of the interstate faces you directly at the sun, which can either be so bright in the morning that it pulses in your eyes like someone thumping a book by your head or so glorious at sunset that it feels like an invitation to testify about a miracle, or something close to it. And then there are the brief stretches where you don't see a car, especially on a Sunday. If you leave your house early, by the time you're driving the small, empty country roads near Richard, it can feel awkwardly deserted, like sitting down inside an echoing church.

Though it can be a lonely drive, anyone lost can easily find the signs on Highway 13 to get to Richard. Along the roads, vivid royal blue signs proclaim the "Gravesite of Charlene Richard" is nearby and with sharp white arrows, point the way. Following the signs takes you on Charlene Highway, which crosses in front of the Richard Elementary School. It's a small school with fenced-in school grounds and a gravel drive shaped like a T, but it's most distinctive quality to a traveler is that it sits at the Richard crossroads. It's almost impossible to drive through the small community and not end up there.

That small community of Richard used to be known as "Light and Tie," earning that name one day when a man rode up to an early homestead near this crossroads and asked to "light and tie," meaning to dismount at the person's property and hobble his horse by tying the bridle around the front legs.[2] The request was a matter of courtesy—dismounting without permission was akin to trespassing back then. Some years later the place became known as Baptist Academy since it was the location of one of the earliest Baptist schools in the very Catholic Cajun prairie. In fact, it was the location of one of the region's earliest Baptist churches, Pilgrim Rest Baptist Church, built near the intersection of two bayous and a spring. So few visitors know that history, though. They come to Richard only for Charlene.

So much so that many travelers here assume the settlement of Richard was named after the Little Cajun Saint, but that isn't true. The little town became known as Richard when Theogene Richard donated land for the Richard Consolidated School. Today, though, Charlene is far and away the reason why so many wanderers find themselves at the Richard crossroads.

Little Charlene was often at these crossroads. The school buildings are newer now, but it all would seem familiar to her. By all accounts, before her sickness, she was in some ways a very ordinary Richard Elementary student.[3] She sat in the classrooms like everyone else, played in the schoolyard, lived nearby in a home on the edge of a rice or soybean field, like everyone else.

She was the second of a big Cajun family, one with ten kids. She worked at her schoolwork, rode horses in the summer, was captain of the middle school girls' basketball team. One of the happiest days of her life was when she made her solemn Communion. It was May 1957. Her grandmother sewed the dress. The skirt was scalloped, with flowers along the trim. She also made the crown of flowers Charlene wore on her head. Her family called her "Sue-Sue," but all her sixth-grade friends called her "Charlie Brown."

With all the things I've read about Charlene, it's a little book that comes to me when I think of her. The book title is her name—*Charlene*—written in the little girl's own wavy, wobbly handwriting. It was her signature, lifted from one of her school papers. A tiny bit crooked, that curly title hangs above a "School Days" photo of Charlene during her days at Richard Elementary. It was taken two or three months before she died. She was twelve.

Charlene's hair was a Cajun's thick black. She had the dark happy eyes and good nose and grin of so many of the Cajun girls sitting in the desks next to me when I was in the fifth or sixth grade. In the rows of yearbook headshots filling my memories, every face my mind's finger stops on is a girl who looks just like her. And all my cousins do too. And my aunts.

Whenever I think of the stories about Charlene, that's the face that stares back at me, and the more I think about it, her black-and-white photo looks most like the pictures of my aunt Wava L. Mouton who owned the copy of *Charlene* I like to look at most. I'm especially careful with it. Aunt Wava died in 1992. When she was alive, she read that copy and loaned it out so often that the glued binding holding it together ruined. She used a rubber band to hold the loose pages together.

If the school sits west of the Richard crossroads, east is St. Edward's Roman Catholic Church, which is held together by flesh-colored bricks. Like it, the other buildings making up the church grounds are small, proud, stout rectangles and squares—dutiful under a bright, early May Louisiana sun.

It's 2020, late in the summer of the pandemic, when I visit her. Nothing feels the same, but that's how everyone wants you to feel, what they tell you to do—get back to normal. But I have no faith that will ever happen again, so I drive there. Maybe I'm looking for a miracle at Charlene's gravesite. Maybe I'm just curious. Maybe I just want the company.

A hunter green ironwork fence surrounds the churchyard grounds. A red brick alcove sits between the graves and the church. Inserted in it is a white carving of Charlene's schoolbook face and the words "Pray For Us." The church building's roof has brunette-colored shingles and there's matching flesh-colored paint on the doors. Seeing it all for the first time, you might shrug your shoulders and say to yourself, "I must be missing it. It's like any regular place." There are days I've done the same. But that suits Charlene.

"She was a neighbor with us, living in the field back there," Frozine Thibodeaux said in 1999 when the *Unsolved Mysteries* vans rumbled into Cajun Country. "She was a nice little girl. She had a long illness," that woman from Charlene's hometown continued. "She died in Lafayette in the hospital, and she did a lot of miracles. And they're going to make a show. . . ."[4]

Unsolved Mysteries focused on a few of the miraculous stories surrounding Charlene: a man with shattered ankles defies doctors and can walk again, a young woman's cancer disappears, a mother earns several more precious years with her child. Since then, thousands have flocked to Charlene's grave, maybe as many as ten thousand each year.[5] Gathering around the grave in huge numbers for her anniversary mass of petition or stopping for a simple, quiet visit on some random afternoon, their voices say prayers and ask her to intercede in their lives.

I never know what to do when I park at places like St. Edward's. Maybe it's a dilapidated Masonic Lodge or a roadside marker for two outlaws built on a lonely hill, but wherever it is, it's a tricky thing to me—dragging my feet through the place where the level of my belief might not reach the depth of other people's faith.

Most of the time I'll leave my camera bag in the car, at least at first. I'll walk around some. I'll try to make as little noise as I can. Even if I'm alone there, I keep my hands cupped behind me. I'm overly careful with my feet. I'm almost always awkwardly tiptoeing around something. I can get so nervous that every breath seems to make a racket. Every footfall a commotion.

That's how it feels on that sunny morning I visit Charlene. As soon as I step through the swung-open churchyard gate, I'm silent and self-conscious, but not confused. I don't need to ask where to go. Not that there are visitors already in a spot, though people do come in spurts during the three hours I spend in the cemetery that morning, but from a distance, I see the iron bench placed near

Charlene's grave and two sun-bleached wooden kneelers. There are the flowers too, of course. Most of the above-ground, marbly gray burials here are decorated with little vases bright with mums and daisies and roses, but the conglomeration of flowers around Charlene's grave is startling. It looks like a flock of tropical birds has settled here.

It's bed-like, Charlene's above-ground tomb, and white, and busy with vases set around the base and blessed candles, some with Mary pictured on the glass, some plain but colored a sacred-heart red. On the upright headstone, at the very top, people have placed several figurines of idyllic children and cherubs. A Blessed Virgin Mother statue stands in the center. Rosaries of every color fall like shawls around her body. In embossed lettering, the headstone's brass nameplate says, "Charlene Marie Richard."

Someone's also cemented a small, white-washed brick onto the top of the tomb's cover plate. The brick has two ovals glued to it, which look like twin lockets sitting side by side. One oval holds Charlene's yearbook picture. The other contains a small prayer. A longer prayer hangs from the headstone. It's a letter signed by a family and laminated, then tied to a vase by a brown cord. Its words recount a miracle received through Charlene's intercession—their daughter being healed of cancer.

I let the laminated sheet fall and direct my attention to a large Plexiglas box near the foot of the grave. On top of that box sits a small wooden treasure chest decorated with bright blue lettering saying, "PRAY FOR US."

I know this is a serious place, the most serious portion being the petitions people write and slip into the Plexiglas box, but I've traveled here to document how people might have turned to Charlene during the COVID pandemic, so despite my tentativeness, I gently lift the plastic lid to study the objects left inside.

I notice the medical mask first. It's lying on the top of a notepad and pens and a sealed letter with "Charlene" written across the flap. I don't open it. That seems a step beyond what I've come here for. I also don't touch the several Post-it notes left in the box, but there's no need. They're printed in large lettering as if they want to be read. One yellow sticky note asks, "Please heal Carl Lewis of the COVID 19," and another petitions for "all the COVID affected patients," and another prays for someone's "breathing back to normal," and another supplicates, "Please heal my family from COVID 19."

A red truck pulls into the parking lot in front of the cemetery, and I close the lid and step away from Charlene's grave. Each time a car or truck drives up, I'm careful to do this. I drift to another part of the grounds or putter around the outside of the church. At one point, when an older woman stops her car near the gate and I'm caught off guard, I have to gather myself up quickly to give her plenty of room. From the back of the cemetery, I watch her as she genuflects at one of the kneelers, stands, bows her head, slips something into the Plexiglas box, then walks away to the church. I don't check the box again when I cross near the grave to leave. I figure I've run history's little errand for the day.

Driving home, though, something different comes to me. I take the road that passes by Pilgrim Rest Baptist Church, then Grand Coulee Road so I can drive through Iota, my mother's hometown, only 10 miles away. Iota has a strange connection to Richard, in its way. People used to visit it for healing too, but it wasn't a saint they were driving there to see.

In 1811, Iota was known as Wolf Point, Pointe-aux-Loups in Cajun French, for the large packs of wild wolves making a home in nearby woods. Wolves actually roamed the whole waterway known as Coulee Pointe-aux-Loups and they were notorious to early settlers, but that wasn't the only reputation the area had. The bayou held a natural spring, and people believed its waters had healing properties.

A man named Placede Richard first discovered the spring in 1812 when he used it to heal his son of scrofula, but it was Antoine Cart who brought the place its fleeting moment of true fame. It came in 1858 when he opened a resort in the town. That's the year the healing began.[6]

Cart announced his discovery in the *Opelousas Courier*. He claimed that the waters offered "relief of dyspepsia (indigestion, to me and you) and the permanent cure of cutaneous eruptions (pimples)." He promised "the afflicted a means through which a shocked constitution may be restored to health." He praised the natural springs as "abounding with Sulphur and preparations of iron," three of "the streams forming a large basin which affords a magnificent bathing place" and another was "furnished with an abundant stream of water the coldness of which can almost be compared to that of ice."

In truth, Cart's good fortune came by way of an accident. For years he had been plagued by an ailment and headed to the dry climes of Texas for respite. It was a slow trip west, especially in Louisiana. Every day seemed to be a new river or coulee or bayou to cross. In Iota, it was Pointe-aux-Loups that made it a pain, but it was its high water that made crossing impossible. For days, weeks, he waited for the water to recede, and as he did, he noticed his sickness did as well. He owed it to the time he spent in the springs, and once he stood witness to their powers, he ached to share it. That's why Cart's words in the *Opelousas Courier* sounded less like an advertisement and more like a testimonial. He trusted in the healing water's power. Their "remedial agency" is how he would proclaim them, these "curative waters." He signed the ad, "Antoine Cart."

But things run out, and in 1877 Cart sold Pointe-aux-Loups Springs Resort. The resort kept going for a while, but around 1900, the springs gave out too. No one knows why one day the spurting waters just weren't spurting anymore, not really. Of course, people had their ideas.

Some thought it was grace that ran low, but most blamed a lower water table, which they argued was caused by long strings of man-made irrigation canals and the wells and the levees people started to dig around that time to transform the Cajun prairie's hardpan into big stretches of farmland. But no one was certain. Not back then. The fact was, the springs had died, whatever the reason, and that was all.

The drive by the springs made me remember the news stories during the height of the COVID pandemic. There were so many, of course, but the ones that stuck were the ones about the residents of the small communities on Louisiana's coast that seemed to be ghosts from the past—not the people, the stories. It was early April in 2020. Everyone's nerves were raw. Everyone was scared, especially in New Orleans. Coronavirus ran thick there, but there wasn't a case in Grand Isle. So, like a tidal surge, Grand Isle's population swelled as out-of-towners flooded the town.

Grand Islanders started to sweat. They started to worry. In short order, Grand Isle officials erected a warning sign at the edge of town, pitched a large inspection tent by the highway, and threw out traffic cones to divert the incoming cars to the police cruisers parked there. They had their blue lights flashing and staggered the cruisers across the lanes, so people had to stop. Then they started checking people's licenses. "It looked like it was something that we wouldn't be able to control," said town attorney Chip Cahill. Grand Isle had plenty of sun, and beach, and clean air, but what it didn't have plenty of was police officers, fire responders, and ambulances, or at least that's the reason the town gave for the decision it made on that Friday in early April. Anybody coming into Grand Isle needed to be from there. Anybody else was kept out. It didn't matter if you owned a camp on the island. The officers checked to make sure any person trying to get into town had a Grand Isle address on their driver's license.[7]

In May of 2020, Cameron Parish officials sent out the same sort of message to the residents of nearby parishes about their bright ideas. A few weeks earlier, Cameron deputies walking the beaches there noticed the out-of-town trucks lined up on the sand. There were fishing poles and ice chests and tents packed in the beds. There were kids perched on the tailgates. There were parents sitting in the cabs. There were people crawling everywhere. It unnerved the locals. It made the deputies antsy. No one could stay six feet apart. The deputies couldn't enforce three. "We would love to have you come to Cameron Parish when this is over," the Sheriff's Office said, "Just not now."[8]

Not just now, I thought, but back then too. And not just here, but everywhere.

In September of 1918 an oil tanker sauntered into the port of New Orleans. A week or two later residents watched neighbors moan, vomit, struggle to breathe. By October, the city was locking up schools and closing churches and extinguishing streetlights. It wasn't long before pointy fingers were flying around. Who was it? Who can we fault? Where should we look?

At first, only certain portions of New Orleanians were at the business end of the finger, but eventually, it was the city itself that got all the dirty looks. Residents blamed the filth found on back streets and dank alleyways. They blamed the unclean air collecting around the close-set buildings and the smoke spewing from industries. They blamed the "miasmas" that strayed from the swamplands encircling the Crescent City, the noxious gasses that crept into town like little black cats on black-cat feet.

There are *Landscapes of Fear*—this is what Yi-Fu Tuan has taught me. Disease, pestilence, the plague—they haunt our dreams, but they also taint the living world, our surroundings, so we tie these fears to "the influence of the environment." We have for a long, long time, Tuan claims, and "when we sicken, so it seems does the world." We can't separate the two. The virulent air made from dank, stagnant water is the fluid in our lungs. Our goopy eyes see the putrid fumes belched from crowded cities as the cause of the infection. The landscape itself is what slips us back and forth from sickness to health.

We respond. We always have. We grasp at what we know to do. We hide, just like "at the height of the Black Death," as Tuan explains, "when a deadly epidemic hit a town, the almost instinctual response of its inhabitants was to flee."[9]

But don't worry. Never fear. That's what Louisianans have told themselves. Because if the closeness at the heart of New Orleans has historically been seen as a place of sickness, places in the outskirts have always been seen as havens from disease—sites of safety full of clean water and stocked with plenty of good air and ripe with dreams of being healed.

For decades and decades during New Orleans's early history, every August residents "fled en masse" to avoid yellow fever, what they called "Yellow Jack."[10] South to Grand Isle they went, some taking the "blood cure" by visiting the butcher every day for a shot of fresh blood, or north to St. Tammany Parish and the Ozone Belt since the pine woods there were believed to emit a "bracing air, impregnated with the odor of the pine" beneficial for "the healthy as well as the invalid."[11]

Others sought the cottages along the Bogue Falaya River, which was also a legendary healing place. Its springs were believed to be "specially endowed by Nature with medicinal properties" and could be "a healing balm for the many ills to which flesh is heir."[12] The nearby artesian wells of Abita Springs, too, they were praised for their "sparkling liquid that gushes from springs." Their "magnesium water" not only "precluded malady but imparted remedy."[13]

And Grand Isle? Down at the coast? Even back then, the spray of beach water "was believed to be exceedingly healthy."[14] Maybe more than at any other place, at

Grand Isle people could fill their lungs with sea air, take brisk morning constitutions on the beach, wade into the very waters of the Gulf. Besides, a body there didn't need to worry about so many other unclean bodies mucking around. The isolation was part of the appeal.

In 1918, when Cheniere au Tigre wasn't yet lost to erosion, people also flocked to that small strip of beach in lower Vermilion Parish. Like Grand Isle, Cheniere au Tigre was remote, but even more so. Fifty miles south of Abbeville—fifteen lonely miles south of secluded Pecan Island—Cheniere au Tigre shouldered the coast itself. Its only neighbor was marsh. It's only natural company was the Gulf water.

Zoe Sagrera remembers. Chenier au Tigre remembers. In 2010, Zoe was ninety-two, but way back when, when she was a little girl, her family operated the Sagrera Home, Hotel, and Health Resort. All her life, whenever she visited Chenier au Tigre, it was a flood, her memories of those little-girl days surging over her. The people's voices, what they did: "Amazingly," she says, "it all comes back like it was yesterday."

She wrote it all down in a book—her reminiscences of the healing waters of the Gulf and the residents and visitors alike using the sand and salt water for body rejuvenation, the couples covered head to toe in black, black mud from the mud baths, the afternoon parties of people wading out into the salt-rich tide, the ladies in hats and their kids shirtless on the beach.[15]

"The body is our most intimate cosmos," Yi-Fu Tuan says. Traditionally people have seen a sick body as being one of "imbalance," one out of harmony. Sometimes the discord spawns internally, but sometimes it propagates from a malfunctioning outer space. Our world and our bodies become a mesh impossible to untangle. It was true for our historical selves. It seems true today.

"Faced with disaster or its impending onslaught," Tuan writes, "the human response is often a combination of good sense and superstitious fear."[16] If a disease goes "creeping about the streets and lanes for weeks," it's common sense that makes us lock our doors and stay away from crowds. But when it comes to the big reasons why sickness prevails, our grasping becomes more unsure. We may blame the stars. We may point to bewitched objects. We may swear against demon rum or bad dreams. But no matter the culprit we condemn, pandemics heighten our fear "more than other natural calamities . . . because their origins [are] less well known, and partly because their courses [seem] more erratic."

It's easy to laugh at the past. It's easy to make light of old ideas. In 1915, the fiery radical Max Eastman spittled about an incident he witnessed in laidback New Orleans. He was jousting with shrines and healing rites and what he saw as a superstitious lot of people who ought to know better, and his outrage focused on that city that time forgot, which seemed rife with it. "In New Orleans when the citizens fought the yellow-fever mosquitoes by pouring oil in all stagnant water," he wrote, "they were brought to a stand before a cathedral font, where the priest contended that he had placed holy water, and if there were any wigglers in it, they were holy wigglers."

It's easy to giggle and say, "I'd never do that," but I've found when my own body is sick, I'll drive almost anywhere. When the soul is sick, I've found I'll go even farther.

Almost twenty years ago, my wife and I made the once-in-a-lifetime trip to England and Wales. My colleague was on a Fulbright in Cardiff, and the three of us took a trip to Bath. I remember the ethereal mist hovering over the pools lined with lead, the water as green as a beautiful woman's eyes who whispers how everything will be fine, and the smooth stone steps leading down into the pools. The steps' surfaces had been smoothed over the years by the bare soles of people's feet walking over them. I remember bending down and touching them with my fingertips. I remember thinking how every footstep of mine seemed to be a long pilgrimage through time.

"Over these springs Minerva presides," Caius Julius Solinus writes about Bath in his third-century compilation of curiosities of the world, "and in her temple the perpetual fire never whitens into ash." Ptolemy goes back even earlier. He records the Bath hot springs of Somerset England as *aquae calidae*, and in his world, those *warm waters* held a temple for Sulis Minerva, a blend of a Celtic deity with a Greek one.[17] The Romans called Bath *Aquae Sulis*.

English writers in the Middle Ages solidified Bath's legendary reputation as a healing site. "Springs supply waters, heated not by human skill or art, but from deep in the bowels of the earth," a twelfth-century writer declared, and the sick came from all over England to "take the waters."[18] Chaucer claimed British Prince Bladud built Bath and "made there hot baths" and "set over them the authority of Minerva" with a temple adorned with "inextinguishable fires."

By the 1740s when "John Wood, the architect responsible for the building of much of Bath . . . wrote a detailed account of the town . . . he identified Bladud as the founder of the order of druids in Britain."[19] In 1912, Ruth Tongue's *Somerset Folklore* recorded from oral tradition "that the young Bladud had returned after his education in Athens afflicted with leprosy." Diseased, contagious, the young prince found himself ostracized, driven from the royal court by his own people, a former prince reduced to herding pigs. One day, though, "while watching the pigs wallowing in the hot mud of Bath's springs . . . he had recognised the healing qualities of the waters." He was restored.[20]

It sounds so easy.

Back in the COVID summer of 2020, a few weeks before Hurricane Laura hit, several of the McNeese faculty in the College of Liberal Arts tried to *restore* our building to working order. We were trying to turn it into a place "safe" enough for everyone to return. We volunteered to transform classrooms so they could handle students sitting at a distance and make signs for the hallways to reduce as much of the traffic as we could. We called it "getting back to normal."

It was early August, a week before students would show up for the first day of classes, when we prepped the place. A handful of faculty went into the classrooms to push desks around. We had a six-foot pole that we used to measure the distance between their legs and squares of blue painter's tape that we placed on the floor. We rolled in giant Plexiglas shields that the art department built. We put up "enter here" and "exit here" signs on the classroom doors. In the hallways, we installed dispensers to goop out sanitizing gel. We took painter's tape and made ghostly blue arrows on all the floors. We bought facemasks and face shields. We took all the precautions we could, then the Sunday before classes started, we unlocked the doors.

Normal lasted all of three weeks before the first hurricane hit. No one needed to worry about social distancing anymore. The storm emptied the campus. It emptied nearly every building in town.

One or two months after Laura, the administration let us back into the building to check on our offices. The power was still out for most of campus. In Kaufman, they kept the entrances propped open and the windows in the classrooms hitched wide to ramp up the airflow. But it was too late. The building had already caught what was going around. You could smell it in the air. Even with every door flung open, a thick musty odor drifted through the hallways, and a film of organic grime covered all the floors.

Three or four weeks after that, workers hauled in generators to power a makeshift A/C. Tubes and tubes of inflatable white ductwork snaked through the halls. But it was late fall by then, so it didn't really matter, except that a month or two later, it was winter. The moisture trapped inside the building started to show itself. Most of the floors sweated, but the spots by the doors were slick sheets. In the classrooms, you could swipe your hand across a desktop and feel the wet. There were beads of condensation on the sheetrock, and on some walls, where the soot and dirt and construction-work particulates gathered, there were ghost lines. It can happen to any place once a little moisture is let in—faint straight runs of stain where dust-filled water drips perfect lines along the studs standing upright inside the walls.

It was the first time I had seen them since I was a kid. My dad was a smoker—Camels, unfiltered. Drying off after a steamy shower, I'd often stare at the brownish lines falling along the bathroom walls. On a Saturday, every once in a while, wiping the sheetrock down with a vinegar-and-water-soaked rag was my morning chore.

I've also seen ghost footprints, that's what people sometimes call them. Petrosomatoglyphs is another name for these mysterious depressions that seem to be an imprint of a hoof or a paw or even an ancient footprint appearing in hard cold stone. King Arthur, Jesus, Muhammad, fairies, saints, giants, the devil—someone's found a supposed footprint in a riverbed or a sandstone slab or a foundation stone for each one of them, or that's how the stories go.

Sometimes the entire landscape can be seen as a ghostly footprint. The First Nations People of Australia see it this way. They suppose that during "The Dreaming" the world was formed by ghosts or presences—Ancestral Spirits who moved over the land and shaped the world, creating life itself and carving the corresponding physical environment. Proof of it waits in the landscape, or really in everything. Mountains, ravines, waterholes, animals, the planets, the stars, notions of kinship and social processes, even people's cognitive and spiritual lives: all of it was made during "The Dreaming," and all the links between things were made then too. Proof of it can be found all around us.

The key to understanding it, many claim, is grasping that "The Dreaming" did not occur in the past. It's timeless. It's enduring. Australian anthropologist William Stanner calls this the "everywhen." "The Dreaming" is always happening, and people are happening in it, creating it.

For the Aboriginal people, songlines connect the current places of the world to the *everywhen* of "The Dreaming." What is a songline? A story of sorts. And is made by a story. A songline travels over the landscape, retracing the movement of an Ancestral Spirit, but also tracing a route from one physical place to another, from here to there, from where you are to where you're going.[21]

Some nights I dream of traveling and traveling until I find my way back to a certain place I recognize. Often, it's a floating platform in the middle of Toledo Bend Reservoir that I visited as a kid. Nothing dripped with summer as much as my family's trip to visit Sweet T and Uncle Paul at their wooden A-frame house sitting on a pretty lot overlooking the water of that lake, the largest man-made body of water in the South.

On his bass boat, Uncle Paul showed me the giant concrete slopes of the reservoir's dam and how to string my hook through the wad of stink bait before I let it plop into the tobacco-brown water. Way, way, way deep below the mirrored surface, my line heavy with lead weights would sink like a body drifting off to sleep until it landed in a watery field of hay fifty miles down. Or into a flooded barn's loft full of waterlogged alfalfa. Or even into a drowned bedroom with vanity, chest of drawers, bed, and all the other furnishings. At least, that's what I shut my eyes and hoped for. Because in all those places, the giant catfish lurked.

"Imagine," my uncle Paul would encourage me, "a catfish feasting on a barn full of hay or an entire field of corn. Imagine, if you're not too afraid, a catfish growing fat enough to fill a boy's entire bedroom."

Half of me hoped of catching one. The other half dreamed of stolen bait.

Some nights I have different dreams, though. It's a flooded rice field and I'm walking the levees. Maybe the field isn't too far from Charlene. Maybe it's only eight miles away in the small Cajun town of Mowata, that sounds just like "more water" when you say it aloud. Legends say that funny sounding name came one year when the little community suffered a three-year drought. To end it, local rice farmers banded together and dug more than fourteen deep water wells. Sometimes it feels like I do nothing but repeat that funny name in my dreams.

Some nights my dreams are of the small cement lily pond we had in our backyard. My mother kept it full of hyacinth and waterlilies. It was fed by a pipe buried in the ground before the cement was poured, so it seemed like our little oasis was fed by a spring, like the one Placede Richard brought his boy to, or the other one near the mouth of Bayou Nezpique, or the one in a town called Hot Wells.

And some nights, especially lately, it's Blaise LeJeune Bayou. Its thick slow-flowing brown water meant it was a good spot for Blaise to finally settle down. I dream of it, and him, and all the earliest settlers who knew the bayou water cutting through the hardpan meant life or death in the Cajun prairie. It meant sickness or health. It meant the difference being going or staying, and it could, I believe, still mean the same for me, if only I can understand how this home can feel like home again.

What I mean is, sometimes, some nights, these ghost places come back to me.

"Sometimes you may see a ghost, or maybe even be able to touch it," is how Larry Jorgensen starts his story about a Louisiana place that used to be a site of healing. "Sometimes it's only a memory," the retired radio newsman says, "a vision or idea which represents the past, and might even provide a look into the future."

It was a town folks called Hot Wells since the mineral springs located there poured from the ground "between 116 and 118 degrees." Jorgensen visited the site several times over the years, but only after he retired did he chase down the whole story of what he swears is "a true Louisiana ghost."[22]

Legend says that the Choctaw and Tensas people often journeyed to the original springs to treat their sick, but the Hot Wells story most know probably begins in 1913 when a man named William Jordan "discovered" the *miracle* mineral water there.

Jordan had suffered nearly his whole life. Crusty skin and oozing knuckles and itchy arms—eczema got him bad. It ate up all of his hands ever since he could remember. To make it tougher, he was an oil crew worker who needed to squeeze and ratchet and make a fist. The dryness made it painful. The thickened skin made it hard. And even though his people never ostracized him for his ailment, Jordan, like Bladud of Bath, had to slog it out on his own. He had no doctor's cure.

But he landed work in a place called Howerton Hill. It was drilling work. The job set before his crew was to plunge a test well through dirt and stone. It was a tricky hole, but his crew still managed to reach three thousand feet. Then, wham! It all went to hell. Suddenly, water "powered by pockets of gas some three thousand feet below" gushed from the bored opening. The crew took cover. The drilling stopped. The whole operation got shutdown.

The men, I imagine, right off were afraid for their pay, but there wasn't much else to do but pack up their gear and walk away. But drilling work is dirty work, and so before he left the site, Jordan walked over to the water and stooped to clean his hands. He didn't think much of it, and nothing much happened, that is until the next day when Jordan noticed that his rash seemed better. The next day he returned to douse his hands in the miracle water again. It was his daily routine after that. Every day, every week, for a string of mornings he bathed his arms in the almost-too-hot-to-touch water until one day he discovered "the skin rash was completely gone." After that, he proclaimed "the magic of the water" to the world and called the place Hot Wells.

Jorgensen claims that subsequent laboratory tests revealed "the water as one of the best mineral water sources in the world." The stuff was loaded with minerals, high levels of them: iron oxide, aluminum, calcium bicarbonate, calcium sulfate, calcium chloride, sodium chloride. "You can still touch it," Jorgensen says, "if you can find it." You can make a pilgrimage of a sort to it. "You can see what remains of a once thriving tourist community."

But that's not why I decide to drive to Hot Wells one Sunday. It's not for tourism. It's not even to see a ghost town or to reconnect to one of the ghost places that come to me in my dreams. I go because I'm curious about curative waters, wherever they are in Louisiana, whether they're close to Charlene or on the other side of the state. And I go, I guess, because I'm curious about faith, about how hard-skinned it needs to be for you to believe that things will be okay and how calloused it needs to be for you to say that even if they're not, they're meant to be this way.

If driving east and west on the interstate feels like something religious, heading north or south from there feels more like a hermitage. The small country highways are mostly empty. The brown roofs of lonely farmhouses or the isolated cloisters of mobile homes line the roads, but people are few and far between. Maybe I'll see the quiet of a flooded rice field or the silent devotion of cattle cudding grass, but at certain spots, walls of pine or hardwood are sure to flank a small side road I'll be made to turn down. Once I do, it'll feel like a comfortable silence.

On a Sunday like this, cars can be a rarity. If I see any that day, they're slowing down to turn into the parking lots of the little churches stationed along Highways 113, 112, and 121. Church seems woven into everything in the middle of Louisiana, and even though I don't visit any of the worship houses this trip, their signs say a lot. These churches have prepared their internal spaces for the virus, or more precisely, they are protecting their spaces by sharing a word against the disease. In St. Clair, when I need to slow down to a full stop to make the hard left turn off 121, the church sign at the crossroads doesn't mince words. "Let Fear Clear the Air With God," it instructs. And in Plainview, Humble Baptist Church sits on a simple two-lane road flanked by longleaf pine and crimson clover and brown-eyed Susan. Speaking plainly, its sign, stiff-necked and in all black lettering, warns, "Dying Without Jesus is a Bigger Problem Than the Virus."

But mostly, I hope the signs are being honest, and that they are earnestly preparing their external spaces too—their fields and schools and graveyards—because the people on the Cameron coast are moving north to South Lake Charles, who are resettling north to North Lake Charles, who are relocating north to South Beauregard, and on and on and on. New Sunrise Baptist's sign says, "Come in and be blessed" and Abundant Faith Church's sign pledges, "Everybody Welcome," and I hope they keep their vows. Because when the Gulf's water becomes no longer curative but the cause of the disease, when waves like a cancer have eaten away all the high coastal land and people start to flood central Louisiana, I hope quiet and secluded Union Hill Baptist Church means it when it says, "No One Turned Away."

During coronavirus, the schemes to turn out-of-the-way places into resorts made more sense to me. I understood the appeal of coastal Grand Isle or the remote Ozone belt. I saw the reasoning behind little Iota becoming a hot spot. I appreciated why in 1917, with the Spanish Flu pandemic raging, remote Chenier au Tigre or middle-of-nowhere Hot Wells might seem ideal for health getaways. Discovering the healing springs seemed to be a bonus, a happy accident.

But turning these natural healing sites into destinations capable of entertaining visitors was far from happenstance. It often entailed an assembly-line approach, something like it. Build a hotel. Construct a bathhouse. Erect a dance pavilion or a nice-sized hall that serves reliably good meals. If you don't have the Gulf, make sure the miracle water collects in a place deep enough for people to wade or swim, or at least have a good sit-and-soak. In a pinch, even a simple footbath will do. Do some eating out-of-doors. Have some picnics or seafood boils. Maybe serve some barbeque. Have a grocery if you can. A doctor too.

And that's how it went down in Hot Wells. In 1917, the mind of Boyce businessman D. K. Texada took the first steps to transform William Jordan's good fortune into a moneymaking scheme. He bought the natural springs and formed Hot Wells Sanitarium Company. Almost overnight, people flocked to Hot Wells "to take the cure."

Things escalated after that. In 1921, Dr. Clarence Pierson bought the Hot Wells resort "where nature's curative magic flows" and embraced it whole cloth. He expanded the accommodations in town and improved the buildings onsite and worked his fingers to the bone promoting it all. He brought in a beauty pageant and hosted Huey Long for one of his stumping speeches. He even penned letters to Franklin Roosevelt so the President would establish "a polio facility at the wells."

Soon, Pierson's vision was catching. Investors built more hotels and restaurants; then, the locals themselves went to fixing up corners of their own houses for people to pay the going rate and stay for a night or two. Or maybe the whole weekend. Maybe a long weekend. Maybe even a whole week. Someone opened a butcher shop. Someone went in as a barber. Then, blastoff. Roosevelt "was elected President." Everyone was so sure about it—Hot Wells was going to erupt with national attention. Then, splat. None of that happened. Roosevelt picked another spot to treat for polio, and "Warm Springs, Georgia, became what Hot Wells might have been."

Dr. Pierson's dream sputtered along for a while, but in 1934, the man fell sick. It was serious. Bad luck turned worse one day when a central pipe coming off the well stopped spewing water.

Congestion. Blockage. Constipated pipes—that's a problem that surfaces again and again in the history of Hot Wells. The minerals that endowed the waters of Hot Wells with their magic also frequently encrusted the pipes. When that happened, it slowed the flow of water to a trickle.

In 1934, the calcification seriously clogged up the workings of Pierson's enterprise when a workman "attempting to change the plugged pipe accidentally dropped the pipe and plugged the well, stopping the flow completely." Just like that, Pierson's good idea had gone to pot. About a week later, he died.

Whatever ghost is left of Hot Wells can be found about twenty or so miles west of Alexandria, Louisiana. There, a narrow concrete bridge about a hundred feet long spans the soupy green clamber of Bayou Jean de Jean. Across that bridge is a thread-worn patch of streets running a thousand feet east to west and half that north to south. That is the space Pierson's faded dream now occupies.

Pacing my car through those five or six blocks takes no time. I drive Swann Avenue first, exploring as far as I can west, which is two blocks, then turn around. I go south for a block after that, driving Ryan Avenue, then drift two blocks west again. I turn around, head south for another block, then turn around again. I take Johnson Street next, wasting two blocks of driving time on that, spin around, then turn around. Finally, I wind my way up and down Boyce Road that cleaves the place in two.

All these streets were named after dreamers, optimists, early landowners, who back in 1925 plotted the town's nine sections and divided them into twenty-six sellable lots. But all that seems gone now. Today, in Hot Wells, a few run-down buildings wait for something to happen, and that's it, unless I count the "No Trespassing" signs bracing themselves against the trees or the fences that scramble through the yards or the vacant lot holding a discarded baby stroller and flat tires and a broken-down car and several other cast-off odds and ends.

And so I drive the blocks again. But the haunting feeling doesn't go away. "This can't be it," I say to no one in the car. "I must be missing it." I drive around two or three more times, then give in. I recross Bayou Jean de Jean's bridge, climb onto Highway 121, and head home.

It takes me all of fifteen minutes until my gut makes me pull off the road at the sign for McNutt, Louisiana. I take out my phone and open a map to look at the block of streets again.

It's a good feeling—to get punched in the gut, and then find your breath. What I mean is, it can feel satisfying to know you took someone's best shot and got back up, so I turn around, eat a little something to stave off the carsickness coming on, and drive back into Hot Wells to try one more time.

This time, after roaming all the city blocks again, I find a different street to turn down. It leads me to a sign that says Bath House Road, which I take, but that route just heads to another dead-end crowded with unworking things.

"I'm going home," I say to myself again. It's a promise this time, though. It's a vow. But I'm a little lost. Instead of being near the bridge running across Bayou Jean de Jean, I'm forty or fifty feet from the entrance of the Cotile Recreation Area built around Cotile Lake. That's where I meet a man named Clifford Clark. As much as anyone, he's a saint, or at least feels that way to me that afternoon.

Cotile Lake is a man-made impoundment. Finished in 1965, it covers almost eighteen hundred acres. All year round people fish the lake and picnic the grounds. As soon as it's hot enough, people will swim. There's a water-skiing area too that's routinely cleared and snagged for safety, or at least it was before Hurricane Laura. The park took heavy damage during the storm. "There was 120-mph wind up in the park," reports say. Work fell behind.

Every now and then the Police Jury will authorize a drawdown, draining water from the lake through its dam in order to make repairs to the structure or to improve the embankments or even to stifle the hydrilla or another invasive aquatic species. Public meetings are held for every drawdown. The process can be pricey, but so was building Cotile Reservoir—1.7 million in the 1960s.

It was an investment, but not in fun. That was only a byproduct. Having a good place to fish and boat and swim, that's just a side effect. The impoundment is insurance against a drought. If one happens, the farmers around get the first five feet of water. That's the deal they struck in 1965.

In the year before the hurricane, the park had seen more visitors than it had in over twenty years.[23] Maybe it was because the largemouth bass that year were biting, hard. But maybe it had more to do with the pandemic. Maybe it was the rush of people aching to be out-of-doors.

On the day I nose my car through the entrance gate, it's ten months after Hurricane Laura. Uprooted trees still litter a good bit of the grounds and some buildings have missing shingles, but there's still a line to enter. I'm stuck behind a husband and wife in a bright white Ford. They're towing a red-and-black Skeeter, and there's no rush to get her in the water, or so it seems.

They have a long visit with the person manning the entrance station, long enough for me to sneak off. A cracked longleaf pine has transmogrified the Cotile Lake Entrance Sign into a pile of splinters, and I step over its broken pieces to run off to the Port-o-John near the gate. I can't wait. I make water, and hustle up, and then quickstep back only to wait in line some more. When it's finally my turn at the entrance station, I learn why.

Clifford Clark drove an ambulance for the State of Louisiana for twenty-seven years. During that time, he managed his way through the streets of New Orleans, Baton Rouge, Shreveport. Shreveport, he thinks, people always seem to forget about that place in Louisiana, but that's a good-sized city too, he tells me, and can be a hassle to navigate around. He's woven through Alexandria more times than anyone could count, and he's been down to Lake Charles. Sure he has, plenty of times. Now Clifford is retired, sort of. He's lucky enough to operate the entrance station at Cotile Recreational Park. It's almost a hobby, this part-time job.

"I bet you didn't even know you were in there," he tells me when I ask him about Hot Wells. I've interrupted his early lunch. On his desk, a barbeque burger squats on some wax paper and a bag of chips reclines nearby, but he doesn't mind. "I bet you couldn't even tell where the springs are," he says with a smile, offering me a cup of coffee from the pot on the counter.

He points out a 1930s refrigerator and stove combo hiding behind a stall. The contraption was used down at the Hot Wells resort a long time ago. Of course, everything there is closed now. Everything, like he says, is gone. The combo appliance is proof of that, but it's also evidence of the small things about the place that hang on.

I'm sure his sandwich is getting good and cold, but Clifford wants to talk about Hot Wells. It's a place worth chewing the fat about. His daddy worked the switchboard up at the resort back in the 50s. He remembers the little hotel where people could stay.

He tells me that if I head back into Hot Wells, take Bath House Road, then swing over to Alexander Street, I can look for the leaning hurricane fences and then the overgrown road and then the paint-flaking white building with the fallen-in porch. The resort's right there hutting up against the street. He means, that's where it was back then.

When Jorgensen wrote his book on Hot Wells, he visited many of the people who had ties to the place. One was the daughter of George Herring, the fellow who nicknamed himself the "million-dollar man" since he believed he could turn Hot Wells around. Herring worked on the drilling crew alongside Jordan and later bought a small hotel on the main street through town. But a hovel of a hotel wasn't George Herring's big idea. His scheme was to have the State of Louisiana purchase Hot Wells. He knew Governor Earl Long, and Earl "loved Hot Wells," loved the "mineral baths, steam room, and massages," sometimes bringing "political 'friends,' state troopers, and staffers along." Hot Wells was Earl's "pet project." Herring believed if the State purchased Hot Wells, they'd have the dough to fix the resort.

But things never worked out the way George imagined. Oh, the state purchased Hot Wells in 1936. The million dollars, though, never poured in like he thought.

Over the years, Hot Wells bounced around from one state agency to the next. In 1938, it landed in the hands of the Louisiana Department of Hospitals, who a month later leased it to the Alexandria Jaycees, and then in 1949, Hot Wells fell to the Louisiana Department of Institutions, which leased Hot Wells to the Jaycees again.

Hot Wells went back to the Department of Hospitals in 1956. Five years later, that agency tossed it to the Department of Commerce and Industry, which held onto to it for three years. In 1964, the State Tourist Development Commission grabbed control. That lasted twelve years.

The Department of State Parks caught the resort in 1977, but after trying and failing to open an aerobic center there and then seeing the main boiler blow and the well clog, in 1982 it batted control to the Department of Health and Human Resources. In 1985, responsibility fell to the Department of Public Safety and Corrections to run Hot Wells.

It became obvious the resort game was one no one wanted to play. In 1986, the final closure of the Hot Wells resort came, and two years later, the land and mineral wells transferred as surplus property to the Office of State Lands. From 1988 to 1995, the area was used by the Louisiana Department of Military as a training facility for the Louisiana National Guard.

I guess it was like George Herring's daughter Geneva told Jorgensen. There's a picture of her in his book. She's standing at Herring Road near her dad's little retirement home, one arm hanging onto the pole of a stop sign. "Hot Wells," she said when he interviewed her, "was the most amazing thing the state of Louisiana never knew it had."[24]

In part, it was the water itself that was the culprit. The constant maintenance of the pipes and wells always did cost money, but run-of-the-mill upkeep wasn't the only issue. Each time a new plan to reinvigorate the facilities appeared, the new owners soon found out how much repair costs they would need to eat. Nearly everything had to be redone. Hard-water scale constantly choked the boiler and ruined the bathhouse fixtures and crusted up the knobs of the doors. The corrosive mineral deposits even ate away the floors. All of that usually dashed any hope of new investors bringing Hot Wells back.

But some truths are hard to swallow. Take Clifford for instance. He never understood why the State did what it did in 2006. One morning, the dilapidated resort, hotel, spa, and swimming pool that stood at the top of the hill found bulldozers knocking at their doors. It could have been that the State considered the derelict buildings and covered wells on the property a danger to the public good, but no one really seems to know the exact reason, at least not here in Hot Wells. To locals, it's like what Clifford says, "For the life of me, I can't see why they tore that down. They could have made a ton of money on this place."

Back on the roads of Hot Wells, whith Clifford's help, I see what I missed, and why. Everywhere there's bushkiller vines and Chinese tallow. It's obviously been a while, but the tallows' trunks were once scrawny enough to weave their way into the hurricane fence lining the road. Now, those trunks have bulked up and cover long stretches of fence in a curtain.

But when I look close, and now that I know where to look, enough of the metal pokes through to tell me where so much of people's old dreams were laid. Here, west of Bath House Road and Alexander Street, the plans were set. Through the thicket, if I squint, I can see the past. It's easier if I close my eyes:

Running along Bath House Road, a dreamer lays out a good stretch of camping grounds. He puts it closest to the lake so campers can walk to the water by a small path through the woods—that is if the dreamer can get the people owning the land to agree to sell.

The dreamer surely can. He is the dreamer after all, and has a way of selling ideas to people.

And so the path gets cut and the way is made and wanderers leave the camp to walk down to a pier jutting into the water. There's a pavilion built there. It's rustic with open walls, but it's also a scenic spot overlooking the splendor of Cotile Lake. Some mornings the view leaves an onlooker breathless.

But the dreamer knows that beauty won't be enough to draw the crowds of his dreams. He'll need to build more, and does. A little north from the campgrounds, sets of motels go down, constructed in stages as more and more visitors arrive and their need grows.

Because of course, the people come. Of course, need grows. It always does because the word of something good spreads—always has, always will. The dreamer knows. Canoe dock, picnic area, a laundry center—in the scrub pine the edifices come alive. The lodge. The lounge. Hot Wells finally starts selling beer.

And ask anyone who comes, anyone who continues to come year after year—the furnishing here is brand new. The TVs are as modern as they come. Who says mineral baths aren't the draw they once were? Who says they hold no appeal to this new generation? The dreamer tells everyone to shake off that doubt the way you shake off a chill.

Right off the main road, some years down the line, the new aerobic and wellness center rises, gloriously. Its walls are white and clean. Its large windows let the full sun in. There's a bath house and conference center and restaurant and pool, but none of that, for privacy's sake, is too close to the entry gate. The dreamer knows not only what will make people come, but how to make them stay.

Once I open my eyes again, I think I find the old entry gate, that is if a small stretch of gravel whispers the truth about where things used to be. It's the ghost of a road appearing in the overgrown weeds and yaupon. There are a few skinny trunks of hackberry and eastern cottonwood, and beyond, air potato vines strangle everything. Still, not too far from me, I can see two tracks of ruined grass made where someone has driven before. It's proof. It's a sign. It's evidence that every now and then a few people still come out to see this has-been, this almost-was, this way-things-used-to-be resort town.

I find another trace of Hot Wells on the other side of the road. It's a faint impression just before Alexander Street curves into the blocks of Ryan and Swann and Johnson, but I think I see the driveway access for the well and pumps. It's only a guess.

The only remains of the resort I'm sure about are the privately owned buildings standing in town. Those I find on Alexander Street once I cross Bayou Cotile and make the curve into town. I missed them before. It took Clifford and a news clip I found online with my phone to point them out to me. It's the old Smith house, which is a two-story rectangle with a walk-out upper balcony and mirrored lower porch. Jorgensen says many former Hot Wells residents claim it was an old brothel more than a home. Behind it, a half a block west down Johnson Street stands what's been made of the Hot Wells Hotel. It's a red, wooden two-story house chopped up into three apartments. Pat Schmitt, the contractor who bought the two buildings in 2003, lives in a mobile home behind the hotel.

The final building I find I'm less sure about. I want to believe it's Nora Shaw's grocery. It's across the road from the Smith home and looks like the Shaw building from the old photographs. There's what appears to be the telltale pitched roof and the familiar benches beneath its two front windows.

Larry Jorgensen calls all these abandoned houses ghosts. I guess they can seem like that—entities pretending to inhabit a past that's not really here, but not really gone.

Every couple of years someone shows up with a new idea wadded up in their hands to restore Hot Wells. Once it was Cajun singer Jay Chevalier, who sang about everything from Huey Long to that "mighty man" Marc Eliché. Once it was Earl Long. There was an owner of a health company. There was a Florida businessman. There were foreign investors too. There's been two separate firms from Lafayette, which might as well be another country. There's been the state park idea and the state tax on soda pop plan. For Hot Wells, there's always, it seems, a big pile of "almosts." It's like former Treasurer of Rapides Parish Police Jury Tim Ware said, "There were a lot of lookers, but no takers."

The most recent looker came around in 2017. In August, Ritchie Capital Management and Price Co Development bought Hot Wells at a state auction for $119,000. "It's a gorgeous piece of property," said Matt Ritchie, owner of Ritchie Capital Management. "Obviously, there's a lot of history there. . . . We see some potential there." After being dormant for nearly thirty years, Hot Wells seemed to be gushing again with new life.

Ritchie and the new owners felt like they had two ways to go with Hot Wells. Option one—find someone to restore and recreate the spa and wellness resort to take the place back to its original use. Option two—subdivide the land and create a residential development.

But then came the *almost*, the one small thing that clogged the pipedream—no one quite knew who owned the rights to the underground waters. The new owners were "researching that." In 2017, they hadn't yet dug up "an answer."[25]

The hope of Hot Wells, to me, is like a lot of ghosts. I guess, it's like a lot of things. It's not that I don't believe. It's that I can't make myself *not believe*. What I mean is, when I try to imagine Hot Wells turning from being a ghost into something real, there's an *almost* every time as something always makes me doubt that it could be true.

If I'm being honest, it's the same way with Charlene Richard, the little saint who's not one, officially, and maybe never will be. I know that during COVID people were turning to the little black-haired Cajun saint. I know they were visiting that flesh-colored church surrounded by blindingly green rice fields. I know that during certain times of the year those fields are flooded in water in the same way faith covers these people's lives, in the same way it blankets my mother's daily routine. I know people are sitting by her marble-white grave. I know they're leaving little handwritten notes for her. I know that in 2020 in the middle of January, the Bishop of Lafayette Diocese officially opened up Charlene's cause again. The information was sent to the Vatican later that year, but by April and May COVID halted all papal reviews. In July, due to COVID-19, Saint Edward Church in Richard also decided to cancel the Annual Mass of Petition for Charlene Marie Richard. They settled for arranging and promoting a garage sale to raise money for the cause whenever it could be resumed.

Charlene's case was resumed in 2021. Even after the hurricanes hit all of southwestern Louisiana, the "consideration" continued, but that's all it was—an almost, a hope, a dream. In fact, the cause for Charlene's sainthood is still being "advanced." That's the word people use. In November of 2021, The US Conference of Catholic Bishops voted to *advance* Charlene's cause for beatification and canonization. The Vatican has it now, but that process might take years, or even a generation.

In the meantime, it won't be the believing I'll find so difficult. It'll be staving off the doubt. And not with just Charlene. I'll ask myself if I believe ghost towns can make a comeback. I'll ask myself if ghosts come back too. And if so, where they might be. I'll wonder if they're in my office building, right there near the ghost lines. I'll ask myself if I believe in that too—my building coming back, the campus being like it used to be, even a little. But mostly I'll search for answers to my questions about healing and places and water. I'll ask myself if I believe in all three swirling together. I'll ask myself if I believe in Louisiana.

A week or two after a visit to Hot Wells and Charlene's grave, I make another one. This time it's with my wife and my youngest daughter Jules. It's Sunday and I'm grasping in the dark. My house is still damaged. Contractors are still ghosting me. At work, the campus is like a ghost town. Between the hurricanes and the pandemic, most of the students haven't come back. Many of the professors haven't either, and it's my job to call them and try to give them faith, give them hope. "Things are getting back to normal," I'm supposed to say. "We gotta have faith that if we do our job, it'll all work out some way." The trip to Richard is meant to be a break from all that, a getaway now that the hurricanes have made money thin.

It's not a religious experience, but it feels good just to drive, to creep out of Lake Charles as a family for a while. After only thirty miles east, the sides of the roads lose their piles of debris, and the trees don't look so sick anymore. The roofs don't have tarps nailed on. The disasters, in a way, seem gone. By the time we get to Richard, there's nothing going on, and that feels good.

Inside St. Edward's we all sit down. The church is rustic, with a very brown interior. The ceiling's made up of finished planks of dark umber wood, and light penny tile covers all the floors. The wooden pews are sienna, and since their cushions have been removed for the pandemic, their curves seem browner somehow, and hollower. Every word someone utters rattles in the exposed wooden rafters running along the ceiling. When the priest speaks, "Amen," it clatters above us.

After the service, my family walks over to Charlene's grave. I want Jules to see it—I guess for the same reason I wanted her to see Poverty Point or churches in Ireland or Trevi Fountain or Disneyworld. Isn't there a power in the products of belief even if you don't know where your own belief falls? It's the same reason that I brought her to tiny St. Jules Church when she was a little girl.

St. Jules sits in the little town of Tee Mamou, Louisiana, the place where many of my aunts and uncles and cousins are from, the place many still call home.

St. Jules was closed that late Tuesday afternoon we stopped, so we didn't go inside. I had figured as much, but it didn't matter. I wanted her to see this place that carries her name—Jules, a family name, a boy's name to them, five or six generations of uncles and grandfathers, of great-, great-great-relatives.

I remember one of my brothers called me when he heard that I planned on naming her Jules Wava LeJeune. He was worried. "You don't want her to grow up to be too manly," he told me over the phone. And Wava? That was a clumsy thing to do, he thought, hobbling all her days with such an old-fashioned, unpleasant, maybe even ugly sound. "Yeah, we all loved Aunt Wava," he groaned, "but Wava doesn't sound very graceful." It was his way of helping, I guess.

My daughter turned out to be a dancer. As a high school sophomore, she was slated to be Sleeping Beauty in the Lake Charles Civic Ballet's production of it. It was rare that a sophomore landed that kind of role. "She's good," the circumspect choreographer told me one day. There were lifts and turns and whole stretches of the show where the light was meant to follow her. A small thing as dreams go, I guess, but it would do for us, for her, for a time.

It was a Friday when we heard the news that the production of *Sleeping Beauty* that was scheduled to open that next Saturday was cancelled. The State had shut down all indoor gatherings. When it first began, the pandemic was worse in Louisiana, in New Orleans, in Lake Charles, than in many places around the country.

In the summer, before school started, her studio started dancing on Zoom again. *Sleeping Beauty* had been pushed back to Christmas. Some of us thought it would be spring 2021 before audiences would be able to gather again, but it was something to wait for, something for which to hold out hope.

I think her dance studio opened for two weeks before Hurricane Laura came and ripped off the roof. For a long time after the storms, most of the other dance studios in town were closed. For months and months and months, no one in town was dancing. For Jules, it would be longer.

The ballet director's house was damaged, and she moved. We found out in November of 2020 the move was probably permanent. It was maybe the following January or February when one of the other dance teachers beat the bushes for a new place to rehearse. Dance dropped to twice a week for an hour or two. There would be no performances, no shows.

Even now, the ballerinas show up, try to stay in shape, go home, come back the next Tuesday or Thursday to practice again, and then go home.

Some days when Jules makes it back after practice I ask her if she wants to leave her "studio" and find something else. I ask her if she wants us to try to find a place out of town, a place maybe we could drive to once or twice a month. But the questions never go anywhere. Some mornings over breakfast, I ask her instead if she misses it, or I used to.

I've learned it's hard for a teenager to answer something like that. Maybe it's the question. Maybe it's the morning that makes her quiet. Maybe the silence would happen to anyone.

Some mornings I wake up with a dream from the night before. Sometimes it's of my wife and the talks we've had. Sometimes it's the face of another woman. The dream-woman's face is nearly my wife's face, almost always her soil-brown eyes and her thick lips, but it's never quite a face I recognize. Sometimes a more youthful face is there, sometimes an older one, but the difference is that in those dreams, the woman looks back at me new each time. We're talking, you see, and it's that she hasn't heard all my stories a hundred times before, a thousand. In the dream, I'm telling her what's happened for the very first time and she's looking at me differently somehow.

Sometimes, though, it's not my wife's face or the dream woman's, but it's one of my daughters looking back at me. Her face is always her own, but maybe always younger than I know it to be when I'm awake, and in the dream, my daughter is staring at me. No one else is around. We're on a boat in the heart of a silent lake, or we're sitting at a picnic table set up in the clearing of a woods, or we're outside in a yard that runs as wide and as far as a field. It's different every time, but we're always alone, me and her or me and her and her sister, and nothing is there to bother us. Every drop of her attention is mine, and my words come out as clean and straight as a casted fishing line or as solid and weighty as a nice-sized skipping stone. It's a good talk. There's time. I'm listening to her, and she's hearing every word of what I want to say. There are places, we both say, we want to go. There are places we think that are worth stopping for. There are places we want to leave, we agree. There are places, we believe, we want to stay.

8

LAND IN THE SLOW MAKING

I save up all my honey-dos and odd jobs and mister fix-it repairs for the three weeks of breathing space I have between the spring and summer semesters. I want to "get back to normal." I want to "come back" after the hurricane. I want to do what the spray paint on the plywood covering the broken windows around town tells me to do: "Stay strong. Louisiana strong. Cajun strong." Yes indeed, I want to "come back better."

I roll up my sleeves and lace my boots nice and tight and I'm just all set to make my house something not to be ashamed of when the neighbors walk by. I'm laser-focused on stopping the water oozing through the cracked siding. I'm zeroed-in on getting the insulation back in the walls. I got my action plan. I'm 100 percent committed to making the living room livable again. There's only the last tidying-up of schoolwork to do, and then I can hit the ground running.

I do commencement and then grades and then grade appeals and then it's the last Friday of work. It's game time now. It's crunch time. I'm rarin' to make my home feel like home again. Let's role. It's go time.

But on Saturday one of the people leaving town needs a little help packing the U-Haul, and on Sunday, I find out someone didn't quite finish a report. A meeting about English Education majors who've fallen through the cracks because of the storms eats up the Monday morning and then a process-mapping conference on bureaucratic inefficiencies swallows the afternoon . . . and that Tuesday too . . . and also the Wednesday because it's never enough. On Thursday, once the efficiency consultant's gone, the ad hoc committee chair calls a recap meeting for 10:00 a.m. Friday and the weekend are gobbled up by the three thousand mold-ruined books at my wife's high school library that need to be boxed up and hauled away.

Apartment-hunting for the here-a-year professor who lost his rental house during the storms and sat stuck out west somewhere . . . moving around office furniture because maintenance is so short-staffed . . . fixing the desks broken during the semester because every dollar helps . . . using the hours after work to wait on the contractor who promised he would show to do an estimate . . . calling around to find another one when he doesn't . . . and one, two, three, four days of the next week are gone.

And then a flashflood hits Lake Charles. It's more rain than the city has seen in fifty years. A hundred. Add to that all the new subdivision developments south of town that didn't need a drainage plan. Add to that the city's already outdated drainage system of sewers and bayous and rivers. Don't forget the storm debris still around which makes bad things worse.

It's not much of a surprise when the basement of my building at work takes on ten feet of water. It's no surprise when all the "free time" I have left goes to dealing with the comeback after that flood.

But self-care is what they call it. Even when the administration at work is screaming for your attention and the building's electrical is shot and the elevator machinery in the basement spills its guts. Even when you know for weeks, for months, you'll have no office to work out of and no classrooms to teach in. Even in the face of all that, they say you ought to get away, even if it's just for a long weekend, even if it's for a church retreat, which with its lectures on spirituality and group-sharing sessions and personal conferences with priests feels like a working weekend. But it's self-care, they say, and so you do that retreat. And for another weekend, your house gets no closer to becoming a home after being partly destroyed.

"God loves me anyway" seems to be the takeaway from the retreat leader's talks. "Even with all the sin I have, even with all my shortcomings, God looks at me but finds a way to love me anyhow." It's a silent retreat so there's plenty of space to ask myself why I keep setting myself up for this.

But there are moments when an early morning walk in utter silence reminds me how transitory this weekend is, or any other, or any hour I have planned a certain way. That evening I sleep deep and the next day, I use a fifteen-minute chunk of nonsilence on a one-on-one session with a priest. The advice I get from him is a quote from Yogi Berra. "If you see a fork in the road," he says, "take it." It's as good as anything I've got to move forward with.

So I don't cancel the camping excursion I have planned for the following weekend, even though four days before I'm meant to be headed out of town, the flood has me packing my office into boxes again and plopping my computer into a bin to wheel its machinery across the quad. The brick sidewalks make the wobbly library cart dislodge my computer's hard drive, IT lets me know, so for the rest of the summer I'll have to hop on the computer in the general workroom when there's not a line, which is just as well since my new office is a closet crammed with a desk. Not a metaphorical one. A literal one. The door has to be kept kicked open so the phone cord is able to run across the floor.

And I don't cancel for a second time, when three days before the trip I find out that other people in my department won't have use of their offices over the summer and it's my job to hunt out any extra space around campus and oversee the move.

And because of self-care, when two days before I'm supposed to leave, I hear my aunt Charlesa has died, I don't cancel for the third time. "You're going to hate me," I text my two camping buddies and just to twist the knife, I let those words sit a while without a follow-up. It's childish, I know, but I guess I'm casting lines out into the dark. Maybe someone will understand all that I'm leaving unsaid.

It's just that it's impossible to explain it all, but I want someone to know, but without the pity, so for one last time, I don't cancel after one of my friends texts back, "What's up?"

"I'm going to have to ditch you Saturday morning for an hour or two because I have a funeral to go to in the next town over from where we're camping," I text back, and it's sort of like self-care because it's killing two birds with one stone.

What I'm trying to say is that it's a long story, I guess, why I keep going at this and don't cancel everything. And I know I've overcomplicated it, but it's a story with a lot of pieces, or is to me. It's a story, I'd guess I'd say, with a lot of stories.

The first one is the story of the day my aunt Charlesa was born. It's the closest thing my family has to a miracle. My dad was born about eighteen months after her, but even he would tell the story of how Charlesa came into the world as if he was there to witness it.

My aunt Charlesa's nickname was Cricket, and my dad would always start his story with how they always called her that, but then he'd say that her real middle name was Hope. That was an important part of the story too, because when the midwife handed Charlesa to my grandmother in that little farmhouse in Egan, she announced to the room that the baby probably wouldn't live. She tsked and shook her head and decided that the family probably wouldn't have more than a few hours with Charlesa. Maybe a day. At most two. She warned everyone to do what they could with the time they had.

Nearly two months premature, Charlesa was so small, they say, my grandmother slept her in a shoebox to keep her close, to worry over her. And everyone was worried. A tiny cold thing with see-through skin and frail as an eggshell, Charlesa's cries were like a faint song of an insect filling the house, like the palest, softest song of a cricket.

But my family hoped too. And I guess had hope in Aunt Wava, who was there and practically a nurse by then. Family legend says Charlesa stayed alive in a shoebox because of that. Aunt Wava had the know-how to build something from scratch to save the baby.

So I don't cancel. Because of that story, I don't feel like I can.

"Don't overcomplicate it"—that's key to self-care, they say, and it isn't complicated. Aunt Charlesa's funeral is going to fall on the very same Saturday we chose for the camping trip months before. It was the only weekend all three of us had free. The services will be in Covington, not more than twenty minutes from where we've planned on setting the tent, a state park north of Lake Pontchartrain because it was a close drive for the guy in Mississippi. A quick weekend camping trip was supposed to be easy, simple. "It still could be," I tell myself. "It should be easy. Life should. It is if I don't overcomplicate it." So I don't cancel. Besides, we picked a camping spot not so much for the woods but to see the ruins of a plantation turned into a state park and the site of an ancient village along a bayou and the remnants of a fort left on a long-standing waterway, and it felt like I needed to resee how some places are older than others and have always been a home for someone.

I mean, isn't that what self-care is? Giving yourself a break from normal. Giving yourself a chance to deviate from the daily routine. When the everyday drive is blue tarps and snapped tree trunks and piles of sheetrock and shingles by the road, isn't self-care driving until it all disappears? Isn't it taking the fork in the road? It doesn't matter if you don't know which path to go. You run away from home because home is debris, and the very sight of it, of home, is a burden.

Isn't that what people mean when they say self-care? It's the small traumas. It's the stress of making reservations. It's the chore of packing. It's the worry about spending money on a vacation now that money's so short. It's loading up the camping gear. It's gassing up the car. It's three hours of driving to a lake that's not a lake, but an estuary. It's the traffic. It's anything that makes you shift focus from the damage of the storms, the damage to yourself. It's self-care. It's radio static. It's June. It's how it steams inside my car. It's the A/C freezing up sometimes. It's being in a stand-still when that happens so rolling the windows down is pointless. It's worse. It's a stand-still on the Atchafalaya Basin Swamp Expressway. *Atcha* is Choctaw for river and *Falaya* means long, and the expressway is that. In fact, it's the third longest bridge in the US, fourteenth in the world, and once you're on it, there's no way off. Isn't that what self-care means in Louisiana?

"Here is a fringe of a continent, land in the slow making," Harnett T. Kane writes in *Bayous of Louisiana*.[1] Were truer words ever spoken about my home? No place seems slower to change than Louisiana does. No place feels as far-flung from progress. Ask Willie Stark if cut corners and kickbacks aren't common sights in the schoolhouse. Ask Jane Pittman how long some Louisiana journeys take. Ask Binx, and he'll say that even when you're doing something normal like going to the movies or settling for the sad little happinesses of drinks and a date and a good pocket-sized coupe, even then living in the Bayou State can feel like you're going nowhere but in circles.

"Peculiar to its place, the bayou is the product of an oversupply of water pouring over a yielding soil, seeking and finding many courses toward a lower level," Kane writes. "Slow, serene, a bayou has no rush and scourging passage." I just nod my head. I don't see how else you could describe life here—never in a hurry to change, calm about the whatever in somewhere that's falling down. Because nothing is as oversupplied as Louisiana. Just come and sit here on an August afternoon after a rain when even the St. Augustine starts steaming. See if you don't feel overprovided with sticky heat, overly oppressed, overwhelmed, overloaded.

There's also so much life here . . . in Louisiana, in the bayous. Freshwater, saltwater, or brackish, the water of a creeping bayou teems. From tiny duckweed to mammoth cypress trees, plant life booms near a bayou. Alligators, of course, but also snakes, shrimp, crawfish, egrets, herons, all manner of birds really, raccoons, even deer call the sluggishness of bayous home. And don't forget fish. Louisiana has more than three million acres of bayous, including Bayou Bartholomew, which is the longest bayou in the world. In it alone more than one hundred species of fish swim, spawn, fin, thrive, get chunks eaten out of them, die—their rot feeding countless other forms of life. Because in a bayou, it's all abundance. And Louisiana is cramped with these bodies of water, oversupplied with them, like a too-big family in a mobile home.

It's a tight-knit ecosystem—these Louisiana bayous. It's a "lacework out of land," Kane says, "a webwork that's a lifeline for Louisiana residents." They never dry up. They offer a steady current. The course of their life is "curving, twisting, curling back on their own curves . . . splitting and resplitting." "Branching to meet others," they connect and reconnect all those living along them.

But despite the bounty and beauty Kane discovered, he also noted the bayou's characteristically strange and befuddling nature. The waterway, he thought, embodied a mindset. *Bayou* is a Choctaw word. It means small creek, but "its philosophy is in . . . the agreeable life," Kane explains, and for him, that's enough to make it seem peculiar. Maybe, he wonders, Louisiana feels the way it does because of the way the water flows in its basins and bayous.

He's not done, though. He lists the other reasons a bayou confounds us. One is that "few know the secrets of their cobweb meshes of water lines," which could be applied to the workings of Louisiana too. A second is that "only one who had spent years in tracing and retracing their patterns could be expected to find his way about them," which also seems true about Louisiana. But the biggest reason appears to be that Louisiana is a "place that seems often unable to make up its mind whether it will be earth or water, and so it compromises."

That, I know. Louisiana is all about compromising. It's about tradeoffs and handshakes and winks and nods and working out a deal, like negotiating what

I'm willing to put up with to live here. It's about agreeing to stick around and wait and see, even though maybe I shouldn't. It's about toleration. It's about tolerating. It's about having the knack to grin and bear it. I guess, it appears to be just like Kane says it is. A bayou creeps the way Louisiana creeps, thinks serenely what Louisiana serenely thinks, embraces what Louisiana embraces—being accommodating, taking your time, strangeness, oversupply, slow meals, long waits in parade lines, languorous afternoons under the oaks both subtle and marine.

My wait on the Atchafalaya Basin is long. Traffic's slow. And it's hot. But it doesn't take much brainwork for me to thank the stars for one lucky thing about the trip—it's that my pal Jack is sitting shotgun. He's checking his phone to see how long we'll be idling in the middle of the basin bridge without escape because once you're stuck on that span of cement, there's no place to go. There are no exit ramps, no alternate routes, no off-roads. It's just a slow sit surrounded by a nowhere.

But the nowhere is dying. Simply ask the traditional crawfishermen working the basin. The drilling companies have built berms and oil-drilling islands and cut ditches that run east-west that stop the water's flow, stop its churn around curves that aerates the water, which means everything is dying—the fish, the crawfish, the plants. And the crawfishermen are being arrested for trespassing on open waters because the companies want to own all the land, and the water too. The only thing to do then is to imagine a Louisiana without crawfish, and then dream what I'm going to do to fix it.

Then the traffic breaks, and after a bit of jockeying, Jack and I find spots in the fast lane. In no time, we're beyond the basin and Baton Rouge and even the insterstate. It's enough to make my head spin—how quickly we can leave all the gummed-up traffic behind, how quickly we can leave everything behind until we're spiriting along the upper rim of Lake Pontchartrain, my Rogue slicing through patches of longleaf pines, our tongues tying in knots. It's Tickfaw and Natalbany and Tangipahoa and Tchefuncte and Ponchatoula and Bogalusa. It's Chinchuba. It happened just that fast. In the blink of an eye, Jack and I find ourselves lost in the land of Choctaw place names.

In 1868, Horatio Bardwell Cushman visited the Texas Choctaws. He marveled at that people's ability to navigate. He was amazed that Choctaws could travel great distances without becoming lost and could reunite with one another without the use of drawn maps or any writing. "Whenever a small hunting party moved camp, they left a broken bush with the top leaning in the direction they had gone," Cushman wrote. "If a wandering-hunter happened to stumble upon the late deserted camp and desired to join its former occupants, the broken but silent bush gave him the information as to the direction they had gone."[2]

But more than this, Cushman envied the totality of their knowledge of the landscape and their connection to it. "Nearly every river, creek, lake, rock, hill and vale was endeared to them, by a name given to it from some peculiarity, some incident, or adventure of the past," Cushman gushed. "Nature's rocks, mountains, hills, dells, woods, and waters" embodied "the remembrance of the heroic achievements of a long line of ancestry.... Every piece of the landscape, every site they named, existed both as a physical landscape and as a marker of history, a piece of their shared memory."

It's in the names. When someone said the place name "Tangipahoa," they said a word that translated to "ear of corn" or "those who gather corn," but they meant the specific people who lived there and the history of that place and the landscape itself. Some people call this "remembering forward" because the past isn't only a single event that happened or even a singular record of that history, but a shared remembering of individual experiences strung together so that the present is an amalgamation of everyone's past. The corn, the harvesting, the Acolapissa people, everyone's memories, the future—it's all Tangipahoa.

Ironically, that mode of thought is the way to get lost. You look down. Things swirl around. You look up. Everything looks the same. Where you've been disappears. Where you're going, you don't know for sure. Where you are has no clear markers or boundaries or limits.

It happens to me and Jack. From Lonesome Road out west on 190, past the Beau Chene Country Club, all the way to Fairview Riverside State Park—it's all Chinchuba. But you wouldn't know it.

Chinchuba is a place without an official name. It's an unincorporated community—a place made up of brick homes with three-car garages and beige condos and strip-mall businesses. It's tucked-away subdivisions and gated communities complete with security stations playing make-believe at being a town. But there are no signs, not clear ones. We don't quite know when we're there, and when we are, we don't know exactly where we are. Maybe we think we're still in Mandeville. Maybe we find our way by accident. But we only know for sure we're where we're supposed to be when we see Fairview Riverside State Park sitting on the beautiful Tchefuncte River and turn in. It's part of Chinchuba too, a Choctaw name that means alligator. It's all Chinchuba.

Fairview Riverside State Park is like a miniature suburb. To drive through the park's series of roads, Jack and I loop and circle and cul-de-sac and dead-end just like we're driving around the ubiquity of a subdivision.

Nearly every slot is stuffed with a camper, an RV, or a travel trailer hitched to the back of a diesel pickup, and each one has dragged along everything that looks like home: motorcycles, ice chests, lawn chairs, bug zappers, pet dogs, picnic tables, propane tanks, barbeque pits and burners, golf carts, insect nets, flags and flag poles, TV antennas and satellite boxes, little iron fences that mark off the rectangle outside the camper's door, and rollout indoor/outdoor carpet to cover it with, and every sort of light imaginable.

But Jack and I are doing just the opposite. We've brought not much more than a tent and a camping hammock, and when we finally make the big sweep along the park's curvy road to find the patch of empty lawn designated as the tent camping sites, we discover the area's empty.

Jack strings up his hanging bed, I spread out my rust-and-tan two-person tent, and in no time the two of us are scrounging around for firewood. First, we tramp into a nearby palmetto stand until the deerflies escort us out; then we cross a small gravel road that separates the tent sites from a playground. There, we find a heap of storm-fallen pine branches bulldozed into a pile and for some idiotic reason choose a log so heavy that it takes both of us to lug it back to the soon-to-be fire.

With one hand each, we grab the beast, and with our free hand, we swat deer flies from our nostrils, the corners of eyes, our earholes. To Jack, this becomes a dance . . . legs moshing up and down, arms and elbows flailing, hands raving around his head. I join in.

The dance ends back at the iron fire ring. I start hacking branches while Jack fiddles with the kindling, and in short order, a glowing fire brings a second job. From our chairs, we toss logs to burn.

But sometimes it's hard to sit still, even by a good-going fire. You can start staring at the flames. You can start thinking.

To build a fire is to build a house, I grouse . . . in some ways. For starters, there's the foundation that can go wrong. It needs to be stacked right. And too many logs can suffocate a fire just like you can have too much house so that you can't come up for any air. You can have too many pockets in a fire to poke at too. You can have too many rooms. You can mess with a fire too much. You can try to fix a fire to death.

They say Chinchuba and Mandeville and really all of the Northshore is like a room for residents of New Orleans. People call it a bedroom community since everyone works in New Orleans but sleeps here.

My own bedroom growing up was always full of people. We had six boys in one room, all of us sleeping in two sets of triple bunkbeds—a top bunk, a bottom one, and a trundle bed on wheels that slid out from the bottom bunk when it was time for bed. I'm the baby of my family. My bed was the in-and-out trundle.

Sometimes, while I was sleeping my brothers would kneel down in the dark and shove my bed under the bottom bunk while I was still lying there. They called it playing "buried alive," and the first couple of times I panicked, but then I learned if I quit squirming, they lost interest. Sure, it took some time and some practice, but I taught myself to make it convincing—how to hunker down, breathe slow, say goodbye to the world outside your new grave, act like you might as well be dead. It's funny how things work out. That's also a pretty good strategy when a hurricane comes. Now that I think about it, it might be the only workable strategy for calling Louisiana home.

It's good to get up from a fire sometimes. It's good to walk around. And here, the only thing to keep my legs busy is taking whacks at the big log, so I stand, stretch out the knee aches, then start with the hatchet and the hacking.

I stop when in the middle of my swinging, a state park agent on an ATV Rhino whizzes up. Clipped cedar branches stack in the carryall bed. He waves. We wave. Then he kills the engine.

Once the puttering stops, he asks us if we could use firewood, that way we wouldn't have to kill ourselves with all that hacking.

"Sure," we say.

"I'll be right back," he goes, "just let me unload this," and zips off to a taped-off section of the park. Later I find out a film company turning the book *Where the Crawdads Sing* into a movie has rented out that section. After about twenty minutes, he pulls up again with the carryall full of wood scrap and waste-cuts of boards left over from a repair project he's just finished. "It's untreated," he says.

Park agent Grayhawk Perkins is part Choctaw, part Houma, he tells us, and when we ask him what's good for keeping away deerflies, it's not a simple question. It's an uncorking of a whole conversation.

Grayhawk has done a lot of things, and knows a lot of things, but he's best at being a good talker. My wife's people might say, "He's never met a stranger." My family might say, "I had a good visit with so-and-so today. So-and-so, he's good company. He makes for good company." That's what my dad might've called that. It's a skill, I think. A gift.

We find out Grayhawk knows Lake Charles well. He's been there several times and has even visited the school where I teach. He's put on programs at several colleges around, even at Jazz Fest. He's given talks on traditional healing practices with plants and demonstrated the traditional drum playing and once even recreated a long march for a documentary. The re-creation was faithful, all traditional—the wagon train, the scouts on horseback, the foodstuffs, the tack. Actually, he's been in several movies, he tells us, like *Last of the Mohicans*, when he almost throttled a kid who was too careless to learn how to shoot blanks.

Grayhawk's not only a park agent. He has a day job too. He's a fourth-grade teacher. The park's a side gig, something to stay busy, something to meet people. He's better than sixty now, and over the years, he has met tons and tons of people, he says, all kinds. He enjoys talking to them, helping them when he can. For instance, for deerflies, he tells us the smoke of green clippings of cedar or cypress branches laid on the coals of a good fire works well.

When he leaves, Jack and I hurry around to break off enough green cypress branches to smoke a fire all night. There's nothing much else to do anyway. It's getting dusk and we're on wait for our third, a friend of mine named Kevin.

I met Kevin when he lived in Louisiana for a while. We talk at least twice a week, but I haven't seen him in over four years. The last time was at his wedding at a state park in Arkansas where my job was to uncap a homemade wooden ring box his grandfather carved and shellacked. A Tennessean originally, Kevin now lives in Mississippi, working at a university where he advises Freshman to think for a second about what they'll do with the rest of their lives. It's a job that has him working till five every Friday, and so he doesn't leave Hattiesburg until 5:30. The hour and a half drive from Mississippi to Fairview Park takes him nearly twice that. When he finally arrives, he and Jack hit it off, just like I thought they would.

If Jack is a puckish roamer of the woods, Kevin is the forest itself come to life, a copse of yews moving slowly across a plain, maybe a coppice of firs moving against a castle. He's tall, lanky. His legs are like cypress knees, his arms a willow trunk that tells you how high a flood can rise. His face is the wonder of Spanish moss and how it stays alive. His heart's a shovelful of good dirt. He's pesky when he's talking about something he cares about, like how an old word should sound or which verb to use to describe what a branch might be doing when it's yawing upwards or how a good parent ought to make their kid stare at a tree for an hour at the slightest chance the child might see something new to them—like a parade of carpenter ants or the whorls that make bark what it is or even something they imagine being there but isn't, which is what the three of us talk about that night until we fall asleep.

It's the stuff of nightmares but the waking kind—the stories of supernatural beings the Choctaw tell. Their beings of shadow who live in shadowy places, like *Na Losa Chitto* or "Big Black Thing," which is deadly and "inhuman-like" and haunts remote portions of the woods or roads at the edge of town or any out-of-the-way places—it's the stuff that'll keep you awake.[3] There's *Hoklonote'she*, who is malevolent, able to shapeshift, adept at mimicking animal noises, and known to frequent far-off places in the thick forest. There's *Hashok Okwa Hui'ga* (grass water drop), who is a "small ball of fire that may be seen moving about, a short distance above the surface of the water" and lives in "marshy places—often along the edges of swamps." Any person "must immediately turn away and not look at it, otherwise she or he will certainly become lost and not arrive at their destination that night, but instead, travel in a circle." There's *Kashehotapalo*, who is "neither man nor beast" but instead has body and legs like a human and feet like a deer. His "head is small and his face shriveled and evil to look upon," and people call him *Kashehotapalo* because the noise he makes sounds like "the cry of a woman." He lives in "low, swampy places, away from the habitations of men," and of all the things he loves, he loves most to torment hunters. When they "go near his abiding place, he quietly slips up behind them and calls loudly, then turns and runs swiftly away."

And finally there's *Nalusa Falaya*, or "The Long Evil Being," the most famous and deadliest of these creatures roaming lost places. Nalusa Falaya is "about the size of a man and walks upright." Its "face is shriveled; its eyes are very small; it has quite long, pointed ears. Its nose is likewise long. It lives in the densest woods, near swamps." Nalusa Falaya . . . the Long Evil Being . . . the Long Black Being . . . the Shadow Being—if it's not shadow itself, the shadows are its haunts. It preys upon children turned around in the woods and hunters "far from their homes, late in the day when shadows have grown long beneath the pine trees." Then, "a Nalusa Falaya will come forth."

In 1908, an eager, outdoorsy, educated but never-formally-trained anthropologist traveled to the breezy north shore of Lake Pontchartrain to interview the Choctaw people living there. He wanted to capture their stories and document their culture. His name was David I. Bushnell.[4] Practically still muddy from an excavation of peat bogs in Switzerland, Bushnell lived in the Crescent City but made "frequent visits . . . to the few Choctaw still living near Bayou Lacombe" on the Northshore. He spent most of his time excavating the mounds he found there, but he also transcribed several of the stories the Choctaw shared with him.

"The oldest member of this small band is a woman, Pisatuntema," Bushnell wrote in his collection. "She is about fifty years of age, the daughter of one of the principal men of the last generation, who, at the time of his death some years ago, was recognized as a chief." Pisatuntema learned many of the ancient tribal myths and legends from her father and led most of the storytelling Bushnell witnessed. "Often, however," Bushnell explained, "while telling the legends, she would be interrupted by others who would suggest or add certain details; but all were familiar with the subjects and at no time did they differ on any essential points."

Bushnell heard animal tales and hunting stories and one story about a Choctaw girl who meets the Devil and is taken to a cave to be killed. Through the help of a frog, she escapes and tricks the devil to climb into a boat she sinks to the bottom of the bayou. The anthropologist also heard a creation story and the long story of two brothers who chase the sun to see where it dies and many, many stories about encounters with supernatural beings. "The dense swamps and forests surrounding the homes of the Choctaw were regarded by them as the haunts of mysterious beings," Bushnell related, "to whom they attributed any injury that befell their hunters while away from home."

Nalusa Falaya—Pisatuntema told Bushnell a great deal about that being. She explained that it has "many children which, when quite young, possess . . . the power of removing their viscera." At night, these children "in this lightened condition . . . become rather small, luminous bodies that may often be seen, along the borders of marshes." She also described how Nalusa Falaya itself waits until it spies a careless hunter who has recklessly drifted far out into the woods or has treated the land thoughtlessly and then "calls in a voice resembling a man." The hunter turns, lays eyes upon Nalusa Falaya, falls to the ground, then becomes unconscious. That's when Nalusa Falaya "sticks a small thorn into his hand or foot, and by so doing bewitches the hunter and transmits to him the power of doing evil to others."

In the late 1990s, anthropologist Tom Mould traveled to Mississippi to collect the narratives of the Mississippi Band of Choctaw Indians. One of the people he talked to was Terry Ben, a former history teacher who at that time was acting superintendent of the Choctaw School system. "I remember one unique story that my grandfather used to tell over and over in the early days, as far as when he was hunting," Terry Ben told Mould. "Toward Jackson, the Pearl River gets wider and wider as it goes to the Ross Barnett Reservoir. The swamp, also in that area, is big even now; it's a big swampy area. And I guess in the past, at some point, they would go hunting there and they'd be just miles and miles away from the nearest house or cabin."

It was around the 1930s, maybe the 1920s or the 1940s. It's hard to pin down the past, but "during that time period, there was a unique creature who supposedly lived way in the swamp . . . a manlike creature that had a tail," Terry explained, and although he couldn't quite remember the name of the creature, he knew that it was familiar to his grandfather and to the men he hunted with, to everyone, really. It lived in "the swamp area where the campfire light was . . . where they were sleeping" and would "come to the edge of the light."[5]

But it's obvious, isn't it, the whole point of these stories? It's clear that it's not over. It's not in the past. In these hunting stories told by hunters, hunters are the main characters, and while the hunting trips may have happened a long time ago, what makes them unique is that they aren't stuck in that time ago. They're a gateway to it. They're the edge of where someone's former encounter opens into someone's recent run-in. The woods are the woods are the woods. It's all Chinchuba. It's all one big black thing. As captain of operations for the Choctaw Police Department Harold Comby tells Tom Mould, "The *na losa chitto* of the past is the *na losa chitto* of the present."

The next morning I'm up before everyone and driving away from camp. Where I end up is basically in the middle of Mandeville, the junction of highways 22 and 190. Mandeville once was a patch of pinewoods but now is a sprawling suburb north of New Orleans. To me, the city mainly seems to be subdivisions and strip malls and too many chain stores, but where 22 and 190 meet, it's a McDonald's that used to be something else.

Back in 1978, it was near this spot where a massacre occurred in a grove of massive live oaks, their branches like a heavy curtain. There are photographs of the scene and reports of what the police and newspapers say transpired here. There are witness statements to corroborate too, and even though it doesn't seem possible, there are clues that are still left behind. At least I think I still see the telltale tire marks in the grass and remnants of the trash the murderers left behind.

It happened on a Fat Tuesday, early in the morning. By 8 a.m. . . . the sound of heavy footsteps. . . . the whine of a motor . . . a thud of something hitting the ground . . . then it was basically over. Surely somebody should have seen something, but like the papers said, "Our judges were in masks. Our lawyers were at parties."[6]

You see, in Mandeville celebrating Mardi Gras means going overboard. You scream. You holler. When someone shouts, "Hail Orpheus," you shout, "Hail Yes." You catch the parade. You catch a Pineloon—a pinecone sprayed too thick with purple, green, and gold until it looks like a doubloon. You stay out later than you plan. You sleep in. Everyone does. And when something bad happens, like it did back in 1978, no one notices until it's too late.

When people did find out, they started calling it the Mardi Gras Day Massacre in the Chinchuba Oaks because the act didn't look like an accident. It didn't seem random at all. The violation was performed with such decisiveness, such swiftness, that it seemed like a desecration because the place they chose wasn't accidental. The grove was once home to a simple cabin that served as a chapel, one of several built back in the 1860s by the poet-priest Rev. Father Adrien Rouquette. A murder here felt like an intentional defilement of a sacred space.

Father Rouquette gave up a life of wealth and ease to preach to and live with Choctaws of Bayou Lacombe. Reportedly the first Creole to be an ordained priest after Louisiana changed hands to become an American possession and affectionately known to locals as Père Rouquette, the poet-priest preferred a rustic life among the Choctaws to the urbane life of New Orleans. He was a "nature lover and servant of man" and, instead of a house, the ecclesiastic preferred "an old oak of giant dimensions which long served the missionary as a place of shelter in its hollow trunk."[7]

They say the Choctaw called him *Chahta Ima*, "like a Choctaw," and loved him. He earned his legendary reputation for baptizing them in the bayous and sleeping in the woods and most famously for building four rustic cabin chapels under the majestic oak groves growing along the region's waterways.[8] Perhaps the best known was Kildara—the cabin built among the Chinchuba Oaks.

And then in 1978, to widen Highway 22, DOTD came in on Mardi Gras Day and cut down all the trees. That's the murder. That's the mauling people refer to as the Mardi Gras Day Massacre in the Chinchuba Oaks.

It was traumatic, sure, but it wasn't quite a surprise. For weeks and weeks and weeks, residents had protested the proposed highway project, but then in the hours right after dawn on a Mardi Gras Tuesday, men with chainsaws and a bulldozer put an end to the "several months of unsuccessful negotiations between the state department of transportation and development and local citizens who had banded together to save the trees."9

When I'm back at the campsite, we drink the McCafés I bought because I'm as guilty as anyone. Next, we ramble down to the river and talk about nothing until I find the campsite bathroom showers and dressing stalls. I smell of woodsmoke and sweat, but I'm worried I'll be late for Aunt Charlesa's services, so I don't waste time with a shower. I pull on tight socks and long pants and a stiff shirt through all of the talking, then try to make good time on the drive to Covington.

My cousin Craig's the first one to recognize me when I walk into the funeral home that morning. He places me as one of Uncle T-boy's as soon as I open the door. "Right, right," he says after I remind him which one I am, "the baby." Craig's good company, like that.

My cousin Cynthia's good company. Her grand-piano smile is good to walk with while you're following a hearse as it creeps through a cemetery. She makes you feel happy, even as you and the rest of the attendees file into a mausoleum with the hallways full of drawers. She's good as anything to be with as you read the names of people carved onto the walls and count the small sconces meant to hang flowers in, but are empty.

My cousin's Lana's good company. Everything's easy with her. She waves off my bad memory and reminds me of her children's names. There's a comfort in the way she crams against the wall next to me while people crowd the room for Charlesa's last rites. With an ease, she asks my cousin Mark for a copy of the "Words of Remembrance" he wrote about his mom. He read it to us at the very end of the service.

In it, Mark confirms what I've already suspected—Aunt Charlesa made for good company too, maybe even more than the rest of us. She served strong coffee in demitasse cups to all her neighbors. She kept her rugs always vacuumed but never worried about people's shoes tracking on them. She liked catching up. She felt lucky for the visiting, the visitors. It came out when you talked to her.

Aunt Charlesa and Uncle Norton bought a small home in Gentilly when they were first married and fixed it up. They did the same for one in Mandeville, and then the same for a burned-down house next door to that one. She liked to redo houses with Norton, but I find out through Mark that the small rural farmhouse in Egan was the home that was the closest to who she was.

She liked to plant flowers; my grandfather was a farmer and gardens reminded Charlesa of that. "That's good dirt," she would say, taking handfuls of earth and showing them to Mark. "Pappa would've liked that dirt."

She liked to play house—Mark tells us that too. "When she was young," he says, "she and her sister Pat built a fort under the house because they wanted to play house, but they never got to play house because of CARL [my dad, his caps] was the 12th child and the youngest."[10]

"He had a cowboy hat and a toy gun," Mark says. "And he always wanted to play cowboy. So Charlesa would find a stick and pretend it was a gun. They spent hours and hours chasing each other under and around that house. 'It wasn't fair,' my mom used to say. She could never win. After all, Carl had a real gun and all she had was a stick."

I stay at the funeral longer than I thought I would, then it's a game of dodge on 190 South. My foot's on the gas, threading traffic, nearly floating above the smooth cement, kicking myself for being thankful for the highway project that destroyed the Chinchuba Oaks back in 1978.

That year the Louisiana Department of Transportation and Development thought about putting the brakes on the $6,353,272 project. Months before the infamous Fat Tuesday, that office agreed to wait and try to find another solution. James C. Moore, the district engineer living in Hammond working on the project, promised everyone that. "We don't just go out and destroy things," he said. "Every place that we can save a tree, we do it."

LDOTD "checked into the possibility of redesigning the highway to provide a greater degree of curvature and save the trees," Secretary George Fischer explained, "but we found this to be unacceptable."[11] The curvature would deviate from regulations, making the department liable for any accidents. They also considered handrails to protect the trees, but those were deemed "unsafe and unacceptable."

Despite all the excuses, if you ask me, the truth is it seems like it was typical Louisiana, typical Bayou State, typical bayou. It all came down to oversupply. "The Chinchuba Oaks were not important enough to save," James Moore told the paper after it happened, "because they have no proven historical significance and there are plenty of other oak trees in the area."[12]

I'm a little blue when I pull into Fontainebleau State Park to meet Jack and Kevin. The park encompasses about twenty-eight thousand acres of the northern shore of Lake Pontchartrain and sits about seven miles from where the old Chinchuba oaks stood. It has a host of camping sites, a little beach, several trails, guest cabins built on pilings out in the lake's brackish water, and a visitor center, which highlights the land's history as not only an 1829 sugar plantation, but also the habitation of the Acolapissa, who were one of the first people here, even before the Choctaw. It's a nice park, but there's just so much to feel.

The acreage of the park is bordered by two bayous—Cane Bayou on the east and Castine Bayou on the west. "The Choctaw called Cane Bayou 'Chela'Ha,'" some of the park info tells visitors, "which translates as 'noisy' because of the sound of the wind rattling the cane grasses along the waterway." Bayou Castine's name "comes from the Native Muskogean term 'Castem Bayouk,'" a park guide says. "It translates as 'Bayou of Fleas' because of the biting insects infesting the banks at the waterway's mouth. Creoles accepted the name Castine Bayou, unaware of its derogatory meaning."

Grayhawk told us another story about that word *castine*, how a part of it wasn't in the past. In the story, he said he laughed when he went to the mayor and found out the City of Mandeville decided to name their new, state-of-the art, upscale, largest-in-St.-Tammany-Parish event center the Castine Center. "You might as well have called it Flea Market," he told the mayor.

One of the other things Grayhawk talked to us about is how bad things used to be for him. He told us when he was younger, he had a chip on his shoulder. That racism could get kind of bad there in Mandeville, on the Northshore, and he carried it around with him. His uncle noticed that and one day told him, "You've only met the bad people. You need to spend some time meeting the good people."

As Grayhawk got older, he started traveling, started giving lectures, started finding himself in movies, began meeting all kinds of people, and after a long year of speaking to crowds and playing music and roaming all around, Grayhawk met with his uncle again.

"How many people have you met this year?" his uncle asked him.

"Uncle," Grayhawk answered, "I don't know. Maybe a million."

"And how many of them did you not like?"

And Grayhawk answered smiling, "Maybe ten."

It's something I think about a lot at Fontainebleau.

There's no trail to Castine Bayou, but there's one to Cane Bayou, which is where Kevin and Jack and I plan on hiking that day. Cane Bayou trail is a tramp through pine-hardwoods and palmetto stands and sweet gums and a lush understory. There are several ways to come in and out of the trail and its entire length has several forks, but the trail's longest route ends in a view of Cane Bayou, if you can make it that far. The three of us try it.

At a mile and a half, the Bayou Cane trail splits, one route wiggling north a little, the other waggling a little south, but both eventually straighten out. After they do, maybe there's three miles left from there to the end of the trail, which is Bayou Cane itself, with its water and noise and its whispering cane.

A long time ago there were two ancient crescent-shaped midden mounds that sat along Cane Bayou, but they were partially destroyed "before the park understood what the large shell mounds or middens were [and] heavy equipment was brought in to gather the old clam shells for use in paving roads."[13] Père Rouquette also built one of his four small cabin-chapels on Bayou Cane, and there was a time when most people sort of knew where it was and a wanderer could still see evidence of it if she or he knew where to look. But it's gone now too.

Maybe none of it matters. Even if we could find our way to see either of these, there's no chance that day of us reaching the end of the trail because that June, there's a gate keeping out trespassers, but it's not what you think. It's a clear roadblock with no bars or wire, but it's sure to keep out anyone who might want to find an old place where people use to live. It's a natural roadblock, and it's sturdy. It's deerflies. Swarms and swarms and biting swarms of them that run us back up the trail and down a different fork until they spit us out not at the visitor center but where the trail exits to an alley of twelve colossal oaks facing each other, all of them draped in moss, and serving a long time ago as shade for "20 double cabins that housed enslaved families from 1829 to 1862," as the nearby marker lets us know. The park has worked to save these oaks, and the small type at the very bottom of the marker clarifies the source of some of what they know about their past: "2019 Eagle Scout Project—Jackson Cantrell."[14]

After a long think under these oaks, Jack, Kevin, and I don't know what to do next. We've walked all of the park we can, and snatches of people are coming beneath the oaks now. In twos and threes and fours, they're arranging around the trunks and posing for wedding photographs or baby pictures, and now a woman is unfolding a blanket at the center of the alley and placing objects there. It is either the start of her process for making art or the beginning of a ceremony or ritual. Without any of us saying it, we each feel like we're in the way.

We move off to our cars full of indecision. No one's positive about what the other ones are willing to do. The prospect of leaving for another place where I can't describe precisely what we'll find keeps me quiet for longer than it should. I don't want to waste anyone's time. When I finally say what we might try, I can barely beat them into the car. At the park's exit, knowing left is where we'll spend the night and right is the sleepy little town of Lacombe, I mutter to myself, "If you see a fork in the road, take it," then turn.

Lacombe is "woodsy with a mixture of fragrant, tall pines and moss-dripping oaks, and houses cozily ensconced under the trees."[15] To me, the town feels like a good hiding spot—cramped, like a closet full of old coats, and full of shadows, like a corner of your house, and motionless in the way a child playing hide-n-seek holds their breath when they hear the seeker step into the room. Père Rouquette called the cabin he built there at the headwaters of Bayou Lacombe something like that. "Le Coin" or "The Nook" was its name. Of the four he built, it was the cabin he "loved best of all."[16]

Most people say that Rouquette was called "Choctaw like" because he not only lived with the Choctaws but respected them, embraced them. The parishioners of Lacombe's The Sacred Heart of Jesus say that "rather than trying to replace the Choctaws' special festivals with a Christian observance," the priest "accepted the Indian rituals and incorporated them into his religious teachings. Today, we still have the beautiful Buchuwa ceremony of honoring the dead because Père Rouquette allowed the practice to continue."[17]

Buchuwa was a ritual Rouquette observed happening "in the Indian village more than a century ago." He identified it by name in his journals and described it, writing that during the Feast for the Dead "the Indians would disperse in the woods, build small fires, and sit and wail until mid-night. While the lamentations were going on, twelve Indian women prepared the banquet at twelve open fires. At midnight, all returned from the woods, and a banquet followed ritual dances." Rouquette thought the Feast was "most impressive and most eerie."[18]

Today, Lacombe's best-known and most striking tradition is its current All Saints Day custom, which seems to be a merging of Buchuwa and a celebration of the Catholic Holy Day of communion between all saints. On November 1st, the faithful in Lacombe buy a good supply of candles and go "at nightfall to newly cleaned and flower-decorated graveyards" to place "lighted candles on the graves to honor the dead."[19] The celebration forms a river of lights, snaking through the cemeteries, the candles eventually finding a place of rest atop the graves. Folklorists Frank de Caro and Rosan Jordan say that in Lacombe, especially in "The Williams Cemetery . . . the custom of lighting candles for the dead has been retained most vigorously by blacks and by Creoles of color (many of whom also claim Choctaw ancestry)."

Several cemeteries celebrate this tradition every year, when the past is remembered forward, and the three of us travelers can see the alluringly intricate iron cemetery gates of La Fontaine Cemetery from the highway. It sits in a picturesque spot, with the oaks of Bayou Lacombe only a few feet away, and hushed by a canopy of moss-covered oaks and holding a clutch of bright white above-ground burials and a dramatic-looking mausoleum, it is a siren song off Highway 190. But it's not November, but June, so the cemetery gates are locked and there's no way for Jack, Kevin, and I to tour the grounds.

That's okay, we say. The summer's no time for cemeteries. It's a time for self-care, and long weekends, and rambles through the woods, and a winding drive around Lacombe searching for something you're not quite sure is there, or even what it is, and maybe couldn't explain why it is you're looking for whatever it is you're trying to find.

Local history says Père Rouquette founded Lacombe's Sacred Heart Catholic Church in 1890, and in 1913, its Knights of Columbus chapter placed a marble cross at a site on Bell Park Road where "the Nook was supposed to be located."

The three of us spend at least a half an hour looking for it, but end up disappointed. Instead of a marble cross, along the Tammany Trace Bike Trail a few blocks from the church, we find a set of six brightly painted benches facing a plaque of thirty or so words describing Rouquette.

The plaque promises a story, but doesn't deliver. It lists his name, the years he lived, his nickname, and not much else. The benches promise a visitor a place to sit, but they're also a letdown. Some pieces of the benches are rotten, and the entire set is encircled by strands of yellow "CAUTION" tape warning people to stay off.

Staring at Rouquette's rotten benches, I think about how easy it is to get lost in expectations. Not just here, but in most places. Not just when visiting something special, but in the everyday things. A good job, a nice career, a reputation, a steady little car with a new smell, a fenced yard and a pool and a garage, a nice-sized house with plenty of rooms, something closer to town than a farmhouse, something bigger than a shoebox. Something good someone might say about you. Something memorable. Something true.

The traditional burial rituals of the Choctaws throughout the South were unlike any other burial customs early travelers observed when they encountered the various native people in America.[20] First, female relatives prepared the body, washing it, dressing it in the best clothes. Then the male relatives erected a funereal scaffolding to hold the body off the ground. The structure would be built about thirty feet in front of the person's home. It might include a roof and walls. Maybe a fence would be built around its base to keep away the animals and curious children. A well-worn clay pot, an elaborate piece of jewelry, a bow and arrow, or other sorts of workaday objects would be placed on the scaffold for the person. A bear skin or blanket might be draped over the dead to cover the body's frame. Benches could be built on the east side of the platform for the mourners.

Once everything was prepared, the mourners would come, every day, several times a day, sitting on the benches, crying, wailing. Along with the mourners, the bone-pickers would arrive as well. The bone-pickers were recognizable by the special tattoos that adorned their bodies and the long fingernails on their thumbs and fingers. They stood at a special place near the funerary stand. They sang certain sacred songs and moved a particular way. People knew them by name—the bone-pickers, the bone-gatherers, the *na foni aiowa*. They were the ones who guided the burial.

Only the bone-pickers knew when the right amount of mourning time had passed. Once they sensed it, they would announce that the day of the last cry had come—the big cry, the *yaiyo chito*, the final day of remembrance. After that, they would pick the bones clean of flesh, and once that job was finished, place the bones into a box so that the scaffold could be burned and a grand feast could be held. At the end of the feast, towards the end of it, the bones would be transported to the family's burial site, its charnel house, its *hatak illi foni aiasha*. There, the box of bones would rest among the other boxes brought over the years. Only the bone-pickers could ensure the dead moved on correctly.

Traditional Choctaw thought seemed to hold that every person has in essence two spirits, or shadows as they were often called, the inside shadow and outside shadow.[21] Much in the way our shadows follow us on a sunny day, these shadows stay tethered to the world of the body, but each in their own way. When a person died, the inner shadow would stay near the body for a time, but eventually travel west to the Land of Ghosts where a gateway to a happy place awaited. The outer shadow remained with the body much longer, sometimes roaming the site where the person perished, and sometimes wandering around his or her former home. Sometimes even staying near a relative's house.

Bushnell wrote that the Choctaw told him the outer shadow could often be seen "moving among the trees or following persons after sunset," but, especially at night, the outer shadow was "wont to travel along the trails and roads used by living men and thus avoid meeting the bad spirit, Nanapolo, whose wanderings are confined to the dark and unfrequented paths of the forest."[22]

The Choctaw also believed, he explained, that a person's spirit or shadow could travel or "leave the body even during life." This type of traveling explained dreams. "At night when a person is resting and all is quiet," Bushnell claimed, the Choctaw believed "the 'spirit' steals away from the body and wanders about the country, seeing many people and things, which are known to the individual when he awakes."[23]

Scientists now say that the hippocampus in our brain probably manages both our sense of direction and portions of our memory. It makes sense that those might be related. So much of what we recall is tied to specific places and what happened there. In a way, a shadow reflects that relationship. In the physical world, the sun shows us where we face in a cardinal direction. In the world of our mind, our experiences and memories follow us like our shadow does. Losing a shadow would be like being unmarked in time and place. To me, the Choctaw stories and beliefs about inside and outside shadows seem to capture this.

For the Choctaws of Lacombe, the bone-pickers don't come anymore. In fact, they may never have. Bushnell found no bone-pickers in Lacombe when he visited. Actually, he found "very little lamenting or mourning on the occasion of a death or a burial" at all. "The body was borne to the grave and the interment took place without a ceremony of any sort."[24]

But maybe remnants of the old ways remained, and Bushnell just missed them. Maybe his obsession was with the mounds he found. Maybe he became so focused on them and on finding proof of early occupancy that he brushed aside everything else, everything he saw as less than authentic or historical or reliable. Maybe he had expectations. Maybe he thought about the work he was doing and what other anthropologists and scholars would say was valuable. Maybe he overlooked something else, something miraculous, like a line of people meandering through the evening, holding candles; a train of bodies snaking through the forest, erecting fires, sitting in the dark around the flames until midnight came, then weaving back home through the trees for a feast.

Along with all the stories of shadows and supernatural beings, Pisatunema and the other Choctaw told Bushnell stories about Père Rouquette too, that man "who lived among the Choctaw, the greater part of his time being spent at either Bayou Lacomb or Chinchuba." Bushnell says, "Chataima, meaning 'Choctaw-like' came from Rouquette's fancied resemblance to a Choctaw. His hair, which was dark and straight, was worn long, his eyes were dark and piercing, and the natural swarthiness of his complexion was increased by constant exposure to sun and wind. The two women, Emma and Louisa, now living at Bayou Lacombe, were children when baptized by Père Rouquette."[25]

Father Rouquette's life and death became part of local legend here. When the priest died, they say his body was brought to St. Mary's Church in New Orleans. Unfortunately, "there was too little time to inform Indians across the lake," historian David Usner writes, "so only those already present in the city were able to attend the funeral." A *Daily Picayune* article described the spontaneous affair: "There were a picturesque group of bare-footed Choctaw women, one among them so old that she could barely walk. Her tribute was eloquent in its simplicity—a cross of the wild herbs of the forest which she carried before her when she followed the hearse to the cemetery."[26]

But legend says something was also hidden in all the ceremony. Stories claim that the Choctaws were intentionally not informed of Rouquette's death and purposefully left out of the celebration. People believe officials feared the Choctaws would want to bury Rouquette in the woods, so the funeral was kept a secret to prevent that. But there's another twist. Legend says that later, when no one was watching, the Choctaw people stole Rouquette's remains and placed them in a secret location near Bayou Lacombe, somewhere in the woods.[27]

After spending a good chunk of our time together hunting around Lacombe for things to see, around 6:00 that afternoon I tell Jack and Kevin, "I don't know what else there is to do. I mean, I don't know where else to look."

By 6:15, the three of us are five miles west of Lacombe, parked at a closed pool installation company. Our plans are to walk the Tammany Trace Bike Trail to see where it crosses Bayou Cane. There, Père Rouquette built another one of his chapels, or so some people say.

The walk's not far, and the bridge is easy to find, but there's a fence stopping us from descending the road bank. Even if we did scale it, we'd have to plow through head-high weeds and walls of trash trees and thick elderberry bushes wired close together with kudzu vine. None of us are in long pants or wearing the right sort of shoes, and I know each of us is worried about ticks and redbugs and maybe even fleas.

"It's okay," I say. "I'm not sure of what we'll see down there anyway."

"Next time," Jack swears.

By 7:00, we're looping around Fontainebleau again so I can drop Kevin at his car. By 7:15, he's following me out of the park. By 7:25, all of us are flying on 190 where it crosshatches 22—the site of the "surprise destruction" scheduled for a Mardi Gras Tuesday when everyone would be away.

It was "a sneak attack," that's how one letter to the editor put it, "reminiscent of the surprise attack by the Imperial Forces of the Japanese on Pearl Harbor."[28]

State Representative Bill Strain of Abita Springs said the go-ahead to cut down the oaks came like a bolt from the blue. He hadn't seen a work order from LDOTD. "They normally would mail me a copy of it," he told the paper, but not this time.[29]

The LDOTD workers also looked suspicious, like they knew exactly where to go and what to do first. In other words, they moved with such purpose it appeared as if they recognized they were doing something wrong because, as one witness said, they made a beeline for the largest most controversial tree, the one the stories said was Père Rouquette's oak, and "got it taken care of first before anyone could do anything about it." By noon, the workers cranked the bulldozer's engine off, having "accomplished their mission."[30]

But the greatest surprise of that massacre was a clandestine memo that a journalist eventually dug up. News-Banner reporter Mike Dowty told his readers that he discovered the Mardi Gras Day Massacre "was first ordered in a secret letter dated January 24."[31] The entire crime could be "traced up the chain of command within the transportation department" until the trail ran cold right before it hit the desk of department head W. T. Taylor. The memo proved the massacre's timing wasn't a coincidence, but no one could quite prove if Taylor was in the dark about it or not.

I'm not sure it matters. It was typical Louisiana. It was oversupply. When everyone looked up from the destruction and wondered how the state could ruin such historical trees, LDOTD cited director of the Louisiana Division of Architectural and Historical Preservation Paul B. Hartwig's report that "indicated the trees had no historical significance . . . Father Rouquette seemed to have preached and converted Indians at several locations throughout the parish."[32]

It's like it always is. Just like how state police Captain William Jourdan said it was when he was called out to protect the bulldozer that Fat Tuesday morning. "A lot of times we do things we don't really like. That's our job," he said. "I like trees as well as anybody."

It's a game—the excuses, the blaming, the way people use words. Everything's a game: the wordplay within the insurance policies, the thumbtacks pressed into the map on the wall I call "Pin the Tail on the Hurricane," the phone-tag with the contractors. The name-calling people do when they label something a *disaster* or not and the Monopoly money that becomes *available* and who gets it when they do. The layers of a new roof are a jigsaw puzzle, and wondering if you can trust the roofers you've hired to do it right is a roll of the dice. It's pressing your luck. The charades you act out with your wife, your kids, your coworkers when you smile and say you're doing okay. The nightly game of blind man's buff where you grope and grab and go stumbling in the dark while you can't sleep. Everything is just one long game of playing house in Louisiana like it always is.

Back at camp, Kevin and Jack and I start feeling the deerflies buzzing us almost as soon as the sun starts losing itself in the sky, and we're not alone. Now, there's a couple in a converted ice cream truck in the tent site next to us, and three spaces down, there's a woman who's built her SUV into a house of sorts. When the back hatch is open, I can see the bed she's built where the backseat used to be and the drawers she's constructed beneath it. The couple's made a fire in a Lil' Smokey, but that's not enough to keep the deerflies at bay. They close the lid and hurry inside the van. The woman, who never makes a campfire, climbs inside her SVU too, but she has screens she can wrap her windows in, so she rolls all the windows down and stays inside for the rest of the night.

My pals and me try to play buried alive too. We first cram inside a tent, but it steams. So we march away from the campsite, as far away from the palmetto stand and cypress grove as we can until we're standing in the middle of the park's main road where it makes a wide fork. That's better, but not good enough. Eventually, the three of us hunker in the park's bathroom, thankful for the sheetrock walls and the shingled roof and shower stalls with benches where we can sit and talk until it's completely dark and fewer deerflies fly around, especially fireside. That's when we go back.

It's a poor fire we make, but it's ours. The scraps of 2 × 4s Grayhawk gave us stack too perfectly almost. We need gaps in the pyramid at the fire's base for enough of the evening air to suck through the wood, so we mix in a few broken logs. In other words, it's letting go of perfect. And it takes a while for the boards to burn down so their edges are ragged enough to stand up unevenly. It's slow-making. It's odd. It's supplying enough broken things, mixed with the three of us shrugging shoulders and giving in to good enough.

The next morning I'm up before everyone again. It's Sunday, the day we're supposed to leave, so this time I walk to the river and sit on a bench until the sun's up and Kevin and Jack are awake. By 7:00, I wander back into the campsite. Kevin's pulling up the stakes for his tent and stuffing it into the laundry sack he carries it in. Jack's gone, so I follow Kevin's lead and start stuffing my junk in my bag.

When Jack shows up, we pack the car, and then the three of us settle at a picnic table to decide if we should just go home.

I think about offering the Boy Scouts Boardwalk of the Big Branch Marsh National Refuge a few miles away. It's a 4-mile loop of raised walkway stretching into a wetland near the edge of Lacombe. There are places on the walkway where visitors can stare into the marsh, like the two kiosked "lookouts" that peer over pockets of open water. "In the foreground are the lilies and reeds and fish that frequent marshes. In the background, a rim of cypress and pine trees frames the scene. As you look out across the marsh," the signage at the grandest lookout says, "notice the cypress trees in the distance. Cypress trees prefer wet sites and can withstand flooding," but pine trees are different. They'll die in watery land. And they're re all dying here. At the grandest lookout in Big Branch Marsh National Refuge, the trunks have turned ashen. The crowns are snapped. The branches are completely bare. In the far background, a person can make out a nearby subdivision and its two-story houses with raised foundations and bulldozed dirt pads and elevated yards and manicured lawns. In the foreground, the kiosks describe it all.

The eighteen thousand acres of the Big Branch Marsh is a place of "transitioning," which doesn't mean the marsh is in the process of being drained and filled to build developments, but that the trees themselves are changing. "At Big Branch Marsh NMR," the kiosk explains, "the scattered cypress brakes are a hydrologic transition between fresh marsh and the pine flatwoods. The dead pine trees near the observation platform indicate that the ground in this area has sunk and become wetter than it was in the past. Now it is too wet for the pines to survive." It's natural— the sinking, the dying pine flatwoods, the rich understory of briars and solidago and saw palmettos becoming marshy bulltongue and wild iris and water lilies. "A natural phenomenon," the kiosk says, this land of transitioning "that results in changes in habitat."

It's normal. It's typical. I'm supposed to accept it. And I do, in part. Louisiana is sinking, and always has, always will. It's life here, and I get it, but I don't have the heart for it. Not now. Not on this camping trip. So I'm on the edge of suggesting we pack it in and all go home. That's when Grayhawk pulls up on his ATV.

It's what you do, not what you are that defines you—Grayhawk tells his fourth graders that. Life's about living, not about sitting around. It's trying things. And if he talks to someone long enough, he believes he'll find a way he's connected to them. He knows it's true. Life proved it to him at 2:00 in the morning in New Hampshire when he stopped at a store and ran into someone who knew him. In France, too, it happened randomly on the street. At Riverside Park, with me and Jack and Kevin, Grayhawk talks to us until he finds the link—that we all know a man named Ray Miles. Grayhawk tells us he has plenty of pictures of Ray when he was a young man and pictures of Ray's son Luke when he was just a baby. In his favorite photograph, Grayhawk is holding Luke.

Ray Miles was my dean, my boss, for years. After my dad died, I'd stumble into Ray's office and ask him every question I had about things. Ray was a remarkable historian. I bet he knew more about the Atakapa than anyone in the world, but I don't know enough to be sure of that. What there's no doubt about is that he knew everything about what I was interested in. He knew Louisiana and its oldest stories, and he also knew about fixing things, the odd jobs around a house.

Once I asked him about the first stories of the Atakapa in Lake Charles. "They're different," he told me. "Maybe even unique." Most origin stories of other Native Americans in the region say they come from the earth, like from clay or a cavern. The Choctaw's origin story say they come from a cave. Their stories even say there's a tilted mound squatting in the middle of the state of Mississippi that is their point of origin. It's called *Nanih Waiya* and is variously translated as *stooping hill* or *place of creation*, but it is sometimes also called *mother mound*. "But the Atakapa," Ray told me, "they say they come from sea foam, a clam shell, the sea."

Once I asked Ray about copper water lines and if I have to replace my pipes, did he think it was worth the money to come back with copper, with something I know will last but might cost an arm and a leg. It depended on where else I could save money, Ray figured. Where else I could make do.

I remember the day Ray left school because the cancer in him made him forget what time it was so he was late for class. Everyone immediately knew something was wrong. That wasn't like Ray.

Ray's funeral was delayed maybe a half a year because of the pandemic and then the hurricane. When it finally happened, and I could walk around the posters full of pictures of him, I stared the longest at the one of him fixing sheetrock. He's on a ladder, splotched with drywall mud and paint, smiling.

When we finish talking about Ray and catching Grayhawk up on how quickly things went south, Grayhawk teaches us the Choctaw words for the places around. He tells us Bogalusa is really hiding another word for bayou—*bogue*—and that *lusa* is the Choctaw word meaning *dark* whether it's in *Nalusa Falaya* meaning "long black thing" or Bogalusa meaning "cloudy" bayou. He says in *Pascagoula*, *pasca* means bread and *goula* means people, which means bread people lived there and that's what that place was, and is. And it was a good place. A place with people who had enough to eat. Had enough to share. A good place to travel to.

I think that must be as old as anything because even though my people's names for places aren't as old as Choctaw words, they're not so different. It's typical Louisiana. It's always the same. LeJeune Cove means the place of the LeJeunes, their neighborhood, their home, and I wonder if it could mean a place with people who made for good company, if people knew them for that, if people went there with that in their hearts.

Carl, Mark, Homer, Michel, Joseph, Blaise, Blaise . . . an uncle came to him long, long ago and said, "We're leaving our home for a new one," and Blaise said, "Okay, a fork in the road, let's go."

My friend Stella always says, "Who is remembered never dies," and I hope that's true.

For Peré Rouqette, there's something about the possibility of his grave being somewhere out in the woods. Yes, the Chinchuba oaks are gone. The chapel cabins are destroyed. But there's something about just knowing there are stories about his body being stolen and buried in a place that keeps the past alive.

For the Choctaw, mourning was always a long affair, and so maybe, even for those who are long dead, a remembrance keeps going today in a way I can't recognize as bone-picking or Buchuwa or something else. Maybe it's at the yearly celebration at *Nanih Waiya*. Choctaw elder Wagoner Amos remembers the oldest stories in the oldest words, and when he tells people about Nanih Waiya, he says, "To think that this was the place . . . where the Choctaws originated is so obvious. It was said that the place where the staff was plunged into the ground shall never be destroyed. That is why it's still there, it is meant to be and we can all see it."

Was it so very different from what my family did for Aunt Charlesa? Even though our gathering lasted for the brief span of one bright morning, in a way that celebration was the best way we know how to care for someone who has died. There were no bone-pickers. There was no scaffolding, no benches. There was no train of candles through the graves. But there were flowers and pictures placed near her body. A rosary entwined in her folded hands. There were chairs gathered around for those of us mourning her. There were people directing us, helping us move from the first stages to the last and choosing how to go from one place to the next.

When we said the final prayers and everyone gathered in the small room positioned right off the hallway, there were so many of us that if you were standing shoulder to shoulder with us, you would've called the room a shoebox, but you would've been happy to be squeezed so close together. When we stood in the mausoleum, even though some of us had tears, there was no one big cry, but when Mark read to us his "Words of Remembrance," didn't we all remember forward about the place that's ours.

"Fortunately, Charlesa was born with something that many people do not have," Mark read aloud at the services. "The day she was born, in addition to her mother and father, she had 5 brothers and 5 sisters," he said. "Exactly how Wava made the incubator and what she used for heat is unknown as electricity had not yet reached their house, but I imagine that Mom became a LeJeune family project. They managed to keep her warm and got her to eat. She not only survived but thrived in that house full of family."

My aunt Wava made for good company; when she stopped in for coffee on an afternoon, she knew the news of every one of her brothers and sisters. My aunt Charlesa made for good company; she welcomed visitors and served her coffee in beautiful demitasse cups and grew a good shareable garden. Near her grave in Covington, there's thick Augustine nearby and the zinnias rush to color every year. She, I think, would have said there's good dirt here.

But when I think about standing in that dirt near Charlesa's grave, what comes back to me the strongest is something Mark wrote, something he read aloud during the services while my relatives crammed together, some of whom I didn't recognize or couldn't place but stood next to happily. "Whenever I imagine heaven, I think of two things," he told us. "One is that old country song 'Will the Circle Be Unbroken.' The other is those LeJeune family reunions Mom would take us to. I imagine Mom walking into heaven now, Dad is there to meet her and take her to the reunion."

And I guess what comes back to me even now is some advice my dad used to give. He used to say, "No matter where you go, there you are."

It's a fringe continent—Louisiana, my home. It's a land of slow making. It's a land of the lying oaks of Pecan Island and Grand Chenier where you live under layered light in a world that almost seems right, but it's not a liar. It's just a "place that seems often unable to make up its mind whether it will be earth or water, and so it compromises." It sinks. It builds an ancient mound. It tears them down for roadway shell. It bulldozes oaks for traffic jams. It's complicated. Almost every night during hunting seasons, agents must go in search of at least one missing hunter, and that seems just about right for Louisiana. For the earliest Choctaw, almost every shadow seemed to have a name, and some would find you if you got lost, and some you wouldn't want to, which seems true for Louisiana—everything seems a shadow of what it might be. And though it might not seem that way, Louisiana loves me anyway, or so they'll console me. I'm simply confused because it's confusing, just like self-care. Louisiana is oversupplying me with small traumas to take my mind off the larger ones. It's good advice, Louisiana is. If you see a fork in the road, take it, no matter where you go. It's all the advice I have, and I have choices to make.

Epilogue

NO MATTER WHERE YOU GO, THERE YOU ARE

Once the person is gone—the body dead and the shadows let go—the bone-pickers come, or did. Somewhere. But not here. Not ever for my family. We had our own ways. Simpler, maybe, but in many ways the same.

And we had our own place—St. Joseph Catholic Cemetery.

It's not ours alone, of course, but there are so many of us buried there it feels that way.

In June, on Father's Day, the year after the storms, I drove out to see my father's grave resting at the far south end of St. Joseph's. I couldn't say exactly why, except Sundays can feel freer than other days, and the Sunday of Father's Day usually means a day without anything scheduled, a day when I can crank the engine of the car before even a shred of sun touches the hood and drive out of town without anyone wondering if I'm around.

Once I'm there, when I'm stepping through the grounds, I'm always struck by how many of the names repeat from stone to stone. The cemetery holds generations of my mother's and father's people, and once my dad passed, we buried him in the cemetery not too far from where his father and mother and grandparents are buried, so there's also a strange feeling that time repeats there too.

Some say that for the Choctaw, whenever the bone-pickers left, whenever someone died, those who passed were no longer thought to be a part of the nonshadowy world, and so that person's name was never spoken again, which seems a shame to me. But what do I know. I only have the experience of hearing the words my dad said the night he passed away. He was in his bed. My mom and brothers and sister were gathered around him. In pain from the pancreatic cancer that was killing him, he asked us to call the priest.

The priest hesitated on the phone when I spoke to him. He visited a few days earlier and that day my dad looked okay, like he might be around for a few more weeks. But my dad knew. He had only seven or eight hours left, and at that moment, as his wife and daughter and sons were standing at his bedside, he needed them to witness something.

I answered the door when the priest knocked and led him to the back of the house. I could see the whiteness flash across his face when he saw my father. Quietly, he nodded to us, then found a chair by the bed so he could deliver last rites.

After the priest finished and made his sign of the cross, my dad had a question for him, a question he wanted us to hear, I think, more than a question he wanted the answer to. "Can those up there watch over those down here?" my father asked, nodding once the priest gave the answer he knew was coming.

The year after the storms, Father's Day was a gray day, and it felt right to stand near my father's cloud-colored stone as a sort of anniversary of recovery. But who was I kidding?

What could I hold up as the cure for the homesickness you feel at home?

With my mother's encouragement, I drove to see my father's grave the following year too. It had been two years since the double hurricanes. My insurance claim still wasn't closed. All the repairs weren't done. My garage was a slab. But the difference, I guess, was that I had accepted that my garage would probably always be that way. I felt lost, and chances were my life was always going to be this way, but I had come to terms with it.

I realized this whole journey of mine had been me trying to figure out how my dad's advice could be true. I started to see it. I started to embrace that no matter where you go, there you are.

It's not a far country, but I've been to the edges of Louisiana. I've stood at a lip of land that juts out into the Gulf, watched the water eat away the sand, went back years later, and stood where the new lip was formed.

The places we have are the only ones we have. It matters what they are. It matters how we treat them. When they're gone, we'll be able to say their names for a time, but eventually, even that will be lost to us. Then their stories will go too.

I think the truth is, there is no cure for what you are. It's in your bones, and you drag that around wherever you go, which means you can be lost anywhere, which means my dad probably knew that I'd feel lost anywhere. I might as well be lost in a place that matters.

NOTES

1. Homesick at Home

Thanks to all the Mardi Gras scholars—especially Barry Ancelet, Marcia Gaudet, Carolyn Ware, Ray Brassieur, Carl Lindahl.

1. For Potic Rider's story, see Carl Lindahl, "The Presence of the Past in the Cajun Country Mardi Gras," *Journal of Folklore Research* 33 (1986): 125–53.

2. John Austin Young, *The Lejeunes of Acadia and the Youngs of Southwest Louisiana: A Genealogical Study of the Lejeunes of Acadia and the Descendants of Joseph Lejeune/Young and Patsy Perrine Ha* (Basile, LA: J.A. Young, 1991), 10.

3. Pierre LeJeune dit Briard is perhaps the earliest member of my family line in Acadie. Growing up, I always heard one of my ancestors married a Mi'kmaq woman. The genealogies seem to say it was Pierre. One of Pierre's descendants was that man mysteriously deported to Maryland named Jean-Baptiste, Blaise's father. When Blaise died, Blaise Jr. took on that land near Blaise Bayou. Blaise Jr.'s son Michel was born in Opelousas. Michel's first son was also named Michel, Michel LeJeune Jr., who married Aglae Fontenot. Their oldest boy was named Francois Homer LeJeune, my great-grandfather, who homesteaded LeJeune Cover, a place that should have cured all of my restlessness.

4. See Charles-César Robin, *Voyage to Louisiana*, printed 1807, translated by Stuart O. Landry (New Orleans: Pelican, 1966). A few quotations come from William Darby, *Geographical Description of the State of Louisiana* (New York: James Olmstead, 1817).

5. William Faulkner Rushton, *The Cajuns from Acadia to Louisiana* (New York: Farrar Straus Giroux, 1979), 134.

6. This book's exploration of place names and culture is indebted to Kent Ryden, *Mapping the Invisible Landscape* (Iowa City: University of Iowa Press, 1993); Mary Hufford's *One Space, Many Places: Folklife and Land Use in New Jersey's Pinelands National Reserve* (Washington, DC: American Folklife Center, Library of Congress, 1986) and her "Telling the Landscape: Folklife Expressions and Sense of Place" in Rita Zorn Moonsammy, David Steven Cohen, and Lorraine E. Williams's edited collection *Pinelands Folklife* (New Brunswick, NJ: Rutgers University Press, 1987): 16–40; and the work of geographer Yi-Fu Tuan.

7. The article was sponsored by the 1999 Congrès Mondial Acadien-Louisiane, a group designed "to develop closer links between Acadians of the diaspora."

8. The children were Jean-Baptiste who was three years old, Blaise who was two years, and a little girl named Marguerite who was two months.

9. James Dorman, *The People Called Cajuns* (Lafayette: Center for Louisiana Studies, University of Southwestern Louisiana, 1938), 16.

10. John Mack Faragher, *A Great and Noble Scheme* (New York: Norton, 2005), 373–76.

11. Carl Brasseaux, *Founding of New Acadia* (Baton Rouge: Louisiana State University Press, 1996), 43.

12. Brasseaux, *Founding of New Acadia*, 73.

13. Carl Brasseaux, "A New Acadia: The Acadian Migrations to South Louisiana," *Acadiensis* 15, no. 1 (1985): 126.

14. Brasseaux, "A New Acadia," 126.

15. Carl Brasseaux and Richard E. Chandler, "The *Britain* Incident, 1769–1770: Anglo-Hispanic Tensions in the Western Gulf," *Southwestern Historical Quarterly* 87, no. 4 (April 1984): 357–70. The quotes about Blaise's trip come from this source.

16. Dana David, "*Le voisinage*: Evolution of Community in Cajun Country," *Folklife in Louisiana: Louisiana's Living Traditions*, https://www.louisianafolklife.org/LT/Articles_Essays/creole_art_voisinage.html.

17. Samuel H. Lockett, *Louisiana as It Is: A Geographical and Topographical Description of the State*, edited with an introduction by Lauren C. Post (Baton Rouge: Louisiana State University Press, 1969), 94–95 and 50–51.

18. David, "*Le voisinage*."

19. Dorman, 25.

20. Brasseaux, *Founding of New Acadia*, 101.

21. David, "*Le voisinage*."

22. Robert L. LeJeune, *From Pointe-aux-Loups through Cartville to Iota* (San Antonio: STPG, 2014), 24.

23. Gerald L. Gold, "The French Frontier of Settlement in Louisiana: Some Observations on Cultural Change in Mamou Prairie," *Cahiers de Geographie du Québec* 23, no. 59 (1979): 272.

24. Gold, "The French Frontier of Settlement in Louisiana," 265.

25. Barry Jean Ancelet, Jay D. Edwards, and Glen Pitre, *Cajun Country* (Jackson: University Press of Mississippi, 1991), 28.

26. LeJeune, *From Pointe-aux-Loups through Cartville to Iota*, 109–10.

27. Most of the story can be found in the depositions and legal documents produced in the suit Ford filed later. It charged the Spanish government with mistreatment of Ford and the Acadians aboard the *Britain* and with malfeasance in its interactions with Tovar and the passengers. Brasseaux discusses this in his article about the *Britain*. Nearly all of the quotations about this story come from that article.

28. Brasseaux, "The *Britain* Incident," 369.

29. Brasseaux, *Founding of New Acadia*, 100.

30. Charles Allen and Sara Thomas, "Observation on Vegetation Changes in Cajun Prairie, A Coastal Prairie Flora in Southwest Louisiana," *Journal of the Botanical Research Institute of Texas* 1, no. 2 (2007): 1141–47.

31. Malcolm Vidrine, *Prairie Cajuns and the Cajun Prairie: A History* (Eunice, LA: Louisiana State University, the Cajun Prairie Habitat Preservation Society, and the Cajun Prairie Gardens, (2012): 54–55.

32. Natasha Daly, "What We Know about the Mystery Bird Death Crisis on the East Coast," *National Geographic*, online, July 15, 2021.

2. The Only Time Ben Lilly Was Ever Lost

1. J. Frank Dobie, *The Ben Lilly Legend* (Austin: University of Texas Press, 1950), 7.
2. The details about Fool River here and at the end of the chapter come from John Q. Anderson, "Some Mythical Places in Louisiana," *Louisiana Folklore Miscellany* 3 (May 1958): 1–10.
3. Dobie, *The Ben Lilly Legend*, 24.
4. Dobie, *The Ben Lilly Legend*, 24. As much as we might rightly accuse Dobie of being prone to exaggeration, some people do seem to be naturals at this. For a discussion of this, see Michael Bond, "Chapter 5: From A to B and Back Again," 95–110, *Wayfinding—How We Find—and Lose—Our Way* (London: Picador, 2020).
5. Dobie, *The Ben Lilly Legend*, 8.
6. The money came from the local Lions Club. The inspiration, or most of it, came from James Rider, who wrote a weekly column for the *Bastrop Enterprise*.
7. Dobie, *The Ben Lilly Legend*, 22.
8. Wes Helbling, "Kindred Spirits: Teddy Roosevelt, Ben Lilly and the Bear Hunt of 1907," *Looking Back: Stories from the History of Morehouse Parish* (self-published, 2012), 41.
9. Neil B. Carmony, *Ben Lilly's Tales of Bears, Lions, and Hounds* (Silver City, NM: High Lonesome Books, 2016), 3.
10. Dobie, *The Ben Lilly Legend*, 36.
11. "Louisiana State Parks, The Problem and the Solution," *First Annual Report to the Governor*, Louisiana State Parks Commission, New Orleans, Louisiana, 1935. Act No. 91 of the Regular Session of the Legislature of 1934 officially began the Louisiana State Parks. One of the commission's first activities was sending the office of the governor their first annual report, "Louisiana State Parks—The Problem and Answer," which outlined the commission's goals and potential projects.
12. "State Parks for All, Another of Senator Long's Constructive Programs," special "memorial number" of the *Louisiana Conservation Review* for Huey Long, Louisiana Department of Wildlife and Fisheries, 1935.
13. "The Beginning," *Louisiana State Park History*, Louisiana State Parks, https://www.lastateparks.com/louisiana-state-park-history.
When the State Parks began in 1934, the new state office assumed operation of three existing sites known for their historical value: Longfellow-Evangeline State Historic Site (the oldest), Camp Moore, and Fort Pike/Fort McComb State Historic Site. All of this was done by official proclamations made by Governor Oscar K. Allen and Attorney General Gaston L. Porterie. In 1934, the total land amounted to 298 acres. None of it offered visitors an encounter with the "primitive." That would change with the addition of Chemin-A-Haut. The Park Commission labeled Bayou Bartholomew a "fine fishing stream."
14. "Motor Tour No. 2—20 miles round trip. North of Bastrop for ten miles on State Highway 204," *Bastrop, Louisiana / Mer Rouge, Louisiana: Compilations by Federal Writers' Project of Works Progress Administration -1935*. Document of Historical Collection of Morehouse Parish, 35-36. Much of the land included in the park site was purchased from the Crosset Lumber Company.
15. "State Parks for All," 21.
16. "Chemin-A-Haut State Park—Bastrop LA," *The Living New Deal*, https://livingnewdeal.org/projects/chemin-a-haut-state-park-bastrop-la/.
17. Dobie, *The Ben Lilly Legend*, 171–72.
18. Quoted in Helbling, "Harrison Left," *Looking Back*, 157.

19. Dobie, *The Ben Lilly Legend*, 7.

20. Wes Helbling, "Centuries old 'Castle' on Bayou Chemin-A-Haut," *Bastrop Enterprise*, March 14, 2012.

When arborist Harvey Stern came to measure and date the old cypress, he counted at least one hundred rings, which would make the tree at least a thousand years old.

21. "Roosevelt May Hunt Bear," *New York Times*, September 8, 1907.

22. "Louisiana Canebrake Lairs of Bears, Boars, and Panthers to be Invaded," *New York Times*, September 20, 1907.

23. Theodore Roosevelt, "In the Louisiana Canebrakes," *Scribner's Magazine* 43, no. 1 (1908): 47–60. See also https://sites.rootsweb.com/~lamadiso/articles/louisianacanebrakes.htm.

24. John A. Barone, et al., "Distribution of Canebrakes in 19th Century Alabama." *Journal of the Alabama Academy of Sciences* 79 (January 2008): 1–11; Steven G. Platt and Christopher G. Brantley, "Canebrakes: An Ecological and Historical Perspective," *Castanea* 62 (March 1997): 8–21.

25. Harris Dickson, "When the President Hunts," *Saturday Evening Post,* August 8, 1908, 24.

26. Dobie, *The Ben Lilly Legend*, 7.

27. Helbling, "Kindred Spirits," 40.

28. Theodore Roosevelt, "In the Louisiana Canebrakes."

29. Theodore Roosevelt, "Letter to Ethel Roosevelt," October 6, 1907.

30. Dobie, *The Ben Lilly Legend*, 6.

31. People in Mississippi have always known of Holt, especially hunters and people who grew up near Greenville, Mississippi, but there's a chance much of the Holt Collier legend might have remained unknown to a wider audience, might have even disappeared, if not for Minor Ferris Buchanan's *Holt Collier: His Life, His Roosevelt Hunts and the Origin of the Teddy Bear* (Jackson, MS: Centennial Press, 2002). Two short years later, the Holt Collier National Wildlife Refuge was established. It ranges 2,200 acres and is only a few miles south of Holt Collier's gravestone, which rests in Live Oak Cemetery on the edge of Greenville.

32. Roosevelt described Clive and Harley Metcalfe as "adopting" Collier once Hind passed away.

33. Buchanan, *Holt Collier*, 185.

34. Buchanan, *Holt Collier*, 140.

35. Helbling, "Kindred Spirits," 45.

36. Dobie, *The Ben Lilly Legend*, 100.

37. Quoted in Buchanan, *Holt Collier*, 190.

38. Buchanan, *Holt Collier*, 188.

39. By the 1980s, most of the Louisiana black bear habitat had been destroyed, but recent conservation efforts have helped save the Louisiana black bear. Around six hundred of that unique species remain.

40. About seven months after the hunt, writer Harris Dickson's article "When the President Hunts" appeared in the *Saturday Evening Post* (August 8, 1908).

41. Helbling, "Kindred Spirits," 44–45.

42. Buchanan, *Holt Collier*, 191.

43. Helbling, "Kindred Spirits," 45.

44. Dickson, "When the President Hunts." In his *Scribner's* article, Roosevelt himself said that the success of the bear hunt was owed to Clive and Harley Metcalfe.

45. Roosevelt, "In the Louisiana Canebrakes."

46. I wonder if it all seemed a little too familiar to Collier. During the famous 1902 hunt, Roosevelt also stood in a stand for a time, waiting there while Collier tried to drive a bear close enough for a shot. Then it happened.

Around 3:30 on a Friday afternoon in November, Collier's dogs tracked a mammoth bear through the woods and bayed it until it was surrounded. Collier blew his bugle, calling for Roosevelt and his hunting partner Huger Foote. In the meantime, the bear caught hold of one of Collier's dogs, killing it in his huge, gnawing jaws. Unwilling to lose any more dogs, Collier took his rope and lassoed the bear by the neck, then fastened it to a tree. The legendary stage was set.

When Roosevelt arrived, he refused to shoot the tied bear, and cartoonist Clifford Berryman cemented the legendary affair in a sketch that made paper after paper, including the front page of the *Washington Post*. It may seem odd, but the national coverage didn't do much to add to Holt Collier's notoriety.

It would take nearly a hundred years for Buchanan to succinctly explain the mistakes the cartoon made. He pointed out that Berryman drew the mammoth bear as a cub and whitewashed the holder of the rope. Collier turned from legendary Black hunter to a simple white man, in a very real way being erased from history.

47. Helbling, "Kindred Spirits," 47.
48. Dobie, *The Ben Lilly Legend*, 5.
49. Robert Marshall, "Priorities in Forest Recreation," *Louisiana Conservationist*, October 1935.
50. "Chemin-A-Haut State Park," *Louisiana Master Naturalist—Northeast*, blog post, November 15, 2017. https://louisianamasternaturalistsnortheast.com/2017/11/15/chemin-a-haut-state-park/.
51. Quoted in Buchanan, *Holt Collier*, 197. See *Theodore Roosevelt: An Autobiography* (New York: Macmillan, 1913), 332.
52. Quoted in Buchanan, *Holt Collier*, 197. See Harris Dickson, "Bear Stories," 52. I have used standard spelling.
53. Helbling, "Kindred Spirits," 51. Helbling explains that "some sources claim he killed about 600 mountain lions and 500 bears during his time in New Mexico" alone.
54. That year, an article titled "Ben Lilly Most Famous Hunter" circulated around the nation's newspapers—Nebraska, Delaware, Wisconsin, Ohio, Michigan, the *Daily Oklahoman*, the *Detroit Free Press*, the *Iowa City Press-Citizen*, the *Western Times* from Sharon Springs, Kansas, the *Reidsville Review* from Reidsville, North Carolina, on and on and on.
55. *Catoctin Clarion*, Mechanicstown, Maryland, August 21, 1919.
56. Kelby Ouchley, "Ben Lilly," *64 Parishes*, Louisiana Endowment for the Humanities. 64parishes.org/entry/ben-lilly.
57. Theodore Roosevelt, "Bear Hunting Experiences," *Hunting Trips of a Ranchman* (Upper Saddle River, NJ: Literature House, 1970), 338–39.
58. Dobie, *The Ben Lilly Legend*, 7–8.
59. Dobie, *The Ben Lilly Legend*, 218.

3. Mister Unlucky, Mister Nobody

1. I take this quotation from the transcription of Revon Reed's story found in Barry Jean Ancelet's *Cajun and Creole Folktales* (Jackson: University Press of Mississippi, 1994), 80.
2. *The WPA Guide to the State*, Tour 641.
3. In *The Forgotten Jews of Avoyelles Parish, Louisiana* (Santa Maria, CA: Janaway, 2012), Carol Mills-Nichol explains that Bunkie's name traces back to a story about an early Jewish resident.
4. Yi-Fu Tuan, *Space and Place: The Perspective of Experience* (Minneapolis: University of Minnesota Press, 1977), 38. For a discussion of the "center" in settlements, see Claude Lévi-Strauss, *Tristes Tropiques*, trans. John Russell (New York: Criterion Books, 1961), 202–12.

5. Quoted in Yi-Fu Tuan, *Topophilia* (Englewood Cliffs, NJ: Prentice-Hall, 1974), 31.

6. Yi-Fu Tuan, *Space and Place*, 128, 149.

7. http://www.rockabillyhall.com/JayChevalier1.html.

8. "Tour Information," Mrs. Stephen Juneau, WPA Project Supervisor, Alexandria District, 1936, State Library of Louisiana, Object File Name: wp004937.

9. For a discussion of luck in place naming, see Ronald Baker, "The Role of Folk Legends in Place-Name Research," *Journal of American Folklore* 85, no. 338 (October–December 1972): 367–73.

10. Joseph Mitchell Pilcher, "The Story of Marksville," *Publications of the Louisiana Historical Society* 10 (1918): 74. This is one of the earliest accounts of Marksville's history. When it was presented to the society, the society's secretary happened to be the noted Louisiana writer Grace King (friend of Mark Twain and critic of Cable's depiction of Creoles). King noted that the essay "was listened to with great interest.... The notes on Indian tribes containing much new and original information." See "Minutes of October 1917," *Publications of the Louisiana Historical Society* 10 (1918): 67.

Pilcher writes, "A sturdy French pioneer from Pointe Coupee . . . a trader and planter, and owne[r] of a considerable tract of land in the great prairie of Avoyelles, part of which bordered the Red. This was Marc Elishe" (134). In Pilcher's account Eliché is not alone. He has a scout named Rabelais and "a few slaves."

11. "Introduction to Avoyelles Parish," *Avoyelles Parish Crossroads of Louisiana Where All Cultures Meet*, compiled by La Commission des Avoyelles with Sue Eakin (Gretna, LA: Pelican, 1999).

12. Historical marker, "Founding of Marksville," Courthouse.

13. Pilcher, "The Story of Marksville," 134.

14. Tuan, *Space and Place*, 157–58.

15. See Charles-César Robin, *Voyage to Louisiana*, translated by Stuart O. Landry, printed 1807 (reprinted by New Orleans: Pelican, 1966); and William Darby, *Geographical Description of the State of Louisiana* (New York: James Olmstead, 1817), 119–21.

16. *History of Avoyelles Parish, Louisiana* is probably the best known and most substantial history of the parish. I can tell you from experience that if you walk into the Avoyelles Parish Library in Marksville and ask about the history of the town or the parish itself, the industrious librarians who work there will hurry from around the checkout desk, smile while they march you over to the two medium-sized bookshelves lining the hallway leading to their offices, and pull three books for you. One will be *Avoyelles Parish* compiled by La Commission des Avoyelles with Sue Eakin. Another will be *Marc's Town* written by Randy DeCuir and published by the *Greater Avoyelles Journal* for the town's 170th birthday. Saucier's will be the third. It's by far the biggest, and it's likely to be the first they hand you.

17. In 1724, the second iteration of the edicts known as the Code Noir outlined the governance and polices of Louisiana. Articles 1 and 3 concerned Jewish people. Article 1 ordered the expulsion of Jewish people. Article 3 forbade any religion other than Roman Catholicism.

18. Grand Pre to Carondelet, September 27, 1796, MS 3, Louisianan Collection, Bancroft Library. See Lawrence Kinnaird and Lucia B. Kinnaird, "The Red River Valley in 1796," *Louisiana History: The Journal of the Louisiana Historical Association* 24, no. 2 (Spring, 1983): 184–94.

19. For a concise review of this, see Stuart Rockoff, "Jews in Mississippi," *Mississippi History Now: An Online Publication of the Mississippi Historical Society*, https://mshistorynow.mdah.ms.gov/issue/jews-in-mississippi.

20. This information is found on the LSU Libraries web page about the *Avoyelles Pelican*, which began publication in 1859. This information is also found on various ancestry sites.

21. We know some of the earliest people to come to Louisianan were Jewish people, some stepping off the frigate *Count of Toulouse* in 1719. Many claim French brothers Jacob David and Romain David were the first Jewish settlers in Louisiana. For an overview, see Samuel Proctor, "Jewish Life in New Orleans, 1718–1860," *Louisiana Historical Quarterly* 40, no. 402 (1957): 110–32.

22. Silvia Marzagalli, "Atlantic Trade and Sephardim Merchants in Eighteenth-Century France: The Case of Bordeaux," in *The Jews and the Expansion of Europe to the West, 1450–1800*, eds. Paolo Bernardini and Norman Fiering (Berghahn Books, 2001), 268–86.

23. Pilcher, "The Story of Marksville," 134.

24. Raymond L. Dale, "Marksville, Tunica-Biloxi to Discuss Future of Indian Mounds Park," September 18, 2020, Avoyellestoday.com.

25. The Avoyel people seem to have been incredibly friendly, or at least ready trading parties. One local history says the first record of interaction with them comes from a 1718 letter written by scout Bernard de la Harpe. It's near the end of January. Harpe and his men are scouting the Red River for Bienville when Harpe takes note of bands of Avoyel on the far bank. "They were of the tribe Tamoucougoula," Harpe writes, "otherwise called anoy." It is "believed that the *n* was meant to be a *v*," the historian notes. Harpe decides to send his pirogue across. "They gave us presents of a few quarters of bears and of deer," he writes. "They also caught a lot of fish for me." Quoted in Saucier, *History of Avoyelles Parish, Louisiana*, from Pierre Margry, *Decouvertes*, Vol VI (1875), 249. The letter also includes a troublesome phrase by Harpe: "I kept them for several days to hunt." He continues: "They killed ten deer and one bear, many bustards, and ducks, a few hares and several squirrels.... I gave them two guns."

26. "*Avoyel* is not a French word for *flint*, so it is not a French term for 'Flint People,' as has sometimes been stated," Chief John Sitting Bear Mayeux says in an interview about his 2004 book *The Avogel Tribe of Louisiana*. He wrote the book to correct his people's history, a history written by "non-Indians who relied on inaccurate information." Mayeux's book is meant "to prove that the tribe is not extinct."

27. Information about Carol Mills-Nichol and her book comes from "Remembering the Jews of Avoyelles Parish," Jewish Book Month feature in *Southern Jewish Life* (Birmingham, AL, November 2012), 23.

28. Corinne Saucier, *History of Avoyelles Parish, Louisiana* (New Orleans: Pelican, 1943), 295.

29. Site marker for Spring Bayou Wildlife Management Area.

30. "Introduction to Avoyelles Parish," *Avoyelles Parish Crossroads of Louisiana Where All Cultures Meet*, compiled by La Commission des Avoyelles with Sue Eakin (Gretna, LA: Pelican, 1999), 3.

31. Jeffery Alan Owens, "Naming the Plantation: An Analytical Survey from Tensas Parish, Louisiana," *Agricultural History* 68, no. 4 (Autumn 1994): 46–69.

4. Into a Far Country . . . Close at Home

1. An instrumental source for this chapter is Lana Jean Fagot Prejean master's thesis, "'Occupy Till I Come': The Redbones of Louisiana's No Man's Land," University of Southwestern Louisiana, 1999.

2. See W. E. Paxton, *A History of the Baptists of Louisiana from the Earliest Times to the Present* (Provo, UT: Repressed Publishing, 2013), reprint. The book saw print mainly due to the intercession of Green W. Hartsfield. See William A. Poe, "The Story of a Friendship and a Book: W. E. Paxton and Green W. Hartsfield," *Louisiana History* 22, no. 2 (Spring 1981): 167–82.

3. Greene W. Strother, "About Joseph Willis," master's thesis, Baptist Bible Institute, New Orleans, 1934, 19–20.

4. The town is called Pitkin now.

5. Quoted in Glen Lee Greene, *House Upon a Rock: About Southern Baptists in Louisiana* (Alexandria, LA: Executive Board of the Louisiana Baptist Convention, 1973), 326. Cited as "Letter to the Author from Greene W. Strother, April 27, 1973."

6. Randy Willis, *The Story of Joseph Willis, His Biography* (Createspace Independent, 2018). Randy Willis details Daniel Willis's maneuvering to disinherit Joseph from Agerton's rather large estate and argues Daniel Willis relied on North Carolina's "An Act Concerning Servants and Slaves" to overturn Agerton's will "written September 18, 1776," a document that not only would "bequeath to [Joseph] most of [Agerton's] property" but also "free him." Randy Willis provides the letter Daniel wrote to Governor Caswell.

7. Paxton, *A History*, 2–3.

8. Marriage documents, bills of sale, birth certificates, legal cases, church minutes, and various ecclesiastical records trace Joseph Willis's life and his work to establish Baptist churches in Mississippi and Louisiana. Much of this material is housed in the library at Louisiana College. For an overview of the collection, see Karen L. Willoughby, "Great Awakenings Focus of Joseph Willis Institute," *The Message* (February 2012). http://baptistmessage.com/great-awakenings-focus-of-joseph-willis-institute; Sammy Tippit, "Land, History, and a People Called 'Redbones,'" *Redbone Chronicles: Redbone Heritage Taking Pride in Who We Are* (January 2007): 7–21; and Mark H. Hunter, "Search Through Own Heritage Leads Evangelist to Story about Enslaved Mixed-Race Pastor," *The Advocate* (Baton Rouge), August 29, 2014. http://www.theadvocate.com/baton_rouge/entertainment_life/faith/article_022813e0-07e1-511d-83bc-219c06286829.html.

9. The Louisiana Association of Baptists wouldn't be established until 1818. Many historians site Willis as one of the founders.

10. Willis, *The Story of Joseph Willis*, 12.

11. Born in 1897, dying in 1943, Crawford was a civil engineer, or at least the initials C. E. follow his name on the title page of his book. Crawford wrote his brief history of the people and the famous Westport fight after spending some years getting to know the people and "lodging in the home of an old 'Ten Miler.'"

The account of the fight itself is labeled as a transcription of an account "as told to him by a Frank Taylor." I suppose copies of these pages have circulated for several years, but in 1993 Don Marler and his Dogwood Press published them. Interested readers should be able to purchase a reprint through that press.

12. Lana Jean Fagot Prejean. "Occupy Till I Come," 89, 109, 1.

13. The book Marler ended up writing was called *Louisiana Redbones* (Hemphill, TX: Dogwood P, 2003).

14. Steven D. Smith, *A Good Home for a Poor Man: Fort Polk and Vernon Parish, 1800–1940* (Tallahassee, FL: National Park Service Southeast Archeological Center, 1999), 90–91.

15. Strother, 19–20.

16. "The Argument" is the title of the work's first chapter.

17. Greene, 325.

18. Tony Maricle told me he lives up in Ten Mile. He has a 126-acre hunting camp, not for hunting but for his grandkids.

19. "Pitkin Grave Marker Cites Early Preacher," *Lake Charles American Press*, January 22, 1961.

20. A fitting inscription for a preacher—Psalm 119:103 is "How sweet are thy words unto my taste! yea, sweeter than honey to my mouth!" (KJV).

21. Smith, 38. Smith argues that "more probably these are a mix of Blacks and Native Americans (Attakapa)."

22. Yi-Fu Tuan, *Landscapes of Fear* (New York: Pantheon Books, 1975), 38.

23. For a discussion of these gravehouses in Louisiana, see Marcy Frantom, "Gravehouses of North Louisiana: Culture History and Typology," *Material Culture* 27, no. 2 (Summer 1995): 21–48 and Rocky Sexton, "Don't Let the Rain Fall on My Face; French Louisiana Gravehouses in an Anthropo-Geographical Context," *Material Culture* 23, no. 3 (Fall 1991): 31–46. For a detailed discussion of this cemetery, see "Talbert/Pierson Grave Shelters," National Register of Historic Places Database: Office of Cultural Development, Division of Historic Preservation, https://www.crt.state.la.us/dataprojects/hp/nhl/view.asp. For the connection between these gravehouses and Redbones, see Don Marler, "Grave Houses: A Review," Second Annual Conference of the Redbone Heritage Foundation in Natchitoches, LA (September 2006). For a broader discussion, see Donald Ball, "Observations on the Form and Function of Middle Tennessee Gravehouses," *Tennessee Anthropologist* 2 (1977): 29–62. For a general discussion of Upland South Cemeteries, see D. Gregory Jeane, "The Upland South Folk Cemetery Complex: Some Suggestions of Origin," in *Cemeteries Gravemarkers*, ed. Richard E. Meyer (Logan: Utah State University Press, 1992): 107–36.

5. At the Shores of Eternity

1. Dan'l Dennett, "Scrap Collected at Grand Isle," *Daily Picayune* (New Orleans), September 1, 1883, 14.

2. R. J. Russell and H. V. Howe, "Cheniers of Southwestern Louisiana," *Geographical Review* 25, no. 3 (July 1935): 446. Two of the earliest geographers to study the cheniers, Russell and Howe, should be credited for retaining the use of the local *chenier* in the academic world.

3. Gay M. Gomez, *A Wetland Biography: Seasons on Louisiana's Chenier Plain* (Austin: University of Texas Press, 1998), 11. Gomez explains that "the oldest cheniers rest 9 to 12 miles from the coast, the youngest within a mile of the shore" (13).

4. The Gulf Coast Chenier Plain encompasses more than 6.5 million acres. For a discussion of the extent of the chenier plain, see James G. Gosselink, Carroll L. Cordes, and John W. Parsons, *An Ecological Characterization Study of the Chenier Plain Coastal Ecosystem of Louisiana and Texas*, National Coastal Ecosystems Team, Office of Biological Services, Fish and Wildlife Service, US Department of the Interior, 1979.

5. Many of Gay Gomez's words come from her two books about the region. That way, readers can get to know her too.

6. In Pipes's day, the trip "required three to five hours poleing in a small boat from Gueydan to reach White Lake, here it will require a sailing sloop and another five or seven hours to cross, providing the wind is fair, with another hour's poleing through the marsh after the south side of the lake is reached, before you have set foot on the island."

7. Both sources are quoted in Gomez, *A Wetland Biography*, 19.

8. "The Chenier Plain," unpublished paper in Gay Gomez collection, McNeese State University Archives, 42. The author of this paper appears to be Timothy F. Reilly.

9. Gomez, *A Wetland Biography*, 14. Gomez explains "a second exists along the north central coast of South America" and "a third chenier complex fringes the north coast of Australia" (14).

10. Daniel Broussard, interview by Gerald Sellers, *Islands in Vermilion Parish*. Vermilion Parish Library vertical files (Abbeville).

11. Ronald Baker, "The Role of Folk Legends in Place-Name Research," *Journal of American Folklore* 85, no. 338 (October–December 1972): 368. Baker explains that "by naming the

topographical features around him, man comes to manage his environment and thus gives some order to what was wilderness, which contributes both to his physical and psychological security" (368).

12. Axel Schou, "Pecan Island. A Chenier Ridge in the Mississippi Marginal Delta Plain," *Geografiska Annaler, Series A, Physical Geography*, special issue, *Landscape and Processes: Essays in Geomorphology* 49, 2/4 (1967): 321. Schou described the landscape as amphibious, extolling the development of the specialized mud-boat, with "a strong automobile motor," a windshield, and "a heavy constructed propeller . . . to work through layers of vegetation" (321).

13. Dennett, "Scrap Collected at Grand Isle," 14. Until indicated, subsequent quotations come from this source.

14. Robert W. Harrison and Walter M. Kollmorgen, "Land Reclamation in Arkansas under the Swamp Land Grant of 1850," *Arkansas Historical Quarterly* 6, no. 4 (1947): 396. For the acquired land in Louisiana, see Ory G. Poret, *History of Land Titles in the State of Louisiana*, Louisiana Department of Natural Resources, 1972, 33–34. Poret was the former director of the Division of State Lands.

15. "The Holland of America: Richest Land in the World to be Reclaimed by Construction of the Gueydan, White Lake and Pecan Island Transportation Canal," *The Meridional* (Abbeville, LA), May 27, 1905.

16. "Pecan Island," *Cameron Pilot*, 1897.

17. "State News—*Vermilion Star*," *Lake Charles Echo*, August 2, 1889.

18. "The Holland of America," *The Meridional* (Abbeville, LA), May 27, 1905. The article explains that the investors bought most of the land from twelve cents to $1.25 an acre. After the canal, "the company will then be warranted in asking from $10 to $15 an acre for strips of land one mile by a quarter wide bordering on the canal."

19. These canals have their own ecological impact—allowing for salt intrusion and erosion. See Don Davis, "Traînasse," *Annals of the Association of American Geographers* 66, no. 3 (1976): 349–59. First, outsiders cut canals indiscriminately without considering the flow of water. Locals also managed the canals, sometimes damming them to prevent saltwater intrusion. Outsiders didn't. Oil companies also used much heavier equipment to dig canals, which made them deeper and larger

20. Kenny Franks and Paul F. Lambert, *Early Louisiana and Arkansas Oil: A Photographic History, 1901–1946* (College Station: Texas A&M University Press, 1982), 184.

21. Quoted in Franks and Lambert, *Early Louisiana and Arkansas Oil*, 184.

22. Dean Tevis, "Pecan Island—Once a Weird Burial ground of Man-Eating Indians Is Strangely Isolated Community of Louisiana Marsh," *Sunday Enterprise* (Beaumont, TX), March 31, 1935, 1. Located in the State Library of Louisiana, Archives, vertical file folder "Pecan Island."

23. While desiring swampland for cattle herds may seem odd, history tells us that cattle excelled in the cheniers' nutritious native grasses, unusually good climate, and habitat containing very few predators. The marsh also had good access to drinking water and access to the Gulf. Thus, for a time, cattle stood as the dominant industry of the cheniers, drawing several early settlers. See Donald J. Millet, "Cattle and Cattlemen of Southwest Louisiana, 1860–1900," *Louisiana History: The Journal of the Louisiana Historical Association* 28, no. 3 (Summer 1987): 311.

24. Beyond naming the island for a positive life-sustaining feature (pecan trees), Jake Cole carries proof of high land back across the deluge of swamp water. Perhaps this story parallels the traditional story of the hero's journey to a terrestrial otherworld, like the English tale of the swineherd who finds terrestrial paradise while looking for his lost sow.

25. Leroy F. Dubose, "How and by Whom Pecan Island Was Given Its Name" in "Pecan Island High School," 2, State Library of Louisiana, Archives, vertical file folder "Pecan Island." I date the version of this story based on the types of documents, which match other works

compiled in the 1930s by collectors contracted to document the history of the area. I also use the age of Sarah Vaughan Koch given in the article, which is 64. Sarah Vaughan Koch died in 1931. The 1930 census lists her as 62.

26. This detail in particular has lasted through the years. Jim Bradshaw includes it in his version of the Cole legend. His words—"alligators 12 to 14 feet long, sometimes as many as 25 of them in one hole"—are strikingly similar to Vaughan's.

27. See for example *The Meridional*, October 31, 1885; March 27, 1886, 1; *Lake Charles Echo*, September 25, 1886.

28. Legal reports appearing after Cole's death say he "passed most of his life on an island off the coast of Vermilion parish, known as 'Mulberry Island,'" *Southern Reporter* 2, May 25–October 19, 1887, 794–95.

29. This type of efficiency narrative appears in other places and times, including the writings surrounding Manifest Destiny, such as John O'Sullivan's 1838 "The Great Nation of Futurity" or his 1845 "Annexation." For other examples, see Douglas Jackson, "The Virgin and Idle Land Program Reappraised," *Annals of the Association of American Geographers* no. 52 (1962): 69–79; Katie Holmes and Kylie Mirmohamadi, "Howling Wilderness and Promised Land: Imagining the Victorian Mallee, 1840–1914," *Australian Historical Studies* 46, no. 2 (2015): 191–213; Erin Kitchell, "Fixity, the Discourse of Efficiency, and Enclosure in the Sahelian Land 'Reserve,'" *African Identities* 12, no. 1 (2014): 110–23; and Sophie McCall, "Land, Memory, and the Struggle for Indigenous Rights," *Canadian Literature* no. 230-1 (2016): 178–95.

30. "The Holland of America," *The Meridional* (Abbeville, LA), May 27, 1905.

31. "Raising 'Cameron Beavers' for Meat and Fur Pelts, Is Next Big Farm Industry in Southwest Louisiana," *Lake Charles American Press*, February 16, 1926.

32. Carolyn Ramsey, "Rats to Riches," *Saturday Evening Post*, May 8, 1943.

33. See Donald W. Davis and John L. Place, *The Oil and Gas Industry of Coastal Louisiana and Its Effect on Land Use and Socioeconomic Patterns*, United States Department of the Interior, U. S. Geological Survey, Open File Report 83–118. Davis and Place explain "in 1951 the traînasse was the leading canal type in the Pecan Island portion of the chenier plain, with a total length of 499 km. More than 30 km of the oilfield canals appear on the 1951 map. Seventeen years later the system has increased to 135 km, an average addition of 6 km per year" (33).

34. Pecan Island's remoteness has always been a part of its character. In a newspaper article for the Lake Charles paper, David Levingston described the remoteness of Little Pecan, one of the small communities near Pecan Island. See David Levingston, "Gulf Breezes," *Lake Charles American Press*, December 13, 1941, 35.

See Val Bowman, "Pecan Island: Only a Natural-Born Liar Could Tell the Truth About It," *Times-Picayune* (New Orleans), May 12, 1946. Val Bowman quotes from a popular comedian of the day who had traveled there on hunting expeditions. Bowman says visiting the "island is like stepping back into the past, into the kind of life your grandfather lived . . . no telephones, no moving pictures, no electric lights." See also Wilfred d'Aquin, "On a Slow Boat to Pecan Island," *Times-Picayune* (New Orleans), March 6, 1949.

35. Margaret Dixon, "Pecan Island Gets a Taste of Civilization," *Morning Advocate* (Baton Rouge), September 6, 1953. To support travel even if the "weather [hadn't] been good for some weeks," the road was also scheduled to be hardpacked at a "cost in the neighborhood of $800,000."

36. New Orleans's *Times-Picayune*, Baton Rouge's *Advocate*, Lafayette's *Advertiser*, the *Beaumont Enterprise*, and papers in the nearby towns like Abbeville and Lake Charles all had articles about the new road.

37. Shane Bernard, "Atomic-Age Cajuns," *Cajuns: Americanization of a People* (Jackson: University of Mississippi Press, 2003), 23–57.

38. Quoted in Bernard, "Atomic-Age Cajuns," 40. Margert Dixon, "Age of Electricity Comes to State's 'Last Frontier,'" *Lafayette Progress*, May 29, 1954, 1. Bernard also cites several other newspaper articles about electricity coming to the island, including one appearing in *Rural Power Magazine*, one of many promotional magazines published by America's electric cooperatives.

39. For quotations see Bernard, "Atomic-Age Cajuns," 40–41 and 25.

40. Margaret Dixon, "Louisiana's 'Frontier' Libraries," *Morning Advocate* (Baton Rouge), August 3, 1952.

41. "Mrs. Conner is a friendly person," Dixon wrote. But based on what the article says, she also sounds tough, resourceful, and savvy. She fought for the town to have a library and hunted down unreturned books, sometimes using kids to help. When the book a kid was sent out to pester someone about got dropped in the return slot, a nickel was dropped in that kid's palm.

42. Margaret Dixon, "Pecan Island Gets a Taste of Civilization."

43. Richard B. Crowell, *Chenier Plain* (Jackson: University Press of Mississippi, 2015), 32–35. 32–35.

44. *Vermilion Parish Comprehensive Resiliency Plan*, 18.

45. Mud Lake in Cameron Parish is a good example. It holds three or four feet of water, but everyone calls it Mud Lake because the bottom is made of this gumbo mud.

46. Gomez, *A Wetland Biography*, 9.

6. Jack and Me and Coochie Brake

1. J. Maxwell Kelley, "Lying Horse Rock," in *Swapping Stories*, eds. Carl Lindahl, Maida Owens, and C. Renée Harvison (Jackson: University Press of Mississippi, 1997), 233.

2. Lonnie White, Assistant District Forester, Letter to State Forester Mixon (March 16, 1955), State Library of Louisiana, "Coochie Brake" vertical file; Eck H. Bozeman, "Coochie Brake: A Most Unusual Spot in Winn Parish," *North Louisiana Historical Association Newsletter* 9, no. 3 (April 1969), 15. Eck was also interviewed in 1992 by a writer for the *Los Angeles Times*. See John Balzar, "Populist Tradition Still Runs Deep in Home of 'The Kingfish,'" *Los Angeles Times*, September 23, 1992. Balzar claims Eck's name was "Ech (pronounced Eck)," but all the sources I have seen have his name as Eck, including a biography of the Bozeman family appearing in a local source, the byline of his article in the *North Louisiana Historical Association Newsletter*, and local obituaries.

3. Wanda Cornelius, "El Camino Real Was Scene of Thievery," *Alexandria Daily Town Talk*, March 5, 1972.

4. Kelley, "Lying Horse Rock," 233.

5. For the use of *brake* in Louisiana, see Randall Augustus Detro, *Generic Names in the Place Names of Louisiana, An Index to the Cultural Landscape*, PhD dissertation, Louisiana State University, 1970, 209–13. Detro explains the earliest use of *brake* in America occurred in 1825, "recorded as 'the cane grew so thick and strong that man, or beast, could scarcely penetrate it. These were called brakes" (210). The term is typically applied to canebrakes.

6. Angela Wendell, "Coochie Brake—The King of Mixon Hill Tells His 83-Year-Old Story," *Alexandria Daily Town Talk*, May 4, 1986.

7. "State Buys Land in Coochie Brake," *Winn Parish Enterprise*, March 31, 1976.

8. Wanda Cornelius, "The Legend of Coochie Brake—Is It Truth or Myth?" *Winn Parish Enterprise*, February 27, 1969.

9. Murphy J. Barr, "Coochie Brake: Buried Gold," *Piney Woods Journal*, February 2004.

10. Darryle K. Lacour, "An Adventure in Coochie Brake in North Louisiana," *Alexandria Daily Town Talk*, December 7, 1999.

11. See Barr, "Coochie Brake," and Cornelius, "The Legend of Coochie Brake."

12. See Jeannie Banks Thomas, "Introduction," *Putting the Supernatural in Its Place* (Salt Lake City: University of Utah Press, 2015). Thomas argues *weird spaces* allow us to be in two places at once: "We are still in and of this world, but . . . simultaneously in another, more ethereal, space" (21), which makes these spaces transformative.

13. "Harley Bernard Bozeman, Obituary," *Winn Parish Enterprise*, May 20, 1971.

14. Wanda Cornelius, "Superstition Hovers Over Lying Horse Rock," *Alexandria Daily Town Talk*, March 1, 1970.

15. The gang exerted supreme authority until local citizens, eventually organized by Dan Dean and James O. Maybin, brought West, Laws Kimbrell, and the entire gang to justice.

16. Richard Briley, *Nightriders: Inside Story of the West and Kimbrell Clan* (Montgomery, LA: Mid-South, 1968). In 2005, Jack Peebles published his *The Legend of the Nightriders* (Metairie, LA: Peebles), which seeks to develop the legend using archival material unavailable to Briley.

17. See Gladys-Marie Fry, *Night Riders in Black Folk History* (Knoxville: University of Tennessee Press, 1975), 3, 74–79. Scholar Gladys-Marie Fry says we must understand Southern stories of night riders and haunted areas as they were historically employed by those in power to control through intimidation, to prey on any fears that did exist in the African American community, and to try to demean that group.

18. Charles Bobuck, *This Is Also for Readers . . . The Wax and Wane of Charles Bobuck*, publisher Charles Bobuck, Itunes, 34–35. Subsequent quotations in this story come from this source.

19. Some of the land seems to be privately owned, but most is posted by the State of Louisiana.

20. Kelley, "Lying Horse Rock," 233.

21. Lonnie White, Assistant District Forester, Letter to State Forester Mixon (March 16, 1955), State Library of Louisiana, "Coochie Brake" vertical file

22. Bruce Shultz, "Winn's Coochie Brake—A History All Its own," *Alexandria Daily Town Talk*, August 19, 1979.

23. Robyn Jones, "Interesting Tidbits Add Flavor to CenLA," *Alexandria Daily Town Talk*, February 17, 1991.

24. Cornelius, "The Legend of Coochie Brake."

25. Eck Bozeman, "Coochie Brake," 15–16.

26. Wanda Cornelius, "Coochie Brake, Early Spanish Fort," *Louisiana Heritage* 2, no. 3 (1970): 22.

27. Cornelius, "The Legend of Coochie Brake."

28. Jones, "Interesting Tidbits."

29. For the fort, see Robert B. Roberts, *Encyclopedia of Historic Forts: The Military, Pioneer, and Trading Posts of the United States* (New York: Macmillan, 1988); and Powell A. Casey, *Encyclopedia of Forts, Posts, Named Camps, and Other Military Installations in Louisiana, 1700–1981* (Baton Rouge: Claitor's, 1983), 50. For the words, see See John L Doughy, "The Hub Lake Gold: An Analysis of a Legend," *Louisiana Folklife Journal* 15 (December 1991), www.louisianafolklife.org/LT/Articles_Essays/LFJhublake.html; and William Alexander Read, *Louisiana Place-Names of Indian Origin* (Baton Rouge: Louisiana State University, 1927). The entry for *Coochie* appears on pages 27–28. For the newspaper, see "Louisiana Gold Mine," *New Orleans Times Picayune*, May 5, 1887, reprinted in the *New York Times*, May 6, 1887. Details about Col. William H. Jack can be found in various sources, but the most detailed version of this story occurs in Harley

Bozeman, "Article 182, Winn Parish as I have Known It," *Winn Parish Enterprise*, May 19, 1960. For maps, see Johann Baptist Homann, *Amplissimæ regionis Mississipi seu provinciæ Ludovicianæ â R.P. Ludovico Hennepin Fransisc. Miss in America Septentrionali anno 1687*, published by Norimbergæ [Hommaniani heredibus, 1759], Library of Congress Geography and Map Division, Washington, DC, http://hdl.loc.gov/loc.gmd/g4010.ar167300; and John Bew and John Lodge, *A Map of East and West Florida, Georgia, and Louisiana: With the Islands of Cuba, Bahama, and the Countries Surrounding the Gulf of Mexico, with the Tract of the Spanish Galleons, and of Our Fleets Thro' the Straits of Florida, from the Best Authorities*, published by John Bew, 1781, Library of Congress Geography and Map Division Washington, DC, http://hdl.loc.gov/loc.gmd/g3860.ar140400. See also J. Frank Dobie's immensely popular *Legends of Texas*, which despite its title, includes legends of a Spanish silver mine near the Red River in Louisiana's Neutral Strip. See also J. Villasana Haggard, "The Neutral Ground between Louisiana and Texas, 1806–1821," *Louisiana Historical Quarterly* 28, no. 4 (1945): 1002–3 for a reference to a mine.

30. For a discussion of placename legends, the landscape, and the past, see W. F. H. Nicolaisen, "Names and Narratives," *Journal of American Folklore* 97, no. 385 (1984): 259–72; and W. F. H. Nicolaisen, "Place-Name Legends: An Onomastic Mythology," *Folklore* 87, no. 2 (1976): 146–59. Nicolaisen notes that place names can become "topographic metaphors," a kind of "shorthand" for an event in the past or the past itself and for feelings about it. When the words are meaningless, the explanatory story becomes even more important (and culturally resonant) because the story itself "tries to give meaning to what appears to be a meaningless name."

31. Quoted passages and information about this plan come from "Coochie Brake Stock Goes on Sale," *Winn Parish Enterprise*. April 23, 1970; Cornelius, "Coochie Brake, Early Spanish Fort," 22–23; "Coochie Brake Company Buys First 160 Acres," *Winn Parish Enterprise*, September 16, 1970; Wanda Cornelius, "Where History Lives: Legendary Win Parish Area Being Resorted as Tourist Attraction," *Forests and People* (October–December 1970): 36–37; "Coochie Brake Featured in *Forests-People*," *Winn Parish Enterprise*, December 10, 1970; "Coochie Brake Development to Be Tourist Attraction, *Springhill Press & News Journal*, December 30, 1970.

32. This address was eventually published in the *North Louisiana Historical Association Newsletter* of April 1969. See also Bozeman, "Coochie Brake," 14–15, and Eck H. Bozeman, "Winnfield Man Is Tourism Buff," *Town Talk* (Alexandria, LA), April 26, 1970.

33. "Sandstone, Not Treasure, Found at Coochie Brake," *Winn Parish Enterprise*, June 26, 1974.

34. "Coochie Brake, U.S. Landmark?" *Winn Parish Enterprise*, August 22, 1973.

35. "Sandstone, Not Treasure, found at Coochie Brake."

36. "Louisiana State Parks: Louisiana State Park History," Louisiana Department of Culture, Recreation and Tourism, 2018. https://www.lastateparks.com/louisiana-state-park-history.

37. *Louisiana State Parks Plan, 1975–1990*, (Baton Rouge: Louisiana State Parks and Recreation Commission, 1975). The plan also included an overview of a new classification system for sites and a detailed proposed capital outlay budget to pay for it all.

38. Yi-Fu Tuan, *Topophilia* (Englewood Cliffs, NJ: Prentice-Hall, 1974), 112.

39. "State Buys Land in Coochie Brake," *Winn Parish Enterprise*, March 31, 1976.

40. "By 1980, Coochie Brake Will Be Tourist 'Preserve,'" *Winn Parish Enterprise*, December 15, 1976.

41. See Lary M. Dilsaver, ed., "Transformation and Expansion, 1970–1980," *America's National Park System: The Critical Documents* (Rowman & Littlefield, 1994), 331–65.

7. The Little Cajun Saint and the Closed Down Resort

1. For quotations from Sister Crowley, Father Brennan, and John Dale Richard, see Barbara Lenox Gutierrez, *Charlene: A Saint from Southwest Louisiana* (Lafayette, LA: privately published, 1988), 9–19. Gutierrez republished the original as *Charlene: The Little Cajun Saint* (Lynd, 2002).

2. Mary Alice Fontenot, *Acadia Parish, Louisiana: A History to 1900* (Baton Rouge: Claitor's, 1976), 195.

3. All of these details about Charlene come from Lenox.

4. Donna McGee Onebane, "Charlene Richard: Narrative, Transmission, & Function of a Contemporary Saint Legend," *Folklife in Louisiana*, http://www.louisianafolklife.org/LT/Articles_Essays/CharleneRichard.html.

5. Julie Darce, "Have You Heard the Story of the Little Cajun Saint?" *Daily Advertiser*, KLFY, August 10, 2017.

6. Mary Alice Fontenot and Rev. Paul B. Freeland, "Chapter VIII Pointe-aux-Loups," *Acadia Parish, Louisiana: A History to 1900* (Baton Rouge: Claitor's, 1976), 155–66. The quotations come from an *Opelousas Courier* article about Pointe-aux-Loups (June 5, 1858), which is reproduced in the Acadia Parish book.

7. Brooks Kubena, "Grand Isle Sparks Controversy Blocking Island Access to Property Owners Amid Coronavirus Concerns," *The Advocate* (Baton Rouge), April 7, 2020.

8. "Cameron Parish Officials Ask People Not to Travel to Beach," KPLC, May 5, 2020. https://www.kplctv.com/2020/05/05/cameron-parish-officials-ask-people-not-travel-beach/.

9. Yi-Fu Tuan, *Landscapes of Fear* (New York: Pantheon Books, 1979), 87–88, 98–99.

10. Richard Campanella, "New Orleans Residents Fled the City En Masse Every August in the 1800s but Not for Hurricanes," *Times-Picayune*, August 1, 2017.

11. Quoted in Campanella, "New Orleans Residents . . ." from an 1855 article in *Picayune*.

12. Henry C. Delery, "Covington," *The Photographic Times: An Illustrated Monthly Magazine Devoted to the Interest of Artistic and Scientific Photography*, edited by Walter Woodbury, vol. 33 (1901), 265. Delery gives a hint of how travel writers described the "primordial" healing place that was Louisiana: "Hidden in the depths of a Louisiana forest, cradled in the odorous pines, breathing their soothing and exhilarating essence, mingled with that of sweet olive and honeysuckle, the little village of Covington slumbers an existence of peace and quiet" (260).

13. Campanella, "New Orleans Residents . . ."

14. "A Visit to Grand Isle," *New Orleans Republican*, August 24, 1870.

15. Zoe Sagrera, *My Memories of the Island; Remembering Life on Cheniere au Tigre* (Baton Rouge: Claitor's, 2010).

16. Tuan, 87–88, 103.

17. Sulis was a Celtic deity, and like many others, specifically attached to a geographic site—a pool, a well, a cleft, a rock formation. Unearthed votive objects and tablets suggest Sulis was conceived of as both life-giving mother and an agent of curses, but the point for the subject at hand is the name, which represents both a topographic feature and religious belief.

18. Quoted in Pat Moore, "Beautiful Bath," *Britain Magazine*, 48–49. www.britain-magazine.com

19. John Clark, "Bladud of Bath: The Archaeology of a Legend," *Folklore* 105 (1994): 44. Clark supplies the Chaucer quote.

20. Quoted in Clark. For original source, see Ruth Tongue, *Somerset Folklore* (London, Folk-Lore Society, 1965).

21. W. E. H. Stanner, *The Dreaming and Other Essays* (Melbourne: Black, 2009). For an interesting discussion of this, see W. R. O'Conner, *Wayfinding: The Science and Mystery of How Human Navigate the World* (New York: St. Martin's Press, 2019).

22. Larry Jorgensen, *Hot Wells: A Louisiana Ghost* (Mansura, LA: GL Management LLC, 2015). Historical information about Hot Wells comes from this source. Unless noted, the quotations do as well.

23. Dylan Domangue, "Cotile Lake Recreation Area Beginning Debris Cleanup Efforts," KALB, February 11, 2021.

24. Jorgensen, *Hot Wells*, 56–57.

25. Jeff Matthews, "Hope for Hot Wells? See What New Owners Plan for Historic Site," *Town Talk* (Alexandria, Louisiana), August 4, 2017.

8. Land in the Slow Making

1. Harnett T. Kane, *The Bayous of Louisiana* (New York: W. Morrow, 1973). Quotations in this section come from this source, pages 1–8.

2. Horatio Bardwell Chusman, "Choctaw Hunting Practices" in *History of the Choctaw, Chickasaw, and Natchez Indians*, electronic resource, edited with a foreword by Angie Debo, introduction by Clara Sue Kidwell. https://accessgenealogy.com/mississippi/choctaw-hunting.htm.

3. Information about these beings and the quotations come from David Bushnell, "Myths of the Louisiana Choctaw," *American Anthropologist* 12 (1910): 526–35.

4. Though untrained, Bushnell was already an accomplished scholar. By 1912 he would be appointed editor at the Smithsonian Institution's Bureau of American Ethnology. Historian David Usner describes Bushnell as an aggressive collector of Native American artifacts and as oblivious to the historical reality facing Bayou Lacombe's Choctaws. The federal government had recently begun enacting its policies of Native removal in that area.

5. Tom Mould, *Tales of the Choctaws* (Jackson: University of Mississippi Press, 2004), 94–97.

6. Patrick Clanton, "Democracy vs. Bureaucracy," advertisement paid for by St. Tammany Taxpayer's Association, found in a collection of articles titled "The Chinchuba Oaks and Mardi Gras Day." *Tammany Family History* blog, created April 25, 2017, accessed July 7, 2021. https://tammanyfamily.blogspot.com/2017/04/mardi-gras-day-massacre.html. Other articles in this collection will be referenced as *Tammany Family History* blog. Additional information provided when possible.

7. Susan Elder, *Life of the Abbé Adrien Rouquette ["Chahta-Ima"], Poet-Missionary of Louisiana* (New Orleans: Graham, 1918), 130.

8. Ron Barthet, "Father Rouquette and the Cabin in the Oak," created November 28, 2020, accessed May 6, 2021, *Tammany Family History* blog. https://tammanyfamily.blogspot.com/2020/11/father-rouquette-and-cabin-in-oak.html

9. "Oak Trees Uprooted," *St. Tammany Farmer*, February 16, 1978. *Tammany Family History* blog.

10. My dad was actually the fourteenth child, but two children died at childbirth. They were "blue babies," as he would always say to me.

11. "Fischer Regrets Chinchuba Sequence of Events," *Tammany Family History* blog, no original author or paper given.

12. Mike Dowty, "Highway Dept. Feels Crucified," *St. Tammany News-Banner*, March 12, 1978. *Tammany Family History* blog.

13. The Eagle Scout Project on the Native People of Fontainebleau explains these sites. https://www.crt.state.la.us/Assets/Parks/parks/fontainebleau/Native_People_of_Fontainebleau.pdf.

14. Jackson Cantrell, "The Enslaved Families of Fontainebleau: A Summary for the 2019 Dedication of the Historic Marker, Fontainebleau State Park." https://www.crt.state.la.us/Assets/Parks/parks/fontainebleau/Enslaved_Peoples_of_Fontainebleau.pdf.

15. Frank de Caro and Rosan Jordan, "Field Notes on All Saints' Day, 1985 and 1986." *Louisiana Folklore Miscellany* 12 (1995): 77–85. This quotation comes from page 82.

16. Susan Elder, *Life of the Abbé Adrien Rouquette ["Chahta-Ima"], Poet-Missionary of Louisiana* (New Orleans: Graham, 1918), 130.

17. Peré Rouquette Day Lacombe, *Commemorating the Centennial of the Death of Peré Rouquette Chahta, Ima*, July 15, 1987. https://sacredheartofjesusonline.org/history.

18. "History At a Glance: Lacombe, Gateway to the Big Branch National Wildlife Refuge," posted by St. Tammany Parish Library, February 5, 2019. https://www.sttammanylibrary.org/blogs/post/history-at-a-glance-lacombe-gateway-to-the-big-branch-marsh-and-wildlife-refuge/.

19. de Caro and Jordan, "Field Notes on All Saints' Day," 77.

20. In his 1899 *History of the Choctaw, Chickasaw and Natchez Indians*, Horatio Cushman remarked that "in the disposition of their dead, the ancient Choctaws practiced a strange method different from any other Nation of people, perhaps, that ever existed" (165). Some very early French writers describe this practice, but trader James Adair provides the first English record of it. His early 1740s account describes "a high scaffold stockaded round" and the "bone-picker" who "scraped all the flesh off the bones; which may justly be called the Choktah method of embalming their dead." Quoted in John Reed Swanton, *Source Material for the Social and Ceremonial Life of the Choctaw Indians*, Bureau of American Ethnology Bulletin 103, Smithsonian Institution (Washington: Government Printing Office, 1931): 171–72.

21. See Alfred Wright, "Choctaws: Religious Opinions, Traditions, Etc." *Missionary Herald* 24 (June 1828): 178–79. It should be noted that some recent sources agree with Wright's general description but say his definitions of *shilup* and *shilombish* are exactly the opposite of how Choctaws use the words today.

22. David I. Bushnell, *The Choctaw of Bayou Lacomb St. Tammany Parish Louisiana*, Smithsonian Institution, Bureau of American Ethnology (Washington: Government Printing Office, 1909): 28. Bushnell claims that before being introduced to Catholic missionaries, "the Choctaw did not agree even among themselves regarding the future state."

23. Bushnell, *The Choctaw of Bayou Lacomb*, 28–29.

24. Bushnell, *The Choctaw of Bayou Lacomb*, 27.

25. Bushnell, *The Choctaw of Bayou Lacomb*, 28–29.

26. Quoted in Daniel Usner, *American Indians in Early New Orleans* (Baton Rouge: Louisiana State University Press, 2018). 108–9. For original source, see "Father Rouquette: The Burial of the Poet Priest," *New Orleans Daily Picayune*, July 17, 1887. In his remarkable book, Usner argues Peré Rouquette provides "the most comprehensive documentation about the Choctaws living near New Orleans" (108–9).

27. Tom Aicklen, *The Rascal, the Rouge, and the Robe*, Lacombe Heritage Center, October 31, 2018.

28. Parker Carrone, "Highway Head Should Quit, Writer Says in Criticism," letter to the editor, *St. Tammany News Banner*, February 8, 1978. *Tammany Family History* blog.

29. Mike Dowty, "Chinchuba Oak Pushed Down by Secret State Orders," *St. Tammany News Banner*, February 12, 1978. *Tammany Family History* blog.

30. For several months, the St. Tammany Taxpayers Association had been working to project the Chinchuba Oaks. During that time, the vice president of St. Tammany Taxpayers Association, Ed Strobe, had developed a peculiar habit. Almost like he had a premonition, he started parking his car in front of the oak to protect it. On that Mardi Gras Day, his car was parked right there, but that morning state police Captain William Jourdan ordered him to move it. Later, once he figured out what was happening, he tried to stop the workers, but then "Pete Fussell from the transportation department drove up to State Police Troop L headquarters 'in a big hurry,'" he told the paper, 'and requested offices to come out to the site of the oak to protect a $250,000 dozer." In his letter to the editor, Parker Carrone claimed that "with several huge pieces of equipment," the workers made "coordinated maneuverers" under the direction of LDOTD Department Head W. T. Taylor, whom Carrone called "the Czar of Asphalt."

31. Dowty, "Chinchuba Oak Pushed Down by Secret State Orders."

32. St. Tammany Parish's official archivist Mrs. Bertha Neff would eventually sign an affidavit that she found an 1894 sale document "from Rev. H. C. Mignot of New Orleans to Rev. Francis Renaudien of a parcel of land bounded by the Mandeville Road, Chinchuba Creek and Kneipp Institute known as the property on which is built the Father Rouquette Chapel."

ABOUT THE AUTHOR

Photo by Carmen LeJeune

Keagan LeJeune is a folklorist, professor of English, and writer who lives in Lake Charles, Louisiana. He has published nonfiction, short stories, and poems in *64 Parishes*, *Gulf Coast*, *Southwest Review*, *Measure*, *New South*, *Louisiana Literature*, and others. He has advanced degrees in writing, English, and folklore, and has devoted more than twenty-five years to the study of Louisiana's unique and fascinating culture. He is the former president of the Louisiana Folklore Society and the former editor of the society's journal. His first book, *Always for the Underdog*, was published as a special book by the Texas Folklore Society. His second book, *Legendary Louisiana Outlaws*, was published by LSU Press. Some of his awards include the 2017 Louisiana Literary Award, the 2016 Brian McConnell Book Award presented by the International Society for Contemporary Legend Research, and the 2019 Arthur Bergeron Award presented for his work in preserving Louisiana's unique history. With a love for all things Louisiana, Keagan enjoys finding those hidden places in the Bayou State, those corners most people don't notice or maybe want to sweep under the rug. He's fascinated by the stories people tell and the connections he finds between those stories and his own.

Printed in the USA
CPSIA information can be obtained
at www.ICGtesting.com
LVHW050855031223
765091LV00002B/17